T0267264

EVERY
DAY
SPIRIT

A Daybook of
Wisdom, Joy and Peace

MARY DAVIS

S sourcebooks

I Believe in Me: A Book of Affirmations.
Unity Village, MO: Unity Books, © 2014.
Used with permission of Unity Books, www.unity.org.

Quotes from Paramahansa Yogananda
used with permission of Self-Realization Fellowship,
Los Angeles, CA., www.yogananda-srf.org.

Diligent effort was made to determine if previously published material included in this
book required permission to reprint. Please accept apologies for any errors. Corrections
will be made in subsequent editions.

This publication is designed to provide accurate and authoritative information in regard to
the subject matter covered. It is sold with the understanding that the publisher is not
engaged in rendering legal, accounting, or other professional service. If legal advice or
other expert assistance is required, the services of a competent professional person should
be sought. —*From a Declaration of Principles Jointly Adopted by a Committee of the American
Bar Association and a Committee of Publishers and Associations*

References to internet websites (URLs) were accurate at the time of writing. Neither the
author nor Sourcebooks is responsible for URLs that may have expired or changed since the
manuscript was prepared.

This book is not intended as a substitute for medical advice from a qualified physician. The
intent of this book is to provide accurate general information in regard to the subject matter
covered. If medical advice or other expert help is needed, the services of an appropriate
medical professional should be sought.

Published by Sourcebooks
P.O. Box 4410, Naperville, Illinois 60567-4410
(630) 961-3900
sourcebooks.com

Originally published as *Every Day Spirit* in 2017 by Mary Davis.
Every Day Spirit: www.everydayspirit.net

Cataloging-in-Publication Data is on file with the Library of Congress.

Printed and bound in the United States of America.
MA 10 9 8 7 6 5 4 3 2 1

For Maya and Mom—

the wind in the sails of my soul.

Introduction: Hunters Road

Between my married years and now, I spent a year and a half in a rented cabin on Hunters Road in the rolling hills of Virginia. I didn't plan it that way. As life would have it, all of my other options dropped away and this very cabin rose to the fore when I needed to move from the house of my marriage. The place was teeming with wildlife, and although I was more alone than I had ever been in my life, I was enveloped by a newfound sense of belonging—to nature, to the earth, to myself, to spirit. Grace seemed to rise up freely from the rocks, the fields and the evergreens, and point the way to just the wisdom I longed to imbibe. The melding of raw loneliness and spiritual exhilaration made for an inner adventure of a lifetime.

Hunters Road is seated near the rise of the Shenandoah National Forest at the foot of the Blue Ridge Mountains. Not only is it exquisitely beautiful, it is radically isolated. For me, anyway. I love silence and I thrive on creating in quiet, but this was a whole new level of stillness. No cell service, no TV, no news unless I drove into town. I had a dish and just enough gigabytes per month to post to my Every Day Spirit pages and do my monthly updates for the wallpaper app. No clicking on videos or opening pages with spinning ads. No surfing my social media. Definitely no streaming.

Most days, the only sounds I heard came from nature, the thoughts in my head and the beating of my heart. I meditated and did yoga. I walked. I worked on the Every Day Spirit app. And I wrote.

Each morning, I sat at the window in the cabin's main room, watching every little movement of nature and listening to my heart. I listened to what the pain and joy were telling me. I listened for spirit and the inner voice of guidance. I made friends with horses, cows, a skunk, a snake, wasps, frogs, bugs and birds. And every day I wrote a story.

I wrote with a connection to you. This journey was for *us*. There was an underlying sense that if I could see my way through the fog of loss and change, disappointment and fragility, all of us could.

I wanted to be able to tell you and my daughter Maya what I had learned. I wanted to report back from the void that gratitude was actually possible in the midst of confusion. I wanted to prove that all was well even when all seemed decidedly not well. I wanted to make an archeological dig into my darkest places and discover what was saving my life. I wanted to be like Thoreau on Walden Pond, on an adventure into the wilderness of raw spirit. I wanted to find beauty in small things when I couldn't find it in big things. And find it, I did.

What you hold now is my survival manual. This is a collection of stories and devotions, musings and lessons, practices and prayers that brought me from brokenness to wellness. This is the ride from barely breathing to confidence. This is the year between surviving and thriving.

I did not worry about what the writings would become. I just knew I needed to write every single day by the window, gazing out on hallowed ground. I knew this was why I was on Hunters Road.

I'm private by nature. It's outside of my comfort zone to share my personal story, but I do this because after all, you were there with me. We made this journey together—I talked to you the whole time.

And I learned that perhaps Hunters Road is not just a place, but a state of the heart. Maybe Hunters Road is where gratitude heals things and where joy grows out of self-love and simple things. Perhaps it's where the peace of our spiritual nature is part of our every thought and action, and where hope rises like the sun.

Daybooks

I have always held a soft spot for the daybook format. Daybooks have been part of my morning spiritual routine for decades. Sarah Ban Breathnach's *Simple Abundance,* Joan Borysenko's *Pocketful of Miracles,* Paramahansa Yogananda's *Spiritual Diary,* Rolf Gates and Katrina Kenison's *Meditations from the Mat,* Sarah Young's *Jesus Calling,* Coleman Barks's collection *A Year with Rumi*—they make a tower near my spiritual practice seat. I never tire of bite-sized wisdom in tandem with the longer, deeper books for devoted spiritual seekers. Daybooks speak to my soul and make a prayer of the precious hours of the day that follow.

Chasing this book has been my pastime for years. I began writing it a decade ago, when I set out to find a daybook of spiritual wisdom for my teenaged daughter but couldn't find what I was looking for. Using a few crafty skills, I printed out ten pages, punched holes in one side and bound it with ribbon. I presented the prototype on her pillow for review. It bombed. "I would *never* read that much every day, Mom." Hmm.

Not to be deterred, I boiled the gems down to a mere paragraph each, printed, punched and ribboned once more, adding a few beads in the binding as a bribe to my audience of one. And again, "Still *waaaayyy* too long, Mom."

One morning, as I contemplated my next move, I watched her over breakfast, eyes riveted on her phone, glued with laser focus on the little box in her hand. *That*, I thought with a smile, *is where I need to be.*

So I distilled the wisdom down even further until there were but a few words left in the pan. With these quotes I created mobile phone wallpapers, and from those, I made the Every Day Spirit Lock Screens app. The side trip took many years and great love, and brought me purpose and positive focus when my marriage was beginning to falter. Each day after Maya left for school and before I taught piano lessons, I focused on creating one beautiful quote for the app. Just one beautiful thing.

Today, the road has arrived full circle, back to the daybook I started all those years ago. We flow, like the hours of the day, like the seasons of the year, toward what we are meant to do. One step at a time, making an offering as we go. We ask for direction, listen for signs, follow the trail, act on guidance, and sometimes we arrive, just for a moment, to receive what we were seeking and to give thanks.

And so I kneel in gratitude.

Gratitude

Thank you, my dearest mom, Tiny Guru, wisdom seeker, strong woman, pioneer, teacher, loving spirit. Your unwavering belief in my life as a writer of songs, poetry, prayers and prose grew me wings. Your unconditional love built a safe haven for failure. Your thoughtful edits in this book illuminated the manuscript, opened my heart and gave me courage. Your constant willingness to love, to help, to protect, to advise and to uphold is my greatest earthly gift.

Thank you, Maya, daughter, gentle soul, courageous woman, spiritual seeker, kind friend, gifted goddess. Your presence has brought out a love in me I never knew possible. Your belief in my mission and your daily—sometimes hourly—counsel with the app made me brave and brought me joy. Your insightful edits elevated each page of this updated manuscript, and your cowriting of the journal prompts brought a newfound richness and depth to the book. You are my life's most beautiful teacher. You are my beloved, my soulmate, my heavenly blessing.

Thank you to my editor, Nancy Griffin-Bonnaire of Mark My Words, Inc., for applying the brilliance of your virtual pen with tenderness, talent and wisdom. Your enthusiasm and keen eye for detail melded to bring a special grace to these pages. Gratitude from the heart.

Thank you to my Sourcebooks editor, Meg Gibbons, for believing in the power of this book to change lives. You brought endless encouragement and compassion to our editing journey and consistently drew me back to my original vision for *Every Day Spirit* with wisdom, clarity and calm. Thank you for the precious gift of bringing her into the world with me.

Thank you to my agent, Michele Martin, for seeing my dream, for going to bat for this book and for your invaluable role in introducing these stories to a wider audience. You had my back from our first conversation, and I treasure having you in my corner and as a companion on this road.

Thank you to author Debbie Macomber, for each gem of advice, for every word of encouragement and for inspiring me, by example, to never give up. Your kindness has touched me deeply and changed my life. And thank you to editor Arnie Kotler, for the grace of your pen on the book proposal that brought me here. You are a shining light in the world.

Thank you, friends and family who supported me along the way, cheered my successes, cried with me in my doubt and fear, encouraged, gifted me with grace and perspective, brought me day by day through the darkness to the light. I love you all beyond measure.

Thank you to my yoga teacher, Susan Van Nuys, for seeing me fully and imparting an understanding of the vastness and beauty of yoga that nourishes me daily in mind, body and soul. It is the gift of a lifetime.

Thank you, community of souls who have gathered here to walk the path of this year. You are in the heart and soul of every word. Your presence is living proof of the unshakable power of love. I walk with you in every step. There's no place I'd rather be.

Thank you, God, for the pain and the light. Thank you for the challenges and the blessings. I offer them all to you.

About God

There are many words in this book that point to the concept of God. Along with the word *God*, you will find *spirit, the divine, divine love, love, the Creator, source, divine source, higher power* and *the universe*. I'm sure you can add to this list, or perhaps for you there is no special name at all, but simply a feeling, a knowing.

I use these beautiful words with consciousness, and without assumption about your beliefs. We will soon embark on a journey through days of love, light, goodness, peace, gratitude, kindness, calm, joy, faith and positivity—and all are welcome. Woven within, I leave space for you to fill in the blank with what you believe. May you take pieces of these ideas to your primary belief system and let them germinate there, rise in a new way and grow you toward an even deeper love.

My mission for *Every Day Spirit*, with each phrase, image, poem, prayer and essay, is guided by these three tenets: to compassionately awaken the soul, to offer unconditional love and positivity, and to be honest to my experience. Everything I do passes through these gates.

There is nothing new here in the following pages—nothing that does not already exist inside of you. But each day's thought will offer some bit of hope, some guidance for your next step, some way to make the world a more compassionate place, some love that thaws the heart for new life or some wisdom that awakens your soul.

Whether we voice it plainly or not, we are all on a spiritual journey. We are all connected to a greater love and to each other. When we align with that, when we lead our lives from this understanding, we live with love and compassion for ourselves and for all beings. Peace within, peace without. When we lead our lives from our highest selves, we bless all others with our light. We change the world with our love. That is the prayer.

This book is for you, my friend.

Blessings,

New in This Edition

JOURNAL PROMPTS: For those of you who love to journal as a means of self-discovery, in the back of the book, you will find journal prompts for every day of the year. Cowritten with my daughter, Maya, they were created to work in tandem with the daybook pages, inviting personal exploration of each day's message in the silence of your heart. May they guide you to inspiration that serves your soul and insight that illuminates your journey.

OFFERINGS: In addition to the journal prompts, this updated edition of *Every Day Spirit* includes twelve brand-new first-of-the-month pages with seasonal themes and new blessings, ninety new quotes, eighteen updated essays and two new pages in "Prayers and Blessings."

A NOTE ABOUT ADAM: The self-published version of *Every Day Spirit* includes stories of a friend named Adam who struggles with alcohol addiction. In truth, Adam is my younger brother, Tommy. In this new edition, I have brought his real identity back into the stories. Together with my family, we hope they might be helpful to someone going through their own personal version of these same challenges. We honor your path and walk with you.

Bless this day

with love and light.

Bless this day

with faith and sight.

Bless this day

with grace and ease.

Bless this day

with joy and peace.

January Blessings

May this year open your heart in new ways, shine light in new places and hold love beyond your wildest dreams.

Thank you, January, for welcoming us to the threshold of a pilgrimage. An open road lies out before us, and each crossroad along the way is an invitation to take a step toward inner peace and greater love.

Blessings for the year that is done. May we remember the gifts and graces amidst the challenges and losses. Blessings for the year to come. May we find peace, possibility and promise, in our hearts and in the world.

Each month, we will revisit some simple reminders to tuck into our souls for the journey. They start here and weave through all the other pages of this book. Every line below is a tool in our spiritual toolbox and a compass to guide our way. Let's walk together on the pilgrimage of this year knowing that all we need for sacred travel is right here within.

Be present.

Let the day flow with grace.

Expect joy. Be positive.

Serve with compassion.

Speak only kindness.

Impart only love.

Never forget you're not alone.

Give thanks for everything.

See goodness in others.

In the World:

* Invite these thoughts into your heart as you begin this precious day.

* Choose a word that will serve as a theme for your month and year.

* Write your intentions for January and for the new year ahead.

In the Heart:

* I welcome the possibility and promise of January. A sunrise of hope lights my way as I begin this journey of the heart and soul.

❧

The Spiritual Sun

Extraordinary love springs from ordinary blessings.

Finding yourself on this path as a brand-new year begins is no small coincidence. We are destined to take this journey of the heart, an adventure of the soul with lessons drawn from simple things—from birds and horses, trees and plants, joys and sorrows, angels and stardust. Nothing big really happens on Hunters Road, yet everything happens here. Extraordinary love springs from ordinary blessings.

Just as these words were given in the complete solitude of a cabin near the foot of a mountain, you were meant to read them in the complete solitude of your heart at the feet of your own wisdom. It is there that you connect with the guidance, insight and love that has always been within you, and that will fuel your life with a hum of joy for having found sacred things in everyday places.

This journey is one of finding the holy in the small, the unseen behind the seen. It's about recognizing the divine flow that seeks to sweep us into her current and assist us in all things. It's about a personal experience with God, with divinity, with our higher power, with our inner voice.

It's all one thing and it's right here; the flow we seek is here. It's everywhere. It's accessible, helpful and made from love. The universe was designed perfectly, aligned in harmony and created in such beautiful order that our only business is to be completely ourselves on a path to understanding our spiritual nature and creative magnificence.

Today marks the dawn of something totally different. As the sun rises in your heart, it illuminates all of the sleeping wisdom within. You have everything you will ever need to awaken your soul and remember who you really are. Face the light and let the spiritual sun reveal the ordinary blessings in this extraordinary day. They are right here in the room.

In the World:

* Journey through today with an eye for beauty. Notice the ordinary miracles that surround you: the tree, the sky, a deep breath, a kind smile. Allow joy to surface. Be in awe.

In the Heart:

* I open my soul to a new beginning, a journey of love, wisdom and contentment. I have everything I need inside of me now.

～∀ﾉ～

Resolve to Release

Live simply. Laugh freely. Give easily. Speak kindly.
Think calmly. Love deeply.

A new year knocks at the door of our hearts and we prepare to receive her. In anticipation of welcoming a beloved houseguest, we might make up an extra bed, tidy the tables and assemble a meal. We might pack away decorations, put away presents and clear our schedules. We make room in our home and open our arms. This loving hospitality can be offered to the precious year awaiting us on the doorstep.

Making space is key to welcoming in the new. Instead of adding to our already overflowing plate of activity this year, perhaps we need to sweep some things away, creating a comfortable and inviting room for a little divine company. Let's make space by letting go of yesterday's artifacts. Let's make a resolution to release what no longer serves us.

It is no wonder that only a small fraction of those who set resolutions at the start of the year see them through. It's another duty in our already dutiful lives and is the first to be thrown overboard when we become overwhelmed.

For now, let's simply open the windows. Welcome in the light that might illuminate inspiration, intuition, self-care, joy, gratitude, creativity and the gift of some delightful unscheduled time for play and adventure.

Then let's answer the door and welcome in the new year with a new language that comes from a deeper place—the voice of the soul. Then we'll be ready for the joy of new blessings and new beginnings.

In the World:

∗ Release old commitments that you have continued out of habit. Release material things in your home by gifting them to those who truly need them. Release addictive or negative behaviors that no longer serve the person you are becoming. Release doubt, fear and negativity. Release any unkindness toward yourself. Release what no longer serves you and make room for beautiful small things.

In the Heart:

∗ I welcome in the light of the coming year, and make room in my heart and home for the transformation of my mind, body and soul.

❧

Light Up the Landscape

Joy is finding the holy in the small and the sacred in the everyday.

There's a brilliant yellow goldfinch outside my writing window, hopping from limb to limb on the old oak tree. They are my favorite of birds, so the sight of her has my heart beating with crazy joy. She's just a tiny flash of brightness, but she has the power to create a big stir. She has me thinking that when it comes to spirituality, a little goldfinch and matters of spirit have quite a bit in common.

For one thing, a goldfinch likes wide-open spaces, like the field, where she can maneuver her roller-coaster flight of ups and downs with ease. Our spirits, too, love wide-open spaces, even when stolen from the ups and downs of a busy day to check in with our inner wisdom. These silent connections can leave us feeling that we, too, can fly. Even a quiet act of tea can be cause for flight.

Our tiny friend is also uniquely radiant. She stands out like a summer flower and can light up a barren winter landscape. Our spirits are like that when we remember that we are an irreplaceable part of an unlimited whole, with divine guidance always present for the asking. Like the goldfinch, our radiance lights up the landscape. Really, it does.

Best of all, the goldfinch came for a visit today to be a living example of the countless small gifts of beauty that surround us in this very moment. Maybe in noticing her presence—like noticing a smile, or a flower, or a kind word—we are reminded that joy is finding the holy in the small, and the sacred in the everyday.

Joy is here, in this moment, right where we are.

In the World:

✳ Be present to small beauties today. Notice, with amazement and gratitude, the countless blessings that surround you. Find them in the miracle of a breath, as well as in a not-so-miraculous mess. See how an average day can become a brighter one when you notice the gift in all things.

In the Heart:

✳ I embrace this day with new eyes and see the beauty that surrounds me now. In simple things, I find great joy.

‚¥‚

Love Is the Road

Peace is the answer. Joy is the goal. Thanks is the prayer. Love is the road.

About half of Hunters Road is unpaved, rattling the bones of my CRV—the one that the local mechanic told me is the only vehicle in town without four-wheel drive. I had arrived here limping in spirit, with no experience in isolation, bearing only a few carloads of stuff plus determination, two-wheel drive and all. The rocky trip down Hunters Road is symbolic of my journey of transformation.

Before I moved here, I had been separated and living alone in the house of my marriage, my daughter in college. My heart was broken, my future feeling like an abyss, and it seemed that everything I thought I knew for sure had completely unraveled. I poured myself into creative projects out of an intense drive to focus on something good—something tangible that I could find hope in. In those eighty-hour weeks, I picked up fragments, once again, of who I might become.

My real transition dawned with the first morning sunrise on Hunters Road. I knew I had to write down the lessons. Not for the sake of being read, but as an archeological dig into what had happened. I wanted to know what I believed in, what brought me joy, who I was beneath the exterior of my circumstances. What spiritual practices saved my life? The answers that were uncovered, dusted off and brought to light, were answers meant for all of us. They became the journey of this year.

The road to ourselves is part paved and part uncharted. It's raw and rocky and full of surprises, especially after it rains. It's also covered in natural beauty that awaits the joy of discovery. On this road, there are no wrong turns. The purpose of the adventure is not to accomplish something or to please others, but to get to the very heart of ourselves—which has always been love. And always will be love. Love is the road.

In the World:

✳ At any crossroads, you have the power to decide what qualities you want to emerge with from this chapter of life. You can always choose to evolve to a higher and more conscious version of yourself when you let love lead in everything you do.

In the Heart:

✳ I am never stuck in one place in the journey of my life. Even through challenges, I am becoming a more loving version of myself.

~⋎~

Perfect Abundance

Gratitude makes sweet miracles of small moments.

Slow down a little. Notice more. Breathe it all in. Give thanks. We are rich with gifts, right where we are, when we begin this day with a grateful heart.

Today, let's register the sight of natural beauty and linger over small moments of tea and friendship. Let's pause to soak up the sounds of laughter or a lilting bird song. Let's be amazed that our spirits are embodied here in the world to feel a soft blanket, a soapy dish, a loving hand.

Let's breathe in the joy of the perfect abundance that surrounds us now.

Sunrise, sunset and the spin of the earth in between are nothing short of miracles. Let's be stunned. Let's be awed. Let's be jaw-dropped by the amazingness of life and pierce the jaded boredom of automatic pilot with a sword of gratitude. Let's greet this day mindfully, noticing the small moments of which miracles are made.

Let's offer up our gratitude on the wings of the only prayer we ever need:

Thank you.

In the World:

✳ See the world today through sacred eyes. Notice the abundance of gifts.

✳ Feel the world today with a loving heart. Allow a layer of defense to fall away and for your heart to open just a little bit more. Breathe into it. Welcome contentment.

✳ Approach the world today with a grateful spirit. Give thanks, aloud or in the silence of your heart, for blessings that are so easy to take for granted.

In the Heart:

✳ I am filled with joy and gratitude. I see the beauty in the small moments of today. I open my heart with words of thanksgiving. I am rich with gifts and miracles.

The Only Offering

Be yourself with all your heart.

It takes a little bit of practice to open our hearts and allow the truth to surface, especially if we've gotten good at stowing things away. It seems that to "be yourself" should come pretty naturally, but not when we've been hiding the light of our soul away from the light of day.

When my Hidden Truths and I got to the quiet of Hunters Road, I gave myself permission to be my authentic self. Since there was not a soul around, it made the most sense. I allowed myself permission to speak my truth, to write from a place of presence and honesty, to listen and follow my inner wisdom, to not second-guess my personal relationship with the divine.

Strangely, most of us need to grant this permission to ourselves, perhaps because this right was stealthily revoked somewhere down the line. Someone implied that our unique version of ourselves was not enough. But we know better.

With permission comes an invitation to allow our personal discoveries to come to the surface and be celebrated. When we accept the birthright of our worth, the doors to a mysterious and eternal grace swing wide. We have invited our truth to the forefront, and a force greater than our own hears our call, feels our alignment and swoops in with a flow of support and insight.

Not only are we enough, but we begin to understand that we are playing a sacred role that was created just for us.

And our hearts are the only offering we ever need to make. Today, just bring your authentic gifts to the table. It's all that's required.

In the World:

✳ You are spirit in human form, filling a role that only you can fill. Make a humble offering of who you are—right here, right now—and it will far surpass good enough. Give yourself permission to love yourself. Accept your sacred role in the universe. Be yourself with all your heart.

In the Heart:

✳ I relax into the knowing that I am a unique and beautiful creation of God.

～∨∕～

The Good Kind of Viral

Every act of kindness spreads peace to the world,
love to the heart, light to us all.

Every act of kindness, each loving word, every peaceful thought changes the energy of those around us. And now there are studies documenting how this beautiful idea plays out in real-life situations. New research shows that when a person sees someone act in a kind way, they are far more likely to engage in that behavior themselves. When we are kind to another in the presence of others, our kindness is multiplied—perhaps infinitely.

A few years ago, there was a kindness campaign in our area, and my daughter and I heard on the radio that people were picking up the tab of the person behind them at drive-through windows. The next time we found ourselves at a drive-through, we told the cashier that we'd like to pay for the car behind us. "Tell them to have an amazing day!" we said with obvious joy from our small anonymous kindness.

A few months later, Maya was a new driver. One day after school, she burst through the door with, "Guess what I just did?" Yep, she had repeated our act of kindness, on her own, with her own money, and with the same feeling of joy.

Even a small act of kindness can bring a big burst of joy. The effects ripple out to family and friends who, after witnessing our kindness, are often motivated to be kinder themselves.

Our actions speak volumes. When we create a world based on kindness and love, we unsuspectingly model that to others, lifting the consciousness of all—spreading peace, love and light to the world.

In the World:

✳ Keep a watchful eye for opportunities to say or do something kind in the presence of your kids or friends. No need to teach or preach. Your actions say it all.

In the Heart:

✳ Kindness flows from my heart with ease. I see the light of these small acts reverberating around the world.

❦

Expect a Day of Miracles

Anticipate beauty. Believe in miracles. Count on grace.
Decide on joy. Expect peace.

You, my friend, are a magnificent piece of work, a powerful consciousness, driven by boundless love and housed in a miracle of a body. Yes, you. Your cells spin like sparkling stars. Your love rises like a thousand rainbows. *Amazing* does not begin to describe you.

So today, we start off by owning our awesome truth—that we are spirits endowed with strength and grace, unconditionally loved and hardwired to grow toward the light.

The story of this day has everything to do with how we perceive ourselves when we rise in the morning. When we acknowledge our vastness, all things are possible. What is *impossible* is to manifest our expansive creativity while anchored to the earth in a place of unworthiness. No, today unfolds from the script of who we believe we are. Let's remember:

We are a sunray of divinity. We are a sparkle in the eye of God's consciousness. We are filled with light and radiate love in every possible direction. We are an extension of divine wisdom, overflowing with joy, knowledge and peace. This is who we are in spite of our earthly challenges—or maybe *because* of them.

Who are we not to believe in miracles? When we align with the truth of who we are, we see miracles as not only possible, but probable. When we *expect* a day of miracles, we *experience* a day of miracles.

In the World:

✳ Anticipate a beautiful day ahead. Affirm that you are a miracle, and believe that anything is possible. Remember the flow of benevolent grace, and count on it to be here when you need it. Know that you are a spirit of joy and peace, then decide on joy, and expect peace today.

In the Heart:

✳ I am in the flow of grace, participating in the miracles that surround me. I am aligned with all good and believe in my limitless potential.

~ ⅄ ⅃~

The Horse That Jumped for Joy

Maybe it's time to run in the rain.

Of the four horses in the neighboring field, Shadow is the free-spirited one, the least predictable, the renegade. I once glimpsed the breathtaking sight of him galloping at full speed in the pouring rain, exhilarated and joyous. After his victory lap, he stopped short and reared up on his hind legs, kicking toward the sky. For the encore, he rolled on his back from side to side until he was caked with mud and thoroughly covered with delight.

Last night, as the sun retired over the mountain and the clouds colored themselves in orange and pink, the horses came up over the ridge to graze. As I cooked dinner, I kept an eye on them, marveling, mesmerized by the gift of beauty. I saw Shadow throw his head back—a sign that he might run—so I left my pot and went to the window in time to see him take off down the hill and out of sight...then gallop back up the hill...*on my side of the fence.* He was free!

Oh, how many days I have balanced on top of the split-rail fence, aching to jump over and stand next to Shadow with no barrier between us. Now here was my giant friend, walking proudly up to my house to see me! Before I drove over to tell his owner of the escape, I busted out of the door barefoot and ran to meet him. We danced around and laughed in the open field together. Carrots were shared in celebration. It was a delicious, impromptu, juicy moment of spirited freedom.

Perhaps the word *spirited* has gotten a bad rap. After all, it means *enthusiastic* (literally, *God within*), *full of energy, determined*. I have been in survival mode for so long that I have all but forgotten this passionate feeling of freedom, arms up, face to the sky. Maybe it's time to decide I am going to wake with joy and enthusiasm each morning and treat myself to simple delights that awaken my soul. Maybe it's time to bust out of my field of habit and sail over the split-rail fence of new beginnings. Maybe it's time to run in the rain.

In the World:

✳ Joy is a spiritual practice. Carve out a few moments each day for something delightful, joyful, playful. Just for you, just because.

In the Heart:

✳ I have the soul of a free spirit—enthusiastic, radiant and uniquely me. I welcome sweet small moments of unbridled joy today.

꙳

The Right Time to Rise

May a ray of hope shine through your clouds today.

Sometimes, healing begins in private—like the kind that follows betrayal or living with someone who has an addiction or any number of unspoken issues. Shedding the thick skin of an old life is slow work. Isolated by the private nature of the secret, you stare down the Big Lonely of not telling your truth and hearing in your very own words what your life has become. But you finally admit it to yourself.

It wasn't really a huge leap for me to move to the middle of nowhere—I was already walled off from all of the seemingly sane, happy people. I had been living in an alternate universe for many years, pretending things were fine outwardly, while dealing with the dissolution of my marriage on the inside. A few friends knew parts of the story, but I held on to the heaviest parts, tenderly feeling the need to examine the secrets, and my role in them, alone. But I was never really alone. *And you're not either.*

Like me, you have a celestial team of guides and angels cheering you on, making like this is the best, most important part of life—this pain. They whisper encouraging words. They make hope visible and grace possible. They keep us in the moment, they ease the pain, they point the way, they remind us there are no mistakes, they tell us that you and I are never a solo act in life's drama.

Through the dense fog of this morning, I could see the outline of only one small bare tree. The little tree seemed like me, my life covered in a fog of unknowing. Nothing was clear—not the past, not the future.

But right now, the sun is rising, and it's burning off the mist, and even the tree knows that the sun was never gone. It was there all along, waiting for the right time to rise.

In the World:

* Just recognizing your truth is a giant step. Naming it is the start of your healing. Many have walked a similar path and survived. The sun is there and will rise for you.

In the Heart:

* I am strong. I am whole. I am enough. I have faith that my pain is meaningful and will help me grow like nothing else in my life can.

Everything We Need

Every moment of this day is a co-creation with the divine.

No book. no teacher, no religion, no guru or saint can teach us how to have a personal experience of God. They can lead us to the doorstep of heaven. They can tell us what it's like to commune with spirit. They can inspire us with teachings of the ages. Great wisdom from experienced teachers is irreplaceable, but there's something even they can't do for us. They can't be a substitute for our own relationship with our own God.

And for that, we have everything we need. We are so infused with spirit, so saturated in the divine, so deeply loved, so magnificently wired that God is impossible to avoid. There is no place where God is not. There is nothing to search for, nothing to remove or to add, only layers to unveil.

My last house was in a neighborhood where each home was surrounded by acres of centuries-old maples and oaks. One morning I woke to the sound of chainsaws. My neighbor had a team of tree workers preparing to fell some of the tallest sentinels. I ran over, distraught. "Ron! What are you doing?" To which he responded, "I can't see the forest from my deck because the trees are in the way."

Which is similar to saying, "I can't experience God today because there are so many distractions." The distractions are also God. Everything is. And when we look at the world this way, where all things are connected, it's easy to initiate a casual conversation and request guidance from a friendly God. We find that we are led, sign by sign, to the right choice in each moment. We need only to remember to start talking.

It's beautifully simple. We were born for this. The wealth of wisdom and guidance is not something that is available only when we're meditating, praying or in church. It's who we are. We have access to a pure connection from within at all times. We never take a step alone.

In the World:

* Look at the world today through the eyes of your highest self. Consider the possibility of co-creating every aspect of today in relationship to a benevolent God who loves you unconditionally.

In the Heart:

* I believe in myself and in the magnificence of my spirit. I am supported and guided in every step I take and every decision I make.

Bless My Eyes

Bless my eyes to see goodness. Bless my words to speak kindness.
Bless my heart to feel compassion. Bless my soul to radiate love.

Bless my eyes to see what is good, loving and kind. Bless them to see what is whole, light and calm. Bless them to see the humble, the quiet and the small. Bless them to see the beauty in nature and in all living things. Catch my gaze when my eyes wander only to that which needs mending. Guard my vision when it strays to that which is dark and discouraging. Restore clear sight when they gravitate to violence. Bless my eyes.

Bless my words to speak only kindness and impart only love. Bless them to be used only to build up and create confidence. Bless them to put light into the world where there was darkness before. Hold my words when they might cause pain. Keep them within when they have the power to tear down and crush. May I never use them to harm. Bless my words.

Bless my heart to feel compassion for every being. Bless me to understand that the suffering of one of us is the suffering of all of us. Bless me to see a spark of divine light in every face. Bless me to see a piece of myself in all others. Keep my heart blind to the faults of others. May I resist a view of the world that creates separation and judgment. Lead me away from comparisons and jealousy for the experience of another. Bless my heart.

Bless my soul to shine love on all who cross my path today. Bless me to express gratitude for the small miracles of daily life. Bless me to joy and contentment for the gifts of this precious day. Gently remind me when I slip into lower vibrations of fear. Let me not linger long in the valley of self-pity. Nudge me out of needless worry. Bless my soul.

In the World:

* Ask for assistance today in gently turning toward the light, the beautiful and the good.

* Choose some lines to carry with you as you plant seeds of kindness, love and peace in the world today.

In the Heart:

* Throughout this day, in thought, word and action, I am in perfect alignment with my highest and most-loving wisdom.

I Am Not My Breasts

Your inner light is what makes you beautiful.

Decked out in their finest, Mom and Dad were on their way down Route A1A in Florida to an anniversary party. They didn't go to many social events and were excited to celebrate this special evening with their old friends. Mom chose flowing blue silk and pearls; Dad wore his best suit. The previous summer, Mom had endured a double mastectomy for breast cancer, and this party marked a return to the small joys of life.

Now several towns from their home, cupping her hands to her chest in panic, Mom exclaimed, "Lou! I forgot the Girls!" Her prosthetic breasts, which she carefully slipped into a specially made bra whenever she went out, had become an uncomfortable fact of life. They were heavy and never felt quite right over her newly healed scars. Well tonight, the Girls were home alone.

Dad, sincere and at the ready to help with this predicament, gripped the wheel and began to maneuver a U-turn. "Wait," she said. "Let's go without them." As she told me later, she had the time of her life at that party and never wore the Girls again. And then she tossed out a phrase that I'll never forget:

"I am not my breasts." Well, amen, Mom.

Our beauty is the light of our soul, the light of our heart, the light of our love and of our spirit. When something knocks us off our game today, let's remember that the wattage of our inner light can be so mesmerizing that what we thought was a glaring imperfection is insignificant when standing in the light of our love. It's not the outer package that speaks the loudest. Our inner light is what makes us beautiful.

In the World:

✳ Take a few moments, right now, to imagine the light of love in your heart center. See it as radiant, glowing, compassionate, beautiful. This is the you that is projected to anyone who crosses your path today. This is the feeling they will walk away with. This is who you are.

In the Heart:

✳ Today I radiate the love and beauty of my inner light.

~✦~

Guardian Angel Friendship

Angels, be with me. Watch over me and guard my every step.
Guide me through the endless details of this day. Let's walk together.

They are here with such tenderness and love. Each and every one of us has a guardian angel beside us right now. There are many kinds of angels, and the angels that are closest to earth, the guardian angels, are here for the sole purpose of assisting us. We can ask them for help with absolutely anything, but we do have to ask. They will never interfere with our free will, and they act on our behalf only when they are called upon. So, when we want their assistance, we just need to have a chat.

To begin connecting, angel author Lorna Byrne suggests, "Have a little faith and be open to the possibility that there is someone beside you who never leaves, even for one second, someone waiting and wanting to help you. Even if you are afraid to do it, acknowledge your guardian angel and welcome it in." We don't have to endure the difficulties of this day alone. We only need to call on our friends in high places. Life changes completely when we make friends with our angels.

In the World:

✳ *Ask often and pay attention.* You can talk with your guardian angel as you talk to your dearest friend—about anything and everything. You can request assistance in all aspects of the day. Then pay attention to the guidance you receive in the form of signs, feelings and intuition about what to do next.

✳ *Ask on behalf of others.* You don't directly communicate with someone else's angel, but you can ask your angel to enlist *their* angel's help with healing, sorting out a problem between you, or helping them with a challenging situation.

✳ *Give thanks.* Show gratitude as if your request has already come to be. *Thank you for helping me with (my challenge) and for guiding me in the right direction.*

✳ *Leave room for something better.* This act of surrender allows you to open to answers beyond your expectations. You can release the outcome with a short prayer: *May this or something greater unfold for the highest good of all,* or *Thy will be done.*

In the Heart:

✳ My angel is here for me today, guiding me in every choice I make.

Grace and the Bluebird

Sometimes when we just stand still, the grace finds us.

For hours I heard the heartbreaking flutter of little wings in the pipe of the wood-burning stove, with no idea of how to help. A friend advised opening the flue and letting the little guy drop into the stove, then fishing him out from there. *Really? Just catch a bird?* This was all new territory for me.

When I opened the stove door, I was shocked to be eye-to-eye with a beautiful little bluebird. He was huddled in the back corner, frightened, and in a fleeting moment, I was within his tender body looking out. I was stuck in the darkness with no sky. I was born to fly free, but not seeing any good options. I recognized myself in him. Then I gently closed the door to ponder my next move.

I retrieved a tea towel from the kitchen and slowly opened the door again. I reached in to cover him, and in a flash he flew out past me into the room and along the ceiling to the first available window. Up and down the screen he flew, then to the next window and to the next, where he stopped, out of gas, alone, scared, checking out the room. And still not seeing any good options.

Stunned by his stillness, I stood motionless as well, only a few feet away. *You are beautiful* was the thought I sent to him. He was sizing me up. *Stay still. Just surrender, little one.* I reached out with the towel in a smooth movement, and he let me pick him up without struggle. Cradling him gently, I took him outside on the front step, where I let the cloth fall open, and he flew up to a tree branch. We talked for a moment, and off he went to new bluebird-of-happiness adventures.

Sometimes when we are cornered, we surrender to something bigger. Sometimes when we don't see a way out, we breathe and wait patiently. Sometimes when we have no answers, we listen for guidance and open to the unexpected. Sometimes when we just stand still, the grace finds us.

In the World:

* Today when faced with an unsolvable dilemma, be still, ask, allow and receive the gift of grace in the form of higher wisdom.

In the Heart:

* I ask for assistance and receive answers in new and creative ways. I am learning to tolerate stillness and the art of allowing.

~⋎⌣~

Meditations on Meditation

Just breathe.

Meditation is one of many tools that can lead us toward a calmer, more joyful day. By resting the habitual thoughts of *Me the Thinker* and giving space to *Me the Soul*, we see how much calamity our thoughts and emotions can whip up, and how calm the space is that lies just beneath that calamity. We understand that this ocean of peace is always available when we turn down the volume of our thoughts. It's not a cure-all for our issues, but we become less attached to them, knowing that thoughts are transient while the soul is eternal. Divine wisdom, guidance and intuition rise to the surface when we take the time to quiet the mind.

In the first few breaths of a seated meditation, you realize how rowdy your mind really is, and it can leave you feeling as if you are not doing it right or that meditation is not for you. No worries. *Me the Thinker* is just doing her job and trying to run the show. Gradually, the mind takes a back seat, and increasingly more time is spent in a restful state of calm. You return to the day feeling refreshed, clear, calm, mindful, aware, kind.

The benefits trickle down to all other parts of your life, including your health, your relationships, your connection with your higher wisdom and your ability to show compassion to yourself and all beings. All that when you just breathe.

In the World:

* Sit cross-legged or in a chair with your feet on the floor. Rest your hands on your thighs, palms up or down. Straighten your spine. Relax your face. Set a timer for five minutes to start, working slowly up to ten minutes twice a day.

* Simply bring your awareness to your breath as it goes in and out. It's a soft, gentle, yet vigilant awareness. You're present with the breath as it goes in, and present with the breath as it goes out. Breathe in. Breathe out.

* When thoughts take over and you find yourself in the frozen food aisle of Trader Joe's buying mahi-mahi, smile and label it *thinking*, and go back to observing your breath. Repeat until your timer rings, then sit for a moment.

In the Heart:

* I meditate with joy and reap the rewards with gratitude.

◞◟

The Gift of Mahi-Mahi

I'm totally trying to meditate but my mind has other plans.

So let's get back to the mahi-mahi from yesterday. We all live with an incessant talker in our heads. According to scientists, our minds generate an average of seventy thousand thoughts a day—that's about forty-nine per minute. No wonder we're all tired. *Me the Thinker* spews thoughts that jump from topic to topic in rapid-fire conversation with themselves. Then there's *Me the Soul,* the witness behind the chatter, observing it all.

Most people who have not thought about consciousness and have never attempted meditation go through life unaware that this distracted "monkey mind," as Buddha described it, is not who we are. Who we are is the peaceful Self, or Soul, or Atman, the eternal consciousness beneath the drama of our thoughts, which will live on after we leave our bodies.

So it makes a lot of sense to get to know her better now, right?

Imagine you are meditating and you catch your mind wandering. And you will. The practice is to label the thinking as *thinking.* I actually go a step further: I tap the thought on its little head with a wand. Really. I lightly hit it with the star end of a virtual wand and see the word *thinking* rise up. Then I smile and go back home to my breath awareness.

If you spend your entire meditation going back and forth between tapping your thoughts and coming back into focused awareness, you have had an extremely helpful practice.

Because at some point, your mind will slow down and absolutely everything in life will seem less dire and troubling. You will know who you are beneath the noise, and you will be at peace. So sit. Stay. You've got this.

In the World:

✳ Persist with your meditation practice. Make it a priority each morning. Just five minutes daily to start. You can do it!

In the Heart:

✳ I am a calm oasis of loving consciousness connected to the divine and to all beings.

~\✦/~

Calm in the Storm

Bless me with a calm center in the storms of my life.

Storms are scary but inevitable. All things are in constant motion, and at one point or another, we will be in their path and will endure suffering. But don't retreat to the storm cellar just yet.

Although we can't avoid the storms of life, it's comforting to know that calm wisdom and infinite support are within reach at any time through the gifts of our spiritual practice. These are beautiful daily practices that become especially valuable *within* the storms of life.

Our spiritual practice does not add something extra to our lives as much as it lifts the veil that hides our natural state of grace. We are, in essence, souls of love, joy and peace. It is from this calm center that we have access to our own powerful inner wisdom, which is part of the endless wisdom of divine love. The calm and safety of the storm cellar door is right here within us. It's always here, and it's always open for business.

There are countless practices that foster this deep sense of peace— practices that help us on ordinary days as well as in our darkest hours. Throughout the year, we will integrate your favorites into a morning routine and discover that the journey to peace is one of life's most amazing adventures. Be patient. Be persistent. The rewards await.

In the World:

* Begin each day with gratitude. *Thank you for this day.* Write it on a note and place it on your nightstand so you remember. Then follow that with a favorite verse or a beautiful quote that inspires your heart. Add a short reading from an inspirational book, a conversation with your angels about the day ahead and a five-minute meditation. You have just started a morning spiritual practice.

* Get a notebook that will serve as a spiritual journal, or use the one you have for your journal prompts to capture insights that feed your soul. As the year goes on, we will explore many spiritual practices, and you can keep the ones that resonate with you close at hand, cultivating your own oasis of inspiration.

In the Heart:

* I am peaceful. I am calm. I am centered even in the storms of my life.

〜✕〜

Silent Sunrise Offering

In a silent morning moment, with a silent voice I pray
to lift a silent sunrise offering on silent wings of grace.

Whatever we offer up in the silence of the morning is magnified throughout the day. Those first thoughts create the joyous momentum for all that follows. When we open to receive our highest wisdom, we continue to access assistance and clarity in the form of intuition, knowledge and guidance as the day unfolds. What a glorious invitation we send out when we empower the dawn of the day with focused attention on practices that reward us with the gifts of joy, inner peace and divine connection.

Our morning spiritual practice is not homework, but an investment in every aspect of our lives. A few minutes a day assist us in making the transformation from our smaller selves to our higher selves. It's as if our perception is shifted from monochromatic black and white, to full, blooming, brilliant HD color.

It doesn't have to be involved or overly planned, just authentic. It doesn't have to be long, but our focus has to be all in. It doesn't have to please anyone else; it is for your soul alone.

As the gift of this day lies out before us, we begin by practicing peace, joy, strength, gratitude and oneness with all things. With a morning moment like that, everything that follows flows with a little more ease and grace.

In the World:

✳ Commit to a few short spiritual practices each morning if possible. After a few days, you will find your ideal time, place and collection of practices.

✳ Consider any combination of prayer, meditation, sacred reading, walking, journaling, gratitude practice, daybook lessons, visualizing, angel cards, yoga or pranayama. Make a list of ideas and inspirations in your journal.

In the Heart:

✳ I create time with ease and grace for contemplative practice each morning. My day is inspired when it starts from a place of spiritual connection with all wisdom, light and love.

January 21

A Winter Night

You are here for a reason, and someone needs your light today.

It happened years ago in the midst of a midwinter blizzard near the end of the evening. The fireplace in the dimly lit barroom cast a golden glow over the dark-paneled room as candles danced alone on empty tables. Behind the bar, Larry was cleaning up, anticipating an early closing time. Behind the keys on the grand piano, I nodded safe travels to the last couple to leave.

As if out of nowhere, a man stood at the door, leaning, arms crossed, listening as I sang what I thought would be my closing number. Before I finished, he was seated by the fireplace, watching me intently. I smiled at him and welcomed him in from the storm. Larry got him a drink as I played a few more songs, guessing by his weathered face and his age what he might like. I wish I could remember what I played. When I finished, I went straight from the piano bench to his table, introducing myself and asking if there was a special song he'd like to hear. No, he said, but could I sit down for a moment?

Then his story spilled out. After a long marriage and years of fighting, his wife had recently left him. The kids didn't come around anymore, and soon he would retire from his job. He had nothing to live for. Calmly, he left his house about an hour ago, intending to drive his car into a tree in the snowstorm. It would look like an accident. As he came around the corner on River Road, he suddenly felt drawn to come into the bar and have a drink. One last drink. Then he heard the music. And in the lyrics, he found hope. And in the hope, he decided he was not going to take his life after all.

I knew in that moment, if I never did another thing in my life, I was meant to be in just that place for a stranger at the crossroads.

In the World:

✳ Perhaps our purpose is not a grand accomplishment, but a small kindness that we don't think much of, that changes the life of another. You are here for a reason, and someone needs your light today.

In the Heart:

✳ Every action and interaction in my life has meaning. I journey through this day mindfully, humbly and kindly.

꧁꧂

Be Present with Peace

Look back with joy. Look forward with hope. Be present with peace.

James Doty is a Stanford neuroscientist who conducts studies in the field of neuroplasticity—the ability of our habitual thoughts to change the brain—in the context of compassion and kindness. Dr. Doty says that some eighty percent of our thoughts are regrets about the past or worries about the future. Eighty percent! But the only place we are living, loving and learning is in the present moment. We are missing the best hours of our lives while we entertain regret and worry.

Although we all have regrets about the past, certainly there are many moments of joy we might rather remember on a regular basis. Dr. Doty reminds us that it's easier to think the thoughts we are accustomed to thinking instead of learning new ones. But isn't it worth learning new thought patterns when the old ones are bringing us down? Instead of dredging up the same painful memories, doesn't it make sense to remember some beautiful ones?

As for our thoughts about the future, many of us have become expert worriers, a sport we need to retire from, as our worry magnifies the negative scene that we are worrying about! We don't want to imagine the worst-case scenario over and over, giving energy to an undesirable outcome. In addition, worrying adds to our stress levels, leading to a cascade of physical and emotional challenges. Let's be mindful about our thoughts and shed some positive light on this precious day. We can all learn to be present with peace.

In the World:

✳ Today, begin to create some new pathways in your brain using mindfulness. Continue to draw your thoughts gently back to the present moment over and over again. Notice details, colors, sounds. Walk and eat more slowly. Stay present with what you are doing.

✳ Release habitual thoughts of the past, and conjure a more beautiful memory. Replace worries about the future with a visualization of a perfect, joyous outcome to the challenge. Send out an affirmation or prayer surrounding the end result you envision.

In the Heart:

✳ I look back with joy. I look forward with hope. I am present with peace.

~‿ ⫰ ⊱

Virtual Hibernation

I am in balance with the wisdom of nature.

From this big window in my tiny corner of the Northern Hemisphere, it's abundantly clear that it's time to hibernate. The trees are bare, the ground is frozen, and come to think of it, so am I. I can't seem to get warm in the cabin without a blanket around my shoulders, which I drag like an ice queen's train from room to room. The sky is gray with clouds that sail on a chilly wind. It's a perfect time to go back to bed—at noon.

My buddies are sleepy too. The horses are moving slower; the bears are fast asleep in their dens; the squirrels are tucked into their nests. Two friends texted me today that they are living their best lives under duvets, willing themselves out of bed in the morning, as drowsy as I am when the rooster crows.

Could it be that people, too, feel the need to hibernate in the winter?

Like our friend the lemur in Madagascar, some of us would love to sit zombie-like in a tree hole and wait it out. It seems perfectly normal that the shorter days would signal a slowdown of metabolism, when we eat and sleep more to conserve energy for the winter chill. If you are feeling this way, it's real, and the best thing to do is to quiet the voice of self-judgment, relax and lean into something soft.

Noticing our natural rhythms as they respond to the seasons is all part of self-care. When our bodies ask for virtual hibernation, chances are that our minds and souls are requesting downtime as well. Accept it for what it is; trust in the wisdom of your body. It's okay to be slow, Ice Queen.

In the World:

* Listen to your inner wisdom as it speaks to the changes of the seasons. In winter, give in to the natural rhythm of slowing down, allowing more space for relaxing, snuggling, reading, sleeping and eating comfort food. Trust that your mind, body and soul know what you need.

In the Heart:

* I listen to my inner wisdom and am in balance with the wisdom of nature. I allow myself to slow down and enjoy stillness.

~\ /~

Take a Break

Today may I judge less and love more.

Judging other people can be a *lot* of work. It's like being in charge of everyone in the world at the same time. No wonder we are all teetering on the edge of overwhelm. What if we relax a little and take a judgment break today?

Our thoughts and words have the power to build up and to tear down. They can sow joy or spread suffering. They can be a reminder of our oneness or build walls of separation. These choices are ours to make every day.

It's natural to think that our way is the right way. We have opinions of how things should be done and are passionate about certain issues. Each of us has an individual view of the world—as it is and as we would like it to be. But it's important to keep in mind that everyone else believes in their own vision just as passionately as we do ours.

When we judge another's choices, we immediately build a wall of division and separation. Judgment and love can't live in the same room or the same thought. When we put our focus on loving more, the habit of judging others falls away. It's helpful to remember that leaning away from judgment doesn't mean we have to agree. Their behavior is not a reflection on our lives, but our negative reaction to their behavior is.

Let's work to change this day for the better without spending all of our energy being in charge of (and annoyed by) others. Let's use our thoughts and words mindfully, and for the creation of a world that we can all share. Today, let's judge less and love more.

In the World:

* Refrain from thinking judgmental thoughts or using words that cause suffering or separation.

* Consider the Golden Rule: Treat others as you wish to be treated.

* Plant seeds of change in constructive ways.

In the Heart:

* I refrain from judgment and focus on ways I can use my gifts and my love to create the change I wish to see in the world.

~↲↳~

A Ripple in the Water

There's always something we can do to change the world.

After listening to the news, I used to have the overwhelming feeling that there was nothing that I could do to make a difference. I am one small voice, one single heart, one tiny grain of sand, one of a million little shining stars. How could I make any impact on the fear, the division, the defeat, the devastation?

Then I received a beautiful image of a stone dropping into a huge still brilliant blue body of water. It created a ripple in the water starting near one shore and traveling far across to the other. The circles grew wider and wider, and their impact arrived in places I could not see or even imagine.

We change the world one by one: one positive thought, action or prayer at a time, rippling endlessly. We change the world with our passionate will. We change the world by clearly imagining it as whole and healed. We change the world with peaceful, compassionate action. We change the world by sending out fervent blessings over and over again. Our souls need not be deterred by the constant repetition of negative thoughts and images. The unseen is vastly more powerful than that which we see.

When we feel helpless to make a difference in the world, or in times of challenge and suffering, there's always something we can do. We can call upon the power of prayer, blessings, love, visualization and compassionate action. We always have a choice. Drop a stone in the river, and be a ripple in the water of love.

In the World:

* Be exposed to news less often. Resist leaving it on in the background. Keep your thoughts and actions focused on positive change.

* Allow news of tragedy to evoke compassion. Use this connection with those who are suffering to send out a blessing or a prayer. Take action to assist in the places that are within your reach.

* Pray for our world and for all beings. Your prayers will reach distant shores.

In the Heart:

* I am a being of light. I spread rays of love and compassion all over the planet.

Be Yourself Bravely

Beauty is born and blooms from within.

Someone's opinion of us is just that, an opinion. It never defines us, and it's not required that we shop in the costume closet of another's expectations. Lasting happiness never ensues as a result of living up to external ideals. And the real dichotomy here is that the pressures of society fade into black and white next to the truth of our own brilliant color palette. Period. There is no point in walking onto the stage of our lives if we are not playing the colorful part of ourselves.

When we slow down and really start to look within, we encounter our essence as the incredible, unique expression of divine love that we are. This is our true self. Trust this. Believe this. And be positively, relentlessly on your own side.

In *The Top Five Regrets of the Dying*, Bronnie Ware reports from the bedsides of those with only a little time left. Many share this number-one regret: "I wish I'd had the courage to live a life true to myself, not the life others expected of me." When we find ourselves asking, *Am I good enough?* maybe the real question is, *Am I me enough?*

Beauty, like confidence, radiance, self-love and joy, is born and blooms from within. Nothing in the external world can teach us how to be our magnificent, authentic selves. It's an inside job. So be an original. Be quirky. Be imperfectly perfect. Be yourself bravely.

You are beautiful just as you are.

In the World:

* Today, begin with just one kind compliment directed toward yourself and repeat it often.

* If self-love does not come easily to you, try this simple tool from Dr. Shauna Shapiro: When you see yourself in the mirror each morning say, *Good morning, I love you.* The results are transformative.

* Be kind in your expression of your true self. It's possible to be both honest and kind.

In the Heart:

* I honor my divinity by sharing my authentic self and unique gifts with others.

Last Day on Earth

Say "I love you" out loud and often.

My neighbor Gene died yesterday. I loved Gene. When he wasn't at his restaurant, you could find him in his garden. Hundreds of tulips and daffodils would sing out joy each spring; topiaries were lovingly trimmed into whimsical shapes; maple trees and rhododendrons looked like they would rather live in his dirt than anywhere else on earth. Everything he planted grew brilliantly.

After my husband moved from the old house, Gene had my back. When he knew I was alone and busy, he would leaf blow so my piano students could find the driveway. He shared vegetables in the spring and plowed me out when it snowed. He was relentlessly thoughtful, kind and generous. Two days ago Gene was in his garden. Yesterday morning, he woke with an aortic aneurysm. Today the garden is gently still. I wish I told him how much he meant to me.

In Gene's honor, I imagine that today is my last day on earth. What will I do differently? The first thing that comes to mind is to do what I didn't do with Gene: Tell my loved ones that I love them. Out loud. And tell them what I love about them. And how they make me feel. And what a gift they are in my life. And how beautiful they are. Rumi's words drift through my heart as if part of Gene's garden: "With life as short as a half-taken breath, don't plant anything but love."

My sister-in-law Julie has lived her entire adult life with a rare life-threatening disease. She is a mom of four. I once asked her how she copes with knowing that her life is so fragile and that tomorrow is not a given. She said, "It's an amazing gift! If only everyone knew what it was like to live every day like it is your last." So I'm starting today. And I want to tell you that I love you.

In the World:

* Take a moment to imagine the scenario of today as your last day. What would you do differently? What words need to be said, what situation resolved, what joy experienced? Say, "I love you," out loud to your beloveds today.

In the Heart:

* I am thankful for my precious life and live today with every ounce of my being. I am generous in my expression of love.

~ᘐ~

Three Grace Notes

Open your soul to grace.

It's comforting to know that grace is always here. Every day, no matter what challenge presents itself, we have ready support and wisdom that far surpasses our mind's ability to see our way clear of earthly dilemmas. Generously bestowed upon us from the divine, grace is an unearned gift that is always present, always free and always ours.

We can think of grace as an extra layer of divine light that illuminates our minds and guides us toward the highest outcomes with ease. It's a North Star that brings strength, courage, patience and heavenly solutions to our worldly challenges. Here are three grace notes to remind us to ask for a helping of grace today:

1. First, we remember that we are not alone and that the gift of grace is already here for us. Stress will begin to melt away as we soften, aligning with the current of ease, allowing an opening to divine wisdom. So, remembering that grace is available is the first step to receiving her gifts.

2. Next, we ask. *Please cover me and this situation in grace. Shine a light on what I need to know today. Provide me with clarity and divine solutions in all this day may bring.* We can be specific, knowing that grace immediately flows toward perfect resolutions. With open arms, we ask and we trust.

3. The third step in opening to grace is noticing and following the guidance that will be clearly given. Through signs large and small, answers will be provided, and we will know what to do from one moment to the next. What we get done in the flow of grace happens easily and effortlessly. What does not get done today is meant for another day.

Relax. Breathe. Our minds can remain free of worry as long as our souls are open to grace.

In the World:

✳ If it resonates with your heart, make a note in your journal to open to grace. Write down the three grace notes. Let them be a reminder to make the request for a lovely helping of grace each morning.

In the Heart:

✳ I am open to the grace that is here for me at all times, assisting, guiding and supporting my day.

The Inner Voice

Ask, listen, trust and receive.

It can arrive as a feeling or as a sense of which way to go. It reveals itself as a vivid dream, as synchronicity or in plain words. It can be as subtle as a soft nudge. Our inner voice or divine guidance provides direction and assistance from the source of all universal wisdom, and therefore is always positive and light filled. It will never lead us to do anything that is negative or destructive as our soul's wisdom only operates on a plane of light.

Perhaps you wonder, as I do, if the inner voice is *my* voice or that of a guide, an angel, a deity or God. It is my belief that it can be any or all of these possibilities. If our pure consciousness, or soul, is connected to all things, then we can access loving information from a wide variety of sources. Each of us must ask for guidance from a deeply personal place in alignment with our most precious beliefs. There is no one right way, only the right way for you.

It's important not only to listen to the inner voice in order to receive the message, but also to listen to what you are being guided to do, and act upon it. The more we act on our soul's guidance, the more we are able to hear it. We hear best when we trust in ourselves and in the benevolence of the universe. Ask, listen, trust and receive.

In the World:

⁎ Listen for your inner voice in every decision today. Your meditation practice will calm your mind and enhance your ability to hear and to feel on a higher vibrational plane.

⁎ Ask your more important life questions during your spiritual practice when your mind is calm. Remain open for answers and clues that may come in unusual ways. Trust and act on the guidance received.

⁎ Use your journal to collect stories about the guidance you requested and the insights you received. They will become uplifting and powerful reminders to look back upon.

In the Heart:

⁎ I trust that I will receive clear guidance and I will follow the promptings of my heart.

❧

Anticipating Abundance

I am thankful for the blessings of this day.

As we now know, the first thoughts that we impress on our subconscious mind in the morning can powerfully direct the course of our path throughout the day. Affirmations ("I am..." statements) are especially effective and can be used as a mantra, or repeated phrase, keeping our intention on track as the day unfolds. Below are a few examples. Affirmations work best when they are personal. If any part of a written affirmation doesn't resonate seamlessly in your heart, you have the creative license to rewrite it until it represents your energy and intention.

I am clear, focused and efficient in my work today.

I am peaceful, joyful and patient with my kids and friends.

I flow through the day with ease and grace.

I have all the time I need for all I need to do.

I listen for guidance and follow my inner voice.

The power of affirmations comes from imagining that we are our highest selves and believing in the best possible outcomes. We don't need to detail how things will happen. The universe will manifest our visions in ways beyond our wildest dreams.

Be thankful for the blessings of this day, and countless blessings will be on their way.

In the World:

✴ In your journal, create a few affirmations that fit your day or use some of the ones above. Close your eyes and sit for a few moments with relaxed breathing, repeating the affirmation, feeling gratitude as if the gifts have already been received.

✴ For more ideas, every **In the Heart** section is an affirmation.

In the Heart:

✴ I am thankful for the blessings of this day. Joy and gratitude radiate from me as I anticipate the abundant gifts of today.

Flight Preparations

*As I walk to the edge of the darkness and take one step over the side,
I believe I'll land on my feet, or I will learn to fly.*

It can take a lot of precious time to make big changes in our lives. It can take many years and thousands of steps to get to the precipice of transformation. Our next destination and the spiritual truths that are required on the journey will unfold at a pace that is right for each of us. But one thing is for sure: When you decide the time is right, it only takes one step over the side to become airborne. And surely you will soar.

Sometimes change is not our choice, and we find ourselves facing inevitable and unforeseen turmoil in our lives. Sometimes it is our choice —we feel stuck and choose to initiate a transition. Should you be facing great change or challenge, know that you are the pilot and ground crew of this bird, and your timing, no matter how long it takes, will be perfect for you. You will fly, sweet bird, with the wings of faith on the wind of grace.

It never hurts to have a short list of flight preparations for when the time comes to spread your wings and take to the skies of your new journey. Know that you are infinitely loved and divinely guided. Have patience with your heart and with your timing. Turn grace into your compass, and take some flying lessons for the soul.

In the World: Flying 101

∗ Sharpen your vision by clearly imagining scenes of your future contentment and peace.

∗ Strengthen your wings by making gradual changes.

∗ Be present and grateful for the moment you are in.

∗ Focus your ability to hear your inner voice by meditating daily.

∗ Rewrite fearful thoughts with encouraging affirmations.

∗ Assemble a navigational team of the finest guides in the heavens.

In the Heart:

∗ I spread my wings with courage, grace and divine assistance. I am prepared for things to work out even better than my wildest dreams.

February Blessings

May the voice of our highest wisdom rise up from the winter stillness.

The dawn of this new month rises in the relatively long dark night of winter. Times of darkness ask us to practice a little extra faith to remember that day by day the light is returning. Times of darkness ask us to practice a little extra patience to remember that there is a season for everything and it's okay to not be okay all the time.

Sometimes we need *a little extra*, and February may be one of those times. We might need a little extra love, warmth and compassion, a little extra self-care and downtime, a little extra soul time and spiritual practice time. When the inner voice is calling for us to slow down, may we give ourselves the gift of a little extra space to answer the call.

May the voice of our highest wisdom rise up from the winter stillness and offer comfort on our journey to loving ourselves within so we might be instruments of love in the world.

Be present.

Let the day flow with grace.

Expect joy. Be positive.

Serve with compassion.

Speak only kindness.

Impart only love.

Never forget you're not alone.

Give thanks for everything.

See goodness in others.

In the World:

✳ Invite these blessings into your heart as you begin this new day.

✳ Choose a word that will serve to illuminate your path this month.

✳ Write some intentions for the month of February.

In the Heart:

✳ When my inner voice calls, I answer the phone.

~γ⅃~

The Making of Miracles

Miracles don't happen to you. They happen through you.

Miracles happen through small moments and great beauty, through small prayers and great faith, through small rays of hope and great love. Through us.

The humble lotus plant grows through the dark muddy water to finally expand into layers of petals and open her blossom to the light. It may seem that the miracle is the brilliant lotus blossom that floats on the surface of the lake. But the incremental journey through the dark to the light is the real miracle. And like the lotus plant, the incremental journey of our lives, day by day through the dark to the light, is the real miracle.

The co-creation of our lives ultimately unfolds through the thoughts we think, the prayers we pray, the intentions we set, the guidance we invoke. We shape this day by the deliberate choice to act in ways that bring us closer to the light, and to allow the light to act *through* us.

Small actions can align us with powerful change and shape this day by transforming us into instruments through which miracles are made. It's all about small things—with great love.

In the World:

The miracle of today lies in:

∗ planting positive morning thoughts of love;

∗ acts of kindness for yourself and for others;

∗ gratitude and awe that awaken your spirit to the beauty around you;

∗ pain or joy that brings newfound depth of compassion and understanding;

∗ the awareness of signs, symbols, divine guidance and insight;

∗ choosing small actions, over and over again, that bring you closer to the love and to the light.

In the Heart:

∗ Today, I am a channel for miracles and a vehicle for positive transformation for myself and others.

❧

Filled to Overflowing

Today I give thanks for all of the things in my life that don't need fixing.

A sweet friend of mine is the dedicated full-time caretaker of a child and a spouse, both of whom suffer from debilitating diseases. She holds down a demanding job while coordinating all of the shopping, cooking and cleaning. She creates time to schedule and take everyone to their medical appointments and to get their medications before the bottles and homeopathic remedies run out. She falls into bed exhausted every night and gets up after a few hours of sleep to do it all again, with great love.

When I ask her how she is, I am always amazed and inspired by her response. After a deep breath, she will let out a long exhale and say, "Well...pretty good! Yes...we're doing *good* over here!" It sounds a bit like a pep talk for herself, but I've noticed as the years pass that she never complains. Not one word. Ever. She cries sometimes from exhaustion or frustration, but she never wishes her challenges away or looks at her life as the movement from one disaster to another as any one of us might.

Continuing to answer my question, she always counts the blessings that she does have. Someone had a good day yesterday. A symptom may have improved slightly with new meds. There was a snow delay, and she got an extra hour of sleep. Noticing the victories first, she always cheers for the smallest step forward and celebrates every inkling of the positive.

The simple act of noticing what's going right opens us to the abundance that lies in and around us all the time.

Today, may we give thanks for all of the things in our lives that don't need fixing, and fill our glass to overflowing.

In the World:

* Notice the tendency to complain. Replace complaint today with the awareness of all that is going well, of all that is beautiful, of the hundred precious things that deserve our gratitude.

In the Heart:

* Today I give thanks for all of the things in my life that don't need fixing.

~✦~

Keeping a Sabbath

The heart deserves uninterrupted time to answer the call of the spirit.

Just think. There can be a day when we can linger longer in our morning meditation. A day when we can stretch, breathe and align without a phone chirping on the corner of the yoga mat. There can be a day when our gratitude practice is not confined to a time of day, but a joyful lingering with the Creator of all gifts. A day to read, to contemplate, to welcome and to allow.

The word *Sabbath* originates in the word *sabat*, meaning *to stop, to dwell* or *to rest*. It honors God's rest following six magnificent days of creation. We, too, need rest after six full days of worldly ways. We need the space to remember the tender truth that most real creation doesn't take place on the phone. It happens in the heart. The heart deserves uninterrupted time to integrate the challenges and gifts of the magnificent co-creation of the past week. We can think of it as soul care.

The Sabbath is a day to honor the sacred spirit, remembering that our wisdom and clarity originate in moments of stillness and listening. After all of our *doing* this week, it is a retreat for the soul to step off the train of constant connectivity to bask in uninterrupted *being*. Consider unplugging each week to recharge your heart, create with your hands, nourish your soul and answer the call of spirit.

In the World:

* Plan for a day or part of a day when you expand your spiritual practice time and refrain from technology. Check your accounts a few times during the day if you need to, but don't feel compelled to answer what can be answered tomorrow. Your friends and colleagues will get used to it.

* Your time can be completely unscheduled, or you can have at the ready a good book, your journal, some cooking or hobby supplies, your kayak, your walking shoes—whatever supports your favorite contemplative activities.

* Plan an activity with your family or with a friend without electronics. Discover each other in a new way.

In the Heart:

* I joyfully allow myself a day of rest and renewal, of lingering and listening, of being and allowing. I welcome a day of soul care.

꧁

Befriending the Dark

Darkness is the fertile soil of the soul.

The first time I came home to the Hunters Road cabin after dark and shut off my lights at the end of the long gravel driveway, I sat in dread. This was a huge mistake. There was no way I was going to walk from the car down the tiered steps through the tunnel of trees to the front door. Nope. It was pitch-black, coal black, not-a-drop-of-light black. Perhaps the universe was sending me down a little joke, handing me a reflection of my life at that time. I sat for long minutes in humorless terror before a heart-pounding race to the door.

So why does darkness provoke fear and light provide safety? Why in spirituality do we equate dark with evil and light with goodness? Why do we dread the dark and race for the light? Isn't it possible that this dark night of my life was the most fertile ground I had ever walked upon?

After a few weeks, I allowed myself not only to tolerate but to befriend my darkest stories. I allowed myself to sit at the table with them. I allowed myself to look into the eyes of losses and see how they took me apart, how they washed me out, how they grew me back again, how they colored me in. And I found that God was in the dark too, shining a light that can only be seen from within it, a lighthouse to the ship. It's a precious place, really, if we can bear to anchor there for a while.

Late last night, I rolled down the driveway and shut off my lights. I got out of the car, walked to the middle of the clearing, and looked up. The coal black served as a backdrop for a glorious rendering of sparkling constellations. There, under the North Star, I knew, for the first time in my life, that I was not afraid of the dark and that within my darkness was also the face of love and courage, the face of beauty and faith. In my darkness was also the face of God.

In the World:

✳ When the dark is asking for your attention, follow her to the table and see what secrets she imparts. Love her as part of you. Learn from her and treasure her wisdom. Thank her, and allow her to leave when she's ready.

In the Heart:

✳ I accept and love every part of myself, the light and the dark. I learn from the dark as I learn from the light.

~\/~

Life Is a Gift

Through the eyes of gratitude, everything is a miracle.

What if, instead of our habitual mind chatter, the background of our consciousness was the rhythm of a constant, soft *thank you*?

This is not merely positive thinking or glass-half-full mentality. This is our soul in conversation with an abundant universe, expressing gratitude for the infinite miracles that surround us now and that will be arriving soon.

It's like floating in a sea of awe. It's like lying on your back under a sky of thanksgiving. It's like seeing everything through the eyes of gratitude.

It is not a stretch by any means to recognize our lives as being made up of an unending series of gifts. From sunrise to sundown, we are being given countless blessings that expand us, grow us, delight us and show us who we are. Even times of pain and suffering can arrive with the radiant awareness of divinity.

It depends on which eyes we use to see.

Gratitude acknowledges the magnitude of our lives as embodied spirit and the real truth of our short time here: *Life is a gift.*

In the World:

* Gratitude Awareness Practice: Beginning today, write down in your journal twenty things you are grateful for each day for three days. It sounds like a lot, and it's meant to be a lot. It will ask you to be aware of all of the tiny gifts and precious moments that might otherwise go unnoticed.

* In three days of Gratitude Awareness, you will lock in the habit of noticing the countless precious gifts that surround you.

* Continue the practice after the first three days, writing three to five gratitudes each day. Begin or end your day through the eyes of thanksgiving and abundance. It's a small practice that will change your life.

In the Heart:

* I see the world through the eyes of gratitude. I am aware of the constant miracles that surround me now.

～✓ ↙

The Greater Plan

Be patient with yourself. There may be a greater plan that you cannot see.

Sometimes the timeline in our mind is not at all what's going on in our lives. We set ourselves up against noble goals with deadlines that come and go without the results we are expecting. Let's be patient with ourselves. There is a lot more happening behind the scenes than we can see from here.

When I was looking for a rental house in the country to begin this new chapter in my life, I found the perfect cabin on a mountaintop. The views were incredible, and I could imagine myself writing there. I even knew where I would put each piece of thrift-store furniture that I didn't have yet. At the last minute, someone swooped in and bought my dream cabin. I had no place to live with only weeks before I needed to be out of my old house. I was devastated and adrift.

A few days later, two acquaintances who knew I was looking for a cabin wrote to me at almost the exact same time to tell me they just heard of a pretty place that would be coming up for rent the next day. It turned out that they were both telling me about the same cabin, where I now sit, bursting with gratitude that I'm here and not on the mountaintop. This is exactly where I need to be.

Prayers, desires and requests are always answered. There are ways of praying and tools of manifestation that we can use to better align with our goals and lay a path to their fruition.

But if we do our best praying and aligning, and still don't meet our goal, it's not a failure. A greater plan is at work. Have patience knowing that everything happens in its perfect time.

In the World:

∗ Know that you are always taken care of for your highest good, and be open to the possibility that your greatest disappointments may reveal themselves as blessings at some point down the road.

In the Heart:

∗ I am patient with myself and have faith that the perfect plan is unfolding for me now.

✕

I Am Moving Tomorrow

Simplify.

Although I don't have big pack-rat tendencies, with a move on the horizon I was stunned by the sheer volume of my possessions. My ship was anchored in place with a heavy load of goods onboard. Relocation would not be easy under these conditions. There was always the option to leave it for others to manage, you know, after I've gone on to the next life—which did sound like an appealing plan for my inner procrastinator. But I didn't want to miss this golden opportunity to lighten up a little.

So, well in advance of the move, I started chipping away at one drawer, one closet at a time. I did it thoughtfully and slipped it in here and there between students. As the move drew closer, I had to get more ruthless. I was not going to drag boxes of I-don't-know-what from the house to the cabin after they had already taken up space, unused for sixteen years. So I took a page from Marie Kondo's *Life-Changing Magic of Tidying Up* and asked of each item, *Does this bring me joy?* And honestly, the answer was usually a resounding *No!*

Even if you're not moving, there is no time like the present. My mom leaves an index card out in her laundry room that says, "I am moving tomorrow." She wants to keep the mentality of living lightly for when the time comes for an inevitable move.

One of my favorite Mary Oliver poems is called "Storage." In it, she tells of how she filled a rented storage space and left it to sit for years without any longing for its contents. One day she was inspired to call someone to come and haul everything away. She felt free as a bird when it was empty!

We, too, can know the feeling of freedom when we lighten our load. And the space we create when we simplify our lives makes room for what we truly love.

In the World:

✳ Do your heart and your loved ones a favor and consider simplifying. Start small with one drawer, one closet, one corner at a time. Make more room in your heart for love.

In the Heart:

✳ I simplify my life, creating space for the expansion of my soul.

You're Driving Me Nuts

Today may I be patient and kind to those who drive me a little nuts.

Patience is in the pause. It's in the heat of that small space right before we react when someone is making us crazy. Yes, I know, when we reach the boiling point, it's very hard to hold back the avalanche of frustration and anger. But that one little saving-grace pause can allow us to respond thoughtfully instead of reacting randomly.

It's easy to be kind to kind people. Not so much with those who seem, by their very nature, to drive us to the brink of insanity. There are times when we all have the right to be angry and express it, but mostly it just fuels the fire.

Anger is multiplied in the presence of anger. Anger is divided in the presence of love.

Kindness gets easier with practice, and as this day unfolds, we'll have lots of opportunities to give it a try. It's always *possible* to be kind. And it's usually possible to fend off anger with a little patience and perspective.

Maybe we owe a debt of gratitude to those who test our patience and leave us exhausted, emotionally waving a white flag. They are our best teachers. Just think, they give us endless practice at patience, kindness, compassion, setting limits and speaking our truth.

Every experience in life can be used as a lesson if we are willing students. And come to class with a little good humor.

In the World:

* *Patience.* Take a breath before reacting.

* *Kindness.* Formulate the kindest response possible.

* *Compassion.* Be open to understanding why they act the way they do.

* *Setting limits.* Respectfully find a way to set boundaries.

* *Truth.* It's possible to be honest and kind at the same time.

In the Heart:

* Today I will be patient and kind to those who drive me a little nuts.

We Invite You, Angels

Where your worries are, put angels there.

Let's begin today with a collective exhale, releasing the companion of anxiety. Take a shorter inhale of clear light, and a longer exhale of all that is troubling. Repeat. Shorter inhale of light, longer exhale of all the worries. Be present in this moment where all is manageable.

We invite you, angels, into this space of uncertainty. We invite you into our fear and rapid heart rates. We invite you into our lack of time and lack of contentment. We invite you into the home of our heart, where the weight of the world has taken up residence. We invite you into our messiness and chaos.

We invite you, angels, into our children's innocent minds, where their fears reside. We invite you to be with us during the influx of bad news and too much information. We invite you here when we feel alone or lacking direction.

We invite you, angels, into every step where help and healing is needed and welcomed. We invite you, angels, into this day.

Our invitation for divine companionship reminds us to surrender and ask for a little backup. In *Angel Letters,* author Sophy Burnham tells us that angels are everywhere. "What will bring their help? Asking. Giving thanks. Who will recognize them? Anyone." She goes on to say that when we "present ourselves, like children, in total trust and love and humble gratitude, then they will pour their blessings on us overwhelmingly. They play with us. They look after us. They heal us, touch us, comfort us with invisible warm hands, and always they try to give us what we want."

In the World:

✳ When overwhelm sets up shop in your heart, take a few breaths of shorter inhales of clear light and longer exhales of all that is worrisome.

✳ Invite your angels or special guardians into the day. Ask for the comfort and assistance you need. Release stress into their arms. Surrender a little and open your heart.

In the Heart:

✳ I am always guided and guarded by the divine presence of angels. They help me to release my worries to the power of love.

~·\~·/·~

The Relief of Impermanence

I flow with ease and grace through the constant change in my life.

After talking about death with hospice patients, I often entertain thoughts of my own transition. It may seem heavy on the surface, but actually, it's a relief to be reminded that everything is impermanent. Life will go on after we have gone, and knowing this while we're still here can really lighten our burden.

Last week during my hospice volunteer time, I had a patient confess that she felt as if nothing would be changed by her death. Yes, a few friends and family members would miss her, but the world would keep spinning pretty much as usual. I assured her that her energy had already changed the world and would be part of it forever. *There, there, dear.*

But wait! She brings up an essential perspective. If we're not in charge of anything truly permanent, why are we pulling our hair out over all these details? *Because our minds are in control.* Shouldn't we put our focus on enjoying the precious moments of this life while we're here? *Absolutely.* Shouldn't we be stressing less and loving more? *You got it.*

That takes a lot of rocks out of the backpack. *Feeling lighter.* So today we delight in a few affirmations, noting the joys of impermanence.

In the World:

* Instead of resisting change, I flow with the blessings and notice the gifts.

* Instead of controlling, I unclench my fists and let go of the outcome.

* Instead of being in charge, I surrender to the divine wisdom of ease and grace.

* Instead of losing my balance, I maintain a spiritual practice to stay centered in the challenges of my life.

* Instead of being angry or regretful, I am compassionate and forgiving.

* Instead of holding on to the darkness, I release it and open to all that is loving and light.

In the Heart:

* I flow with ease and grace through the constant change in my life. I relax, ask for guidance, listen for direction and respond from a place of love.

Lovey and Dovey

*You are loved, valuable, blessed, beautiful, enough and worthy—
every day of the year.*

Once mourning doves fall in love, they vow to stay together for life. When Maya was small, upon learning this, she named a pair of mourning doves Lovey and Dovey. Well, this morning, a new Lovey and Dovey are visiting outside the window, reminding me of what I'd rather forget— that Valentine's Day is coming.

For twosomes across the land, Valentine's Day is a time to express love for each other through greeting card sentiments, flowers, chocolates, a special dinner and time set aside for just us two. The Loveys and Doveys pair off and enter their own world of love, sweet love.

So what happens to Lovey on Valentine's Day when Dovey is off in another field?

I'll tell you what happens. Come to think of it, she's totally fine. In fact, better than fine. She is perfectly capable of buying her own chocolates and flowers, and she absolutely loves the idea of making it a special night of self-care. Right. That's what Lovey is going to do. She's going to make it a night to remember the love that she's made of every single day of the year. Lovey does not need a holiday to know just how loved—and how lovable—she is.

Lovey knows her worth and she honors her unique gifts by taking care of herself, mind, body and soul. She does this so that the love within her can flow freely from source energy to the world. It's a pretty big job.

Lovey wishes Dovey a lifetime of peace and love in the other field—then thinks no more about it. Lovey is busy radiating love to fields all over the planet.

In the World:

* If you find yourself solo on Valentine's Day, make it a special day for you. Ask yourself what you need, and respond to your inner knowing. Treat yourself to something special, and lavish abiding love on the beautiful soul that you are.

In the Heart:

* I am loved, valuable, blessed, beautiful, enough and worthy—every day of the year.

Happy Sailing

Love is the wind in the sails of the soul.

You, my friend, are a boat, and not just any boat. You are a beautiful sailboat with sails up, ready to catch the wind. The boat is your body, offering protection from the water and containing you as you make your way through the ocean of this day. The sails are your soul, moving you in the right direction, propelling you on the path to your most adventurous life lessons.

You might be facing clear, open waters or maybe choppy seas or a full-blown storm. But no matter what your beautiful sailboat faces today, it can be an amazing day when your sails are filled with the wind of love. And yours already are.

It's easy to drift off course when we fill up on too much daily news and social media, where the images and stories paint a seascape of fear. We see the ocean differently though the eyes of love, which is the most important thing we will do today. It's what we're here for. Love is the endless power behind all creation and the gentle essence of our radiant spirit.

Love is the wind in the sails of the soul.

It is not where we are going or how fast we get there that gives this day worth. It is how much we are able to radiate love to everyone who crosses our path, no matter who they are or what we are trying to get done. Love is what a successful day is built upon.

If we could lift up above our lives and see as the angels see, we would see that love is all that shines through the haze of humanity. The love of our soul is all we really leave behind. Happy sailing!

In the World:

* Just for today, speak only loving words and think only loving thoughts, taking a break from negativity, complaint and constant media.

* Refrain from judgment, offering compassion to all beings.

In the Heart:

* Today, all of my thoughts and words are empowered by love. I leave behind the light of love in all of my travels.

~✣~

Love Letter to Saint Valentine

Love is always the answer.

Dear Saint Valentine: You, my dear, have captured my heart with your steadfast faith, limitless love and unfortunate beheading. Now we live in a brighter world where today, in honor of you, true loves will be showered with flowers and chocolates. It seems we got the better deal.

Although your life remains quite the mystery, some stories tell us that you were a priest or bishop who met your gruesome end in Rome on this very day back in the third century. You found yourself imprisoned by following your heart and illegally marrying lovers in the church.

Then there is the tale of you restoring sight to the blind daughter of your jailer. It seems you had an unwavering belief in doing what we must in the name of love, regardless of the consequences. When it comes to love, you didn't hold back and you didn't back down. And you paid the ultimate price. What appears to be an airy-fairy holiday in your name down here on earth may have more depth beneath the surface than it first seems.

I like to imagine that you believed in the magic of love. I like to imagine that you knew there were no conditions to love's generosity. I like to imagine that you elevated love as the most beautiful and sweetest gift ever given. Maybe the flowers and chocolates aren't such lightweight symbols after all; they are the beautiful and sweet gifts of love.

The big ideals that you contemplated before you gave your life are only beginning to dawn on me, dear Valentine. That it's imperative we follow the heart. That it's honorable to value our beliefs as sacred. That we can actually love our enemies and their families. That amidst all her contradictions and complications, no matter what the question is, love is always the answer.

Thanks for showing us what it means to be someone's Valentine.

With all my love. 🖤

In the World:

✴ Today, celebrate the beautiful and sweet blessings of love.

In the Heart:

✴ I believe in the magic of love and the unconditional gifts of love's generosity.

Compassion in the Ambulance

We are one family, made of love.

I had been sick for weeks with relentless internal bleeding from a uterine fibroid. My scheduled surgery was still a week off, and I was trying to power through my days, anemic and determined. I looked like the walking dead. Then I fainted and actually looked like the *dead* dead.

In the ambulance I left my body.

I was hovering outside myself, over the young EMT's shoulder, watching her as she tried to set up an IV in my left arm. She was panicking. "I can't get a vein! I can't find anything! We're losing her!"

In the clarity of pure consciousness, I had an overwhelming flood of compassion for her. I could feel her distress as if it were mine and was filled with empathy. I was overflowing with an incredible love and wanted to console her, to tell her everything would be all right. Years later, I can still feel my compassion for her.

Isn't it interesting that in spirit form, our thoughts are not of ourselves first but of others? I wasn't thinking, *Hurry up, you fool! I'm dying here!* Instead, I wanted it to work out well for her also. She and I were one. I was filled with the greatest love imaginable.

This experience confirmed my belief that our essence is made of light, beauty, kindness, love, generosity. In order to love one another, we need only to sweep the dust off our everyday lives and look under the veil.

We are one family, made of love.

In the World:

✳ Move through the world as a being of unconditional love. Be reminded of the light that you are made of, and you will shine your love in all of the dark places—and on all of the people—that need your light today.

In the Heart:

✳ I am made of light and love, and am connected to all beings. I share uplifting energy with all who cross my path and my mind today.

Winter Faith

Everything is unfolding in its perfect time.

If you are waking within, feeling the stir of a new beginning but not yet the actualization of the dream, today is a good day to have Winter Faith. New beginnings stir in the mind, body and soul before they ever break ground in our outer lives.

They start with faith in possibilities. They start with small steps and big dreams. They start with a knowing that you *can* do this. They start with a belief in yourself and in the seeds you have been planting and nurturing with love through the dark days of winter.

Sometimes we ration kindness toward ourselves, basking in the rewards of contentment only when we feel we have accomplished something tangible. It is during these times, when no rewards are visible, that we need our kindness and inner support most of all.

Last week, after two isolated winter months in the cabin, I wrote myself a note. Higher self to earth self. It addressed me as a kind friend: "Be patient. You have all the time you need. Your work is meaningful, and you are being guided by a powerful connection with the divine. Enjoy the journey and the questions. There is no race or struggle. This is only a path of love." I read it every morning.

Today, let's look at our dreams and our creativity in a new way. Let's believe in the germinating of ideas. Let's be patient as we create space for growth. Let's get comfortable not having all of the answers yet. Let's reach for an understanding that allows us to be grateful even when there are no tangible results. Let's open to Winter Faith and see the void, too, as sacred time.

In the World:

* Hold strong to an unshakable belief in your dreams, and be gentle with yourself in their time of gestation. Believe that everything happens in its perfect time and that you are where you are meant to be.

* Write yourself a note, higher self to earth self. Tell yourself in kind, loving words what you most need to know.

In the Heart:

* I have the heart of patience and the soul of faith. I believe that everything is unfolding for me in its perfect time.

Forgiveness

*Forgiveness is not an action we have to take
but an attitude we can choose to adopt.*

Over the years I have created a lot of quotes on the art of forgiveness in the process of trying to figure it out for myself. During the birthing of Every Day Spirit—the app, as well as the daily social media posts and the website—I have been making my way through the land mines of marital separation and have only recently arrived in a little home of my own. It's been a road—oh yes it has.

The actions that brought me here changed my world as I knew it and gave me a golden opportunity to look at forgiveness from every angle. I found myself wondering if there was a way around it, an option to do it partway and still get to hold a little grudge, because after all, I was the victim, right?

Nope. By holding on to my hurt, pain and anger, I was doing more harm to myself than anything that had happened in the marriage. By not fully forgiving, I was interfering with my own growth and interrupting my own healing. Shards of hate, anger, fear and retribution remained in my heart, and their presence within was making me into someone that I did not want to be.

I came to realize that forgiveness was not an action I had to take, but an attitude I could choose to adopt. I didn't *have* to do it; it was the next best step to healing. Not only did the change of attitude free my soul from the negative storyline, but my heart seemed to open to even more compassion, love and peace than I ever dreamed possible. Forgiveness was an amazing gift—to me.

In the World:

✳ Make an effort to understand the art of forgiveness, discovering articles and books that resonate with your beliefs. Take gentle steps toward forgiveness and freedom from past drama as you are ready.

✳ Practice relentless self-care and self-compassion as you make your way through the journey of forgiveness. In your journal, create some affirmations that encourage you on your way forward.

In the Heart:

✳ I have the power to choose to forgive and release myself from the pain of the past. I have the strength to forgive freely and fully.

Ahimsa

From the deepest valley to the sky above, let's cover the world with love.

The other day at a busy eye doctor's office, a woman ahead of me at the reception desk said in broken English that she needed help understanding her bill. In the most compassionate way, the receptionist took her aside and explained everything slowly, respectfully and clearly. Although the line was growing, there was not a note of impatience in her voice.

As I was leaving, in front of me was the same receptionist walking an elderly man all the way to his car. Chatting joyfully with him, she exuded pure love. I waited for her to gently close his car door and I told her what a beautiful person she was and how she changed several lives today by her kindness. She smiled shyly and said quietly, "That's just who I am."

I was reminded of an ancient little Sanskrit word that takes on the depth of the receptionist's love. *Ahimsa* translates to *noninjury*, and it is a key virtue based on the belief that we are all sparks of divine love, so to harm any living thing would be to harm all living things. When we take away all violence, what we find is the essence of abiding love. So, not only is ahimsa the absence of cruelty, hate and injustice, it is the deliberate presence of love and kindness for ourselves and for all beings. Yes, on the soul level, that's just who we are.

The purest love flows up from the endless well that resides in all of us. By walking gently on the earth, taking care to harm as few of God's creatures as possible, we become instruments of that great love, spreading kindness to all who cross our path.

In the World:

✳ Walk through today with a gentle step, spreading pure love while doing no harm.

✳ The yogic sage Patanjali described an eightfold path to enlightenment of which the *Yamas*, ethical codes of conduct, are the first step. Ahimsa is the first *Yama*. If you are drawn to yoga, you might be enriched by learning these guidelines to a peaceful, loving and enlightened life.

In the Heart:

✳ By a spark of divine love, I am connected to all other beings. With a kind and loving heart, I take care not to harm any living thing.

Be at Peace

A calm connection is just a moment away.

Be at peace, and let go of all attachments to outcomes.

Be at peace, and know that love always lives right here, right now.

Be at peace, and open to divine timing.

Be at peace, and let the world spin without you.

Be at peace, and breathe, just breathe.

Be at peace, releasing stress, anxiety and worry.

Be at peace, allowing each moment to enter without resistance.

Be at peace, shoulders soft, heart open, spine aligned with heaven.

Be at peace, knowing you are never alone.

Be at peace, and call on angelic assistance for any task.

Be at peace, and listen for guidance.

Be at peace, imagining the highest good for all.

Be at peace, and make an offering of your day.

Be at peace, and feel how infinitely loved you are.

In the World:

* When you have reached the bottom of the well and there is no more for you to give, or when stress has robbed you of your composure, remember that a calm connection is just a moment away. Stop. Breathe. Be at peace.

* Step back for a moment of perspective, bringing serenity to your mind and body, welcoming your soul wisdom. You've got this. Peace. Love. Joy.

In the Heart:

* I am peaceful. I am calm. I am eternal. Today, divine grace protects me, strengthens me and leads me on my way.

Date Night with the Soul

May I quiet my words and listen. May I calm my thoughts and be.
May I soften my heart and open. May I still my soul and receive.

When I sit down to meditate, the noise of the world can be insanely jarring. My ears are ringing, my thoughts are galloping, my body is buzzing. I can be so filled with motion that I require a transition, a place of in-between in which I gently put on the brakes and roll to a stop. To that end, I sit for a few minutes, breathing in deeply, and exhaling longer than my inhale to remind my body that it's okay to slow down, and to announce to my mind that she is going to be offline for a bit. I feel my mind resisting—*Can't you see I'm busy here?*—so I must tell her that she can have my plans and concerns back just as soon as I'm finished meditating. She usually behaves after that.

Yes, there is Her and there is Me. There is the Little i, and the Big I. There is the Thinker and the Observer. There is the judgmental, controlling Ego Mind, and the limitless, unbound Soul. Meditation is when the Soul plugs into the source energy and recharges so it can intuitively lead the Mind.

When I don't give time to Me, my Mind takes control of everything and powers through in a Blitz of Doing. I become too serious and sometimes, seriously off track. There is infinitely more fun and flow under the insightful direction of the Soul.

So now that we've decided who's boss, I just watch my breath flow in... and out...gently floating a mantra or phrase over the top. I breathe in. I breathe out. In. Out. It feels like a very cool mini-retreat.

When my Mind gets unruly and tries to jump in, I tap her on her little head with the wand—call it what it is, *thinking*—and go back to the wide-open Soul space. This little tapping game is like gymnastics for the Mind, training her to chill while the Soul gets a date night. After I'm finished, we say goodbye at the Door of Noisy Thoughts, and I know that I bring a greater piece of Me, and of love, into the world.

In the World:

✳ Keep up your daily meditation dates with your soul. You will fall in love again and again.

In the Heart:

✳ I make time for the sweet pleasure of finding peace within.

꙳ᢣ

Unfailing Strength

Live with gratitude for the gift of time.

Last week, my friend Olga sent me a beautiful essay that was written by one of her former students, Gabriela, who was diagnosed with cancer. As a thirty-eight-year-old mother of six, she broke down under the weight of her thoughts, imagining her husband and children living on without her. The future was inconceivable, and her anxiety was unbearable.

A friend of Gabriela's shared with her the following passage from Saint Francis de Sales: "Do not look forward to what might happen tomorrow; the same Everlasting Father who cares for you today, will take care of you tomorrow and every day. He will either shield you from suffering or He will give you unfailing strength to bear it. Be at peace, then, and put aside all anxious thoughts and imaginings."

She pinned it on her fridge and read it every morning. As she meditated on the words, she asked that her fears about the future be lifted and to have faith in what she could not understand with her rational mind.

Eventually, peace came over her. She found ways to stay in the moment and to appreciate, with gratitude, the blessing of each day. Gabriela reordered her priorities to spend more time with her family at home. In her words: "Most importantly, I also learned to live day by day. I learned to savor each moment, not to dwell on the past, not to grow anxious about the future, but to appreciate the simple, small moments of my daily life and to trust that with God, there can be peace amidst distress."

When faced with a frightening diagnosis, we are also given the chance to change the way we think about our lives. It offers a precious chance to surrender in faith to the divine and to live with gratitude for the gift of time.

This lesson is ours, right here and now, even without the diagnosis.

In the World:

✷ As an extension of our call to peace from the last two days, offer your greatest trials and fears to the divine. Have faith that you will find peace within your challenges. Savor each moment with gentle gratitude and courageous trust.

In the Heart:

✷ Today I surrender my challenges to the divine and live with gratitude for the gift of time.

The Garden of the Future

Every act of kindness plants a seed.

Thoughts are energy, and as we learned in physics class, energy stays around forever; it is neither created nor destroyed. What they didn't tell us was that our thoughts have great power, germinating into new buds that grow endlessly into the future. We all change the world whether we intend to or not. And we always change the world for the better when we plant the seeds of kind thoughts and words.

As our spiritual awareness grows, we pay more deliberate attention to our thoughts and actions because we are aligning more and more with our shared humanity. In connection with all beings, compassion is our most natural state of consciousness. We come from one love, so to lift up one of us is to lift up all of us.

It begins with the smallest offering of a smile or an encouraging word. A seed is planted and paid forward, perhaps from hand to hand as the result of a single kindness shared. Our everyday actions of love propagate and spread infinitely.

Today each of us contributes to the garden of the future. Even if we don't see the results of our actions, no kindness, no act of love, is ever wasted.

We leave the world a more beautiful, a more colorful and a more loving place when we sow kindness generously and freely.

Because every act of kindness plants a seed.

In the World:

* Spread kindness abundantly today. Keep your heart open for chances to share a kind word or action, no matter how small.

* Include yourself in your acts of kindness.

* Look for nothing in return. Give with an open hand and share with an open heart.

In the Heart:

* Through generous acts of kindness and love, I sow never-ending seeds in the garden of a loving future.

Lessons from a Fire-Breathing Bull

Be in awe of creatures great and small.

I crossed the one-lane bridge and caught sight of the enormous black bull who lives in the bucolic field next to a lake on Hunters Road. Walking up the hill, I wonder, *What is your name, Big Bull?* In rhythm with my steps, I roll over possible names for him. He needs a regal name. A big name for a big guy. A name for the ages. *Abraham. That's your name.*

Standing at the split-rail fence, I call him bravely but sweetly. "Abraham! Abraham! Come here, honey! Come on, boy!" He stares at me, then slowly and thoughtfully, the ginormous bull lumbers my way, male parts sashaying with each thunderous step. I stand my ground, holding on to the fence until Abraham is standing directly in front of me, within arm's reach. I can see his beautiful brown eyes, with hundreds of eyelashes over each one. His body is over three feet wide; his head towers over mine. Surely this is the biggest animal I've ever been this close to.

I'm not sure at what point I lose my senses, but I am overtaken by the sudden desire to reach out and pet Abraham on the head. He has a little tuft of curls where his third eye would be, and I think, *Oh! I must touch that!* (So much for inner wisdom.) I reach out my hand to give him a little pet, and he instantly inhales and exhales with such hurricane force that—like a dragon—a cloud of steam comes from his gigantic nostrils! Straight out of Harry Potter. I scream and jump back (I have no wand), rolling backwards down the hill. *Oh, Abraham.*

You might think that the moral of the story is: Do not touch a bull on the third eye. Good one. I'm also trying a few others on for size: 1. Our uniqueness makes life an adventure of discovery and awe. 2. Don't assume. Just because one thinks they are offering love does not mean it will be received as such. 3. Respect all living things, and be humble in their presence. 4. Always carry a wand. Since that time, as I pass Abraham, I send him a blessing and continue on up the street, marveling at my insanity—and his incredible beauty.

In the World:

⁕ All creatures, from the bulls to the bees, need our support, love and protection to thrive and survive. Assist in ways that resonate with your heart to respect their uniqueness and protect their habitats.

In the Heart:

⁕ I honor the miraculous design of every living inhabitant of the earth.

꧁

The Art of an Apology

An apology is an act of grace, a soul truth, a gift of the heart.

I vividly remember making my first real apology as an adult. I was in the car with a friend, and as he was talking, I was working on how to phrase my wrongdoing. His sentences were like double Dutch jump ropes—I couldn't find a way in. I couldn't blurt something out into dead air or thread it into a lighthearted conversation. As we crossed the 14th Street Bridge into DC, I was losing my breath and my nerve.

Then, a light bulb. I needed a "bridge" line to introduce my apology. It's funny that I can't remember what I was apologizing for, but I remember the way I figured out how I was going to do it. These bridge lines are an essential part of my communication toolbox to this day.

An apology is an act of grace, a soul truth, a gift of the heart. It's hard, but beautiful. It asks us to get humble and (oh, no) vulnerable. It asks us to accept our imperfections and the inevitable screwups that come with being human. It asks us to put someone else before us. It asks us to lay down our pride and confess honestly. It asks us to take responsibility for the way our actions feel to others. If it is sincere, an apology is a nonnegotiable part of our spiritual integrity and a bonding thread of light between one soul and another.

Being forgiven is not the goal of an apology. We apologize because we can see with new and more compassionate eyes that what we have done has caused harm, and we are truly sorry. If the art of an apology does not come easily to you, join the party and start practicing. It's one of the most beautiful actions on earth.

In the World:

* Try out a few possible bridge lines to introduce your apology: "I'd like to tell you something important. Is this an okay time?" "I've done something I don't feel great about, and I want to tell you about it." "I feel badly about what I said yesterday."

* Then without excuses and with heartfelt love, jump right in with the naked words: "I am so sorry I..."

In the Heart:

* I apologize from the heart and embody an openness that is honest, vulnerable, freeing and healing for all.

The Same Sky

The darker the night, the brighter the stars.

I was forty weeks pregnant and a few hours this side of my due date. My doctor's office in Vienna, Austria, was humming with the polite buzz of German and my long flowered dress made an irreverent statement in the sea of fitted black and brown. Funny the things we remember.

After I was called in, a flurry of worried hands took turns on the Doppler. Then the world stopped. Time. Stood. Still. I could see my doctor shaking her head. "I'm sorry…" I heard only clanging in my head.

The next many years saw me drowning in an ocean of crushing grief. And strangely, some unexpected moments of hope. First came the relentless search for God. If my child was *there*, I wanted to know exactly where *there* was. I searched until I found her through the veil, within me, in all things beautiful. Next came compassion. I was now in fiery solidarity with all loss—great, small, different—and these were my new people. I understood more about the precious nature of humanity and was united with all suffering beings.

Small talk and surface living burned away along with my old self. The depth of my grief was the darkest of nights, yet my capacity for joy seemed to reach the same distance in the other direction, to the stars. Life was an ocean of feelings that words could not touch. One step at a time in what was an eternity, I inched toward trusting life again.

There are dark nights of loss and dark nights of the soul. Dark nights of betrayal and dark nights of fear. In that night, the stars will beam their light and, with it, the grace of an insight, an illumination with a prompt to feel, to grow, to change, to be in awe, that would not be felt or seen were it not for the darkness. Look up toward the stars. We are all here with you, looking up at the same sky, shoulder to shoulder, never alone.

In the World:

✳ We all have our own path through grief. There is no wrong turn or right way. This sacred road is not linear but one of blinding darkness and flashes of stars. Be where you are, and be patient with your heart.

In the Heart:

✳ I am the guardian of my own unique grief process. I am patient as I come to understand who I am becoming. I feel everything with an open heart and know that I am never alone.

∽⅄⊱

Faith is Winning

May my faith be stronger than my fear.

I have lots of faith. I also have lots of fear. The fears tug at me relentlessly. Real ones like the illness of a family member and finances, and not-so-real ones like slipping hopelessly behind in some imaginary race to get through the piles on my desk.

But on most days, faith is winning. Not by default, but because each morning I roll out of bed at dawn to lock in practices that I can pull out of my back pocket when fear strikes.

Each day I remind myself to watch for the sacred woven through the small moments. Each evening I give thanks for the divine order and its perfect timing. Every hour in between, I remind myself that I am not alone in this. These things seem to shore up my faith stockpiles and straighten up my shoulders a bit.

Faith is not really an underdog when we realize that we have a pretty strong faith practice already. Most of us don't have much fear about waking up or breathing, right? We have faith that we will be here to open our eyes in the morning. We have faith that air will fill our lungs without too much conscious effort. We take for granted this daily testament of trust in the universe.

Faith doesn't have to wrestle fear to the ground or banish it from the kingdom. It just needs to have the upper hand. And we have everything we need to make faith the victor.

Use your spiritual practice as a candle of faith in the dark room of fear, and voila! Fear is illuminated into obsolescence.

In the World:

✳ When worries threaten to rob your peace of mind today, call on the faith tools of your spiritual practice. Enlist prayer, affirmations and patience. Activate thoughts of trust and light; surrender to a higher plan, and they will gradually illuminate the situation. Stay with the practice until you feel the shift. Fake it 'til you make it if need be. Fear doesn't know the difference.

In the Heart:

✳ I focus my energy on positive outcomes for the highest good of all. My faith is stronger than my fear.

Just Play Monopoly

Find joy in small things.

When Maya was fifteen, a historic snowstorm dumped more than two feet of snow on the DC area, and we became frozen in time. I rejoiced in what seemed to be a windfall of freedom. Maya found Nirvana in a series of canceled school days and in the prospect of not having to work so hard for so many hours a day. It was like an impromptu vacation in our own home. Oh, the gift of unscheduled time.

As several days went by with still no school opening in sight, I began to see projects in the house that I "needed" to do. It seemed that the house was suddenly begging for a serious facelift. I wanted to scrub the kitchen floor, wipe down the cabinets, clean baths, set up the basement for recording projects. My list gathered more steam to include painting the baseboards, organizing files and practicing piano. I found myself feeling quite busy in our formerly relaxed vacation house in the snow.

On the third Snowmageddon afternoon, Maya made a proposition. "Mom, let's play a game of Monopoly." Without missing a beat, I said, "Okay, honey, but I have to get some things done first. I need to put some laundry in, vacuum upstairs and..."

She interrupted me with an annoyed expression and said, "You know, Mom, no one would care if you didn't 'get things done.' None of the things you think you have to do really need to be done *now*."

Don't you hate it when your kid nails you? I had made a list and given priority to crossing things off. And it dawned on me in that moment that she probably wouldn't ask me to play Monopoly many more times. It was fun for her today, on a snow day, with none of her friends around. Suddenly it became clear that there was nothing more important in the world.

We should just play Monopoly. And find joy in small things.

In the World:

* Be where you are today. That's where the joy is.

In the Heart:

* I am flexible with my plans, following love's lead. With lightness in my heart, I am present for joy in the small moments of this day.

~✎~

The Computer Coma

I surrender my small plans to divine order.

When we call on the divine for ease and grace in the midst of our busyness, we are always met with support. Trouble for me is, I lose consciousness and forget to ask.

My daughter tells me that when I'm at the computer, I'm in a coma. I'm staring so rabidly at the screen and my focus is so white-hot that fire comes out of the top of my head. Not really, but she can stand at the door and ask me a question, and I don't hear, don't move and don't even flinch.

Then comes the exasperated, "Blink twice if you can hear me talking."

When I get up after hours of making art, updating the app or even answering email, I feel disoriented. *Where was I?* The more disturbing thought is, *Why did I try to muscle through all that work without constantly calling on the divine for assistance as I went along?*

So here's what I do now. I set my phone alarm for every hour as I work. When the alarm rings, I bring myself to the present moment and surrender my work to the divine.

My prayer usually starts with a surprised, *Hey there!* As in, *Wow, God, are you still here?* I get my bearings and continue, *I know you are assisting me in all my work and bringing light through my hands, my eyes and my thoughts. With your help, everything happens with ease and grace. Please send extra angels for ___. Thank you!* And bam. I'm back to work.

What I surrender is my small self, the one who thinks she's in control and has all the answers. It doesn't feel like I'm giving up power but instead releasing control and allowing the power of a much greater force to step in and take the lead.

The results of teamwork are remarkable.

In the World:

✳ Set your phone alarm for every hour while you work. Take a minute each hour to ask for companionship on your daily round.

In the Heart:

✳ Wisdom and grace from my higher power guides all my actions today.

❦

Leap Day Prayer

What you pour into this precious day,
you will receive back in a cup of beauty.

May this day be especially blessed.

May this day be grounded in the radiant energy of love.

May this day use my gifts for the work of the divine.

May this day be the best day of the rest of my life.

May this day bring the opportunity to lift someone up with kindness.

May this day remind me that I am unique, worthy and irreplaceable.

May this day flow with ease and grace through every activity.

May this day be one of peace and patience.

May this day be a constant prayer of gratitude, no matter what I am given.

May this day bring moments of hope, joy and laughter.

May this day give me the chance to let someone know they are loved.

May this day reflect my faith in the perfect imperfection of all events.

May this day find me humble in my thoughts and words.

May this day be especially blessed. Amen.

In the World:

✳ What you pour into this precious and unique Leap Day, you will receive back in a cup of beauty. Pour in your most magnificent self.

In the Heart:

✳ I step into this day knowing that infinite love is mine in every moment, and that I am especially blessed in all things.

March Blessings

In the garden of my heart is the promise of spring.

Today we welcome into our hearts a new month that includes the spring equinox. On the first day of spring, the hours of daylight equal the hours of darkness, and for the rest of the season, we are gifted with a little more light each day. With every new leaf and bloom, we witness nature's glorious co-creation with the divine. And we are reminded that this co-creation with the divine is happening within us too.

We open to the promise of March with a gentle invitation for this new month and new season of the heart:

May we invite love to think through us today. May we invite nature to be joyful through us today. May we invite faith to walk with us today. May we invite grace to act through us today. May we invite kindness to speak through us today. May we invite new blooms to grow through us today. May we invite our highest wisdom to work through us today.

Be present.

Let the day flow with grace.

Expect joy. Be positive.

Serve with compassion.

Speak only kindness.

Impart only love.

Never forget you're not alone.

Give thanks for everything.

See goodness in others.

In the World:

* Invite these thoughts into your heart as you begin a new chapter.

* Choose a word that will be a guiding light for your month.

* Write your intentions for the month of March.

In the Heart:

* I welcome the creative beauty and light of spring into my heart.

❧

Presence

May your path be clear before you. May you be at peace with yesterday.
May you be present in the moment for the blessings of this day.

For just a moment, let's set down the burden of the future. Let's take that box, with all of its concerns and dreams, close the lid and set it down. Now imagine a clear path before you, illuminated in brilliant white light, where the perfect experiences manifest for your future.

And for just a moment, let's set down the weight of the past. Take that box, with all of its regret and sadness, close the lid and set it down. Now looking back, bless your experiences, surround them in brilliant white light and allow yourself to be at peace with yesterday.

Here we are, present in the moment for the blessings of this day.

In *The Power of Now*, Eckhart Tolle explains, "Unease, anxiety, tension, stress, worry—all forms of fear—are caused by too much future, and not enough presence. Guilt, regret, resentment, grievances, sadness, bitterness, and all forms of nonforgiveness are caused by too much past, and not enough presence."

In other words, it's not possible to be completely present while we worry about the future. It's not possible to be completely present while being regretful about the past.

Today, let's leave those boxes alone and be here now. Let's stay in the present as it unfolds and experience the wonder and the gift of each moment.

In the World:

* Practice presence by taking any routine activity and giving it your fullest attention. When washing the dishes, driving your car or making coffee, notice your actions with all of your senses.

* Notice how your inner peace grows along with your ability to be present.

In the Heart:

* My path is clear before me. I am at peace with yesterday. I am present in the moment for the blessings of this day.

The Circle of Love

May love rise in your heart and shine on your day.

We can be the kindness that reminds someone that the world is a loving place. Today, we can be a ray of sun in someone's darkness. Into this day we can weave a simple kindness that gently eases the pain of another while bringing a lightness to our own hearts as well.

Through small offerings and acts of kindness, we activate the flow of love from ourselves, into the heart of another and back to our hearts in a circle of divine love without end. Today we can show unconditional love to others that will fill our hearts with love in return.

In the World:

* Lift up others by preparing yourself in the morning for a positive day. Your spiritual practice sets the tone by bringing you home to your highest self.

* Be aware of the energy you bring with you as you leave the house.

* Be generous with compliments to family, coworkers and strangers alike. It only takes a few genuine kind words to awaken someone's inner joy.

* Listen well when someone is talking. Consider waiting a little longer before adding your thoughts. Ask a question that shows your interest.

* Assume everyone comes from a place of love, even when it seems otherwise. When you are present without judgment, you bring out the best in others. Wayne Dyer put it beautifully when he said, "See the light in others and treat them as if that is all you see."

* Smile easily. A smile almost always evokes a return smile and raises the energy of the room.

* Be encouraging to those who are struggling. If you know someone is going through a challenging time, ask about it. Offer some words of support.

In the Heart:

* Today I have the power to lift the spirits of anyone who crosses my path or my mind. I find it easy to spread love and feel the flow of love back into my heart.

⤳⤲

Horse Whispering at Dawn

Sometimes silence says it all.

On a frosty morning, I woke in near darkness to see that the sun, pregnant with light, was just under the ridge. I heard a silent message that there was something going on in the field, so I wrapped myself in a blanket and moved to the window. I gasped in awe at the scene.

Three horses were standing in perfect formation on a hill near the house, heads bowed, facing in the direction where the sun would soon rise, totally still. I felt I had been transported to an important ceremony, one of reverence, wisdom and grace. I watched, barely breathing, then in a note of solidarity I sat as near to them as I could—at the kitchen table—and parked my consciousness on the fence next to them. We meditated together. It was as if I was right there. Sounds crazy—I know.

I peeked at the brightening sky, and the moment the first ray of sun broke over the mountain, the horses began to gently stir. Without another thought, I pulled on my rain boots with the blanket still wrapped tightly around me and walked, ever so slowly toward the field. One foot crunched on the frozen leaves. Then I stopped. Then another step, slowly, mindfully, head down, in reverence for the silence of the dawn. I continued my slow march as all three horses stood still watching my approach, grooms on the altar.

I arrived at the fence and looked up. They were walking slowly toward me. Shadow put his head down on the fence, and with arms still enclosed in the blanket, I bowed and put my third eye on his, and stayed, connected like that, joined and still. Ever so slowly, the two other horses put their heads on either side of Shadow. I lifted my hands to the heads of the outer horses, and we all four stayed bonded in a silent group hug for minutes. I looked up with grateful tears.

No words necessary.

In the World:

✳ Follow your instincts. Allow stillness at times when words seem small. Notice something beautiful, and receive the beauty in silence.

In the Heart:

✳ I open my heart to experience moments of amazement, wonder and awe. I am one with life's beauty and surprise.

~⋎⁓

Becoming Something Beautiful

Even in the dark soil, a seed is becoming something beautiful.

Sometimes we need to be underground before we can bloom. Maybe our life as we know it has unraveled, and we are in a dark place, uncertain of our next move, frozen in time, dormant.

When we are in a place of darkness, we put pressure on ourselves—with the help of our loved ones—to be fixed, to snap out of it, to bring our old selves back to life.

The most healing thing we can do in troubled times is to be patient and compassionate with ourselves. Our time in the dormant underground is essential to the bloom. It is not that the darkness has to be fixed, *but it's the darkness that is fixing us.* We just need a little more time in her presence.

Depending upon when a seed is exposed to water, sunlight and warmth, some will germinate very quickly, and some will remain dormant for long periods of time. Some seeds, like common vegetable seeds, are immediately ready to germinate. Then there are seeds from a unique lotus plant that are thought to be over two thousand years old and will still germinate, transforming into incredibly beautiful and unique flowers under the right conditions.

Even in our darkest challenges, before a tiny ray of light shines in, we are already transforming, bursting with the possibility of becoming something brand-new. Something more authentic. Something bigger. Something lighter. Something unique.

Even in the dark soil, a seed is becoming something beautiful.

In the World:

＊ Have patience with yourself today. If you feel stuck—not seeing any outward growth—know that you are growing within and will break ground into the light any day now.

In the Heart:

＊ I am a unique expression of love, and I am patient with myself as I grow at my own pace and in my own time.

⤙⤚

The Power of Prayer

Our prayers are always answered. But not always in the ways we expect.

We are always heard—every request, every plea, every note of gratitude, every song of joy. Each and every prayer propels energy toward our intentions in rays of healing light and grace. Our prayers set off an immediate response that sweeps us into the flow of assistance. Every prayer arrives safely at its destination. There are no exceptions.

With our endless needs for healing, comfort, love, guidance and protection, it may seem that prayer has limited power. We don't see results as fast as we would like. Plans do not unfold in the ways we expect. We want the kind of miracle that we imagine.

After a passionate prayer has left our heart, it is powerful beyond our imagining. Energy shifts, grace is unleashed, divine order conspires to assist. It is not given to us to see the plan that is set in motion. Prayers are always answered, but often in ways that we can't fully understand. There may be a higher good at work that does not include perfect healing, ease and calm, or our version of the end result. Our challenges, too, can be part of the plan.

Prayer requires from us a twofold faith: It asks that we wholeheartedly believe that the prayer is heard and answered, and that no matter what answer we receive, the path that follows is for our absolute highest good.

So we send off our intentions and let go, knowing that the prayer we impart has been received and is already manifesting some powerful light in our lives.

In the World:

✳ Prayer is concentrated thought connecting us with the divine. A beautiful time for prayer is after meditation when the mind is calm and the vibration is high.

✳ Give thanks as if the prayer request has already been granted.

✳ Release the idea of a certain result and open to answers beyond your expectations. Have faith that the right path is unfolding for you now.

In the Heart:

✳ My prayers are powerful messengers of light, hope and healing. They are heard and answered in perfect time for the highest good of all.

~\/~

Road Rage Resolution

Give peace a chance.

There has not been peace on earth in my lifetime, but I'm still holding out hope. Like John Lennon, I'm a dreamer, and I believe that one day the world will be as one. Meanwhile, there are concrete ways we can practice peace in our daily lives to bring us closer to the global peace we dream of.

When I was in nursing school, we had classes on communication centered on interviewing sick people under stressful circumstances. That's when I learned the beauty of "I" statements. Used to convey a feeling or belief, they're an easy way to let someone know how they are impacting you or the situation, without placing blame.

For example, you are in the car, and your partner explodes into road rage, cursing out another driver. If you say, "You are such an angry driver!" it will feel like an attack and fuel the fire. When you say, "I feel really unsafe when you yell at people while you're driving," you are stating the fact of your feelings. Your partner can't argue with your feelings—they are yours.

Marshall Rosenberg takes it a few steps further in his important teachings on nonviolent communication. These steps can be applied in our relationships or in the workplace, and they can lead to conflict resolution even in the most protracted arguments. It won't hurt to try. Give peace a chance.

In the World:

* There are four parts to the practice of nonviolent communication: (1) observations, (2) feelings, (3) needs and (4) requests.

* Using the example above, it might sound something like: (1) *We've been fighting almost every time we take a car ride together and you yell at other drivers.* (2) *I feel anxious and angry when you yell, and I'm sad that our time in the car isn't more relaxing and fun.* (3) *I value my peace and have a need for more kindness.* (4) *Would you be willing to stop cursing out other drivers while I'm in the car?*

In the Heart:

* I am contributing to peace on the planet by taking meaningful steps to bring peace into my daily life.

❧

Infinitely Grateful

Help me to be infinitely grateful for how fortunate I am, how much good there is in the world, and how much love I can create. —*Maya Davis*

Maya wrote this prayer after her high school choir raised up tender hearts of song at a memorial service for the brother of one of their members. Ryan lived on earth for only twenty-two years. He was a unique and beloved soul. His presence lives on through his great love, his beautiful smile and the unspoken reminder that our time here is temporary. We must live our lives in a way that takes nothing for granted.

Ryan's life and Maya's prayer remind us that from a place of infinite gratitude, we can honor this precious day by appreciating all we have been given. We can honor this day by training our eyes on goodness in the world. We can honor this day by giving and receiving love freely and unconditionally. As we live each moment in appreciation and awe, we honor those who have gone before us.

Ryan and so many of our loved ones can't be present today to live out their earthly lives, but we can. They can't stand on solid ground and offer gratitude for the gift of life, but we can. They can't wake in the morning and admire beauty or seek goodness, but we can. They can't give and receive love as an embodied spirit, but we can.

Let's allow our losses to remind us to live deeply and fully, treating each moment as the precious gift that it is.

In the World:

✳ Begin the day in the deep, rich soil of appreciation. *Thank you for this most amazing day.*

✳ Seek out joy, beauty and goodness by noticing it in the simple things that are near you, like nature, art, music or a kind face.

✳ Express your love generously. Say, "I love you," often. Send off a loving text or email to someone who might need to hear it. Work toward repairing a relationship or patching an argument. Live and love deeply.

In the Heart:

✳ I am infinitely grateful for the blessings of this precious day. I am generous with my expression of love.

Beautiful Soul

You are not what you have done. You are what you have become.

We are all in the process of coming into alignment with the beautiful perfection of our souls.

We are all in the process of discovering that none of us has a better, purer or bigger soul than another. When we meet up in the afterlife, we will greet each other as divine, radiant, unique reflections of God, perfect as we are.

We are all in the process of remembering who we really are and sweeping off the dust that covers the brilliance, wisdom and joy of the spirit.

We are all in the process of working though the lessons we need to learn for our soul's development—lessons learned through joy and pain, dedication and devotion, friendship and love, being and doing.

We are all in the process of becoming. We are always in the midst of change, evolving slowly into greater versions of ourselves, expanding and growing toward an understanding of our essence, which is love.

We are all in the process of realizing who we are at the deepest level and finding joy right here, right now.

One step at a time, we become a little more compassionate, a little more peaceful, a little more loving.

So forgive yourself for any past transgressions and turn your thoughts to what you have become—and who you are becoming.

And have a beautiful day, beautiful soul.

In the World:

*   Release the burdens of past mistakes and seek the gentle peace of the present moment.

*   Make a plan for moving one aspect of your life into greater alignment with love. Become a higher version of yourself one step at a time.

In the Heart:

*   I am a beautiful, radiant, unique reflection of divine love.

~⌣~

The Intention of Love

Bring love wherever you go. Shine light wherever it's dark.
Leave blessings wherever you've been. Be kind wherever you are.

After I had my first daughter, I asked my mother how she did it with four children under the age of six. Her answer surprised me. She said that when you have one child, you give your all to that child—one hundred percent. And when you have four, you still only have one hundred percent, so you give that. And here's the key: You give the best of you, and the power of the *intention* of love does the rest.

Imagine a speaker in a large auditorium or a band in a stadium. Everyone, even those standing in the back, receives the impact of the energy coming off the stage. Every person in the place has access to the same intensity of the message because of the intention of the giver.

Even on those days when we feel fractured by the juggling act of work, school, childcare, spiritual practice, shopping, cooking, cleaning and keeping up with friends, we have incredible untapped power within. Power that is easy to access.

Our clearest intentions are unleashed in the simplest way—by a mere pause during which our energy is centered and refocused. Even a few breaths will open the heart to empower everything that comes after.

We just need to pause, connect with our calm center, then direct our love to the next task. When we continue to check in with the source of our love, the intention finds its way to the places where we can't always be. It makes up for those moments when we feel that there just isn't enough of us to go around.

Bring love wherever you go, and know that it is more than enough.

In the World:

* Between activities today, take a short pause to center yourself, open your heart and ask for guidance for the next event. It's not one more thing to do. It's what will make everything else go more smoothly and gracefully.

In the Heart:

* I am peacefully centered and bring the best of myself to this day. The intention of my love goes exactly where it is needed most.

꧁

Life Is Fun

May I approach all work in the spirit of joy and creativity.

Whenever we put our attention on what we are doing in the present moment, we are living our lives fully. Conversely, when we are wishing we were somewhere else, we are letting our lives slip by while our minds are off in another place. Right here, right now, in simple things, is where the joy is.

Buddhist nun Pema Chödrön encourages us with this practical advice: "Constantly apply cheerfulness, if for no other reason than because you are on this spiritual path. Have a sense of gratitude to everything, even difficult emotions, because of their potential to wake you up." (Those in the midst of acute grief and pain get to take a pass here.)

Applying cheerfulness is merely a matter of showing up to all of our tasks with love and a lightness of spirit. We don't have to do a *Sound of Music* twirl through the horse field or living room, although that might be helpful. Put on music that you love. Be a domestic goddess, and clean the house as if for an honored guest. Slow down as you do the yard work with an eye for the miracles of nature. Bring a positive attitude and a smile to the office.

We are all weighed down by our lists and duties, homework and yard work, housekeeping and bookkeeping. "When you discard arrogance and complexity...sooner or later you will discover that simple, childlike, and mysterious secret known to those of the Uncarved Block: Life is Fun," offers Benjamin Hoff in his classic book, *The Tao of Pooh*.

Life is fun. *Really?* Well, it's all in the way we think about it.

It's about applying cheerfulness, being present and being grateful. It's about doing small things with great love. All else becomes lighter. On the journey of today, let's find creative ways to remember that our souls are joyous and that life is fun.

In the World:

✳ Today, bring yourself back to the present moment and to your spiritual path by applying cheerfulness and gratitude.

✳ Smile inside and out. Create fun ways of thinking about your work.

In the Heart:

✳ I approach all work in the spirit of joy and creativity.

The Soul Remains Whole

Be gentle with yourself. Listen to your inner voice.
Trust that grace is here. Don't hurry the healing.

To add to the joy conversation from yesterday, it's okay not to be okay. We live in a culture that puts a priority on happiness, and if we are not happy, something must be wrong that needs to be made right to return us to the correct state of happiness.

But joy and sorrow don't live in separate worlds.

Some wounds run deep and can't be healed with any fast and efficient therapy. They take untethered time and an open heart; patience and self-love. Sometimes there is no closure in the healing process, yet joy and sorrow find a way to mingle, coexisting within us in a deep, rich mix of humanity.

During times of grief or challenge, in our anger, vulnerability and humility, we might feel that God is ever so near—or completely absent. Crisis might drive us to rely heavily on spirituality, or to feel abandoned by it. In those dark nights of the soul, remember this:

The spirit is never broken.

While seasons of pain may leave us feeling as if we are shattered into a thousand tiny pieces that will never be put back together again, the soul always remains whole. We may become a new version of ourselves, but on the soul level, we are always complete and made of love.

In the World:

✳ Keep facing the light. Even when it is a long way off, know it is there.

✳ Take small steps toward integrating your pain into your new life. Have patience with yourself, and be exceptionally kind to yourself.

✳ Be an advocate for what you need from family and friends. Your journey is yours to experience in whatever way you choose. There's no right way. Just your way.

In the Heart:

✳ I have all the grace I need for whatever life asks of me. I face the light and take steps in the direction of healing as I am able.

꜀꜀

Universe at Work

You don't have to figure it all out today. Take one step, one breath at a time.

My friend Lyndy is leaving in three weeks on a cross-country spiritual journey. She called last night, worried and wondering how she was going to manage to get ready with all that was going on in her life. In addition to the trip planning, she is also selling her parent's home, sifting through the remnants of a divorce, figuring out her finances and working as a caretaker.

Sounds familiar, right? At some point or another, most of us are immobilized by the daunting weight of daily demands.

This time, however, the answer she needed was right in the house. Last year when I visited Lyndy, she gave me some Abraham-Hicks CDs to listen to in the car on the long drive home. So I reminded her of an inspiring story that Esther Hicks relates about a day when she was out of sorts with a long to-do list. She was strongly prompted by her wise guides to make two lists.

On one side, she was to list only what absolutely had to get done that day. On the other side, she would list everything else. She would be in charge of the "today" side, and the universe (God) would be in charge of the other side. Off she went to accomplish her side of the list.

Esther did this each day, revising the lists as she accomplished things, until she realized that by the time she turned her attention to the items on the universe side, they had resolved themselves or had very simple ease-and-grace solutions.

After dividing up her lists last night, Lyndy saw that the trip planning was robbing her peace, and if she could concentrate on that for a few days on the "today" side, she would have more focus for her other duties before the trip. And surely the universe is already working out miracles and creating resolutions for its side of the list.

In the World:

✳   Break it down. Make your lists. Your part on the left, everything else on the right. Do your work, and allow the universe to work miracles in perfect time.

In the Heart:

✳   I handle one breath, one hour, one day and one miracle at a time. I am in the constant flow of spiritual assistance.

꒼ᐛꒌ

Stand Like a Mountain

I align with the divine.

There's a small thing we can do right in this moment that will make a big difference in our health, our confidence, our openheartedness and our spiritual energy: Sit up straight.

Even if it's a little uncomfortable at first, be mindful of your posture today. Your muscles and bones will thank you, your heart will open wide and your healing energy will flow freely.

It's a fact of life that many cell phone users who look down for hours a day at their devices are creating rounded spines. "Computer slouch" is not only a problem for the youngest among us. We should all be paying attention.

There is a pose that is usually taught from the beginning in yoga classes called *tadasana,* or mountain pose, which is a beautiful example of the art of healthy posture. It emphasizes our built-in harmonic balance when we stand as our bodies were created to stand. And when we stand tall, our bones and internal organs are positioned for optimal support, blood supply and alertness.

The spiritual bonus of being in our best possible posture is that an amazing amount of our life force is held within the spinal column. That's why we meditate with a straight spine. Our chakras, or energy centers, are meant to stack up, one atop the other, for the maximum flow of wisdom and healing energy. We can align with the divine by straightening our spine.

In the World:

✳ For increased joy and energy today, practice mountain pose every chance you get. Here are the basics: your feet are parallel, legs straight and strong without locking the knees; your hips are over your feet; spine lengthens long from sacrum to crown of the head; shoulders are slightly back with shoulder blades flat on the back. Relax your face. Ahh.

✳ At your desk, be mindful to sit tall, or consider a standing desk.

In the Heart:

✳ My body is in perfect health; my bones and muscles are strong; my spine is straight and strong; my cells spin with joy and radiant energy.

Free to Sing

Today is a symphony of miracles, and we are the instruments.

There was a long period of time when I could not sing. A few reedy notes would come out, then my throat would close completely, and I would feel like I was choking. It mystified and embarrassed me even when I was alone. I sang for a living for twenty years. Where did my voice go?

I traced it back in my mind and realized that when the illusion of my marriage was becoming clear, I was not speaking up. There were years when I tiptoed around the deck of the truth, trying not to rock the boat and incur a storm of change. I knew there were circumstances that I could not live with, but I was stuck, immobilized by the status quo and a child who needed stability. Everyone else came first. I closed off the voice of my intuition because I didn't want to hear what she was telling me. *Speak your truth*, she would say.

Coming to live alone on Hunters Road changed that. I met Paul and Cheryl, and whenever we got together, they wanted to sing. I was resistant at first. "I don't sing anymore," I would say. But coaxed further, I would find that I was no longer constricted. I was living my truth and exposing my heart to the ultimate sadness of my story, and my knot untied. I was free to sing—and to speak.

We are here as expressions of our truth.

Although it seems that going into our pain will break us into a hundred pieces, instead, when we walk right into the bones of our honesty, we get a hundred miracles. Go figure. So whenever we are ready, we can open the door of the heart and face the pain that we have kept at bay. We will find our truth there.

We can take a small step toward living in alignment with our new selves and discover that today is a symphony of miracles. And we are the instruments, free to sing.

In the World:

✴ Today, find at least one small way to speak up for yourself. Begin the process of listening to your intuition.

In the Heart:

✴ I am free to speak my truth and know I will be guided as I navigate my way with honesty through life's changes and challenges.

I Believe In Me

I am not just enough. I am magnificent.

When Maya was four years old, my friend Pauline gave her a book for Christmas, *I Believe in Me: A Book of Affirmations*. Written and illustrated by the whimsical and talented artist Connie Bowen, it became one of our all-time favorite children's books to read together.

On one side of the page is a captivating colored pencil drawing, and on the other, a simple affirmation. "I am wonderfully creative. I give with joy. I have a place of stillness within me." Slowly, we would examine the sweet detail of each picture and soak up the good feeling.

"I follow my heart. I am thankful. I share my love and watch it grow." We would feel better and better as we read on, expanding, laughing, remembering.

"I am filled with greatness. I am whole and perfect just the way I am. I am one with all life." Yes!

The book reminded us, over and over with every read, of who we are.

In our daily life, we have all become familiar with the phrase, *I am enough*. And yes, you are. But that's not all.

You are magnificent. You are the enormous and beautiful spirit behind the worldly one—watching, knowing, being love in all things—and shining your light on all who cross your path.

You are not just enough. You are magnificent. Remember that always.

In the World:

* Today is the day to remind yourself of your beauty and your magnificence.

* Affirmations are a powerful way to lock in the attributes we wish to enhance on our spiritual journey. Revisit your affirmations or copy some of these to your journal, and use them throughout the day.

* From a place of love and simplicity, allow joy to flow. Beam that joy on all who stand in the light of your sun.

In the Heart:

* I am a magnificent reflection of divine love.

Irish Blessings

May the road rise to meet you. May the wind be always at your back.
May the sun shine warm upon your face, the rains fall soft upon your field.
And until we meet again, may God hold you in the palm of His hand.

Today in celebration of Saint Patrick's Day, we welcome some traditional Irish blessings. May these gentle prayers settle into your soul like a sweet, soft mantra of comfort and serenity.

May love and laughter light your days
and warm your heart and home.
May good and faithful friends be yours
wherever you may roam.
May peace and plenty bless your world
with joy that long endures.
May all life's passing seasons
bring the best to you and yours.

With the first light of sun, bless you.
When the warm day is done, bless you.
In your smiles and your tears, bless you.
Through each day of your years, bless you.

Calm me, Lord, as you calmed the storm.
Still me, Lord, keep me from harm.
Let all tumult within me cease.
Enfold me, Lord, in your peace.

For every storm, a rainbow. For every tear, a smile.
For every care, a promise and a blessing in each trial.
For every problem life sends, a faithful friend to share.
For every sigh, a sweet song, and an answer for each prayer.

In the World:

✳ The little we know of Saint Patrick's life is marked with courage and faith. And so can yours be. Press on with your convictions today with a loving heart. And may you be blessed with peace and plenty wherever you may roam.

In the Heart:

✳ I am strong. I have faith. I am guided. I am blessed.

Divine Timing

May I be a little more patient today than I was yesterday.

I used to be a little hard on myself. Really a lot hard on myself. I set my expectations high and was impatient when I didn't meet my goals. I know. We've talked about patience. But I continued to forget that my timing is not the only timing to consider.

So I decided to boycott the pressure I place on myself and apply a bit of divine timing to my daily routine. A reprogramming of the internal GPS was in order.

The result of my little experiment is the happy discovery that I'm getting more done and having more fun when I exercise a healthy dose of patience and faith. I suspend judgment and trust that all is well. Even when it doesn't look so well from here. I'll share my road map below.

Opening the door to patience changes the philosophy from *making something happen,* my mantra before, to *allowing it to unfold in its perfect time,* my mantra now.

For today, may we relax a little in our expectations for ourselves and others, and invite divine timing to settle into our souls. Tomorrow is another day.

In the World:

✳ In the morning, write down the three most important goals for the day.

✳ Send up a prayer requesting assistance. It could look something like, *I know there is a beautiful plan for today and that you will help it unfold with ease and grace. Thank you for showing me the way.*

✳ Flow toward the path that seems most open first. When you come up for air, pause, center yourself and repeat the process of a prayer followed by action toward the clearest path.

✳ If you hit a wall or end the day without meeting all the goals, release it with the pure knowing that today was not the day for it.

In the Heart:

✳ I flow in union with divine timing and am patient in allowing all good things to unfold with ease and grace.

~᠆ノ᠆

Bless My Mind

Bless my mind with calm and sight. Bless my heart with love and light.
Bless my day with grace and ease. Bless my world with hope and peace.

No matter what kind of day stretches out before us, we could all use a little inspiration to stay on track. It's easy getting lost in the jungle, right? The mind loop can spin false tales of fear and cast us in a drama where we face an uphill battle alone.

On the path of spirit, there is a simpler way. We gently awaken to our unlimited nature and practice the ultimate expression of self-love—we ask for blessings for ourselves. It's easy to forget who we are, but it's equally easy to awaken over and over again and ask for the blessings we need.

Shining the light of a beautiful blessing on ourselves wipes out our temporary amnesia. It enlists divine support in connecting with our highest selves so we can view all aspects of the day through the most loving light. It allows us to let go of the idea that we have to control all of this on our own.

We are a team now. We can create something beautiful together. Shine the light of blessings on yourself so you may shine your light on others.

In the World:

Here is a short blessing for you today. After a few calming breaths, repeat silently:

✳ *Bless my mind with calm and sight.* Imagine having clear, focused, calm thoughts sourced from your highest wisdom.

✳ *Bless my heart with love and light.* Imagine your heart center opening, filling with the light of love on the inhale and freely giving love out on the exhale.

✳ *Bless my day with grace and ease.* Imagine the day flowing with easy flexibility when challenges arise.

✳ *Bless my world with hope and peace.* Imagine the world surrounded with light and in perfect peace.

In the Heart:

✳ May I be blessed with all that I need for the best possible day—for myself and for all those who cross my path or my mind.

~\/~

A Thousand Miracles

To walk in nature is to witness a thousand miracles.

Spring is in the air, and nature invites us to notice her.

The patient brown and gray of bare trees. The lime green tint of tiny new buds. The carpet of last fall's leaves. The hawk circling on the wind current. The dense forest that lives in harmony. The soft path of pine needles under a splash of turquoise sky.

The call of birds and the answer of bird friends. Sunlight making God light through the trees. The spicy, healing scent of pine. Grass. Rolling hills. Mountains. The clear creek water flowing over stones to create baby waterfalls. The color of any flower. The persistence of vines. The singing of tree frogs. Cardinals and finches. Herons and eagles. Berries, acorns and cones.

The sound of leaves dancing in the breeze. Ferns on the forest floor. The view from the mountaintop. The hills of the hollow. Foxes and deer. Moss on tree bark. Wind on skin.

Nature's welcoming arms are always open. They allow our spirits to expand outward from our hearts into her safety, holding space for our wildest dreams and our most intense emotions. She accepts them all and gives them back to us in an awed exhale of peace.

When we need a fresh perspective or a jump start for our creativity, nature waves flags of infinite beauty. When emotions loom large and problems seem daunting, nature invites us to walk with her in peace. For spiritual connection, wellness, strength, wonder and focus—nature donates her gifts. With infinite divine kindness, nature offers us beauty, health, respite, meditation and solace from our worldly demands. There is no better medicine. Along with the birth of spring, open to receive, in gratitude, a thousand miracles.

In the World:

∗ In celebration of the spring equinox, walk in nature with a keen eye for beauty. If that's not possible for you today, use your imagination, a video or a window. Notice the miracles. Give thanks.

In the Heart:

∗ I am one with the beauty of all natural things and allow nature's peace to flow through me like the wind flows through trees.

~\/~

The Worry Tree

I let my worries go so I can be here for the beauty that surrounds me now.

When my daughter was small yet filled with anxiety, we created a guided meditation called The Worry Tree. In her mind's eye, she would walk down a beautiful path, surrounded by colorful flowers, to a grassy spot where the gentle and compassionate Worry Tree always stood in wait. Then she would name her fears, one at a time, and ask the Worry Tree if he would mind holding them for her until she might want them back. She never did.

Through this meditation, Maya was able to release her worries and come back to the present moment feeling a little more peaceful. She was able to fall asleep imagining beauty instead of her fears.

Energy flows to where the mind goes. Train her well. When we generate more beautiful thoughts, we create more beautiful outcomes. Ours is a benevolent universe that responds to where we put our attention.

To banish worries, we don't *turn them off* as much as we *turn our head* gently back home to the present moment. As we free ourselves over and over from negative imaginings, we find ourselves doing one thing at a time with love, presence and gratitude.

May we release our worries so we can be here for the precious gifts that surround us right now.

In the World:

* If you are a worrier, look into guided meditations to reduce stress and relinquish worries. Or create your own version of the Worry Tree meditation and practice it nightly before bed. You can also find beautiful guided meditations online and in apps.

* An affirmative prayer in lieu of worrying might be: *I am thankful for the divine plan that is in place for ___. Perfect solutions are now manifesting with ease and grace.*

In the Heart:

* I release my fears and worries with ease, knowing that all is well and in divine order. I gently bring myself to the beauty and the blessings of the present moment.

◦⌄◦

Where God Is

Right where you are is where God is.

There's nowhere to go. Nothing to search for. No teacher to find. No separation. There's no train that will leave us behind. No platform where we will ever stand alone. There's no place and no situation where God is not.

God is in the details, in the deadlines, in the deaths.

God is in the moments, in the mothering, in our smallest steps.

God is in the wind through the trees and the crashing of the seas.

God speaks through our love and creates through our hands.

God walks through our journey and guides all our plans.

We are a ray of the sun of divine creation, and we have, shining within us, divine love. We naturally reflect the love we are made of. We can't escape it or hide from it. We can't lose it or run from it.

We can forget it, but still, it is here. We can ignore it, but still, it remains.

Listen and know. Right where we are, broken and messy, joyous and celebrating, God is here.

Of all the earthly promises broken and disappointments carried, we can trust this one constant. We do nothing alone. We are surrounded and supported right here, right now, just as we are.

In the World:

✳ Be still. In moments of silence, feel your connection with all things.

✳ Be in awe. In beauty, find the signature of God.

✳ Be patient. In all that is challenging, find divine order leading you to new growth.

✳ Be loving. In daily actions of love, notice divine creation working through you.

In the Heart:

✳ I see the imprint of the divine in all things great and small, right where I am.

~\/~

The Peaceful Warrior

The world is in need of our peace today.

Where I live in the country, I have no cable or data connectivity. I have just enough Wi-Fi to make it through my social media postings for the month, but not enough to read articles and watch videos. Once a week on Tuesdays, I get my news driving to and from town to volunteer with hospice patients, and each week the dying people lift my spirits and the news leaves me in despair. The heartbreaking sadness, low-minded controversies, violence and scary weather reports can render us worried and hopeless. This can't be good.

So how do we become a warrior for peace? There are countless ways we can contribute to the cause of spreading peace on our planet. It begins with making peace within ourselves. From this place of light, we can spread the energy of our love consciously in meditation and through our every action in the world.

On my way home, the news turns to static, the static is replaced by a frog chorus, and the world rights itself once more. Today, let's listen less to the spin and allow the peaceful warrior within to get to work in a world that needs our peace. We have the power to lift the vibration of the planet.

In the World:

✴ Peaceful thoughts: Notice negative thinking about yourself and others, and gently guide your thoughts to what is loving, kind, encouraging, calm and life-affirming. Imagine our world emanating loving light.

✴ Peaceful words: Our words, like our thoughts, have the power to shape our experience and guide the universe to manifestation. May all of our words today carry the power of love and peace.

✴ Peaceful actions: Move through today with a gentle footprint, exuding calm energy to all who cross your path. Led by the wisdom of the heart, take peaceful action for beliefs that you are passionate about.

In the Heart:

✴ I bless the world today with my peaceful light and powerful healing energy. I keep my focus on that which is of the light.

~ᗄ

My Manager and the God Box

From challenges grow miracles.

My mother, who we affectionately call "Tiny Guru" for her small stature and great spirit, takes pride in being my manager. There's nothing much to manage as I am a hermit writer living in the country, and that suits us both nicely. On a daily basis, she gives me the priceless gift of her enthusiastic support. No matter the project, she is all in.

She also does a particularly vital task for me: She prints my Facebook posts and sends me hard copies of them. Receiving those papers every few months allows me to organize my stories for this book. I can lay them out on the floor, reorder them and take notes on them. They are invaluable, thus making her an extra-great manager.

Facebook occasionally changes things up, and recently they restructured the Photos section. Mom's usual procedure of printing out one post at a time was not working. She was deeply troubled and spent hours trying new settings and printing out "that damn frog" over and over. The pages were a mess of ads.

Then came a lightning bolt. "I'll put it in a God Box," she mused. The fact that she didn't have a God Box did not deter her. She searched the house and found a container deemed perfect for the job and carefully worded her short message: "Dear Angels of the Computer, thank you for Mary's printing job. It is lovely. xx Tiny xx." She then left it in the box to percolate for the weekend.

Monday morning, full of faith, Mom fired up the computer, settings as usual, and the print job came out "halfway better." She said softly to the angels, "If this is the best it can be, it will be all right. But I'd really like it to be perfect for Mary." She printed it out again, and it was perfect—and has been ever since.

In the World:

* Make your own God Box. Place your worries inside, send up a prayer and forget them. In Tosha Silver's *Outrageous Openness*, she explains: "During the period of offering, solutions often spontaneously arise. When the mind is no longer grasping for an answer, space opens. The Box gives room for a divine plan, even in impossible messes."

In the Heart:

* I trust that the divine has a plan in progress for all of my challenges.

Fourteen Steps to Calm - Part 1

I unveil the serenity that is within me.

A friend called yesterday and shared how she was suffering from daily anxiety and panic attacks. She was the third person to relay a similar story in past weeks. Embodying calm seems like an elusive dream, but have faith. It's not out of reach. Before we accept anxiety as a companion, there are tools that can bring us closer to our always-calm center. These tools will span the next several days.

1. Make your exhalations longer. Start by counting four on the inhale and six on the exhale, with a goal of four in and eight out. Do this for a few minutes, and you will feel the difference immediately. The hallmarks of the fight-or-flight response during a panic attack are rapid breathing and heart rate. By increasing the length of the exhalations, you remind your body that there is nothing to fear and that all is well.

2. Use positive affirmations. There's an extensive body of research that supports the theory that what we think, we create. The body will default to pathways it already knows, so it takes a little retraining to create new thought habits. Here is a starter list of affirmations, and you can add your own. Your journal, phone notes or index cards are good places to keep these. Word everything in the positive, and smile with your whole body as you think or say them:

I am in perfect health.　　　　*Today will be an amazing day.*
I am calm and serene.　　　　*I am in the flow of love.*
Everything is in divine order.　*I am relaxed and focused.*
I am safe and all is well.　　　*I am in the flow of grace.*
I am joyful and peaceful.　　　*I love my life.*

In the World:

* Take a few moments several times today for a few rounds of long-exhale breathing followed by positive affirmations. Set a timer for frequent reminders to stop what you're doing for this practice. Take two minutes for renewal.

* In stressful times, your daily spiritual practice, even when shortened to meet time constraints, is especially important.

In the Heart:

* I am filled to the depth of my soul with calm joy.

~⋎~

Fourteen Steps to Calm - Part 2

I listen to the voice of my inner wisdom.

3. Ask for help on a soul level. There's unlimited help available in spirit realms for the asking. The prayer might go something like this:

Thank you for putting a perfect plan in motion to relax my mind, body and soul. Assist me in using my inner tools to find deep peace. I trust that a beautiful plan is unfolding in my life today and that I have nothing to fear. Thank you for helping me return to my natural state of calm.

Divine grace is benevolent and is always here to help us out. But we must ask clearly and positively. After asking, know you have been heard and assistance is on the way.

4. Stay connected. Stay connected with your family and closest friends. Share your journey with them. Stress can be isolating, and it's important to keep an open heart. If you had a physical issue, your beloveds would want to help you out. The same goes for stressful times.

5. Be kind to yourself. Anxiety is exhausting, so skip the self-criticism. Think only loving thoughts of yourself. You are doing the very best you can. You are not alone in this.

6. Exercise. Yoga, walking, kayaking, dancing, tai chi—pick something relaxing that you can do outside or facing a window. Calm your body and soak up the beauty of nature while you release endorphins.

7. Drink lots of water and less caffeine. Flush toxins and hydrate your cells with plenty of fresh water throughout the day. Cut out soda and limit caffeine to two cups a day, max. Your mind, body and soul will thank you.

8. Visualize your wellness. You don't have to figure out *how* to get to where you want to go. Jump right to the result, and visualize the joyful, healthy, calm, vibrant you. Just a few minutes of positive visualization a day is incredibly powerful.

In the World:

＊ Continue the practice from yesterday with long-exhale breathing and affirmations, adding the new practices that resonate with you. Set a timer to implement your calming routine several times today. Ahh.

In the Heart:

＊ I take positive steps toward inner peace.

~ㄴ৴-

Fourteen Steps to Calm - Part 3

I am filled with peace and calm. I approach my day with joy and clarity.

9. Treat yourself. Now is the perfect time to treat yourself to a massage or Reiki session. With the right practitioner, you may find that a monthly bodywork or energy-healing session is not a luxury, but a necessity. Another relaxing treat is an Epsom salt or essential oil bath. This has a calming effect and releases toxins from the body.

10. Use good posture. A couple of weeks ago we talked about mountain pose and the importance of good posture for optimum health and spiritual connection. Sitting and standing with a straight spine is especially important for stress relief because it allows the lungs to inflate fully. When your lungs are inflating fully, you can take calming breaths.

11. Spend less time on screens, more time in nature. Technology can short-circuit our energy and leave us mentally and physically tense. Spend as much time in nature as possible. Implement a daily walk while leaving the phone at home. Notice your surroundings and be present.

12. Practice yoga nidra and play music. There are many beautiful recordings of yoga nidra, or yogic sleep, that gently guide the body into a deep and healing relaxation. They range in time from about five minutes to one hour. Experiment with a few until you find one that you love. Relaxing music also has proven to have antianxiety effects.

13. Get more sleep. You may find that you need extra sleep. Adjust your schedule to make sleep a priority. Yoga nidra at bedtime is the perfect setup for a peaceful night's sleep.

14. Meditate. This is the single most important practice for overall mental and spiritual health, and it is suitable for nearly everyone. Learn more about it. Take a class, get a book, download an app or read a few articles. Keep it simple. Start where you are. Start today.

In the World:

✳ Use your journal to create your own calming practice. Enjoy the adventure of discovering the built-in tools that stock your virtual medicine cabinet with calm.

In the Heart:

✳ I am filled with peace and calm, and I approach my day with joy and clarity. I am healthy, safe and have faith that all is well.

~✵~

Feeling Small

Sometimes it's good to feel small. —Maya Davis

It was a perfect early spring morning with a crystal clear sky the color of Santa Fe turquoise. Hiking up the fire road, my new friend asked me about my work. How to explain? Should I say that every flat surface of my cabin is exploding with a creative project? There's a reason I don't talk about my life much in new company. I wear a lot of hats, and it's complicated.

But I forgot that, and with a touch of confident swagger (must have been the altitude), I began to explain about writing a daybook of inspiration and developing an app of mobile wallpapers. I told her I also do retail, have an Etsy store and license images. I went on. I'm writing songs again, producing a CD, and I...

I turned around and became mute, deferring to the stunning view of the valley and the rising rounded curves of the Blue Ridge Mountains. Hawks circled. The brilliant sun danced in shimmering drops of light on several lakes. So small. I am so small!

What was I thinking? That *I* was doing all that creating myself? Clearly not. I'm a tiny drop of water in the universal ocean of love, and I would not be doing anything of value if not for the infinite flow of grace that aligns me with the creative power of the divine. Little Me. Big God. Little Me suddenly got very quiet.

It can be a mountaintop view, a mighty ocean or a starry sky that reminds us of the impossible power of that which is greater than we are. It reminds us of all we are part of and all that is part of us. From this scenic overview of humility, with the perspective of our place in the greater whole, we enter the flow of this mighty love. Through humility.

Yes, sometimes it's good to feel small.

In the World:

✳ Imagine the great vastness of the universe, and allow yourself to contemplate the interconnection between you and the energy of all things.

In the Heart:

✳ I witness and am one with the greater power of the universe. I am grateful for my daily co-creation with the divine.

~∨~

Create Today

May this day be grounded in love, illuminated by light
and graced with blessings.

May this day be guided by divine wisdom, aligned with goodness and filled with joy.

May this day be guarded by angels, softened by patience and raised by kindness.

May this day be lifted by gratitude, deepened by compassion and calmed by inner peace.

May this day be grounded in love, illuminated by light and graced with blessings.

Starting to feel a little better, dear one? Well, good. We are off to a beautiful start in creating a most amazing day.

You see, what we dwell on, we create; what we imagine, we attract; what we ponder, we empower. So surely starting the day with a prayer for all good things will set the momentum for more grace, more blessings and more peace.

We create today one thought at a time, so it's never too late to take a U-turn and change directions. The path is yours to draw; the painting yours to paint over.

Start right here, right now, in creating a day where heaven reaches right down and touches your face, or one in which you reach up and touch the face of God.

In the World:

✳ Use the prayer above or create your own to get in the flow of grace first thing in the morning. Take a moment to get back on track at any time you need a divine energy-boosting break. Create the day of your dreams.

In the Heart:

✳ When I keep my thoughts on the blessings and the good, more blessings and goodness flow into my life.

─╲╷╱─

Garden of the Spirit

Every day of your life plants a seed in your soul. Grow roses.

Every day we can till the soil in the garden of the spirit with gratitude.

The rich grace of thanksgiving permeates the day with an expectation of abundance.

Every day we can sow seeds of love and joy.

The seeds arrive in gardens seen and unseen, traveling on the wind to wherever they are needed most.

Every day we can fertilize the garden with kindness and peace.

Every day we can water the thirsty soil with the rain of generosity and compassion for all humanity.

Every day we can shine the light of the sun to warm and feed the sprouts as they grow into seedlings of patience, forgiveness and faith.

Every day we can weed the garden with mindfulness and meditation, nurturing strong, healthy blooms that reflect the bounty of our gentleness and goodness.

Every day we can harvest beauty from the garden of the spirit.

Every day of your life plants a seed in your soul.

Grow roses.

"The fruit of the spirit is love, joy, peace, kindness, goodness, faithfulness, gentleness and self-control." —*Galatians 5:22–23*

In the World:

✳ Honor this day as the precious gift that it is.

✳ Sow the seeds of love and joy today, and imagine planting something incredibly beautiful in your soul.

✳ Invite opportunities for spiritual growth and soul nourishment into your day.

In the Heart:

✳ I bless this day by scattering and nurturing seeds of love and joy that travel to where they are most needed.

Friendship

*Friends are like the sun in spring, shining the light
that makes our souls blossom.*

My neighbor's yard awes the senses with a field of miraculous flowers. Hundreds of daffodils and tulips pop up with brilliant color in a joyful display of natural beauty. Each one is unique and irreplaceable, arriving just in time after a long winter, radiating love to remind us that life is precious and beautiful. Much like our dear friends do.

In his famous poem, "On Friendship," Kahlil Gibran tells us, "Your friend is your needs answered. He is your field which you sow with love and reap with thanksgiving." The unconditional love of a friend is one of life's most generous gifts. In their presence we find safety from the judgment of the world. In their company is the freedom to be ourselves. They support, confirm, protect and encourage us in the safety of their love. They are willing participants in our joys and laughter, challenges and pain. They are our needs answered.

"For you come to him with your hunger, and you seek him for peace," he continues. Through our best friendships, we learn to know another—and ourselves—with a deep and enduring love. True friends reflect our inner light back to us, allowing our hearts to be seen, bringing to awareness the magnificence of our inner truth.

Gibran finishes the poem with, "And in the sweetness of friendship, let there be laughter and sharing of pleasures. For in the dew of little things, the heart finds its morning and is refreshed."

To those precious friends who make this day beautiful, bearable, meaningful, joyful and new—thank you, dear ones, thank you. My heart finds its morning and is refreshed.

In the World:

* Tell a friend how much you treasure their friendship in your life. Call, write, text—find a way to reach out with your gratitude.

* Share the truth of your most important joys and sorrows with a friend. Honesty is a healing gift for both souls.

In the Heart:

* I am completely free to be honest and uncensored with my dearest friends. I can be vulnerable knowing my heart is safe in their love.

April Blessings

May the sun rise in your heart with love, peace
and the hope of new beginnings.

April opens up with the playfulness of April Fools' Day, then travels on a sacred journey through the holy days of many faith traditions. Nature is waking up under the newfound warmth of the sun and the rains of spring. Gratitude rises for the miracle of new life all around us.

We begin this month with some loving words to welcome in the colorful and radiant gifts of April:

May the warm sun rise in our souls and illuminate the precious nature of life. May the gentle winds of change blow through our uncertainty and remind us that we are beings of infinite possibility. May the newness of spring awaken our hearts with love, peace and the hope of new beginnings.

Be present.

Let the day flow with grace.

Expect joy. Be positive.

Serve with compassion.

Speak only kindness.

Impart only love.

Never forget you're not alone.

Give thanks for everything.

See goodness in others.

In the World:

✳ Invite these April blessings into your heart as you begin this precious day.

✳ Choose a word for the month that awakens your heart in new ways.

✳ Write some intentions for the month of April.

In the Heart:

✳ I open my heart to the miracle of new beginnings in my life. From a place of joy and gratitude, I shine my love to all beings.

Dear Guardian Angel

My guardian angel works overtime.

Dear Guardian Angel,

I'm not trying to overwork you; really I'm not. I'm closing down earlier in the evenings. I'm not answering messages after dinner. I'm not looking at social media more than a few times per day. But still, I know you must be having fits over me. There are not enough hours in the day, and I'm constantly testing the limits of my strength.

All around me, I see faces with dimming eyes. So many of us seem to be overwhelmed by the demands of connectivity, wells running dry from so much output with so little self-care and connection to spirit. I long for more serenity, more joy, more peace. And I know I can find what I seek with the help of your loving assistance, a slower pace and some self-love.

Oh sweet angel, guide me on a path of wellness today. I seek balance between doing and allowing, between effort and surrender. This means that with your help, I'm going to have to implement some realistic limits. There's only one of me, and there's always more work to be done. Please help!

Love, Me ♥

In the World: Guardian angel requests for support:

* Help me to honor my limits and listen for signs of burnout. Help me to slow down before I wear thin. Remind me to enjoy relaxation.

* Help me to trust that if I can't get through my list today, you will help me accomplish things easily and in their perfect time.

* Help me to know that this journey is meant to be fun and that joy is a spiritual practice. Remind me to take myself lightly.

* Help me to always lead from spirit, nourishing my soul so I may be able to share with others from a place of abundance.

* Help me to wake up every morning knowing that I am supported and guided, and that when I listen, I will always know the way.

In the Heart:

* My guardian angel guides me, protects me and answers every call for assistance with loving attention and joy.

Ease and Grace

When there is an endless stream of to-dos, there is no time to simply be.
Seek silence to nourish the spirit.

Today is a good day to rethink our to-do lists. Or better yet, let's put them aside. Perfect harmony and balance will be revealed to us moment by moment when we listen to the guidance of our inner wisdom and divine support. The right things will happen in just the right time provided that we surrender to the flow of grace and ask for what we need.

As we have seen, when we start the day in the silence of a short spiritual practice, work unfolds smoothly because we are connected to our highest wisdom. Taking a few moments throughout the day for quiet breaths and an invocation for assistance can keep us on track, bringing us instantly to our natural state of joy and light. With spirit in the lead, all else unfolds with ease and grace.

The transition prayer or request might look something like this:

> *Thank you for pointing me to the best ways to use my energy right now.*
> *Show me what to do next, and help me to accomplish everything with*
> *ease and grace in its perfect time.*

Although on the outside, it might seem that we don't have time to stop and connect, we soon discover that we accomplish twice as much in half the time when we are in the flow. This process of circling back again and again to our divine assistance and intuition works like a charm.

So today, relax into the river of grace. Ride the flow of the current, and you'll never want to swim upstream again.

In the World:

✳ Do a test run. For today, put the lists aside and set your phone timer for every hour or two. When the alarm rings, take a few centering breaths and say the above prayer or your own personal prayer for assistance, adding in any specific details you choose.

✳ If it's feeling good, continue the test run for the entire workweek. You may never want to stop.

In the Heart:

✳ Everything unfolds hour by hour in perfect divine timing. I have all the time I need for all I need to do.

~✢~

Joy and the Coffee Cake

Celebrate small moments and find joy in small things.

As I sit in the morning sun considering ways to celebrate joy in small moments, I imagine a colorful tube reaching from the sky to me. Through this open joy-transmitting tunnel, I feel beams of sheer bliss coming right into the top of my head and landing with laughter in my heart. My joy channel is getting a strong signal, but strangely, it's only sending one thing down through my tunnel. Coffee cake. Yes, indeed. I'm channeling almond coffee cake.

Since taking all things gluten out of my life some years ago, I dream of my former favorite breakfasts, which all happen to be coffee cake related in some sweet happy way: cheese Danish, scones, banana bread, and the queen of all breakfasts, almond coffee cake. The mere thought of them makes me feel the presence of a happy divine goddess within.

The great news for humanity is that seeing as we are all threads in the same tapestry of oneness, my joy is also your joy. Your joy is mine. We celebrate life's small moments and lift the energy of everything around us in a vibrational fireworks show.

As I drive up the winding mountain road not far from my cabin, I pass a sandwich board sign near a small house that says, "BAKERY—GLUTEN FREE." Last week I stopped in to find an adorable room with ten tables adorned with fresh flowers and happy customers. I walk up to the counter, laden with gorgeous baked goodies, and say, "So, where is the gluten-free section?" I think I'm dreaming when I hear, "All of it is gluten-free." *All of it?*

I lift my arms overhead as if I have just seen a vision of Mother Mary in Medjugorje. Recovering my voice, I sing out, "Have I told you how much I LOVE you?"

In the distant background, I can hear the happy table people cracking up. But me, I'm busy ordering almond coffee cake and lifting up the planet with some big joy fireworks.

In the World:

✳ Be on the lookout for small moments of joy today. Give us all a lift by celebrating what makes you smile.

In the Heart:

✳ I celebrate small moments and find joy in small things.

Plant Seeds

We can't change people, but we can plant seeds
that may one day bloom in them.

Although many of us have been warned that we can't fix people, it's hard to resist the pull to want to change people for the better. We want to impart our wisdom and see the result of our efforts, especially with our loved ones. It's frustrating when changes don't happen when we think they should. Like immediately.

It helps to remember that the energy of every word we speak, especially those empowered by love, has impact that lasts long after the conversation has ended. Every seed of kindness, love, joy, grace, comfort, wisdom and protection is planted in the heart of another to bloom when the time is right—for them.

A few weeks ago, there was no sign of the buds that are now bursting forth from every bush and branch. In the winter hush, these very plants and trees appeared lifeless. Deep within, the buds were a mere possibility of a bloom—creation gestating in the dark.

People are full of possibilities too—creation gestating in the dark. Sometimes they're just not ready to apply the lesson, but the seed of our love and caring lies in wait. Be patient with the seeds you have planted in another. They may one day bloom in them.

In the World:

✳ When there is little you can do to help someone evolve, imagine them as their highest self. Imagine the traits and qualities you know they could possess. Imagine them being blessed with these qualities.

✳ Remain kind. Use words phrased in the positive. Even when results are not visible, know that you have planted a powerful soul lesson in them.

✳ Planting seeds of change does not mean you need to stay in the presence of intolerable behavior or abusive situations. It's possible to plant transformational seeds—and move on.

In the Heart:

✳ I change the world daily with words and actions of kindness, love and peace that are not dependent on the outcome. I have faith that seeds of change will bloom in others when the time is right for them.

Faith over Anxiety

I choose faith over anxiety, hope over worry, love over fear.

Today we can make choices that align us perfectly with what we know to be true: Spirit speaks in the language of solutions, not problems.

When we make an offering of our challenges with a brave, patient and open heart, we will be led to the answers we seek. With affirmations of faith, hope and love, we can turn this day into something beautiful. Starting now.

Today I choose faith, and when I do, my anxiety dissolves and my focus becomes the right outcome for the highest good of all. I believe that all things are possible, and I trust that incredible blessings walk the path right beside impossible pain. I know that I will live through this, thrive through this, become new through this. Today I choose faith.

Today I choose hope, and when I do, my worries retreat and my focus becomes a better outcome, one beyond my ability to see. I imagine a future where my concerns are solved with the ever-present support of spirit. I surrender my need to control, and I offer my problems, great and small, to divine guidance, knowing I am heard. Today I choose hope.

Today I choose love, and when I do, my fears fade and my focus becomes seeing all things through the eyes of love. Every decision I make today comes from a heart of love. Every thought I think today is sent out on the wings of love. I have nothing to fear. I am an eternal being, and by the power of love, all things can be solved. Today I choose love.

In the World:

✳ Choices are made only in the moment you are in. Today when you recognize the signs of doubt and fear, stop and affirm: *I have faith that all will be well.* Send light and imagine the highest outcome for all concerned. Then let it go, and open your heart to the blessings that are yet to unfold.

In the Heart:

✳ I always have a choice, and today I choose faith over anxiety, hope over worry and love over fear.

~\⁄~

As We Grow Wings

I remain calm, centered and grounded in divine wisdom.

At one point in my yoga studies, it seemed that divorce was a limb on the sage Patanjali's eightfold path of yoga. As those in my teacher-training class experienced the joy of spiritual growth, there was a stream of stories about students and teachers in various stages of marital separation. It seemed like a strange prerequisite to enlightenment, but even so, four out of five of my spiritual and yoga buddies were seriously not going to survive this cocoon-to-butterfly thing with their marriage intact. I didn't know what was in the air. Then it dawned on me. Some of us are still in cocoons, while others are growing wings.

As we raise our vibrations and see the world from a higher perspective, our partners who are not on the spiritual path can feel heavy. They might be stuck in the lower-vibrational drama of the world. Our souls are busting loose, and our loved ones are not keeping up with the changes. The transformation on the planet now is bringing about rapid growth, and at times we feel like we are expanding out of our old lives.

This is a personal journey. We don't all grow at the same pace. Our partners don't have to *get it*, but it is essential that they *respect it*. They don't have to believe it, but they may not belittle it. Thankfully there are bridges that ease the growing pains. These tools help us to show love, patience and compassion to our loved ones—as we grow wings.

In the World:

* Surround yourself with a protective aura of white or golden light. See the shield as impermeable to lower vibrational energy.

* Lighten the energy of your home with sage. Bless each room with the love of the divine, allowing the smoke to rise into all corners.

* Seek to be calm and centered in the heat of drama. Use your practices of mindfulness and compassion to stay grounded.

* Pray for the person and speak to them with your inner voice, from your soul to theirs. This is a conversation from your higher self to their higher self. Speak your truth. This is a transformative practice.

In the Heart:

* As I energetically expand, I use my light for the highest good of those I love. I remain calm, centered and grounded in divine wisdom.

APRIL 8

Be Still My Soul

The harvest of this day grows from the seeds of sacred silence.

Precious, sacred silence is one of our most essential friends. Our silent time reminds us of who we are and gives us access to infinite wisdom from which we are guided when making our daily decisions. So why is it so difficult to write it in on today's schedule?

Many of us now have a spiritual practice during which we meditate, focus on gratitude, pray for assistance, and inspire the heart. But as we know, the world pulls ferociously at our shirttails, begging us to pay attention, to divide our time, to distract our focus and be busier than is good for the soul. It takes a mindful effort to revisit our priorities often, and make the time to connect with spirit. It's the most important thing we will do in the day. And when we do it first, the rest of the day is driven by the ongoing intuition gained from mindfully connecting with the source of all love.

This is not a duty or an effort. We don't work to be more spiritually connected; *it is who we are.* We merely set aside time to check in and let the noise drop away for long enough to reveal the beauty and calm that resides within. And if we can just hover there...open...for a moment without jumping in with a thought, within that stillness, we activate our soul's wisdom.

Our lives can be driven by our schedules or by spirit. They can be driven by the constant chatter of our minds or by a place of calm. They can be driven by impulse or by wisdom.

May we quiet our words, calm our thoughts, soften our hearts and still our souls daily, so that we may listen, open and receive. And let spirit lead.

In the World:

* Meditation can be your most life-changing daily practice. The rewards will reach across all aspects of your being. Every day is a good day to begin learning or to recharge your practice. One morning at a time. As health guru Kris Carr says, "Progress over perfection!"

In the Heart:

* I have a calm center from which all wisdom arises. I still my soul and receive.

❧

In Giving We Receive

We change the world one by one: one positive thought,
one compassionate action, one prayer at a time, rippling endlessly.

When we fill out the volunteer form at a homeless shelter or nursing home, we often go in thinking that we will use our time and talent to help someone else. We are strong, loving, able, and have a gift to give or a skill to share. But there is another important truth of service: The gifts of volunteering are really gifts to the soul of the giver. We are fulfilled through our generosity.

The very people we think need our help become our most radiant teachers. Facing poverty, illness, unfathomable loss or impending death can bring God so near that we can find ourselves at the intersection of heaven and earth.

We are here to love one another and to serve those in need with a compassionate heart. We can do this in small ways every day through an act of kindness and the simple art of being helpful. There are countless ways to experience the gift of service.

Giving is inherent in our nature. And today, someone needs what we have to give. Let's change the world one by one: one positive thought, one compassionate action, one prayer at a time, rippling endlessly.

In the World:

✳ Consider first what hours you can commit to volunteer work and ease in gently, offering one or two days a month to start.

✳ When donating clothing and household goods, everything should be clean and in good working order. Treat your donations as gifts to a precious friend.

✳ Contact local organizations, and find out what they most need. When you act locally, you make a greater impact.

✳ Self-care is an important part of serving. This is not selfish, but essential. You can only give of yourself when you are in balance.

In the Heart:

✳ I am generous, loving and able to be helpful. I give of myself in small ways throughout the day and seek opportunities to use my gifts in service to others.

When It Rains, It Pours

Lift up my worries and rain down peace.

Did you ever wish that it would rain down exactly the element of grace you need in this very moment? No, money doesn't count. Imagine asking for an extra portion of strength or patience—and it pours down, infusing you with everything you need to move forward. That's the thought from which this arose:

Lift up my fears and rain down love.

Lift up my tears and rain down joy.

Lift up my blindness and rain down sight.

Lift up my darkness and rain down light.

Lift up my doubt and rain down faith.

Lift up my grief and rain down grace.

Lift up my challenge and rain down ease.

Lift up my worries and rain down peace.

And I do believe that's how this grace thing works. We ask—or beg, as the case may be—knowing it's there, knowing it's coming—standing out in the middle of the field looking up at the clouds.

In the instant that we ask, it begins. And when it rains, it pours.

In the World:

✳ Ask for what you need today, then soak in every ounce of it. You don't have to deserve it or earn it. It is grace with your name on it.

In the Heart:

✳ Grace is present for me in every moment. I ask for what I need. I receive it with an open heart. I give thanks.

~✦~

A Rainbow in the Dark

Everything is in divine order.

My brother Tommy has an easy laugh and a soft spot in his heart for those who are hurting. He is strong-willed, smart and funny, and he was my first best friend. He is also struggling with alcohol addiction. It's an incredibly helpless feeling to watch someone that you love harm themselves, and it's especially hard if you love them with a mother's love.

Our mom, Tiny Guru that she is, can be a worrier. She's totally plugged into the divine, with one foot in both worlds and a deep understanding of all things spiritual, yet when it comes to her loved ones, the Great Mother in her rises strong and she worries about her lambs.

Yesterday in the mail, I received the latest pages from her spiritual journal, written during her most recent at-home contemplative retreat, which she calls her Silent Week. Just as I sat down at the table to read, an incredibly strong storm blew in. The sky turned black, thunder cracked, lightning danced, wind whipped through tall trees, torrents of rain fell. I latched all the windows and lit candles, expecting to lose power.

I sat back down. And there I read, and wept. Mom's sadness about the state of my brother's life tore at the tapestry of my heart. There she was, confiding in her divine guides about her most intimate sorrow, confessing her fears. She even invoked the help of Saint Monica, mother of Saint Augustine, who himself was a bit wayward until he saw the light through the grace of his mother's prayers. "Please show me how I can help," Mom implored. She *was* the storm outside.

But then, in the last entry, she surrenders. She decides to trust in divine order and put all things in God's hands. She releases the remnants of resistance and ends with: "Again the words of Saint John fill my heart. I leave my cares forgotten among the lilies." At that moment, I turned to look out the window, and there, within the dark rainstorm, at 8:45 in the evening, was an incredible glowing rainbow.

In the World:

✳   Even in impossible situations, have faith that a higher plan is at work and that your requests for assistance have been heard.

In the Heart:

✳   I have faith that all things are unfolding in perfect divine order. My prayers are heard and answered for the highest good of all.

~\ ⁄~
∨

The Holy in the Small

Joy is finding the holy in the small and the sacred in the everyday.

When we want to find something, we begin by seeking what was hiding or lost for some period of time. *Finding* is the adventure of looking and experiencing the joy of being reunited with the lost thing.

So how do we *find* sacredness in the small moments of everyday life? Fortunately, this is one adventure that allows us to pack lightly, as what we seek is right here with us. All we need is our full attention plus a little resolve to find some amazing beauty today.

We see what we are in the habit of seeing—and we create what we concentrate on the most. So if we want love, miracles and blessings, we first decide to notice them. When we turn our attention to finding the beauty and the good, beauty and goodness appear everywhere.

It's hard to fathom that God would even want to be present in the mundane moments of our mosaic lives. But what if God is already in them? What if all of those tiny tiles are made up of some sort of divine clay and paint?

With a little mindfulness, the tiles of the mosaic catch our eye, fill our hearts, show us beauty and lead our way to joy. The morning light, the bird on a limb, the thought of a loving friend, the kindness of a stranger. The bite of food, the soft shirt, the trusty car, the needed rain. The smile of a child, the spoon in the pot, the broom on the floor, the tear over loss.

The common miracle here is love—which always wants to be found. So look. Really look for what you want to find. And you will experience the joy of being reunited with the lost thing—the holy in the small and the sacred in the everyday. Which were there all along.

In the World:

✳ Decide that beauty surrounds you today. Will yourself to see goodness and light. Watch carefully for beautiful happenings. Stay where the love is.

In the Heart:

✳ I notice the sacred in each small moment and find joy in everyday miracles. My life is a brilliant mosaic of divine love.

The Water Is Wide

Life can bring mighty challenges, but you came here with a mighty soul.

Yes, there are moments when wings would be good. There are nightmares that we wish we could wake from. There are days when the wall of water is so high that the only way to travel is by taking a leap of faith into the next wave. And when you do that, remember something.

You are not alone, and you have all the strength you need to get through this. Ask for guidance through the storm. Believe in the power of the divine to do all things and in yourself as a piece of that divinity. Invoke the assistance of some powerful angels to guide your way to the other side. Persevere by holding on to hope and the crystal clear image of the best possible result.

When faced with a challenge, something important is demanding your attention. So instead of looking the other way or looking for a way out, face it straight on. Ask for guidance and listen to your intuition. Stay alert and watch for signs. Be patient with your progress. There are some valuable lessons to be learned that will serve you in meaningful ways in the future.

And most of all, believe in yourself. Everything in your life so far has prepared you for this moment. All of the wisdom and strength you need is within.

Life can bring mighty challenges, but you came here with a mighty soul. Consider the possibility that there are many more blessings to come as a result of this journey through the deep water.

And that you have everything you need to make it to the other side.

In the World:

✳ Create some positive affirmations for the challenges that you face. Write them in your spiritual journal. Say them often today.

✳ Enlist divine support and be open to all possible forms of guidance.

In the Heart:

✳ I have everything I need for the challenges I will face today. I have a constant stream of support and love that is always available to me.

❧

Perfect Harmony

My mind, body and soul are aligned with health and harmony.

My friend Lyndy started the weekend focused on sorting out her finances, specifically on finishing her taxes. She had taken an extension, which was now a looming deadline, and it hung around her neck like a fifty-pound bag of rocks. No wonder she pulled a back muscle leaning down to pick up a box that was not very heavy.

As she sat to do her taxes, she now had the added worry of back pain, which clung to her all weekend. But as she made her way through the task, as distasteful as taxes can be, she started to feel a lightness of being. When the forms were completed, her back pain miraculously disappeared also.

Medical intuitive Carolyn Myss teaches us that financial stress often takes up residence in our stomach or back. In fact, all of our emotions and traumas, concerns and dramas are not only housed in our thoughts, but also in our bodies. No disease happens in isolation. Our mental, emotional and spiritual health resonates through all aspects of our being.

Our mind, body and spirit are meant to work in harmony. Learning to associate physical pain with our emotional attachments is a valuable spiritual tool that can serve us for a lifetime—as well as during tax time.

In the World:

∗ For long-term or recurring illnesses, we can augment medical science by aligning mind and soul with the body. Enlist meditation and the healing power of positive affirmations.

∗ Consider a wide range of alternative healing practices in addition to traditional medicine, including acupuncture, homeopathic medicine, Reiki, massage and other bodywork from experienced practitioners.

∗ Look into nutritional changes as well as vitamins and herbs.

∗ Research the chakra system. Some classic titles are *Anatomy of a Spirit* by Carolyn Myss, and *Eastern Body, Western Mind* by Anodea Judith.

∗ Consider learning integrative movement like yoga, tai chi or qigong.

In the Heart:

∗ My mind, body and soul are in alignment and in perfect harmony. I am happy, healthy and whole.

APRIL 15

Amazing Grace Please

May this day wrap you up in grace and hold you up in hope.

One of my hospice patients says she can talk to God. And He answers her right back. She slipped this little gem into a conversation as if it was an everyday occurrence. I leaned in close.

"I always start with *please* and end with *thank you*," she whispered. I pelted her with questions: "What exactly do you say? How often does this happen? How does He answer?"

"I say to God, 'Please take this pain away from me now. Thank you.'"

That's it?

"And then something changes," she says with a gleam in her eye. "Right away, something changes. It's hard to explain, but it is immediate. Everything feels better. Everything feels different. Everything is lighter. And that's the answer. He changes things."

He changes things.

We go on to talk about how that *thank you* at the end does not depend on the answer. It is a *thank you* in advance, because she knows that He will answer her. She assumes that she is heard, and if she surrenders and asks, it will be given.

The grace at the heart of this exchange is available to all of us, at any time. The more we open to it and align with it, the more access we have to *feeling* the answers.

It is not that God is here sometimes and not others. God is always here, and it is up to us to align with the ever-present gift of amazing grace.

In the World:

* Have a running conversation with spirit today. Try out using the very powerful *please* and *thank you*.

* Surrender, be vulnerable and ask. Suspend judgment and notice how you feel after.

In the Heart:

* Today I open and align to a power far greater than myself, knowing that grace is a gift freely given and assistance is always here.

Joy in a Puddle of Mud

*Joy is the sound of love, the color of gratitude
and the song of your favorite things.*

I'm beginning to think that joy is a slow simmer, slightly under the radar of life's noise, popping up into our consciousness as a sweet sound, color or song that awakens us with a smile—like the Little Guy on the driveway.

I heard his happy announcement as I was walking to the car for my daily trip to the post office. He was so small that at first I didn't recognize him as a bird. Tiny as a butterfly, he was chirping mightily as he hopped in a circle around a mud-puddle gift from yesterday's rain. A combination of surprise, elation and a shout-out to his friends, this was one joyful Little Guy.

Joy is the sound of love.

With the arrival of spring rain this week, it's possible that a newly minted bird was finding his first bathtub. *Could I be so lucky?* he might have been thinking as he danced the blue stone perimeter. His gray wings fluttered in a dry run of what he might do in the water. *This is too good to be true.*

Joy is the color of gratitude.

A great light of courage rose up from Little Guy. With me, a giant human standing not five feet away, he took the leap of faith. Stunned at first, he stood still in the puddle. Then with a flourish, he dipped his head in and shimmied the water between all of his feathers. Again and again, he delighted in the practice, tasting the freedom of trying something new for the first time and getting the hang of it.

Joy is the song of your favorite things.

In the World:

✳ Today, be an excavator of joy. Let your eyes be vigilant to delights of the soul. Let your heart be open to signs and symbols of love, gratitude and hope. Try something new for the joy of it.

In the Heart:

✳ Joy is not dependent on my circumstances, but arises through sweet, simple moments of love, gratitude and hope. When I seek joy, I find joy.

~\/~

Prayer Is Light

Prayer always matters. Prayer always bears light.
Prayer always changes things. Prayer always changes us.

Imagine this: Prayer is a brilliant light that grows in proportion to our focus on the intention. The more we focus, the bigger and brighter it gets. This light has amazing power to heal and manifest positive change. This light can support and guide, bring calm and peace, and can only be used for good.

It matters not if our prayer is in our own words, from a sacred text, a loving-kindness meditation or a blessing. What brings the *real* power to our prayer is when the energy of our love and intention is empowered by divine energy. By enlisting divine assistance through prayer, our ray of light becomes a brilliant sun shining on our intention. Our souls can radiate a lot of light. Add divine light—and anything is possible.

Prayer always changes things.

From where we sit, we don't see the whole story of life's challenges. We don't understand the deeper purpose in our trials. We often don't know what the end result of our prayers should be. So we make an offering of the outcome. We trust that the divine knows the way. We accept that our prayer might be answered in ways we don't expect. We invite surrender, faith and acceptance into our hearts.

And we are changed from within.

Prayer always matters. Prayer always bears light. Prayer always changes things. Prayer always changes us.

In the World:

* Everything you do today can become a prayer. Allow divine light to work through you and use you to lift others—and yourself—where needed.

* When praying for a specific intention, focus your light on perfect healing and the best possible outcome, no matter what form that might take.

In the Heart:

* My prayers are working to spread light, love and healing. My prayers hold the power to manifest positive change in the world.

~∨~

The Engine

Be kind to your beautiful self.

This goddess of all spiritual lessons was a little late coming to me. After all, I was busy giving of myself in service to others, creating, learning, living, being and doing. Self-care always seemed to be the last car on my train. The caboose. A cute addition to my spiritual track, but nowhere near engine status.

Oh, how wrong I was.

I now see self-care as the foundation of all spiritual practices. If we don't honor ourselves, we can't possibly honor our oneness with all creation. If we don't care for ourselves, we are unable to serve others from the empty well. If we don't see that we are a magnificent reflection of God, we can't be God's magnificent reflection in the world.

We can only become what we accept ourselves as being. So let's accept our magnificence.

In the World:

∗ Be kind in the way that you think of yourself. Edit out any negative or unkind thoughts.

∗ Be kind to your body in all ways, fueling it with healthy foods, exercise and plenty of joyful activity.

∗ Be kind to yourself by imagining yourself on the soul level to be a radiant, powerful expression of divine love.

∗ Be kind to yourself by taking downtime when your mind, body and soul request it from you. You will know when you feel resistance— that feeling of dragging yourself from one event to the other. Stop, check in with yourself, get present and treat yourself as a beloved. All else will be accomplished with greater ease.

In the Heart:

∗ I practice loving-kindness as a gift to myself, prioritizing self-care in mind, body and spirit. When I am clear, rested and healthy, I enjoy life more deeply and I love others more fully.

꙳ ꙳

Confessions of an Insomniac

May we be at peace in our hearts. May we be at peace in our homes.
May we be at peace with each other. May we imagine peace in our world.

It was hard to feel peaceful when I wasn't getting any sleep. I could fall asleep unaided, but would wake at 2:00 a.m. and be up for torturous hours. Worries swirled madly in my mind, proliferating midair, whipping up a Kansas-sized tornado of worst-case scenarios right there over the bed.

Sometimes, I'm embarrassed to say, I'd take copious, messy notes in the dark about problems, solutions, things to say, things to do. After tossing around my fears and turning around in bed, I'd finally fall asleep and awaken to a pile of crazy fear notes.

In the light of day, nearly everything seemed manageable. I'd toss out the notes and question my sanity. And do it again the next night. Until I found a calmer solution. The rosary.

I had never been a big rosary person. Although I grew up in a Catholic family and was named for Mother Mary, I left my Catholic roots behind in college and embarked on a spiritual journey that took me around the world of faith traditions, only to land me back in love with Mother Mary. I even offered her a seat on the board of Every Day Spirit. (I really did.) So the rosary is a sort of salary.

Mostly, though, it is her gift to me. As soon as I awaken, every night now for years, I reach over, eyes closed, and get the rosary from my night table. Before any worry thoughts possess me, I silently pray: *Thank you for divinely solving all problems in the highest possible way.* Then, bam, I start.

In my Dad's little leather rosary book, it says that every prayer can be like a rose gently placed at Mary's feet. So I offer them with that kind of love—until I fall asleep that is—in which case I finish in the morning when I awaken, without a single fear note in sight and with major peace inside and out.

In the World:

✳ Any repetitive prayer or mantra can be used on any kind of beads. When you awaken, hold thoughts at bay and begin your prayer.

In the Heart:

✳ When I have peace within, I contribute to peace in the world.

Darkness to Flight

Just as she thought this was the hardest day of her life,
she turned into a butterfly.

In the twenty years since the stillbirth of our second daughter, Angela, I have gradually integrated an important lesson: Healing has the power to transform us when we bring our suffering to the light of day.

Through my infant loss support group, I have learned that healing begins when we weave our hardest truths into the tapestry of our lives. This means telling our story, unedited, to a compassionate listener. In the process of telling it, we own it as an essential part of who we are. Instead of being walled off in a dark cocoon, our sorrow lives as part of a whole—where grief and love can eventually coexist—and where there is hope of great pain living alongside a fulfilling life.

Major loss and traumatic events are some of the most important things that will ever happen to us. They change us irrevocably and force us to come to peace (or not) with our lack of control over our lives. They also offer us the opportunity for soul growth and transformation when we compassionately share our experiences with others.

By writing our greatest sorrow into the pages of our lives and by gently accepting her constant presence here, we weave these events into our souls—made ever deeper and more expansive with each and every experience we endure.

Given the chance to see the light, to feel the sun, to expose the soul to transformation, there is no doubt that from the darkness will rise an amazing, powerful, strong, precious set of wings. Yours and mine.

Let's allow the pain to grow us and color us in. Let's emerge from the dark, look up toward the light—and fly.

In the World:

✳ Seek a compassionate soul with whom you can share your true story and bring the whole of you into the light of day.

In the Heart:

✳ Each day I take small steps toward opening my heart to the truth of my experiences. I accept my sorrow as an essential part of life and I weave it into the tapestry of my soul.

﹍ᐁ﹎

More Gratitude, Less Worry

Keep your eyes on beauty, your body in the breath,
and your soul in gratitude.

Soon after I moved to Hunters Road, I noticed something of grave concern: There were wasp nests under many of the eaves of the cabin. Most were fairly small starter homes, but nonetheless, they were there, and I was not going to peacefully coexist with them. Peter, the supremely helpful owner, offered, "You can knock them down with a broom, but they'll just come back. They're pretty benign."

Benign? Are you kidding me? In my mind, they were dive-bombing the plate at mealtime, chasing me down the hill as I gardened and keeping me from entering the front door altogether. Before I caught sight of their scary little legs dangling down in hot pursuit, I got online and spent hours researching my options, dutifully reading blog threads and finally settling on a batch of earth-friendly fake paper wasp nests. I dragged out the ladder with a determined air about me and hung them around the doors to discourage any new wasp activity in places where I needed to tread. That'll teach 'em.

As winter thawed, I watched, fascinated, as the wasps built nests again under the eave of my writing window. They stayed on point and focused on building, floating just above head level, their long legs making them look less like scary creatures and more like dancing ladies. They didn't dive-bomb; they didn't chase; they didn't block the door.

It was I who had dive-bombed worry. I spent a precious day of my life accusing, dreaming up worst-case scenarios and implementing solutions where no problems materialized. I could have chosen to be present for life's beauty and invitations. I could have been grateful for a hundred small precious things. But no, I was busy being chased by scary legs in my mind. Next time, I will come home to the moment I am in. I will reside in the only place where gratitude is possible. Right now.

In the World:

✳ Until it's truly time to take meaningful action, consciously release worries as they arise. Choose to be right here where the blessings are.

In the Heart:

✳ I release my worries and bring myself back to the present moment. I release my fears and trust that I will be guided to the next right step.

Tattoo the Earth

May your footsteps be gentle and your imprint be love.

With each step we take, we change things. Our presence on the planet impacts our surroundings and leaves a permanent imprint—a tattoo—that lives on after we are gone.

Each of us is connected to all other beings and to all of creation as reflected in this traditional Navajo prayer: "As I walk, as I walk, the universe is walking with me. In beauty it walks before me. In beauty it walks behind me. In beauty it walks below me. In beauty it walks above me. Beauty is on every side. As I walk, I walk with Beauty." As guests on the earth, we honor her hospitality by walking in her beauty and leaving behind for our children an earth that is healthy and vital.

The natural beauty that surrounds us is our most treasured resource. Every living creature can be cause for admiration, and each glorious scene appreciated as an awe-inspiring gift.

Our natural world is one of the greatest sources of joy to our souls, rising with the sun every single day to remind us of her miracles.

As we celebrate Earth Day today, may we commit to respecting our beautiful home. May we leave behind the imprint of our awe and gratitude. May our presence impact our surroundings in a positive way.

May our footsteps be gentle. May we tattoo the earth with love.

In the World:

✳ Be a steward of the earth. Leave her as you find her—or better.

✳ Be frugal in your use of natural resources.

✳ Be diligent about recycling and use of plastics.

✳ Be mindful of the energy you use each day at home and for travel.

✳ Be involved in protecting the environment.

In the Heart:

✳ Today, I notice and offer appreciation for the magnificent gifts of nature. I treat the earth with love and respect, and tread with a light footprint.

꙳

Effort and Surrender

The very act of surrender makes us stronger.

The theme of effort and surrender plays out in many aspects of life. A good example is on the yoga mat. Before a pose, our breath creates space —a surrender and an opening to grace. Then we use effort to achieve the physical form of the pose. Once in the pose, we surrender, opening the heart once again, allowing the pose to soften while breathing in this new, expanded energy. We again assume effort to go a little deeper—to expand a little further.

This cycle of effort and surrender can continue as long as we hold the pose. The alternating balance of effort and surrender creates a circle of ever-widening exhilaration and strength.

The same thing can happen in our spiritual lives. We are surprised to find that, much like in the yoga example, when we surrender and soften—the very actions we associate with weakness—we find deeper stores of strength and energy. The moment we let go and open to something greater than ourselves, we tap into the source of infinite peace, strength and renewal.

Most of us are willing to make the effort it takes to achieve our goals. We live in a world that favors precision, perfection, striving, attaining and grasping. But using effort alone can block that which we seek.

Through the act of surrender, we find our strength. It is by releasing and opening that we are filled beyond all expectation.

In the World:

* When we surrender perfection, we open to vulnerability, the key to unleashing our gifts and talents.

* When we surrender the outcome of our efforts, we work for the joy of working and give for the joy of giving.

* When we surrender control, we open to the perfect plan of the divine, having faith that we will have all the strength we need for all we need to do.

In the Heart:

* In the moment of surrender, I feel a strength that is greater than my own. I release control and put my life in the hands of divine guidance. I open to possibilities beyond my wildest dreams.

The Truth of Who We Are

No one shines like you do.

Sometimes it's hard to believe that we are beautiful, shining lights, that our souls are glorious, that our essence is brilliant love. I know, it can feel like quite a stretch. If this is one of those times, listen up. We all need to be reminded about the truth of who we really are.

You are here to shine your unique rays of light and share your magnificent gifts. No one can replace you. No one has your fingerprint. No one reflects love the way you do. No one expresses divine radiance like you.

Truly believing in our magnificence is not an easy practice. We are trained to be self-critical and to seek beauty in external ways. But if we want to share our gifts with the world, it's essential that we recognize the truth and beauty of who we are.

When we understand the magnitude of our light and the value of our unique talents, we are free to reach out and share our gifts for the good of all who cross our paths. When we accept the greatness of our love, we can offer great love to others.

Acknowledging our amazingness also enables us to make the powerful connection with divine wisdom. It is from this place of self-love and soul truth that we plug into all of the assistance we will ever need.

You are a magnificent, glorious, beautiful reflection of divine love. You are an irreplaceable part of the whole. No one shines like you do—and someone needs your light today.

In the World:

✳ Take a moment to imagine yourself as a channel of radiant light. Everyone you come in contact with today feels your inner beauty, and you lift their vibration by your very presence.

In the Heart:

✳ The brilliant light of my soul is unique and raises the frequency of the energy of all those who cross my path today.

～╲┃╱～

It's Safe to Be Happy

Keep an open heart for joy, beauty and the gift of small things.

My friend Maria called me the other day and shared a phrase that had been going around in her heart all day—*It's safe to be happy*. So many of her yoga students came to class feeling tender and worried, weighed down by the stresses of their lives and a barrage of negative news stories. Maria's phrase offered a kind of permission slip to allow joy into the mix. She told them that it is okay to exhale and create guilt-free moments for the simple pleasures of life.

Bringing out the joy in our day isn't a result of the things that happen to us, but of the way we treat ourselves along the way. Joy is already present within us as an integral part of our spirit. When we treat ourselves as the precious beings that we are, we align with the joy within.

Self-love is the key.

The people of Denmark, a country often listed as one of the happiest countries in the world, have a word for cherishing yourself by making your surroundings as comfortable as possible. *Hygge* (pronounced "hue-gah") is the feeling that comes from nourishing the soul in an unhurried atmosphere. It's visiting with friends, enjoying good food by candlelight. It's the contentment that arises when we bask in small delights like a savored coffee or a cozy quilt with a good book. It's relaxation, togetherness, presence, enjoyment, appreciation. We might all do well to channel our inner *hygge*.

Honor your right to the pursuit of happiness, and allow yourself the pleasure of the things you love. Sometimes it takes a little letting go to realize how tightly we hold on to our worries.

Remember, it's safe to be happy.

In the World:

✳ Treat yourself lovingly today. Take an extra moment to enjoy a sweet, simple indulgence. Soak up the feelings of deep satisfaction, contentment and joy.

In the Heart:

✳ I cherish myself and show myself love by making time for the simple pleasures of life that bring me joy.

Improve a Life

*Speaking a few kind words might be the most important thing
you will do today.*

When we think about our purpose in life, we would all like to be able to list lofty goals and accomplishments. We want to know we are here for a reason and that we will make an impact on the world. Discovering the cure for cancer, working as a counselor, or giving helpful workshops are the path and purpose for a select few. But what of the rest of us with less definable ways of making an impact?

It's not too much to ask to want to change the world. It's important that our lives have meaning and that the echo of our love will remain when we are gone. As creatures of connection, we are wired to want to lift others up and be of assistance on a daily basis.

And we can.

Perhaps we underestimate the power of our kind words. Just this morning, I had a challenging situation that threw me off. I was moping and wandering, stuck trying to work out an unexpected problem, until I got a lovely note of encouragement that became the wind in my sails. It shifted the energy, helping me to relax enough to see the resolution and get back on track. A few kind words changed my day.

Every day, each of us has the power to improve the life of someone else. That's an important ministry. We have the ability, through our kind words, to change the perspective of another. As the poet Rumi so beautifully reminds us, "Be a lamp, a lifeboat or a ladder. Help someone's soul heal. Walk out of your house like a shepherd."

Let's endeavor to improve a life—to change the world for someone today. Let's help someone's soul heal. That's the real-life definition of purpose.

In the World:

⁕ Give the gift of kind words today. Speak them. Text them. Call them. Email them. Write them in a handwritten note. Be the change.

In the Heart:

⁕ Speaking a few kind words might be the most important thing I will do today. I lift others with thoughts and words of kindness.

The Circle of Abundance

Abundance grows from the seed of every thank-you.

Giving Thanks: When we keep company with a constant inner *thank you* for the blessings of this day, we are appreciating the gifts of our lives exactly as they are. We do this when we notice the smell of morning coffee, the needed rain falling on thirsty plants, the special song that plays at just the right time. Every tiny whisper of thanks for the coffee, the rain and the song magnifies the extraordinary riches in the ordinary moments of today. Our sense of lack is replaced by the awareness of countless blessings.

When we express gratitude, we plant seeds of abundance.

Giving Credit: Built into every *thank you* is alignment with the divine. After all, who are we thanking, anyway? As we offer our thanksgiving in small moments throughout the day, we are humbly acknowledging the source of all things and the reality that we are always being showered with gifts in the form of support, beauty, love, joy and guidance.

When we align with the divine, our seeds of abundance bloom.

Opening to Grace: After we give thanks and recognize our co-creation with the source of all abundance, we surrender our grasp on circumstances and control over outcomes. Things go a little smoother when we relax a bit and allow the blessings that are meant for us to flow toward us. Now we've opened our souls to the possibility of even more to give thanks for.

When we open to grace, the roots of our abundance spread, and even more blessings begin to flow our way.

In the World:

* Today, give thanks for this precious and amazing day, planting the seeds of abundance.

* Give credit by recognizing your co-creation with the divine.

* Surrender control over outcomes, so that the grace of abundance can unfold in ways that are beyond your wildest dreams.

In the Heart:

* I am blessed in countless ways by gifts from the divine. I give thanks as I notice the beauty and see the good that surrounds me now.

Bless Them

When someone crosses your mind, bless them.

Blessings are a powerful, transformative gift that we can offer to others—anytime, anywhere. When given generously from a heart of love, they shine the light of comfort upon the receiver. In his inspiring book *The Gentle Art of Blessing*, Pierre Pradervand tells us, "To bless means to wish, unconditionally and from the deepest chamber of your heart, unrestricted good for others and events." To bless is to uplift.

Whenever anyone crosses our path or our mind, we can get in the habit of offering them a quick blessing. *Bless Johnny in his work. Bless Tommy and Becky with smooth travels. Bless Bill's meeting. Bless Bob and Katie with ease and grace. Bless Brenda to perfect health.* It takes only a little mindfulness to recognize the countless opportunities we have in a day to lift up others in ways that are beyond the scope of our material world.

Pradervand puts it beautifully when he tells us, "To bless all without distinction is the ultimate form of giving, because those you bless will never know from whence came the sudden ray that burst through the clouds of their skies..."

Blessing others gives us a positive alternative to aggravation and complaint, helplessness and fear. There is always something we can do to change the world for the better and, in the process, become an instrument of healing.

In the World:

∗ When someone crosses your mind, bless them.

∗ When a friend is grieving, bless them.

∗ When you hear a troubling news story, bless them.

∗ When you see images of war, bless them.

∗ When someone you know is having a rough day, bless them.

∗ For every blessing you offer, you are blessed in return.

In the Heart:

∗ Today, as people cross my path or cross my mind, I bless them, imagining for them their highest good and happiness.

APRIL 29

The Gift of Saying No

Say yes to what inspires you. Say no to what depletes you.
Your heart is listening.

Recently my mother sent me a short article on speaking "the language of no." She often tells me that I can't be "all things to all people," and this short piece was in keeping with her advice. I reassure her often that I am not overextended, but in truth, I am always feeling behind and groaning under the weight of the long list of tasks on my to-do list.

Many of us have the lovely tendency to put others first. While this show of love brings with it countless rewards, I'm coming to see that if we give of ourselves to the point of exhaustion and leave little time to recharge our own batteries, our giving energy is short-lived and our divine purpose shortchanged.

I know what fills my well and charges my spirit batteries. I'm sure that you do too. Be it music or meditation, yoga or prayer, reading or walking with a friend, we must honor this as our soul food—for these are the very activities that nourish who we are and support our road to self-discovery and purpose. When we follow our curiosity and joy, we are always coming home to our inner beauty. This is the place from which all creation springs forth. If we don't nourish it, our lights become dim.

Saying no is not selfish. It's spiritual self-care. When we have more energy, we can share our light in ways that best use our gifts.

So, let's say yes to what inspires us and say no to what depletes us. Our hearts are listening.

In the World:

* What we study, what we think, what we say, what we do, what we watch—we align with. When we say no to what is not in alignment with our authentic selves, we honor our deepest truth. Today, let's begin to tip the scales in favor of who we are and what we love. Enjoy having more energy for friends and family, and for experiencing the beauty and joy of this precious day.

In the Heart:

* I let go of all that does not feed my soul. I see clearly what should remain in my life and what can be released.

❧

The Offering

The gift of your love is always enough.

I may have painted a rosy picture of meditation, neglecting to mention that on some days, it might feel like a complete disaster. You sit and the dog sits on you. You sit and your mind just won't quit. You sit and you remember you forgot to do that thing for your boss. You sit and your leg cramps or you fall asleep or big emotions rise up and you cry. This, too, belongs. Whatever arises, just notice it with compassion and tenderness.

We are making an offering of our effort, and the offering is received. No matter how humble, no matter how messy, no matter how sleepy, no matter how sad, we showed up and we offered our love. This is what we do every day. We show up. We ask for guidance. We surrender our small selves and make an offering of love to something greater. We offer everything we do. *Take it,* we say within. *Use it for good.*

Great power lies in a humble offering. It's the key to unlocking the doors of spiritual support. That's what holocaust survivor and psychologist Viktor Frankl meant when he said that success and happiness cannot be *pursued* but must *ensue* as the result of our surrender to something greater than ourselves. Grace flows when we make an offering.

We don't own our success or failure—we give it back. Botanist and inventor George Washington Carver was born into slavery and rose to become one of America's most influential voices of agriculture in the South. Every day, he woke and asked God for a plan. He was a prolific inventor who offered every invention and every day of his life back to God. And the grace kept coming.

We do what we can, moment by moment, hour by hour, day by day, to make the world better because we have lived. What is undone or partly done or done through tears, we offer. *It's okay.* Because the strength to show up the next day will be provided. The grace is unleashed. The flow is open. Tomorrow will come, and we will sit once more in meditation practice and make another beautiful gift of our love.

In the World:

✳ Offer your practice and offer the day. *This is yours. What would you have me do with it? Show me the way. Love through me.*

In the Heart:

✳ Each day I offer my love to be used for good. It is always enough.

May Blessings

When we turn our attention to finding beauty and miracles,
we create more beauty and miracles.

The month of May arrives as a gift wrapped up in nature's abundance. New growth sprouts up all around us, reflecting the new growth we feel within. In her bountiful daybook, *Pocketful of Miracles*, Joan Borysenko says of May, "It is a call to gratitude that everything in the universe is continually being re-created, including ourselves."

Like nature around us, we, too, are always creating, always changing, always growing. Where we put our focus is what we create more of in the world. So if we want to find more beauty and miracles in our lives, let's turn our attention to the beauty and miracles that surround us now. They are right here waiting for us in every new bud and bloom.

May the creation of new life in our world remind us of the glorious creation that is always manifesting in our hearts.

Be present.

Let the day flow with grace.

Expect joy. Be positive.

Serve with compassion.

Speak only kindness.

Impart only love.

Never forget you're not alone.

Give thanks for everything.

See goodness in others.

In the World:

* Invite these May blessings into your heart as you begin a new day.

* Choose a word for the month that encourages your inner growth.

* Write your intentions for the month of May.

In the Heart:

* I am an eternal creation, growing each day toward the light.

~\ /~

A New Perspective

When you're feeling stressed, count the ways you're blessed.

It's comforting to know that when we turn our attention toward all that is going right, we disarm the beasts of stress, lack and discontent pretty quickly. It just takes a little focus, a lot of trust and the revving up of our spiritual practice of gratitude.

It's essential to remember during stressful times that what we focus on will grow. What we worry about stays present. What we dwell on, multiplies. When we complain, we whip up more of what we complain about. And when we focus on the gifts, that's exactly what we find—more gifts.

When life gives us something unexpected today, we've got all the tools we need to handle it. Really we do. We are all infinitely blessed. Let's receive this day with a grateful heart and welcome an immediate shift. Let's reframe our story to be less stressed and more blessed.

In the World:

* *Take a breath.* Take a deep breath with a long exhale to center yourself and to mark the start of your new perspective.

* *Count your blessings.* Release your focus on fears, and mentally name some of the ways you are blessed. Look around you and notice them. Feel the joy of having these blessings in your life. Inwardly smile and count them; the soft shirt, the hot tea, the quiet moment. In less than a minute, you have connected with your infinitely wise center and empowered the feelings of calm, abundance and joy.

* *Return home.* When anxiety or lack creeps back into your consciousness, gently stop the thought loop with a breath, and notice a few beautiful things around you and all that is going right.

* *Train your eye on beauty.* Unless you are actively working on a solution to the stressful problem, train your mind to return again and again to all that is well with your world today. Vibrate high, and you will attract the highest vibrations.

In the Heart:

* I shift my experience today by changing my focus from lack to abundance. I am infinitely blessed, and more blessings are on their way.

The Art of Listening

To listen with compassion is to give a precious gift.

Speaking our truth is one of the best ways to get to know ourselves. Many a heart can be healed by the simple act of uncensored expression in the presence of quiet compassion. While it may seem passive to be on the listening end of a conversation, you are giving a precious gift.

I'm not sure when my self-conscious veneer started to crack, but I must admit I talk to horses a lot these days. They don't interrupt me when I'm talking; they nod between bites of grass; they have compassionate eyes. They can handle a wide range of emotions without getting squirrelly, and their silent kindness reminds me of the gift given by a good listener.

Yesterday I had a long chat with Floyd. After much thinking, I had come to the conclusion that self-love is the foundation of spiritual practice. When we acknowledge the beauty and divinity within, we open to beauty and divinity in all things. I was working through this, wondering how I had missed the obvious for so many years.

It started pretty innocently. "Hi Floyd. You're SO beautiful...*and so am I!*" And with that I started to cry. Why? Because I haven't thought of myself as beautiful in a long time, and saying the words had played a tender chord in my heart. I went on to tell him how we have radiant light that shines out from within, that does not stop with this skin or these bones, or that fence or this field, that our radiance connects with divine light and becomes infinitely vast. And off I went, going all cosmic on him. He stood there listening, then walked closer and lay down by the fence near me. I talked on until I felt my heart crack open and integrate the lesson. What a blessing to be able to speak it. Great listener, that horse.

We can all take a cue from Floyd and listen patiently while someone sorts something out, or vents, or cries, or rambles on. Sometimes we just need to speak the fears out of our minds to disarm them. Sometimes we just need to speak the dreams out of our hearts to empower them. With a small act of words and a big gift of listening, the healing begins.

In the World:

∗ Active listening is easy. Relax, listen, nod between bites of grass and convey understanding. Your loving presence is all it takes.

In the Heart:

∗ I give love to others through the gift of compassionate listening.

∿⋎⋍

Friends Are Diamonds

*May we be grateful for friends who remind us who we are
and who we are meant to be.*

Friends are diamonds who reflect the light of our spirit. They illuminate our souls and recognize our beauty, goodness and love.

Friends are those who listen compassionately and hold our stories with a tender heart. They reflect back to us what we need to know.

Friends are those with whom we can be completely ourselves and totally uncensored. Nothing we confide will ever be used against us.

Friends are those who guide us when we lose our way and offer perspective when our path is not clear.

Friends are those who allow us to have our fears, but remind us that somehow, the light will shine again.

Friends are those with whom we share the hilarity of our messy days and the humor in our drama.

Friends have a smile for us when we need to lighten up and are the keepers of joyful memories.

Friends are those who are present for us in times of suffering. They listen and hold space through seasons of grief.

Friends are those who lift us up and remind us who we are and who we are meant to be.

Friends are those who grace us with unconditional love and solidarity, keeping company with us on earth until we keep company in all other realms.

In the World:

✳ Make an effort to connect with your dear ones. Find a small but meaningful way to let them know how much they mean to you and how grateful you are to have their companionship on this journey.

In the Heart:

✳ I am thankful for the precious friends who love me unconditionally through the seasons of my life.

The Spiritual A-Team

Carry with me the heavy burdens and the joyful moments of this day.

It takes a village to raise a child, and it takes saints and sages to raise a soul. My divine guides have been assisting me all my life, and I could not manage without them. That's why I decided to put them in charge of my life and work—as an honorary board of directors. Enter my Spiritual A-Team. What began as a fun idea many years ago evolved into one of my most precious soul support systems.

After contemplating which of my divine guardians would hold the major roles, I set up some job descriptions. I wanted the CEO to support my spiritual growth and be in charge of my work. It's a big job, and I humbly invited my most beloved spiritual guide to hold this position and work through my thoughts, words and hands each day.

Other jobs that I filled are Chief Prayer Officer, who oversees my prayer life, Chief Meditation Officer, who helps me to stay on track with daily meditation, and Chief Lighting Officer, who keeps me in the present moment with light and love as I wade through the details of the day.

Next, I turned to the Angel Officers. I asked special angels to help me with all kinds of tasks, and now they are everywhere—guiding, guarding, nudging me in the right direction, patiently waiting for me to ask. With their lighthearted sense of humor, they have a way of translating the power of divine love into gentle guidance and endless support.

Here's the best part: Every Sunday, I call a board meeting. Starting with the CEO, I invite my special board members, out loud, to please be present with me for the meeting. That moment of roll call feels so exquisitely beautiful that I often have tears in my eyes before I get to the agenda. Then I speak from my soul as I review the happenings of the week—sharing, asking, begging, laughing, crying, thanking. Each week I am reminded how incredibly, tenderly, unconditionally loved we are.

In the World:

* Today, forge a personal relationship with your honored ones, thinking of them as friends and coworkers. Keep a running conversation, and enjoy the blessings of a Spiritual A-Team. Use a page in your journal to assign indispensable positions of importance to your team.

In the Heart:

* I open my heart to the loving assistance of my guardians and guides.

Listen to the Heart

Listen to the heart. It always knows.

I rose from bed this morning expecting to do my usual spiritual practice followed by a full day working on the app. As I have been on the path of ease and grace these days, I took note when I felt resistance to my familiar morning routine of yoga, spiritual reading, gratitude practices, meditation and writing. I felt off—encumbered by the organized plan I had been following for some months. Busy day or not, it was time to listen to my heart, and she was telling me to streamline my workspace.

I pulled out all of my supplies from the yoga area, the meditation area and the writing area. I tucked away everything that I was intuitively done with. I put some photos away and pulled others out. I got rid of all lists and extra notes designed to tell me what to do next. *I will know what to do and what to write,* I told myself. I even made a different kind of tea and did a sage ritual to energize and bless the cabin.

Change is in the air.

It's after noon now, and I'm just getting to the end of my morning routine, but I'm feeling clear and new. Tomorrow I will start fresh with a simplified morning practice that will lead to more connected and efficient work.

When we relax and lean into the flow, knowing we are unconditionally loved and clearly guided, we access that place in the heart that always directs us toward our highest alignment. We know because we are, in our essence, connected to the source of all wisdom, always flowing toward a higher vibration and greater authenticity.

Pay attention to how you feel. Notice the sense of ease or resistance. Listen to your heart and respond. You will not be led astray.

In the World:

* Take at least a few minutes for silent meditation and relaxation. Then ask a question or ask for guidance, and trust that the answer will come clearly. And it will! Stay vigilant for signs and guideposts.

In the Heart:

* In all situations, I listen to my heart and believe that my intuition is valid. I trust in the wisdom received.

A Froggy Hallelujah

I am resilient, and I flow with what life offers me today.

My tinnitus came on gradually as a result of a long music career standing next to a guitar amp and in front of a drum kit. The first few times my right ear made a shrill scream, I was not alarmed. I thought it might be my angel daughter communicating from heaven. No worries, just a hallelujah.

When it came on full force and full-time, with both ears emitting many wavy, high-pitched siren sounds in tandem, I was sure a spaceship had taken up residence in my head. It was so loud that nothing in the world was louder than my ears. Not a rock concert, not an airplane, not the ocean, not fireworks. My ears could always be heard over the sounds of the world.

Until, that is, I moved out to the country and witnessed the frog choir coming from the small pond outside the back door.

I do not exaggerate when I tell you it is deafening. After a rain, it only takes one frog to start singing, then a friend joins in, and within minutes, the place goes haywire. They fill the night with nonstop, earsplitting, mighty joy. Yep.

I use the same technique to manage the frog choir in my yard as I use to manage the spaceship in my head. I pretend it's a hallelujah. Instead of folding under the anxiety of my loud ears, I imagine it's a choir of angels singing of love to me and to God. And instead of waking up at night rustling for earplugs with a sleepy complaint, I imagine a mighty hallelujah rising from the pond.

And roll over and give thanks that the frogs can out-sing my angels.

In the World:

* Put a fresh spin on your greatest aggravations. Make light of what sends you over the edge. Welcome the noise instead of steeling for battle. Have the serenity to accept the things you cannot change.

In the Heart:

* I am calm, resilient and filled with inner peace. Instead of resisting, I flow with what life offers me today.

~ ⅄ ~

Everything Is Possible

Have faith. Dream big. Lead with your heart. Follow your bliss.

To all the new graduates and brave adventurers who are setting off on a new journey in life: Change brings with it the opportunity to begin again and move one step closer to who you are and what you love. Face your transformation with enthusiasm, courage, reverence and an open heart.

And know that everything is possible.

In the World:

* *Have faith.* Those of great faith who are able to imagine the impossible are those with the foundation of the essential twin beliefs: belief in yourself, and belief in a benevolent universe that conspires to support and assist. Aspire to great faith. Believe with your whole heart in your magnificence and in the highest, most unlimited version of yourself. Know beyond all doubt that grace is always lifting up your plans and dreams.

* *Dream big.* If you can dream it, you can be it. If you can imagine it, you can build it. In one of my favorite passages by Paramahansa Yogananda, he says, "Tune yourself with the creative power of spirit. You will be in contact with the infinite Intelligence that is able to guide you and to solve all problems. Power from the dynamic Source of your being will flow uninterruptedly so that you will be able to perform creatively in any sphere of activity."

* *Lead with your heart.* Develop the ability to silence your thoughts so you might recognize the voice of your heart through your intuition and higher guidance. Then listen to the promptings and follow them. When the heart leads, you will always have a North Star and an inner compass of authenticity and integrity.

* *Follow your bliss.* When Joseph Campbell came up with this phrase in *The Power of Myth*, a generation of seekers resonated with its truth. Joy is the most important signpost affirming that we are on the right path. The future goal is not your life. The path is your life. Create a life that makes you happy now.

In the Heart:

* I face transition with excitement and an open heart. I know I am always supported and guided toward my highest dreams.

You Will Know

The door that closed was not your door. Your door will invite you in.

"What do you want to be when you grow up?" We have all been rehearsing answers to that question since we were small, and still our high school and college grads are torturing themselves with it, thinking the answer should be clear. Oh, the pressure.

Our outward measure of success is hitchhiking on the back of our degrees, or lack of them, making the future look mighty heavy. From a spirit point of view, finding a job in our field when we graduate does not define who we are. *Because what we want to be when we grow up is happy, compassionate, loving, kind, peaceful and authentic.* At any age, this is alignment and is the place from which to start.

After I graduated from nursing school, I began playing in bars as a full-time musician—and twenty years went by. It might have seemed like a financial failure to some, but it's exactly where my heart was pulling me. I've never regretted a moment of it. Every day was a celebration.

We are not our titles, our jobs or our salaries. We are so much more than that. We are infinite possibility. When we follow the authentic yearnings of the heart, we can't miss. When doors close, it means others are meant to open.

Believe, pray, pay attention, be the absolute best version of yourself, and life will unfold as it should. Really it will. "Have patience with everything unresolved in your heart and try to love *the questions themselves*," Rainer Maria Rilke advises in *Letters to a Young Poet*.

Love the questions themselves. Start where your heart leads you, and allow life to be a joyous adventure.

In the World:

✳ Be patient with yourself, and believe that you will know what to do. You will be led by what unfolds with ease and grace. You will be led by what feels joyful. You will be led by following your inner wisdom. Ask your angels and guides for direction, and open to gratefully receive it. You will hear the call. You will know.

In the Heart:

✳ I am unlimited possibility. I follow the authentic yearnings of my heart, and I am led to the experiences that are meant for me.

~╲╱╱~

A Degree in Reinvention

It's your life. Paint the world in the colors of your love.

Not only can we support the transition from education to the real world with patient excitement, we can also open to the infinite possibilities that await as life unfolds in the jungle out there. You see, it's possible that just when you think you've found your calling, a change will occur that sends you careening on another vine. And where your heart goes, you will go, even if it takes a lifetime. My neighbor Thelma went to art school at the age of sixty-nine and graduated first in her class. My mom published her first book at eighty-five. There are no limits to what we can pursue.

Some of us manage to find our purpose early on and stay with it, but the vast majority of us grow and evolve in ways that make it impossible to stay planted in one place. So we find ourselves in the school of life with a fine arts degree in reinvention. I, for one, can speak from experience after a menagerie of careers that have left me with something of a PhD in reinvention. And why not? We have but one precious life and so many amazing choices.

Don't ever put a ceiling on your dreams; you are always *becoming* and will transform many times. Life is a garden of chances in which we are planted, germinate, grow, bloom, release seeds of wisdom and plant ourselves again. There are infinite shades and varieties of you.

And your gifts will color the world in incredibly beautiful ways.

In the World:

* If you are feeling stuck, go to the library and hang out in the biography or memoir section. Thumb through the lives of some inspiring limitless souls. The choices are endless.

* Try something new, even as a volunteer, that you have been passionate about. Begin the path to reinvention, each small step leading to the next. Allow yourself to be inspired.

In the Heart:

* Today I open to all the possibilities my life has to offer. I believe in myself and in the power of my dreams. I am unbound.

Life's Most Important Secrets

Inhale: Love in. Exhale: Love out.

Life is out of control. It doesn't take many years of living on our own in the world to glean one of life's most important secrets: We have little control over most of the events in our lives.

We could go down the rabbit hole looking for meaning in the challenging things that happen to us, but the bottom line is that sometimes things appear to be random and unfair. And in response to this unpredictable reality, I have come up with a secret of my own:

I always hold within my control what kind of energy I'm going to put into this day.

Simple as that. Am I going to radiate love and her family, or fear and hers?

This is a huge thing to be in control of. If my constant question is *How can I react to this with love?*, then all day long, I am vibrating love. The question itself opens the heart and exposes the deep wells of unending, unconditional love.

Two things happen when we deliberately act with love. We instantly make contact with the divine, the infinite source of all love. Secondly, our capacity to love *ourselves* magnifies as we align with our magnificence as beings of love. Magnify our magnificence. Love does that. It connects us with our divine source and renders us feeling pretty great.

When we bring the energy of love to this day, we become the energy of love to everyone who crosses our path and crosses our mind. We become a catalyst for infinite love, waking it up in others and lifting the vibration of the planet. Maybe life's not so out of control after all.

In the World:

✳   Throughout the day, breathe love as a beautiful mantra for yourself and others. Inhale: *Love in.* Exhale: *Love out.*

In the Heart:

✳   I breathe in love to the center of my heart, magnify it, and send it out into my world today.

MAY 12

The Gift of Life

Enjoy life. It's a gift. Unwrap it with gratitude and love. —Tiny Guru

Last night I had a talk with an old friend who is recovering from alcohol addiction. She sounded clear and bubbling over with life. The purpose of her call, probably part of a Step Nine mission, was to voice an eloquent apology for any hurt she may have caused me. I'm guessing we both flashed back to some messy times, but the present moment was so energetically beautiful that I was quick to assure her that whatever happened in the past was long over, and that I always knew anything hurtful did not come from her true self anyway.

She went on to tell me that life had become joyful. After a decade of self-destruction and darkness, she was now, after a year of sobriety, able to look back and see herself on the precipice of losing everything—her family, her health, her home and her life. Yes, she almost lost the precious life she had been given and nearly everything in it.

The shock of that vision completely reordered her priorities. Problems became bumps in the road instead of constant drama. Her family became all the more treasured. Waking up seemed to be cause for celebration. Love was literally pouring out of her.

We are not our mistakes. We are beautiful souls who have come here to experience this precious gift of life together. We are who we have always been: eternal beings of love. It's never too late for a transformation and another chance to unwrap the gift of life with gratitude and love.

In the words of Ralph Waldo Emerson, "Write it on your heart that every day is the best day in the year."

In the World:

* May we be reminded, no matter what today might hold, to be grateful for the gift of life and to use it to reflect to ourselves and others the joy of who we really are.

In the Heart:

* I am infinitely grateful to be alive. Each breath reminds me of the sacred gift of life.

꙾

Forever Love

If today is a hard day, let it be a gentle hard day.

Dear Angela, Mother's Day is a tumultuous day for mamas who have lost children. Because I had only nine months of carrying you while you were growing inside me does not make me less of a mother to you. You live on daily in my thoughts and in my heart. I am your forever mom, and you, my sweet child. Although many bereaved moms would rather avoid Mother's Day entirely (and I respect the individual nature of grief), I have always taken the day to celebrate your time here as my daughter.

Your loss had already taken so much from me: my joy for so many years, my faith in future plans, my connection with those who couldn't understand, my hope, really. I was not willing to let this day, too, be rooted in pain and loss. Every other day might hold an element of your absence, but not this one. No, I'm claiming this day to remember the radiant love that comes with the honor of being your mom. I want to allow your loss to *find* something new in me.

Twenty years ago, my forty weeks with you were an intense and beautiful adventure. We meditated each morning. We walked on the cobblestone streets of the pretty Austrian town and talked about every little thing. We imagined and we made big plans. We sang, we danced and we read together side by side. And most brilliantly, you brought out a love in me that is unlike any love I have known. A love I would trade my life for. Yes, little one, I would. My love for you is one I didn't know I was capable of, coming in waves of grace and waterfalls of joy. You expanded me.

So on Mother's Day, I celebrate being your mom. I've got some flowers here, and this card I'm writing to you. And that's enough. The gift of the love you brought out in me is worth celebrating because it's a love that won't ever die. I've got it tucked safely right here in my heart—and within every cell of my being—as one of the most precious gifts I have ever received in my life. With forever love, Mom 💜

In the World:

✳ If your parent or your child has left the earth before you, write them a letter or write your thoughts about Mother's Day or Father's Day.

In the Heart:

✳ On Mother's Day (and Father's Day), I allow the best of my memories to come to the surface and keep safe company with my love.

꧁

Gratitude in Advance

I am thankful for the miracles that are yet to unfold.

From the moment we utter those sunrise words, "Thank you for the blessings of this day," we change the energy of the morning to one of prosperity. Our heartfelt *thank you*, rising up through the sleepy dawn of today, is a deep and transformative acknowledgment that we are not alone in the creation of our experience, and that this day will bear countless gifts.

Through the lens of thanksgiving, small moments become precious, simple things become sacred and life itself becomes a gift.

In the midst of the pain and uncertainty of my separation, I started a Gratitude in Advance practice. In a spiral notebook, I listed all the blessings I wished for my future life as if they had already happened. I felt the joy of their fruition as I wrote the same list out every day on a new page. To my complete amazement, everything on the list came to pass.

The more grateful we are, the more we have to be grateful for. Waking with a heart of gratitude and giving thanks *in advance* for the gifts of the day is one of the most powerful habits we can practice. Fasten your seat belt, and keep an eye out for miracles!

In the World:

✳ Dedicate a new spiral notebook to the Gratitude in Advance practice. Really get one. This is worth it!

✳ After today's date on the first line, write, "Thank you for the blessings of this day!" Then make a list of future blessings that you are thankful for. For example: "I am in radiant health. The house sale flows with ease and grace. I have all the money I need for all I need to do. The app sells millions worldwide." (Still working on that one.) "I finish my book with divine guidance." You get the idea.

✳ Make daily entries, each on a new page with the day's date, as part of your morning spiritual practice. The items are exactly the same from day to day until one comes true and another item takes its place.

In the Heart:

✳ I am thankful for the blessings of this day and for the miracles that are yet to unfold.

Celebrating the Sunrise

There is grace in the sunrise, in the light of a new day.

This morning I wrap myself in a blanket and pad out to be with the sunrise. The early birds begin with tentative melodies, and the answers arrive with joyful enthusiasm. They seem to know something I don't know. They sing, *Are you awake?* Friends join in until it becomes a symphony of birdsongs, with the rooster and the ravens throwing in their loud solos. They are insistent. *Are you awake?*

The wind in the trees sounds like a distant waterfall as it blows through the towering sentinels. All of the leaves on Hunters Road clap for the sun. Each blade of grass shimmers wet across the horse field. There is a faint *om* coming up from the very earth.

This is what I think the birds know: Everything is starting over. Just like me. It is the dawn of a new beginning. New life. Every morning we get another chance—and they sing about it. There are two sunrises, one over the field and one in the soul. The birds have somehow figured this out.

Wispy pink clouds gather expectantly around the place where the sun will come up over the ridge, receiving her, beholding her. The Beatles' "Here Comes the Sun" sings in my heart with the first beam of light. "It's all right," the lyrics tell me. *Really?* Yes. Right now, everything is all right.

There is grace in the sunrise, in the light of a new day. There is space now, while worries wait, for hope to rise. There's a chance now, to create beautiful things from the ashes of night. There is faith now, that anything is possible in this brand-new world. There is peace now. *Am I awake?* I am awake to the possibilities.

The sun breaks free like confetti of gold shining between the branches of the big tree in the field, and the earth stands still for the tiniest of moments, in awe of this precious day. *We are awake.* And here is our chance to begin again. Because every morning the birds sing, and grace pours in with the light.

In the World:

* If it has been a while since your last time, make a date to experience a sunrise outside. Bask in the sights, the sounds, the colors, the grace.

In the Heart:

* I rise each morning grateful for possibilities and new beginnings.

MAY 16

The Currency of Love

May the blessings of this day radiate through your smile,
be helpful through your hands and shine through your heart.

We are infinitely blessed—alive, awake and empowered with the ability to give and receive love. May we freely allow the gifts of this day to pour through us like waterfalls of grace, accepting them with a grateful heart and passing them on to wherever they are needed most.

We are not created as containers to catch, collect and carry our riches. We are created to transform energy by opening to the gifts of life, then allowing them to freely flow through us. Rich with a deep well of love, we receive these blessings and give them back to our world in an endless circle of beauty, transforming our blessings into service for others.

In order to facilitate this exchange of love, we don't need to possess any extraordinary talents. Martin Luther King Jr. once said, "Everybody can be great, because anybody can serve. You only need a heart full of grace. A soul generated by love."

We already have a soul generated by love.

When we are open to being of service, opportunities organically appear. We are given the chance to include or compliment someone, to listen in a way that makes another feel important, or to share our time, talents and resources.

We are made for this, to give and to receive. The currency is only and always love.

In the World:

* May the blessings of this day radiate through your smile, giving joy to everyone you encounter today, lifting spirits with light and love.

* May the blessings of this day be helpful through your hands, serving where you are needed, lifting spirits with skill and generosity.

* May the blessings of this day shine through your heart, raising the vibration of the world, lifting spirits with energy and grace.

In the Heart:

* With gratitude for the blessings I have received, I serve freely and joyfully, creating a circle of abundance for all beings.

An Unexpected Surprise

Kindness changes the world one heart at a time.

Today, someone took time out of his busy life to write me four short lines letting me know that I had a positive impact on him during a hard time. Those words of kindness were a gift to me in that moment, filling my heart and lifting my spirits. This simple, loving act brought immense joy to my work today, knowing that I had helped one person.

We all go through the day putting out love in the best way we know how, but we rarely know how our actions affect the lives of others unless they tell us. And what an unexpected surprise that is. We are delighted to learn that something we did made an impact. We mattered. Someone's heart changed because of us, and they took the time to pause and share it.

We have all been changed for the better by the kindness of others. It might be a teacher or a counselor, a contractor or the checker at the grocery store. It could be a doctor or a friend, a bus driver or a caregiver. It may be a parent or a mentor, a neighbor or someone in a support group.

When we acknowledge their impact on our lives, we become part of the ripple effect of kindness, changing someone's day while we change the world.

One heart at a time.

In the World:

* Take a moment out of your day to write a short note to someone who has made a difference in your life. Let them know how they changed you. Tell them how special they are.

* Encourage your children or students to do the same, helping them to identify how someone has changed their lives for the better, how they might express that in a few simple lines, and how it might feel to receive a note like this.

In the Heart:

* I let others know how I feel, freely and openly, taking the time to express simple kindness through words of gratitude.

Light in the Darkness

Send your light into the darkness and your peace into our world.

May God bless those whose lives are touched by war. Protect them, comfort them, and grant them a moment of peace.

May God bless those whose lives are touched by grief. Hold them in tender arms of love, and grant them a moment of peace.

May God bless those whose lives are touched by illness. Cover them with healing light, and grant them a moment of peace.

May God bless those whose lives are touched by trauma. Encircle them in strong wings of safety, and grant them a moment of peace.

May God bless those whose lives are touched by injustice. Fill them with resilience and mighty grace, and grant them a moment of peace.

May God bless those whose lives are touched by depression. Lift them with a ray of hope, and grant them a moment of peace.

May God bless those whose lives are touched by poverty. Fill their needs through hearts of compassion, and grant them a moment of peace.

May God bless those whose lives are touched by addiction. Lift them up in health and light, and grant them a moment of peace.

May God bless those whose lives are touched by anxiety. Lead them to still waters of safety and calm, and grant them a moment of peace.

May God bless those whose lives are touched by loneliness. Cover them with the kindness of friendship, and grant them a moment of peace. Amen.

In the World:

* Our light and prayers are a powerful tool for healing and peace. Send your light into the darkness and your peace into our world. It will be felt.

* Add your own personal intentions to today's prayer.

In the Heart:

* In communion with divine love, I send my prayers and intentions of peace around the world today.

Phone Down, Chi Up

Peaceful energy is just a breath away.

In Chinese traditional philosophy, *chi (qi)* is our life force, the vital energy of our being. Similar to the concept of *prana* in Indian culture, it translates literally as *breath* and metaphysically as the creative flow of our energy in the world. It is inherent in all of us, but the strength of our life force may vary depending on how clear and healthy our channel is on any given day.

On days when I'm using screens a lot, I feel a drain on my chi. Sometimes I can literally feel my lights dimming. I might be accomplishing a lot of work but at great cost to my spiritual energy.

It's helpful during our workday to balance the effects of technology by taking short breaks to still the mind and connect with spirit. We can center our souls with a few deep breaths, a quick prayer, some affirmations or a phone-free walk in nature.

For many years now, I have powered down all electronics on what I call Spirit Sundays. It was a little stressful at first, but I quickly got used to dialing down the worldly drama and opening up to the simple joys of the soul. I have no doubt that Spirit Sundays alone magnify my clarity and replenish my energy for the entire week ahead.

Disconnect to reconnect. Unplug to get centered. Step away to come closer.

Peaceful energy is just a breath away.

In the World:

✴ During your spiritual practice, silence your phone. This is your sacred time.

✴ Balance the effects of technology by taking micro-breaks today for a few deep breaths and a connection with spirit.

✴ Consider going tech-free one day a week. It's the best gift you can give to your beautiful self. Find more details on February 4.

In the Heart:

✴ I am a radiant soul powered by the creative energy of spirit. I gift myself with undistracted time for peace and spiritual connection.

Calling Your Power Back

Your inner beauty shines.

It doesn't always feel like our inner beauty is so shiny. Sometimes that powerful inner lighthouse is socked in with fog, and our searchlight becomes more like a flashlight. Life events have a way of covering up our shine by insidiously chipping away at our intensity, and we don't realize it until it's almost dark and we are searching for the shoreline in vain. At just these times, we may need to take matters into our own hands.

Which is what my mom did. She has a tool she refers to as *calling her power back*. The first time she used it, she was rather desperate. After seven months of dragging through the effects of an autoimmune disease, broken bones and sleepless nights, she was sick and tired of being sick and tired.

So she became inspired to change things, and one morning, she lit some candles and called on her loving spirit guides. She then pronounced, out loud and with great force, "I call my power back NOW!" (Think Gandalf in *Lord of the Rings:* "You shall not pass!" But she didn't fall off the bridge.)

She proceeded to call her power back repeatedly, in no uncertain terms, until she felt a shift. She called her power back to heal, to sleep, to dream. Then she played some sacred music and completed the ceremony by blessing the invocation. And it was the turning point in what had been an exhausting, protracted illness.

Our shining inner beauty is always there—a radiant, beaming, powerful light. Never worry that you have lost your mojo. You can't lose it. It's who you are. It just gets covered by the weight of the world, and when you're ready, you have the power to reclaim what is rightfully yours. Shine on, beautiful one.

In the World:

✳ When you are in need of a recharge, find a sacred, quiet moment to call your power back. Keep this ceremony in your spiritual toolbox, and use it whenever your lights grow dim.

In the Heart:

✳ I reclaim my radiant light and the power of my spirit.

Moment by Moment Creation

When we focus on beauty, we reflect light.
When we focus on harmony, we reflect love.
When we focus on gratitude, we reflect blessings.

Our thoughts have more power over what happens today than almost anything else, more than our families, more than our schedules, more than the weather. They shape our moods, our feelings of self-worth, our capacity for joy, our sense of abundance. They are constant companions that can be guided to serve us in creating this beautiful day.

Absolutely everything we do is commented on by our ego minds. We are accustomed to this cohort in our heads, defaulting to her usual rhythms and projections. These thoughts color our perception of the day.

With every thought and action, we co-create with the divine, drawing toward us compatible thoughts and actions. We create when we speak, when we think, when we wish, when we give thanks. We create when we have faith, when we feel compassion, when we smile, when we assist. We create when we are silent, when we trust, when we are kind, when we bless.

Our thoughts are the energy of manifestation. The clearer the thought, the more powerful it is. In *The Whole Elephant Revealed*, Marja de Vries explains, "Focused attention strengthens the power of our intention, because focused attention makes the waves we emit more coherent, that is, more unambiguous and therefore more powerful." The more clearly we focus, the more powerful the thought wave.

Focus mightily on all things light and all things love, and you will create a most beautiful day. Treasure every minute of it.

In the World:

* Start the day with a grateful heart and a positive prediction for your ideal day. Repeat your affirmation often. Allow negative beliefs to float by, then turn them around to reflect the hope of your desires.

* Flow with what arises—surprises and all.

In the Heart:

* I co-create this day with every thought. My thoughts are positive reflections of my most beautiful imaginings.

~\/~

Thank You, Scuba Man - Part 1

Behind every online conversation is somebody's soul.

It was my first all-out attack on a social media post. I had just started my business, and was a newbie with a brand-new platform. My post for that day announced, "Every moment is a sacred moment." Dreamland, I know, but it's my truth. And although a sweeping generalization, it never occurred to me that it could be hurtful. My serene little desk chair tipped over from the weight of my jaw dropping to the floor, horror-struck by the angry comment that went something like:

"That's utter bullsh-t. I have no clue who wrote this preppy cr-p, but whoever it was needs to take off the rose-colored glasses, throw them on the ground, stomp on them and wake up to the real world. Obviously they've never carried the lifeless body of their friend to a coroner's wagon... Go stick your head in the sand like the rest of the preppy do-gooder idiots!"

Ouch. My first thought: *I am so not preppy.* My second thought: *I had no idea it might feel that way to you.* I clicked on his picture to do a little reconnaissance and saw he was a scuba diver. *Me too.* This guy can't be all bad.

In the coming days, I thought about Scuba Man a lot. He wasn't just an angry troll; he was a real person. We both felt misunderstood. He felt I was belittling his experience by throwing fairy dust on the most traumatic event of his life, and I felt like he was accusing me of throwing that fairy dust from a naive, pain-free seat of privilege. Neither was true. But we were both sure that the other was out of line.

Email, social media and texts are our main form of communication, yet without our physical presence, intentions can be easily misconstrued. How can we bring more peace into our writing? More thoughts on that tomorrow.

In the World:

✳ Our written words can lift and can wound. We can't predict the way they will land in a heart, but we can be aware of their power as we write today.

In the Heart:

✳ I consciously use the power of my words for peace.

⤙⤚

Thank You, Scuba Man - Part 2

Walk a mile in someone else's shoes. Understand more. Judge less.

After deliberating, I apologized to Scuba Man by private message:

"I'm the one who wrote the post that you blasted. Sorry that hit a bad spot. I wanted to let you know that I'm far from preppy (more of a hippie), a lifetime scuba diver (but not nearly as trained as you!), and although I have not carried the lifeless body of a friend (I'm so sorry for your loss), I have held the lifeless body of my child. But I had to make a choice when I realized that there is really only one thing I can control. And that is the energy I put into the world. I've been a student of spirituality all of my life, so that's how I process pain. If those are rose-colored glasses, oh well. It's the best I can do. I do believe that even through the tears, holding my daughter in those traumatic moments was sacred. For me. I guess I just wanted to tell you that things aren't always as they seem, and we all have a story. I wish you the best."

I said a short prayer, hit Send, and didn't hear back. When he crossed my mind, I'd think, *Bless you, Scuba Man*, and let it go. Months later, this appeared:

Thank you very much. Your comments and story clear the air. Best wishes!

We were strangers, bonded by similarities. We didn't define our experiences in the same way, but we shared the feelings of loss, emptiness, pain, confusion and grief. Knowing how my words could be felt by a newly grieving person taught me an important lesson. When we imagine what it would feel like to walk in someone else's shoes, the common thread of our shared humanity makes us less likely to assume and to judge.

Thank you, Scuba Man.

In the World:

✶ Remember the soul behind every unique opinion.

✶ Choose your battles and consider disagreeing in a private message.

✶ Be open to unexpected lessons of spirit from the most random places.

In the Heart:

✶ Today, with an open heart, I love more and judge less.

~v~

Unconditional Love

*May simple acts of kindness and unconditional love
light your way today.*

Imagine you are running late for work in rush hour traffic when someone cuts you off and nearly causes an accident. Or the person ahead of you in the express checkout line at the grocery store has about thirty items in their basket instead of the limit of fifteen. Or you have your blinker on, patiently waiting for a parking space at Trader Joe's, when someone swoops in from the other direction and slides neatly into your space. We all know about them—people whose aggravating behaviors test the thin limits of our developing patience.

For those who hold a special place in our lives, it's natural to extend our goodwill and to support them, even when they are not in the best of moods. When a friend is sick or a family member is in a challenging situation, we might send up a prayer and offer them a special kindness in hopes of bettering their situation. But what of those who are not in our inner circle? Or those whose behavior is incredibly annoying or extremely rude?

We have no way of knowing the stories behind the absent-minded or even deliberately negative actions of strangers. But if we assume the best of all people and consider that they may have an important story behind their behavior, it's evident that they also need a kind heart.

There is an endless well of love and light within us that is always ready to be shared. The more we give away, the more we are able to receive. Be generous in doling out blessings. They are so needed and are always received on a soul-to-soul level.

Your kindness and gentle blessings lift up the hearts of others as a silent but powerful prayer, and as a gift of unconditional love.

In the World:

✳ To anyone who enters your orb today, in a positive or negative way, send them a little love and bless them on their way.

In the Heart:

✳ I am a being of light and have an infinite amount of love and positive energy to share. I freely bless all those who cross my path today.

~*~

Life Is Beautiful

Music unwraps the heart, sings out the prayer,
dances the spirit and opens the soul.

Whenever I feel the urge to wade through the waters of self-pity, I snap out of it when I think of Alice. "Every day, life is beautiful. I am full of joy!" So said Alice Herz-Sommer, the concert pianist, mother, teacher and longest-living Holocaust survivor, living to the age of 110. When I heard her speak these words in an interview, tears welled up in my eyes for the sheer beauty and impossibility of her statement. How remarkable that someone who had lost so many of her beloveds and witnessed one of the most traumatic chapters of human history, could exude such love, enthusiasm, delight and gratitude.

Alice credits music with saving her life, and saving it even after the war was over. When the Nazis first occupied her town and took her mother to her death, Alice poured herself into the Chopin *Etudes*—challenging compositions of the classical piano repertoire.

She practiced sometimes as much as eight hours a day, choosing to see and hear beauty, focusing on the light in an ocean of despair. The hungry and hopeless prisoners who witnessed the more than one hundred performances during her two years in Theresienstadt concentration camp said her music was food for their souls, transporting them to another, more hopeful place. "Music is magic," she explained simply.

So when we wonder if we can bear the unbearable, Alice tells us we can. "The music, the music! It brings us on an island with peace, beauty and love." When we wonder if we can ever know joy again after a loss, Alice shows us it's possible. She expresses little bitterness, choosing instead to turn to beauty and love. "It is up to us whether we look at the good or the bad."

In the World:

* In the face of her darkest days, Alice turned to music. Her music could be our pottery, our garden, our cooking, our knitting, our wallpaper app. We, too, can choose to look for the good. Every small step is an offering of love.

In the Heart:

* I feel the joy of being alive and allow myself to expand through beautiful works of nature, music and art.

~y~

Made from Love

Your mistakes do not define you. Your love does.

If we could lift up off of the earth and see as the angels see, all we would see is the radiant light of our love. And it's a beautiful sight.

No one is free from mistakes and missteps. Some of us even bear the burden of knowing that our actions have hurt other lives. And we need to let all of that go. Without delay.

Isn't it possible that those very actions have allowed us to come to a more enlightened place? Berating ourselves on top of the guilt and shame does not assist in our growth; it only serves to exhaust our souls by grounding our flight with a storm of self-doubt.

It's not what we do, or how we do it, that matters in this world. It's how much we love. And every single day, we have a chance to begin again and make it a day in which our thoughts are empowered by love. What lives on until the end of time is the love we share. Our mistakes do not define us. Our love does.

Even in the depths of despair, when we offer a small token of love to another, we begin to heal. Even after a regrettable circumstance, when we ask for forgiveness with love, we begin to heal.

We learn, we love, we heal, we grow, we love more. We can't go wrong. We are made from love.

In the World:

* Disable destructive, self-critical thoughts as soon as you recognize them.

* Replace them with affirmations of kindness and encouragement.

* Make amends for past mistakes. Then let them go.

* Live today from a place of love. Start by reaching out to someone with one loving compliment.

In the Heart:

* I am a being of love. All of my thoughts and actions today are empowered by love.

~⌇~

Contagious Kindness

Be the kindness that reminds someone
that there's still plenty of love in the world.

Some months ago, when running errands in the nearest city about twenty miles from the cabin, I found myself filling a prescription at an unfamiliar pharmacy. There were many people in line, and I resigned myself for a long wait at the end of a long day.

But something was very different here. The energy was incredibly... happy. There were four women behind the counter, two taking orders and two filling them. They were constantly checking in with each other —pharmacists assisting cashiers and vice versa. They were upbeat and friendly with one another, and most wonderfully, they were especially kind to their customers.

They noticed if someone wasn't feeling well and tried to expedite their order. They took care to listen well to each customer and to be patient in answering questions. Next thing I knew, all of us who were waiting in line were in conversations with each other, complimenting an outfit, remarking on the weather. Someone even let someone else go ahead of them in line. The kindness that the ladies were showing to each other and to us—was contagious.

Yesterday, I had to fill another prescription, and of course I went to the Kind Pharmacy. The same four women were there, and once again, they were rockin' the line with kindness and joy. And, no lie, the same thing happened. We who were in line began to chat, with compassion and smiles spreading from one to the next, faster than a virus.

We have learned that people who witness acts of kindness are more likely to show kindness to others, but it was a special gift to see it playing out in a humble line. Who knew? The ladies behind the counter are changing the world with contagious kindness.

In the World:

∗ Every act of kindness will be multiplied exponentially as it spreads from soul to soul. Let's change the world with our kindness today.

In the Heart:

∗ Each day, I have the power to change the world for the better.

One Miracle at a Time

One breath. One hour. One day. One miracle at a time.

If the drama of life seems overwhelming today, welcome, dear one, welcome to the party. Sometimes the most important thing we can do, literally, is breathe. And focus on one thing at a time, with love. When we feel ourselves spinning out, we can stop the downward spiral with one...mindful...breath...at a time.

It seems like a small thing, but in truth, our breath is our connection to everything. It has the power to slow our autonomic nervous system, which can ease panic and fear. It has the power to oxygenate our every cell, bringing renewed energy and health to the body. It has the power to focus our racing thoughts on the present moment. It has the power to align us with our spiritual selves so we may access the wisdom and grace of our highest love and support.

It's okay to break things down into manageable scenes today. Especially if we are overloaded or in a painful situation. Our bodies and souls are telling us that this moment needs attention. This moment needs us now. This moment wants tea and grace. This moment wants us to be open to whatever it asks of us. To be still and present *is* getting something done. Maybe it's the most important thing we will get done today.

We don't have to figure it all out right now. We have all the help we need when we step back and ask for it. Our job is to keep our hearts open and to act from a place of love.

Simply start with one breath. Then one hour. One day. One miracle at a time.

In the World:

* Take a centering breath. And another. Then just be fully in this hour. You can do an hour. Pain and all, messiness and all, grief and all, you can stay in it for an hour. Keep your heart open.

In the Heart:

* For now, I take it one breath at a time. I stay in the moment while believing that I have all the strength I need for whatever life asks of me today.

~∖⋎⁄~

May They Feel Our Love

May the infinite light of our prayers shine into the darkness of those
who need them today. May they feel our love.

I once read the true story of a near-death experience where a woman had "died" in a car accident. She floated out of her body, and her consciousness was above her car. She said she could see, hear and feel the prayers coming from the long line of cars that were now stopped on the congested highway behind the scene of the crash. The prayers looked like lights beaming out of the cars, and the incredible transcendent love she felt from them convinced her to return to her body, where she recovered and was able to later share her story.

There are countless anecdotal accounts of how prayer has changed the course of circumstances. Some believe these to be true and some don't. But if you choose to pray, there's no halfway. We need not even speak the words without pure passion and love behind them. Having faith that the prayer is indeed working for the highest good of all is where its power and grace comes from.

So when you pray, do it all the way, with all the focus you have.

For those in the wake of life's storms and those who have left this world before us, our prayers can make a difference that we will never know about. This is a gift we can give to our families, to our friends, to strangers, to our world.

They will feel our love.

In the World:

∗   May the infinite light of our prayers shine into the darkness of those who need them today. May they feel our love.

∗   May the infinite light of our prayers reach into the hearts of those with special challenges today. May they feel our love.

∗   May the infinite light of our prayers reach out to the spirits of those who have gone before us. May they feel our love.

In the Heart:

∗   With compassion for all beings and fueled by divine love, I offer the light of my prayers to all those who might be lifted by them.

꧁

Too Good

The story of your life is written with kind words, helpful hands and a loving heart.

If you are out in the dating world, you might want to lean in for this one. No, I don't have tips for profiles or anything like that. But in the increasingly judgmental world of division and separation, there are a few things we might want to keep in mind.

My mom and dad, each from a different political party, canceled each other out at every major election. On top of that, Dad was deeply Catholic, a lay minister who served Communion at Mass, while Mom fled the Church at the start of the sex abuse scandal, never to return. She immersed herself in the pursuit of God and developed a deep spirituality of her own making. The Pope and the Buddha, I would call them. But their marriage endured. Being of differing beliefs did not deter them.

In fact, it's imperative that we maintain respect for various political and spiritual beliefs. We all have to make our own decisions about what we can or can't live with. But know that souls like ours are present across all aisles in politics and in worship, and our personal partnerships do not have to match if we allow each other the honor of independent thinking. That said, bigotry or hatred of another group on the basis of their appearance or belief system *is* a dealbreaker, but we know that.

On another note, once, Maya described a guy who was interested in her as "too good." I almost crashed the car. *Are you kidding me? There is such a thing as too good?* As you can imagine, I opened the floodgates on that one. "Too good is desirable. Too good is amazing. Too good is what you're looking for, honey! Too good is the deal. You want to be treated like the goddess that you are. Go for too good!" She listened well, and dated Too Good for years. I never once worried when they were out together because I knew he had her back.

That's what we want. We want a beautiful soul. One that is Too Good.

In the World:

✳ Surround yourself with people who respect you, who treat you with love and compassion, who would never dream of being unkind to you, who protect and cherish you.

In the Heart:

✳ In all things and in all ways, I am worthy of great love and kindness.

~⋎~

Today's Grace

Open the window of your heart to today's blessings and grace.

Today's grace is already here, and we have been generously provided for. In all we do today, we will have a bountiful *helping* of grace.

Today's grace only asks that we love ourselves enough to open to it. That we soften the angular edges of our plans and reimagine the day as a benevolent road with choices and chances.

Today's grace is all that we need to experience beauty and love. It is all we need to mobilize the strength to do the hard things. It is all we need to give thanks for whatever arises and to meet life with an open heart.

Today's grace flows toward ease. Like energy, it will channel us to the path of least resistance, so we may accomplish our tasks with enthusiasm and synchronicity.

Today's grace is all we need for all we *need* to do. We can gentle up and soften a bit. Some things might flow smoother tomorrow, or if we have the assistance of someone else.

Today's grace works well with laughter and a light heart. It points the way with flexibility and surrender. It revels in our joy. It lifts us in our sorrows.

Today's grace is already here, and there's always enough.

Let's open the window of our hearts to today's blessings and grace.

In the World:

✳ Open, allow and welcome the lightness of flowing with grace. Trust that today's grace will lift you in small acts of tea and big acts in the boardroom, in the classroom or with the kids. Remember it's here for you, in every moment.

In the Heart:

✳ I am surrounded and cushioned by the gift of grace. In all I do today, I flow with ease and a light heart.

June Blessings

Happiness is not about fixing big things that have gone wrong.
It's about finding small things that have gone right.

June beams in with the summer solstice and the promise of more daylight than any other time of the year. And oh, how our souls welcome the light. Gratitude rises with the heat and the hope of vacation days and a schedule that unties our knots a bit. Even if we can't take time off, our souls love to celebrate the small moments and playful delights. Summer rejoices in slow, simple things and our celebration for the first day of June can begin with one little thought: There is only one today.

There is only one today to offer gratitude and open to grace. There is only one today to be kind to ourselves and compassionate toward others. There is only one today to be ourselves bravely—riding the waves of joy and challenge. There is only one today. Let's be awake for it. Let's be all in. Let's celebrate the small moments.

Be present.

Let the day flow with grace.

Expect joy. Be positive.

Serve with compassion.

Speak only kindness.

Impart only love.

Never forget you're not alone.

Give thanks for everything.

See goodness in others.

In the World:

✳ Invite these thoughts into your heart as you begin a new chapter.

✳ Choose a word for June that will light your way.

✳ Write some intentions for the month ahead.

In the Heart:

✳ I am grateful for the gift of this precious moment in time.

~·\/·~

Dolphin Dreaming

Open your heart to the wisdom that dreams leave for your waking life.

I have always been a dreamer in more ways than one, entertaining nightly mini-dramas of all kinds. My dreams range from random to vivid —dreams that seem nearly real, in which I remember every detail and color—to lucid dreams, where I consciously realize I am dreaming and can direct the dream. I even had a complete song come through me once, singing it in the dream and writing it down in its entirety when I woke.

Much about dreams is not well understood, but there is agreement that they are an important means of learning about ourselves, that they consolidate our memories, that native peoples throughout time considered them an important source of cultural wisdom, that dreams can lead to creativity and problem solving, and, my new favorite, that sometimes people dream in tandem.

Last week, while visiting my forever mother-in-law Kay for her birthday, Maya and I stayed in her basement bedroom. We slept side by side in twin beds, heads not three feet apart. In the morning, as a group of us chatted on the porch, I told of my vivid dream the night before.

I was flying over a beautiful landscape when I was drawn to a body of crystal blue water. I looked out over the water to see three dolphins. In my mind, I called them and they swam happily to shore. They lifted their heads, bodies vertical in the water, so I could reach out and pet each one. I looked up and Maya stood, jaw dropped, in the doorway. "I had the *exact same dream!*" After comparing notes, we realized that in our dreams we came to the water from different places, but joined there and dreamed the exact same dolphin story in tandem before waking.

At night, just about anything can happen. We rest, we travel, we learn, we are guided and we are refreshed. Pay attention to the signs and the valuable wisdom that our dreams leave for our waking lives.

In the World:

✳ To remember your dreams, try using a dream journal. When you awaken, record any images that you remember. Soon full dreams will unfold in your memory upon awakening.

In the Heart:

✳ I dream nightly and absorb wisdom from the gift of my dreams. I allow my sleep time to help me access my deeper wisdom.

~\/~

Blue Mind

I am calm. I am content. I am connected.

Imagine slipping into an easy meditation, where you are awed by the overwhelming beauty of life; feeling calm, relaxed, content and at one with an inexplicable power greater than yourself. This is your brain at the ocean.

Marine biologist Wallace J. Nichols has spent years researching and lecturing about the uplifting effect of water that he calls "Blue Mind." He writes, in his book of the same name, that when we are in or near water, we enter into a mild meditative state that brings us peace, happiness and the sense that all is well. Water provides a precious break from the noise and overstimulation of the world—an antithesis to our time with tiny blue screens. It mellows our minds with much-needed downtime, allowing creative solutions to rise to the surface, and for healing to take place on many levels.

We don't have to be on vacation at the beach with our toes in the sand to receive the benefit of water for our souls. All bodies of water have restorative powers. Rivers, waterfalls, lakes and streams have a comforting, calming effect. Pools and mineral springs, even showers, tubs and apps that play the sound of waves crashing on the shore soothe our inner tension. We are hard wired to become more peaceful when our senses are resting in a water element.

More than seventy percent of our blue planet is covered with water. It is one of God's greatest gifts to us. Let's dive into the abundant blessings of Blue Mind.

In the World:

* Think of exposure to the sight and sound of water as a spiritual practice.

* Make an effort to be near water in nature as often as possible. Take a hike by a river or have lunch at the lake in the park.

* Notice and appreciate the peaceful and balancing effects of water today.

In the Heart:

* Water centers me, calms me, heals me and restores me.

∽⋎⊱

Vacation Packing List

For yourself, patience. For everyone you meet, kindness.
For fun, a sense of humor. For the soul, relaxation. For plans, flexibility.
For the journey, gratitude. For all of the above, grace.

Vacations are not always what they seem. While most people look pretty serene in their travel photos, many of us can admit to at least a little vacation stress. It can be a lot of work to prepare for the trip with all the laptops, tablets, phones, chargers and earbuds. When we arrive, we face spotty cell service, no free Wi-Fi connections and slow upload speeds. Okay, just kidding about the tech stuff...but there's some truth here!

Vacations provide a precious opportunity to open the soul to inspiration. One of the beauties of getting away from our daily routine is not being available in the usual ways. So consider traveling light and tech-free in mind, body and soul. With a virtual suitcase that won't cost extra, we can put in a little pretrip prep that will serve us in all stages of travel and reentry. Happy trails to you.

In the World: Vacation Packing List

✳ *Patience:* Vacations come with lines, sometimes long ones. Come prepared with a fun way to occupy the time with your loved ones that doesn't involve a phone. Be creative. Or just talk to each other.

✳ *Kindness:* Start by being especially kind to yourself. Show kindness to all those you meet on your journey. Every server, guide and driver was meant to cross your path. Honor them all. Be extra kind to your travel companions.

✳ *Sense of Humor:* Choose joy. This can really save the day—yours and others. Be generous with your smiles. Let your heart be light.

✳ *Relaxation:* Get a massage. Do yoga. Read. Meditate. Walk. Let go.

✳ *Flexibility:* Things change. We can change. Go with the flow and ride the current with ease and grace.

✳ *Gratitude:* For everything about this new experience, be thankful.

✳ *Grace:* That you might have all of the above.

In the Heart:

✳ I allow my vacation to be a time of joy and rejuvenation. I am present for new experiences with an open and loving heart.

JUNE 5

Soul to Soul

*Blessings are silent beams of love that magnify our thoughts
with the light of grace.*

Every time we bless someone, we send them a beam of love. Imagine beautiful light extending from your heart to theirs, lightening their load, lifting up their burdens, providing strength and healing. They feel lifted. You feel lifted.

The tender gift of blessing others and our world makes a beautiful addition to our daily spiritual practice. My friend Maria blesses people in the silence of her heart as she walks the dog. My brother Bill blesses "everyone I can think of" after his morning meditation. Whenever I am troubled about a situation or something crops up as a challenge, I bless the situation and the people involved. When someone randomly enters our mind, we can bless them. It takes on a sweet momentum once we get into the flow of the practice.

Every single time we send out a blessing, we are also connecting with our own spiritual power, invoking grace from our highest self and a higher source. In his book of blessings, *To Bless the Space Between Us*, Irish author and poet John O'Donohue shares, "When you bless another, you first gather yourself; you reach below your surface mind and personality, down to the deeper source within you—namely, the soul. Blessing is from soul to soul. And the key to who you are is your soul."

Today, let's use the art of blessing others as a spiritual practice, beaming love to all who are in the midst of deep challenges—all those who are exhausted, isolated, sick, grieving, anxious, fearful. We can't solve the world's problems today, but we can offer the inexhaustible power of blessings from soul to soul. And that matters. More than we know.

In the World:

* Use the art of blessing others as a spiritual practice throughout the day today. Try it in all circumstances, sending blessings to loved ones and strangers alike—in situations of ease and in ones of challenge.

* Add the practice of blessing others to your spiritual journal.

In the Heart:

* I bless all who cross my path generously and in connection with unlimited divine source. Blessing others brings me joy.

~✢~

Frannie Makes a Comeback

*Mix a little faith into your doubt. Light a little candle in your dark.
Put a little hope in your heart.*

Oh gosh, Frannie, I'm so sorry. That haircut. What can I say? I don't blame you for running away and hiding in the woods at the corner of the field for two days. It was a bit of a disaster. Even for a llama.

I felt like that the other day. I had just finished working on a big app update, putting everything I had into it. I was worn down from two months of twelve-hour days. For me, the app is the representation of my best effort, and it was as good as it was going to get. The testing was done. The early reviews were in. It was time for marketing to begin. It was exhilarating...and terrifying.

All I wanted to do was run into the woods at the corner of the field and lie down. I was asking those "daring greatly" questions. *What if my best work isn't good enough? What if I have created what I think of as my best work and nothing happens? What if it's embarrassingly horrible? What if it's a terrible bad hair day and I have to face the sheep?*

Today, you are back at your post. You look thin from the shearing but you are proudly guarding your flock. I can see in your eyes that you are confident and alert, no longer self-conscious, ready to rise to greatness should a bear enter the field.

I think I'm ready now too, Frannie. Because the only judgment of my work that really matters is my own and that of my inner circle. I'm ready to come out of the woods and stand tall. I'm ready to walk back to the sheep and to be myself bravely.

In the World:

* Be prepared to fail and to rise up again. But most importantly, be prepared to succeed, knowing that the effort is a success in itself.

In the Heart:

* I let go of all negative thinking and self-judgment that does not serve my highest good. I am a unique expression of divinity and am unchanged by all exterior judgment.

~⌣~

Loving-Kindness Meditation - Part 1

May I be well. May I be happy. May I be loved. May I be at peace.

Today is one of those days. We are the camel, and the last straw just got added to the pack on the hump. And we know what happens next. The cumulative demands on our body and soul have gotten the better of us. Mama said there'd be days like this.

For starters, this is a *good* day to remember our morning spiritual practice. Just sayin'. Meditation, gratitude journal, inviting in the angels and divine grace—these practices are beckoning now. We know this. Beyond that, there's the rest of the day looming. And the loving-kindness meditation is here for us.

It's a kind and gentle practice, easy on the heart and mind. It's here to flood our aching places with tender love and kindness, and to wrap our brokenness in wellness and safety. It invites peace and self-compassion.

As with all of our spiritual tools, we first connect with the joy, love and peace within; then we can go outside ourselves with compassion for all beings. First things first. Let's start on the inside.

In the World:

∗ This is a simple version of the traditional loving-kindness meditation, which evolved from the ancient *metta*, or *maitri*, practice of benevolence toward all.

∗ Sit upright and gently relax, releasing preoccupations and distractions. As you repeat these words, allow them to evoke the feeling behind them:

∗ *May I be well. May I be happy. May I be loved. May I be at peace.*

∗ Repeat over and over, allowing the phrases to fill your mind, body and soul. Feel wrapped in loving-kindness. Be easy with this. Float in your goodness. Take a moment for yourself.

∗ Use these phrases as a soothing balm anytime during the day when you need gentle soul rejuvenation.

In the Heart:

∗ I love, honor and care for myself through the difficult blessings.

~·\/·~

Loving-Kindness Meditation - Part 2

May you be well. May you be happy. May you be loved. May you be at peace.

Hopefully we have all arrived breathing a little deeper today, with hearts opened a little wider and feeling less like a camel. Or a llama. Llamas sometimes have to carry heavy things too. And don't forget donkeys and horses. In any case, if you haven't done so already, take the pack off, dear one.

It's a beautiful day to share some love, and the loving-kindness meditation is a lovely way to do this. It is a three-part meditation, and traditionally the second and third parts are for others.

Today we look at Part 2 of the practice. Here, we direct our thoughts to those closest to us, offering the beautiful blessing of these words to our loved ones.

Then we turn our compassion to those who are, let's say, not so easy to love—those we disagree with and those we might even consider our enemies. This doesn't hurt a bit, and it just might deepen our well of love.

In the World:

✳ Like yesterday, start by sitting upright, gently releasing tension and allowing the breath to calm your thoughts. Begin with Part 1:

✳ *May I be well. May I be happy. May I be loved. May I be at peace.*

✳ Repeat in a continuous, relaxed flow until you feel love and compassion growing like a beautiful light within. Close your eyes and take a moment for yourself here. Then move to Part 2:

✳ *May you be well. May you be happy. May you be loved. May you be at peace.*

✳ Repeat for a few minutes, directing your thoughts to loved ones, family, friends and those closest to you. Then repeat it for a few minutes for those who are harder to love.

In the Heart:

✳ I am loving and compassionate toward myself. I offer this same love and compassion to others from the infinite well of my heart.

Loving-Kindness Meditation - Part 3

May we be well. May we be happy. May we be loved. May we be at peace.

Here we are, in the unfolding of another precious day, with another chance to offer some gifts from our endless well of love. With the addition of Part 3 of the loving-kindness meditation, we reach out to all beings, including nature and the earth upon which we walk. Look out, world. Big love coming your way.

Combining all three parts, we start by directing compassionate thoughts to ourselves, then to our loved ones and to those who are difficult for us to understand or agree with, then on to include all beings.

If you like the idea of spreading light and using your love to lift up the vibration of all others, you will love the complete meditation. In doing all three parts of this practice, know that within minutes, you have given a magnificent gift to yourself, to all beings and to the planet.

In the World:

* Begin by sitting upright, gently releasing tension and allowing the breath to bring you to quiet. Longer exhales are helpful for grounding. Begin with Part 1:

* *May I be well. May I be happy. May I be loved. May I be at peace.*

* Repeat in a continuous, relaxed flow until you feel love and compassion growing like a beautiful light within. Then move to Part 2, directing your phrases first to loved ones, then to those harder to love:

* *May you be well. May you be happy. May you be loved. May you be at peace.*

* Repeat for a few minutes for each group. Then move to Part 3, for all beings and all of nature. Imagine your love wrapping around the earth as you repeat silently:

* *May we be well. May we be happy. May we be loved. May we be at peace.*

In the Heart:

* I am a being of limitless love and compassion. I wish for all beings to have the same love and compassion that I wish for myself.

~⌄~

Holy Downtime

How beautiful it is to do nothing and then to rest afterward.
— Proverb

Maybe it's staying in my pj's and floating from yoga to meditation to a steaming cup of Earl Grey. Perhaps it's the freedom of having no schedule to adhere to. Or it might be that I've shut down the computer for the day. Whatever it is, the mere thought of my tech-free Spirit Sundays makes me light up with pure Mardi Gras joy. After years of practice, the art of allowing and receiving only gets better.

In the wise words of Anne Lamott, "Almost everything will work again if you unplug it for a few minutes, including you."

Your body and soul know when you need unplugging.

Listen to that wisdom, and when it raises the red flag, schedule in some holy downtime. Without any effort at all, the walls that we have built around us to fend off stress swing wide-open to divine wisdom. We receive more focus, clarity and intuitive guidance when we step away and open up the channels once again.

Some of us can't afford the luxury of a whole day without the demands of work or family. But it's essential that we carve out an oasis of even a sacred hour once a week where nothing is required of us and we choose what to do or not do during that time.

Within these open moments, our souls speak and our hearts listen.

It's not selfish but necessary to enjoy the glorious blessings of resting, being and allowing.

In the World:

* Allow yourself guilt-free, do-nothing time at least once a week and as often as needed during demanding times.

* After unplugging, notice how all that you need to accomplish happens with greater ease and grace.

In the Heart:

* I honor myself enough to stop and rejuvenate when my body and soul are in need of rest. It is an essential part of receiving my highest intuition.

From Survival to Joy

All I have is all I need.

In 1943, Abraham Maslow created a stir when he put forth a paper called, "A Theory of Human Motivation." He wanted to know what made us tick—what impassioned the spirit when there were no external rewards dangling in front of us. Maslow came up with what he called the Hierarchy of Needs, whereby after we attain one level of need, we are able to turn our sights to the next, moving from physical survival to safety, love and belonging, self-esteem, and finally on to self-actualization and self-transcendence. Not everyone goes through all the steps, but in general, we move from survival to joy.

I have friends who make yearly mission trips to a third-world country, and they are always moved by the apparent joyful nature of those with very few possessions. It's not merely happiness because supplies and loving faces have arrived—they feel it lives within them before and after their visits. Perhaps when there is little hope for an abundance of *things*, contentment for what *is* settles in. The focus moves up the ladder to love, belonging, self-esteem and beyond.

When we are in excess of what we *need*, we can get tangled in our *desires*. There's nothing wrong with collecting things, as long as we realize that things are not going to raise us up to higher levels of love and lasting fulfillment.

The first stop in the search for contentment is to simply stay in tune with the spark of divine light within. Then lift our eyes from the inner world to others. From our place of divine connection, we can truly love. Through love, we find our connection to all beings, our value, meaning and purpose. The journey to spiritual fulfillment is not about our desires; it's about love and connection. It's never too late to learn that *things* are not the source of lasting joy. Love is.

In the World:

✳ Ask to be shown what to let go of to create space for spiritual growth. Keep what you love. Hold on to what you need. Allow the rest to fall away.

In the Heart:

✳ Right here, right now, in this moment, I am complete. I am content. I am joyful as I am. All I have is all I need.

Red Flowers

All the colors of my love coexist within me.

There's a picture I adore of a befuddled guinea pig standing next to red flowers. "I'm totally trying to choose joy," he is saying, and we can almost see his eyes roll and hear his thought: *How can I choose joy when I'm sad?* Or a thousand other reasons why choosing joy is hard today. His expression says it all. He's not quite there yet, but he's trying, even staying near to something beautiful and happy. The red flowers are helping a little.

At our infant loss meetings, we have occasional moments of comic relief. Newcomers are sometimes shocked to see laughter flying in the face of grief. But the truth is, love, joy, sorrow and grief can occupy the same heart. We learn to carry it all. We accept and live with what is honest, real and authentic in each moment. There is no right answer and no one path. Only what is true for us right now.

Living with loss can feel like carrying a heavy backpack wherever we go. In time, we grow more used to the weight. When we open to all aspects of our grief, we begin to allow her ebb and flow. To consider the thought that someday great love and tender joy can coexist in the space of sadness and raw grief opens a window.

Sometimes choosing joy is easier said than done. We can only accept where we are and take some guilt-free time to nurture the soul. If you relate to the hero in the children's book, *Alexander and the Terrible, Horrible, No Good, Very Bad Day*, just be with it. Know that divine support and unconditional love are always right here in the room with you. You are never alone as you carry all the colors of your love.

In the World:

✳ When you feel ready, consider what might lift your spirits. You could try being especially kind to yourself, formulating a hopeful thought, doing something you love or allowing a smile to occupy your face for a moment. Red flowers might also be helpful.

In the Heart:

✳ I open my heart to the possibilities of this day and allow myself to connect with the whole of my spirit. I take small steps toward welcoming a range of emotions back into my life and my heart.

JUNE 13

An Army of Love

The most powerful force in the universe is love.

It was a perfect day yesterday. A blue sky with crisp air worthy of Santa Fe welcomed in the late spring morning. Joyous and free on my Spirit Sunday, I was off on a kayak adventure to a nearby lake when I heard the news. The car radio was a harsh messenger of yet another mass shooting. My heart broke. Tears welled. Precious, innocent lives were lost and countless others indelibly changed.

The world—my world—still appeared perfectly beautiful on the outside. But the temperature immediately shifted within. Heat began to rise, and energy enveloped me in a huge ball of light. This was not an emotional explosion of rage. This was the rising up of incredible love.

The changes in our world are reflected by great changes in our hearts. It's natural that along with these changes comes a shift—with some of us contracting and some expanding. The continued stream of violence asks us to look within and to stand by our beliefs in this new world. We will choose to empower love or to empower fear. To empower love means we remain relentlessly focused on maintaining our own inner peace and bringing that peace to all who cross our paths in each small moment of this day. To empower love means taking compassionate action in the world as we follow the guidance of the highest wisdom of our hearts.

On some days, no matter how brightly the sun shines, it seems like the world is falling apart. But perhaps it is an opportunity to fall together in an army of love. Everyone is invited. It's a perfect day to change the world.

In the World:

∗ Allow each step and every breath to be one of loving-kindness. Promote positive change without harming others.

∗ Be mindful of the ways you can foster inner peace in your daily life so your peace may expand out to others within your reach.

∗ In a moment of stillness, ask how you can best be used to bring light to the world. Every action, great and small, illuminates the way.

In the Heart:

∗ I have the power to focus on creating more healing light in the world. The way I live my life raises vibrations in all beings.

~∨~

The Gift of Time

Today is a gift wrapped up in sheer grace. It's a hallelujah.

In the weeks that my father received cancer treatment, my parents stayed at a facility called Hope Lodge, where they bonded deeply with other patients. One day, my parents and a dear friend went on an outing between treatments. They wanted to visit a place called the Angel Gardens but realized there wasn't quite enough time before their friend's radiation appointment. Then came the happy discovery that her treatment had been pushed back forty-five minutes and they had time to visit the gardens after all. My mother said, "We have the gift of time."

For the duration of their stay at Hope Lodge, these words became a beloved symbol of the precious nature of life. The three friends reminded each other often that their time together was a gift.

Along with the diagnosis of a terminal illness often comes the sudden realization of the gift of time. Our future is uncertain, and it becomes more important to live our lives fully, to spend time with those we love, to do what we've always dreamed of doing. When we know our time is limited, we recognize the precious nature of each day.

Even without a terminal diagnosis, the future is uncertain, right? We like to think that tomorrow will proceed as planned, but, hey, my tea leaves aren't talking. And today, right now, we've been given a gift. We can choose to live this day fully, to love well and to be joyful.

We don't know what tomorrow will bring. But today is wrapped up in sheer grace. It's a hallelujah. Today, we have the gift of time.

In the World:

A Gift of Time Prayer

✳ *Thank you for this precious day and for the gift of time. May I use it well. May I have a keen eye for joy, beauty and the delights of small things. May I spread love and kindness generously, laugh easily and feel the ever-present peace of your light with every breath and with every step. Amen.*

In the Heart:

✳ I am in love with life and live this precious day deeply and fully, being ever mindful of the gifts and graces that surround me now.

❊

Your Friends Are Like Frogs

Lift up someone else, and you will lift yourself.

The frogs in my little pond didn't leap into the water today when I approached. They held firm to their rocks, smiles plastered on determined little faces. Maybe it was a dare to see who could remain in place the longest.

It could be that they finally became accustomed to my footsteps on the bridge. Or perhaps it doesn't escape them that I always return their babies back to the pond when I'm cleaning the filter. When the snakes come out to boldly sun on these same rocks, they might notice that I'm the one who chases them off.

I'm pretty sure that frogs don't overthink and what's happening is that they no longer *feel* afraid. I am sending out the message that they are safe and loved, and they receive it and are free to be themselves fully and do whatever good frogs do. Like sing, loudly, all night long. But I digress.

At the risk of comparing your friends to frogs, I believe that we all send out energy that makes others feel safe or, on the other hand, guarded. We vibe the language of love—or fear.

What a gift you give to others when you make them comfortable enough in your presence to be completely themselves. What a gift you give yourself when you give love and create a loving response in return.

In the World:

* Today, look for opportunities to be kind. Be the first to encourage, compliment, help out, cheer for, praise, have faith in, mentor and lift up those in need of your light.

* Notice and offer gratitude for the good feelings that come from offering kindness to others.

In the Heart:

* I put others at ease, offering love, kindness and assistance freely, knowing that what I put into the world returns back to my life.

JUNE 16

Calling All Angels

Remind me that the night is always followed by the light.

It's been a morning, oh yes it has. My car has a flat in the driveway. Very hungry caterpillars stripped three trees overnight and are marching on. Tommy needs to go to rehab. My friends are on a crushing journey through infertility. My cousin has cancer. One of my oldest friends faces life-threatening heart surgery.

There's more. You too? If we sat down with a legal pad, I'm sure we could fill the page with today's concerns. It's an impossible, unfixable list. When we are alone, that is.

As I stood in the kitchen, my eyes landed on my grandmother's chipped Mother Mary statue, sent to me recently by my godmother Crissey. Under her base, I have been slipping prayer requests since she arrived. Mary is actually levitating upon the tower of worries. On the black stone counter, I spread out the notes. I blessed and released those that were resolved, and tucked the rest back beneath her mantle.

I implored, *Mary, Queen of Angels, send an army of your angels to those in need today. Big and small, please send them all for the highest good. Thank you, my dear Mary. Amen.*

I can't do this alone, but I can surely organize my mind to *focus* on asking, with all of my strength, for divine assistance. So I asked. And asked. I paced, asked and cried until I was empty—and full of hope, strength and joy. I am not alone and neither are you.

Angels are at your side ready to beam radiant rays of light and hope into your heart. Just ask.

In the World:

* When you surrender control of your concerns into the hands of divine grace, all things are possible. Focus is key. Be crystal clear. The more you focus on the offering, the more powerful the request. Be easy about it, exercising your faith. Then release it, and you will be shown the next step. Wait not in expectation, but in openness.

In the Heart:

* Angels surround me to guide my every step and support the lives of those I love.

꧂

Heart of Divinity

*There is no scale on the planet grand enough to measure
the importance of your life and your love in the world.*

I used to have the sense that I was pulling divine light from outside of myself, through my heart, and out to the intention of my prayer. I was like the pipe of an organ. Divine light and love would pass through me, and I was the channeler, not the source, of the music. God existed only outside my being.

Then I began investigating a more personal experience of God. If we truly are a spark of divinity, if we are connected to the source of all love, if we are made of the same molecules, then God is not just outside of us, but within, through and around all things. Right here within me is a ray of divine wisdom, power and light. So how can I more deeply experience God within?

By honoring myself. By valuing myself as a beautiful, worthy being. By nurturing my mind, body and soul with loving images, foods and inspiration. By loving myself deeply, cherishing my uniqueness, forgiving my mistakes and continuing to turn back to the joyful work of learning how to move peacefully and passionately through life.

We can only heal ourselves from a place of love. We can only ease the suffering of others from a place of love. We can only find our passion and creative gifts from a place of love. When we love and honor ourselves, nothing external in the world can sway our calm.

We know who we are, and that is unchanging. We are a ray of the divine sun capable of sowing healing light and worthy of great love.

In the World:

﹡ Honor your beautiful being by talking to yourself as you would your most precious loved one.

﹡ Bind your self-worth not to external goals and success, but to your inner light, which cannot be changed or diminished.

In the Heart:

﹡ I embody the love and light within and around me now. Divine love is sewn into the tapestry of my being.

꩜

An Instrument of Peace

Unveil the love that is at the heart of you.

One night on *The Tonight Show,* Johnny Carson was interviewing a great spiritual teacher. I'm going back to the archives here, but I have long remembered the essence of this sweet exchange. Toward the end of their conversation, Carson leaned over the desk and said something like, "How did you get it to be so quiet in there?" To which the teacher crinkled into his beautiful smile and replied, "It *is* quiet in there!"

We don't make ourselves peaceful inside. We *are* peaceful. So our work in the world is to release the things that are hiding our peace, to pull back the curtain of what is covering our calm, to unveil the love that is at the heart of us all.

Peace Prayer of Saint Francis of Assisi

Lord, make me an instrument of your peace.
Where there is hatred, let me sow love;
where there is injury, pardon;
where there is doubt, faith;
where there is despair, hope;
where there is darkness, light;
where there is sadness, joy.

O, Divine Master, grant that I may not so much
seek to be consoled as to console;
to be understood as to understand;
to be loved as to love;
For it is in giving that we receive;
it is in pardoning that we are pardoned;
it is in dying that we are born to eternal life. Amen

In the World:

✳ Today release one thing that might be interfering with your peace. Pull back the curtain on one thing that might be covering your calm. Unveil the love.

In the Heart:

✳ From the calm place of peace in my soul, I am an instrument of peace in the world.

◟◞

The Daily Conversation

Ask. Believe. Receive. Give thanks.

Conversations with the divine arise not only in times of trouble but in the small moments and miracles of daily life. Any time is a good time for a chat. Already this morning I have had a few conversations, starting with, *How should I work out this morning? Should I do yoga or weed a garden bed? I felt* that I should open the back door. Immediately the smell of the air intoxicated me, and off I went to get my gardening gloves. Not something I usually do at 7:00 a.m., but it was a most beautiful hour outside. I gave thanks.

I also asked for guidance about when to make a sensitive phone call, and soon after, I asked how to direct my prayers and energy for a friend in need. As always, I asked what to write as I sat at my desk today. It's only 11:00 a.m. and I've done a lot of asking.

The power behind the asking is the belief in the right result. That seemingly insignificant and silent surrender to divine will is the key, setting into motion the receiving part: the hints, signs and inner promptings that steer us in the right direction. The feeling before we even get the question out of our hearts is that the perfect answer is already on its way in the perfect time. It's pretty exciting stuff.

Giving thanks is an ongoing process, given at all stages and phases. We can give thanks for helping when the question is asked, thanks for the signs and surprises of received guidance, thanks for answers and the delay of answers because that, too, is a gift.

Ask. Believe. Receive. Give thanks. Enjoy.

In the World:

✴ Carry on a constant conversation with the divine today. In all things great and small, seek wisdom and guidance, notice answers, allow yourself to flow with grace and give thanks.

In the Heart:

✴ All things unfold in the perfect way and in their perfect time when I seek divine assistance.

JUNE 20

~✲~

Bad Is Not All Bad

Be grateful before the gift. See blooms before they grow.
Feel light before the sun. Have faith before you know.

My friend Thelma was ninety-six years old when she shared what she considered to be one of her greatest life lessons: *Everything that we think is good has a little bad in it, and everything we think is bad has a little good in it.* Okay Thelma, let's think about this.

We tend to want to judge our experiences and label them as either good or bad. If we get into a great grad school, marry the prince or land an incredible publishing deal, we consider that a windfall of good fortune. If we don't meet a goal, if a relationship fails or if our dreams don't come true in the way we imagine, we consider that to be a bad chapter in our life.

When we examine what we consider to be our greatest failures and heartbreaks, we can see from the clear vantage point of hindsight that most of them were leading us to a more authentic path. Each twist of fate and synchronistic set of circumstances changed our direction. Not all seemed *good* at the time, but difficult passages can grow us and ultimately lay out stepping stones that lead to greater courage, compassion, insight and often, contentment.

Patience asks us not to judge things *yet*. Patience wants us to wait until we have a little distance from the experience and can see wisdom at work in our story. Patience begs for faith in a greater plan, a higher power, a well of benevolent grace with our name on it.

Patience, and Thelma, reminds us that bad is not all bad.

In the World:

✳ Take a moment and give thanks for the experiences you have endured through what seemed like failure or defeat.

✳ If you are going through one of those times now, ask to be shown the next step in the greater plan for your life. Ask to be led. Refrain from judgment. Have faith that blessings can emerge from the pain.

In the Heart:

✳ I trust that my challenges hold meaning. I have faith that a perfect plan is in place for me now. I wait in patient openness for miracles that are yet to unfold.

~⋎~

Summer Spiritual Streamlining

Solstice Blessing: May the longest day of sunlight fill you with rays of hope.
May the growing nights of moonlight bring rest upon your soul.

It's summertime and the livin' is easy. The sun is standing still, and so should we. Since December, the days have been growing longer above the equator, culminating in today, the summer solstice, when the sun is at its highest point in the sky. *Solstice* means *sun stands still*. With the change of season comes the perfect opportunity to pour an iced tea and gain a little perspective. It's an auspicious time to revisit spiritual goals and release what no longer serves us.

Taking stock is a way of spiritual streamlining. The broad questions are: *What worries are occupying my heart? How can I release them? What can I be doing to bring more peace and joy to my days?* If we answer these questions honestly, we can allow ourselves to release some habits that are getting in the way of our peace of mind, and step up a few of the practices that contribute greatly to our sweet connection with our better selves. And all of this can be accomplished from a lounge chair.

One summer, while sitting on the sand I wrote, "I send my worries out to sea and open my soul to an ocean of peace." This is not big work, so go easy on yourself. It's a small change in course that brings us into alignment with who we really are. It's the reset of the spiritual compass.

In the World:

Contemplate the following questions and allow your answers to steer you in the direction of greater peace:

∗ Is there an activity in my life that I can do without or make more simple?

∗ Are there spiritual practices I could add or release that might bring more joy and peace to my life?

∗ Am I spending time with uplifting people?

∗ Is what I'm reading feeding my soul?

∗ Am I holding on to worries and concerns that I can let go of?

In the Heart:

∗ With gentle compassion, I guide my life toward greater alignment, authenticity and simplicity.

~⋎⋌~

A Few Morning Moments

Gratitude makes everything grow.

I woke early this morning and took my tea out the back door. The sun had just risen, but my thinking mind had not, so I stood there in pure consciousness, soaking in the glorious morning. Everything was wet and waking from the storms last night; birds conversing across the yard saying, "I'm okay! You okay?" Bugs busy at work. Frogs in position on their rocks. Horses circling a hay bale on the field.

Gratitude grew in me like the unfurling of a prayer plant. Slowly, softly, I felt a whole-body thank-you for just the awareness of this one early-morning moment. And as my leaves spread out, they reached out to the other plants and the birds, bees, frogs and horses. Under the sky, in the glorious light of the sun, we all offered a unified *Yes! This is glorious. Thank you!*

Later in the morning, as I sat at my desk, a ray of light landed near my hands and my heart returned to the few minutes outside at the start of the day. The feeling of gratitude rose within me once more.

When we greet the day in gratitude, the silent prayer will take flight and set the day off on the right path. The impact expands for hours as seen in the ray of light across our desks and our hearts. The lingering song of morning gratitude will be magnified all day long.

Gratitude makes everything grow.

In the World:

✳ Plan to get out of bed ten minutes early one day this week and just softly breathe gratitude as the day begins.

✳ Delight in it as a special time for you. Look forward to it as a gift that you give to your spirit. Put on your soul sandals and walk out the back door.

In the Heart:

✳ I awaken today with great joy and gratitude for my very existence and for the chance to live and to love once more.

~√√~

Complaint-Free Day

If we could see the power of our thoughts,
we would only think loving thoughts.

I once had a roommate who could lead the Olympic complaining team. Her complaints could flawlessly follow a storyline from a single person, to a dramatic situation, to a whole country. Nothing was out of bounds. It was woven pretty well into conversations, so at first I didn't notice it. But once I tuned in, it became impossible for me to ignore. It was dark and negative, and most importantly, it had the power to change the energy of the room almost immediately. Complainers thrive on company, and when I began to respond with silence to her complaints, our friendship drifted apart.

As beings of light, we can all be students of our own highest teaching. What is repeated becomes habitual, and it is essential that we become mindful of our tendency to complain, and lean instead toward positive, affirmative, light filled thoughts and words. This is something we can actually control. Step-by-step we can guide ourselves in the mindfulness and training of our own thoughts.

With every thought, we make a choice about what kind of energy we bring to this day and what we create for our future. A single phrase has the power to encourage, lift and inspire, or to discourage, dampen and block. If we could see the power of our thoughts, we would only think loving thoughts.

In the World:

∗ Today is a complaint-free day. Catch yourself in any complaints and rephrase them in the positive. If today works well, continue into tomorrow. With a little practice, the habit will drop away.

∗ Be vigilant about negative phrasing. Challenge yourself to phrase thoughts and words in the positive. This carries over into prayer and all divine communication—and has the power to create a dramatic shift toward joy and the manifestation of your dreams.

∗ Let love be the power behind every thought.

In the Heart:

∗ I make a conscious choice to bring radiant light into the world today.

Bless This Day

Bless this day with love and light. Bless this day with faith and sight.
Bless this day with grace and ease. Bless this day with joy and peace.

On the phone today, Olga lamented that the news was full of viral coverage of people acting cruelly toward each other in the name of defending their beliefs. It was upsetting to witness the lowest vibrations of humanity. From my porch in the country, with no cell service or TV, I assured her that the world was doing just fine, and we laughed. She reminded me that often we do not see the world *as it is*, we see it *as we are*.

Changing the world on the outside means remembering who we are on the inside. Together as beings of light, we can pour love into the world through our thoughts, words and actions. We can be powerful activists for change without being negative or destructive, and without attacking other people personally. We can channel love toward compassionate action and transformation. The world feels better this way, right?

Today, before we get caught up in the energy of the world, let's recognize the divine energy within.

In the morning, before the phone gets checked and the computer gets turned on, let's set the day right with silence, gratitude and a blessing. The way we start the day is often the way our day goes. See today unfolding with grace and hold up to the light all intentions, great and small, to be blessed.

In the World:

* Bless this day with love and light, lifting the vibration of all beings.

* Bless this day with faith and sight, keeping divine perspective, seeing all things through sacred eyes.

* Bless this day with grace and ease, releasing, flowing, opening and surrendering to divine order.

* Bless this day with joy and peace, smiling freely and calming others with serenity.

In the Heart:

* I begin my day in a place of love and light, blessing all of my thoughts, words and actions. I am a radiant channel of divine healing.

❦

Your Own True Current

Through waves of transition, we find the flow of our own true current.

When we least expect it, we find ourselves starting over.

Life's transitions can sweep us out to sea and toss us on the waves, sometimes for long stretches of time. Seasons go by and still we feel unmoored. We might raise a new sail or test out a new port in search of that which resonates with our souls. We seek to dock where the authentic spirit can thrive.

We traverse many oceans in our journey from high school to college, college to independent living, through marriage, divorce, changing jobs, illness, moving to a new city, having a child, losing a child, a friend or a spouse. Stowed away in these times of transition are chances to make some brand-new choices based on the promptings of spirit.

When I moved into the cabin on my own when I least expected it, I took with me only the things that truly spoke to my new life. The colors, the books, the clothes, the blankets, the angels—I only brought the treasures that represented what I loved, what brought me joy and what aligned with my authentic self.

As unsettling as they are, transitions offer us a unique opportunity. They present us with the chance to style our new lives in a way that more deeply reflects our true selves, and to create a life more in keeping with the flow of our own true current.

We have all of the tools we need to navigate from the waves of transition to the peaceful harbor of transformation. One wave at a time.

In the World:

❋ Write down the traits that you want to embody when you have come to the other side of this transformation. Answer the question: *Who do I get to become as a result of this transition?*

❋ Write down or imagine what your new life and your new self might look like.

❋ Add your discoveries as items on your Gratitude in Advance list.

In the Heart:

❋ Every day I take steps toward becoming my authentic self and aligning with my true voice.

In Perfect Harmony

My mind, body and soul are in perfect harmony.

At first sight, our visceral response to the affirmation above might be along the lines of, *Not in this lifetime.*

Stepping back, it's clear that it doesn't feel like most affirmations, which paint a picture of an ideal world in a way where it is *obvious* that we are stating a goal, and are not actually there already. For example, "I flow with ease and grace through the constant change in my life." Most of us don't do that yet, but it's a good idea and one we want to aim for. It's an affirmation that will bring us closer to the manifestation of that goal.

We are used to talking about the integration of mind and soul in universal language, but bringing in the body can be less comfortable for a lot of us. We'd rather consider our spirituality as separate and leave the body out of it. After all, we are ruthless in the critique of our bodies, drowning in a sea of relentless marketing that pressures us to look or behave in a certain way. Our negative self-talk reminds us constantly that we can't possibly ever look or feel good enough.

Let's bring this home for a minute and consider something really important: Why can't this affirmation be true for each of us *now*? Having our mind, body and soul in perfect harmony does not mean having a monk's calm mind, an Olympian's healthy body, and a soul connected to the divine at some random date in the future when we get it all together.

It means being exactly who we are, right in this moment, loving our body with compassion and gratitude, and opening our soul to the divine right here and now. This we can do. By welcoming the harmony that is within us now, we will continue to integrate greater and greater harmony.

In the World:

✳ Thank your body for housing your soul, for communicating your intuition and for facilitating your creativity. Love your body with compassion and gentle kindness today.

In the Heart:

✳ There is no wrong way to be in my body. Like everyone, I am enough and I am beautiful. My mind, body and soul are in perfect harmony.

Presence as Prayer

To be present in the small moments of daily life is to pray.

Sometimes Sacred stands at the stove; the Divine cheers from the bleachers; Meditation folds the laundry; Holy falls exhausted into bed. Even on the days when we don't say prayers, we are living them.

Gunilla Norris reminds us in her lyrical book *Being Home*, "Sometimes saying prayers keeps us from *being* prayers."

So as we face a full schedule, let's *be* prayers.

Life asks much of us in a day, and being present lifts up even the most demanding of them, making an offering of each small moment.

Within the gift of time that today is giving us, let's be fully awake. Let's notice, appreciate and be delighted. Let's be present wholeheartedly, bravely and completely. Let's stay in the moment that we are in without worrying about all that is left undone.

May our presence be our devotion, our love and our prayer. May our presence welcome this day as an honored guest with open arms.

May our presence weave our prayer into the fabric of the little things.

In the World:

* Be where you are. Stay in the moment. Let your heart be light. When you notice your mind rushing ahead, call it back to the present.

* Keep a running conversation with the divine. Ask for guidance on what to do next and next, allowing yourself to be gently led from moment to moment.

* Have faith. Know that you have all the time you need for all you need to do. Feel it in your bones. Assume it. It is here.

In the Heart:

* The prayer of my day is in the fabric of each small moment. I rise to greet the day with the flexibility of ease and grace as I flow with inner guidance and mindfulness.

A Deep Well of Faith

Everything happens in divine order.

We are not asked to exercise our faith muscle when all is well. In joyful chapters of our lives, our inherent awe and gratitude bubble up to the surface unbidden. When there are no emergencies, we are not required to trust that all is right and good with the universe. It just is.

Then there are those times when we put forth our very best effort toward an important goal that never comes to fruition. Or we endure a seemingly random tragedy, and it feels like we have been forsaken. We are frustrated and devastated, and we are sure that divine timing has passed us by. Believe me, I know. These are the moments that beg for a deep well of faith.

It's possible that what is meant to come to us will come to us, and what is not meant for us in this lifetime will not. In either scenario, our job is to believe that in all things, there is a hidden perfection that is stacked in our favor.

Maybe not in all of it. It's hard to find it in the trauma and the tears. But we can believe in the possibility that one small corner of our hardest days may someday reveal itself as a holy moment, something that brings us closer to love. Our job is to open our clenched fists and surrender a little so exactly what is needed can come fill our hands and hearts.

We are being asked to exercise nothing less than faith during the challenging times as well as in the good times. We may be covered in a fog of earthly challenges, but in the field of divine order, we are infinitely loved and never forsaken.

In the World:

✳ Just for today, try on the feeling of faith, and be with your life exactly as it is.

✳ Be flexible when challenges or gifts arise that are not expected.

✳ Consider the possibility that there is hidden grace working in ways you can't yet see.

In the Heart:

✳ I open my heart to this day with trust, tenderness and faith in possibilities.

✧

Shine Brightly

Shine brightly. See beauty. Speak kindly. Love truly. Give freely.
Create joyfully. Live thankfully.

I wrote the above quote on a napkin last night. *This is why I'm here,* I thought. I wanted to remind myself of the power of sharing light and love. I wanted to remember when I woke up today that the *way* I live my life was the most important thing I could align with. I wanted to remember beauty, kindness and joy. I wanted to remember love, generosity and gratitude.

My friends and I talk about the hazards of too much *doing* and not enough *being.* Our lives get busy in waves. We get distracted by work and travel, by changing schedules and the needs of others. Our spiritual practices suffer as other things take priority. We are running and spinning, accomplishing and nurturing. It can be exhausting and draining on the inside.

But we can handle all of this if we remain connected to our source energy. It's like plugging into the wall socket. We need it. We have to have it. The Creator of the universe gave us all things. We can squeeze in ten minutes several times a day to sustain our quality of life. *Spirit first* is the nonnegotiable priority.

Our *doing* is always informed and empowered by our *being.* Never the other way around. When we are fully our soul selves, there is nothing we can't do. We need to be who we are and be that well. That is why we're here.

In the World:

∗ Write down or think up some phrases of your own that help you to align with the way you want to live your life.

∗ Take a moment to come into balance and connect with your highest energy. Bring the joy with you as you go about your day. Tune up several times today by finding a moment of solitude to put spirit first, to breathe, to meditate, to pray and to see life through the stillness of the heart.

In the Heart:

∗ I connect with my spiritual self often today so I may approach all activity from the place of my highest good and with the guidance of my inner wisdom.

To Be Loved and to Love

You are infinitely loved just as you are.

Unimaginable love. Unconditional love. Blinding, expansive, amazing love. It's hard to believe, but we all have this. Divine love directed at us. Every day. Just as we are.

Living proof exists in the growing body of research into near-death experiences. Seekers and searchers unite in the love of these heart-pounding sagas—firsthand experiences of life after death spanning all religions and cultures.

Although each story has its individual characteristics, most have one hallmark in common: the amazing love radiating from the conscious source of the universe—God. The person having the near-death experience feels immediately overjoyed, welcomed and instantly healed by unconditional love and the realization that they are, in their essence, part of this love.

Infinite love exists for each of us from the divine. So who are we to not honor the magnificence of our spirit?

May we open to the gift of being truly loved and rise to the humbling honor of being one with the Creator and with all creation.

In the World:

* May you allow the infinite light of unconditional love to enter and take up residence in your heart.

* May you be in awe of a magnificent love that is directed at you, just as you are.

* May you accept the healing power of this love, and may it work through your eyes, hands and heart for the highest good of all beings.

* May you find incredible joy in the knowing that you are always, no matter what, infinitely loved.

In the Heart:

* I am tenderly, infinitely and unconditionally loved by God in every moment, just as I am today.

July Blessings

In our soul backpack, we always carry with us an act of kindness,
the light of love and a ray of hope.

Today begins a new month and a new adventure of the spirit. May we open to the light, the warmth and the brilliant flowering of nature that invites us to experience her beauty. Wherever we find ourselves today, we carry in our virtual backpack the higher perspective of the soul. A gentle, unconditional love is right here with us to assist in all of life's surprises. When spirit leads, we always find our way home.

We welcome July with a blessing that floats in on the warm summer breeze of this new month and new journey of the soul:

May simple acts of kindness and unconditional love light our way today. May remembering our magnificence quiet the inner voice of judgment today. May small acts of self-care and self-love nourish our souls today. May amazing grace lift our spirits and bring us a ray of hope today.

Be present.

Let the day flow with grace.

Expect joy. Be positive.

Serve with compassion.

Speak only kindness.

Impart only love.

Never forget you're not alone.

Give thanks for everything.

See goodness in others.

In the World:

✳ Invite these blessings into your heart as you begin this precious day.

✳ Choose a word for July to keep in your virtual backpack.

✳ Write your intentions for the month ahead.

In the Heart:

✳ Everything I need for the adventure of today is with me now.

The Real Priority List

Be kind. Be calm. Be joyful. Be humble. Be thankful.

I have always had a wacky ability to rise up over the earth and look down on my life, Google Maps style. Sometimes I go way up, and I can see the whole East Coast. (Seriously.) Mostly, I just go a little way up and watch what's happening in my life. It's not always a pretty sight.

This short list came from looking down on what my long list had been for that day and considering what it *might* have looked like had I been a little more connected to spirit. "Be kind. Be calm. Be joyful. Be humble. Be thankful."

Whenever I lose sight of what's important—and my precious agenda, instead of love, drives my decisions—I take a look at this list and remember what a real priority list looks like.

In the World:

* May I be kind today, seeing the world with a compassionate and gentle heart. May my presence be comforting and helpful to others, especially those who are hurting. May I refrain from negative thoughts and comments about myself and others, and may I embrace myself with the same respect and kindness that I give to all other beings. May love lead my decisions.

* May I be calm today, spreading peaceful energy to all who cross my path. May the peace I feel within be a healing light to others and contribute to their joy and wellness.

* May I be joyful today, knowing that the light of my smile is contagious and lifts the spirits of others. May I see the positive and the beautiful in this day and remember to take myself lightly.

* May I be humble today, recognizing that all souls are radiant in the eyes of the Creator and that all paths are of equal value. May I be an attentive listener and a loving encourager of others.

* May I be thankful today, allowing the blessings of this day to expand my heart and render me abundant and grateful.

In the Heart:

* My loving actions throughout this day are my gifts to the world.

❧

May I Be Blessed

May I be blessed today with wisdom, patience and strength.

No matter what surprises today might hold, we could all use a little extra assistance. These four small words are packed with intention and make for a powerful start to any request or offering: *May I be blessed.* This. Let this become our mantra today.

These are words that open doors and windows, and let flow waterfalls of grace. They combine a polite request with a dash of surrender and the feel of an affirmation—a sense that the request has already come to pass in real time.

We are born with a direct line to universal wisdom beyond our wildest dreams. We are connected to the source of all that is. But the window to wisdom is opened by the admission of need. The well of patience is filled by the awareness of emptiness. The door to strength is opened by the act of surrender.

When we meditate, we surrender our thoughts and the illusion of control over our lives. Similarly, when we ask to be blessed, we admit that we could use a little divine backup. We open our hearts and whisper, "Help," and we open the flow of assistance.

Whenever we pray these words, we get an immediate answer before the prayer has even left our hearts. We can ask for our precious portion of daily gifts and be assured that we will have all that we need. That is what grace is—an endless supply of blessings.

May we be blessed.

In the World:

✳ Set up some reminders on your phone, in your journal or on sticky notes to help you remember to ask for blessings and assistance throughout the day.

In the Heart:

✳ May I be blessed with wisdom, patience and strength. May I be blessed with all the gifts I need to flow through this beautiful day with ease and grace.

~\\/~

Pursuit of Happiness

To have peace, be calm. To have love, be loving. To have kindness, be kind.

I haven't even told some of my closest friends the details of the dissolution of my decades-long marriage. I was not treated in the way that I deserved. Let's leave it at that. Because the exact reasons are not nearly as important as how we dealt with the fallout.

It was the Fourth of July when I told him we were done. Finished. No more tries. How's that for an Independence Day announcement? I had to stop the bleeding, and although I dread speaking my truth when I know it will not be well received, this had to be the day. Sometimes the truth will tell itself when it can't stand the confines of the dark any longer.

I lived alone in the house during the hardest part of hammering out an agreement. The first lawyer I saw actually rubbed her hands together and laughed, "Well let's see if we can make him miserable for the rest of his life!" I never went back. Why would I want to live with that? Instead, we figured it out together at the kitchen table. Even though we were both hurting, we didn't take it to the next level of pain by suing each other. We cried, but we didn't get mean. I asked for what I needed but didn't take things for spite. It took months, many meetings and a lot of work. Then we had it notarized and went out to lunch.

I have watched friends go through grueling and expensive divorce battles. It's the most stressful thing on earth because it goes against everything we know within. We use money as a weapon, we grasp and protect, we divide and conquer. Any time we inflict pain on another, we wound ourselves also. Even in despair, we can act from a place of love.

As for us, we have salvaged a loving friendship out of the deal—a real treasure that will last a lifetime. In my heart, that's pursuit of happiness.

In the World:

✳ If you find yourself here, remember, self-care first. We access our better selves when we eat and sleep. Write out affirmations and carry them with you. Pray like crazy. Journal for sanity. Find one friend, counselor or confidant you can be honest with. Seek out a wise mediator to guide you through the process. Be honest and kind.

In the Heart:

✳ Calm me, Lord, as you calmed the storm. Still me, Lord, keep me from harm. Let all tumult within me cease. Enfold me, Lord, in your peace.

~✢~

Actively Calm

Slow down and lighten up.

Once upon a time we said *yes*. We said *yes* to the job, the classes, the children, the dinner, the event. Our calendars are therefore packed with beautiful symbols of the richness of our lives and loves. They reflect our connection with others and the fruits of our labor. Oh, so many fruits.

Being a little swamped can be a beautiful thing if we can somehow exempt ourselves from the dreaded feeling that we have way too much to do and not enough time to do it. We have all the time we need. Really, we do.

If we were given a whole bag of gifts at once, we wouldn't want to race through them. We would want to savor the moment, the wrapping and the unwrapping, as well as the friends who gifted them. Today is like that. It asks for presence, not speed. It is an adventure of the spirit, a journey that is meant to bring joy. Paramahansa Yogananda had great advice that makes me relax and breathe a little deeper just thinking about it: "Be calmly active and actively calm."

So today is all about peaceful, lighthearted energy. It's about appreciation without complaint. It's about being in the moment and listening well, inside the heart and outside to those we love. It's about accepting our abundance, even if it involves rush hour traffic. It's about fun and peace combined. We can do this when we slow down a little—and let our hearts be light.

In the World:

* Appreciate: We can't be truly grateful and be worried at the same time. Express gratitude today in all things, even the mess on the desk. Say *thank you* out loud and often.

* Smile: A smile and some laughter can change our biology and lift our anxiety.

* Exhale: Making your exhale longer than your inhale calms the body and reduces stress. Just breathe. And ask your angels for help.

In the Heart:

* I have all the time I need for all I need to do. I am mindful and grateful. I release anxiety and open to the joy that is present in my life today.

Alone but Not Alone

Your spirit is on a human adventure.

As exhilarating as it is to walk a spiritual path, it's not always easy to discuss it with others. It's one of the most personal things we do in our lives. Nothing makes words feel small like trying to explain the vast insights of your journey.

My mother, who is immersed in spiritual teachings, lives independently in an assisted living facility. She has countless wonderful friends who are bursting with life. They go to plays, concerts and movies, and take part in book clubs, art and computer classes. They go to the gym and take walks around the lake. Mom meets a different group of friends most weeknights for dinner in the dining room. But after three years, no one really knows the extent to which she has spent her entire life with one foot on "the other side" as a devoted spiritual seeker.

What a gift to have even one friend who understands our spiritual yearnings. To be able to share signs, symbols, synchronicity, insights, prayers answered, dreams, healings, energy awakenings, angelic assistance and all manner of manifestations of spirit in our lives, is one of the greatest blessings of being a spirit on this human adventure. I wish for you this gift, but if it is not to be, you are not alone. We walk alone with you.

In the World:

* Keep an open heart for like-minded souls. Introduce the topic gently to investigate their understanding and interest level. If it feels right, offer to share a spiritual book or talk that resonates with you.

* Never judge another's interest or lack of interest in spirituality. There are infinite ways to express ourselves in this life. Souls find their way to spirituality when the time is right for them.

* Your heart knows when you've had a spiritual experience. No one can dispute your personal knowing. Even if you are the only one who feels it, it's real. Believe what your heart knows to be true.

In the Heart:

* The deep wisdom of my spirit illuminates my earthly path with love and joy. I am never alone in my truth.

～√√―

Gratitude and Gate 23

I am thankful for this precious life, this precious day, this precious moment.

It started as a simple weather delay on a flight from Orlando to DC, but as afternoon gave way to evening, the captive audience at Gate 23 began to mill around and chat. I left my seat for the window ledge, where I spied an outlet to charge my phone. A young woman nearby had the same thought and as our tired, hungry souls rested, her story spilled out.

Ayan is the youngest of seventeen children born to Somali parents. The whole clan, which includes scores of nieces and nephews, now live in Dubai. Ayan moved to Washington, DC for her college years, and since she was the only unmarried child, her mother moved with her. They both stayed on after Ayan finished her schooling, and they had shared a house in the city for fifteen years.

Missing her family, Ayan planned to spend the entire summer in Dubai. After just a few weeks there, she received the shocking call that her mother was in the hospital, having been diagnosed with a terminal brain tumor. She wasn't expected to live out the week.

When I met Ayan on the window ledge at Gate 23, she was two sleepless days into her journey home. Her mother had slipped into a coma a few hours ago. Her hope now was to see her mother's body before she would be quickly buried in accordance with their Muslim faith.

We finally boarded before midnight and, after a harrowing flight, landed at the now gridlocked National Airport. All of the delayed flights had come in together, and as I waited an hour outside for the shuttle to the parking lot, the skies let go another torrent of rain. By the time I found my car, I was soaked to the bone. Yet all I could think about was how *precious* life is. The inconveniences of the trip were insignificant when I thought of my new friend, now on her way to the hospital to say goodbye to her beloved mother. I could not formulate a single complaint. Instead, I counted precious blessings, like streetlights, all the way home.

In the World:

* Our challenges today come into perspective when we consider the plight of those who experience greater suffering. Allow your thoughts to go to such a soul, and count your precious blessings all day long.

In the Heart:

* Gratitude fills my heart for the gift of this moment in time.

⭒

Diving Deep

Do one thing at a time with love.

The spiritual journey is not one that swims on the surface of life. We know there is a deep ocean within, and we are ready to plumb the depths of our power and connection. There are brilliant colors, and we want to see them all; the colors of joy, of peace, of healing, of awe and even of pain. In order to do this, we have to transport ourselves to the only place where life is happening. Right here.

Vietnamese monk and mindfulness master Thich Nhat Hanh defines mindfulness as "the energy to be here and to witness deeply everything that happens in the present moment, aware of what is going on within and without." So the trick is to release our concerns and fears, and gently bring our awareness to where we are. Then we notice how we feel and what is happening. And incredibly, we can always find a moment of peace in the land of presence.

Being mindful means that when we are washing dishes, we are not thinking about getting the car fixed. When we are listening to a friend, we are not thinking of what we are having for dinner. So much for our pride in multitasking.

What we gain by not dividing our attention is the gift of peace and joy. When we practice mindfulness, we move from task to task feeling grounded and refreshed. When we practice mindfulness, we offer a beautiful gift of healing to others with our compassionate presence.

Today, let's not swim on the surface of life. Let's dive deeply into one thing at a time with our attention and our love, and discover all of the brilliant colors that are right here, right now.

In the World:

✳ With a calming breath, bring your awareness into the present moment over and over today. Notice how you feel, and the details of your surroundings. Allow a gentle calm to envelop you.

✳ Offer others the precious gift of your undivided attention. Embrace them with your compassionate presence and patient love.

In the Heart:

✳ Today I am deeply present to my experiences. I do one thing at a time with great love.

‿〜⁀

Ode to a Stink Bug

Walk with a soft step, and love with a warm heart.

When I texted Maya this morning, telling her that Jessie had died after a long illness, she wrote me a sweet condolence with little emoji angels. Then, confused, the question: *Remind me who Jessie is?*

Jessie is a stink bug in a world where it's not good to be one. They have a terrible reputation for taking over homes and businesses, for dive-bombing people while they are reading in bed at night, and for, well, stinking the place up.

But in all my life, I have never had anything but respect for our little armor-clad friends. In the cabin, there are never more than three or four visible at any one time and they are very agreeable about walking onto the paper for transfer to the outdoors. They don't land on me and they don't smell bad if you don't hurt them. And they are wildly unique with their dinosaur style, feathery wings and stripy antennae.

I greet them with, "Hello, my fearless leader!" They laugh.

Four days ago, Jessie was happily flying around when, to his grave misfortune, he came in for a landing in the pillar candle on my desk. It had been going for hours and held a deep pool of hot honeysuckle wax. The second he submerged, I scooped him out with a pencil eraser, but he sat still, his waxy covering now encasing him on the desk with only his antennae free to move. He meditated in his honeysuckle tomb for four days until passing on. The poor little guy. Or perhaps poor little great spirit.

Crazy, I know. For me, it's not part of a particular don't-kill-bugs philosophy. I simply feel their consciousness and can't imagine treating them with anything less than honor and awe. Same goes for birds and fish, trees and plants, and every creature on the planet. We are our brother's keeper. Goodbye, Jess.

In the World:

✳ Today, walk with a soft step, and love with a warm heart. Extend the net of your compassion to cover all living things.

In the Heart:

✳ I love and respect all of nature, the creatures great and small.

~✓~

The Voice of the Heart

Don't let the noise of the world cover the soft voice of the heart.
—Tiny Guru

The voice of the heart is always talking to us. Really. It's there just beneath the action and chaos, the work and play, the full schedules and busy days. Our highest wisdom is ever-present. No matter how busy we remain or how much we ignore it, she will just keep on talking.

We need only remember that the voice of the heart is a whisper, not a shout, leading the way with equal parts humility and grace. She responds to a few long, slow breaths and a simple invitation. She always answers to the song of gratitude and a request for guidance. She awaits our attention, and the very simple and focused invocation:

I'm listening. What do I need to know right now?

When we get used to her gentle way of answering, through signs, symbols, nudges, feelings and intuition, we find we can carry out this entire day in constant communication with a power much greater than ourselves. "Your vision will become clear only when you can look into your own heart," Carl Jung reminds us. "Who looks outside, dreams; who looks inside, awakens."

Let's be awake to the language of the heart.

In the World:

✳ Your heart speaks when you take a moment to turn down the noise of external sound and open an internal window of quiet.

✳ Your heart speaks to you in crisis, in anxiety, in depression, in joy, in gratitude, in peace. She is guiding, lifting and loving you into wholeness. She is always present. You are never alone.

✳ Your heart speaks to you as the voice of the calm, ever-present companion of your higher power and responds to every request.

✳ In the silence of your heart ask: *What do I need to know right now?*

In the Heart:

✳ My highest wisdom is available to me at all times. I make space to quiet my mind. In the silence of my heart, I tune in, ask and listen.

~✓✓~

Please Stay

No matter how dark it seems, remember that you are loved,
that you are never alone and that life is a precious gift.

Some of us appear to be a calm sea on the outside, going about our daily round privately, while volcanoes of suffering explode painfully on the inside. Life becomes dark, ash-covered, achingly lonely, and after days disappear into months, the journey becomes unbearable. No one else seems to notice the devastation. There's hardly enough air under the ash to make life habitable, and you imagine the end of it all.

Last week, I had someone share with me that they were contemplating taking their life. Part of me had a hint, aware of their long relationship with depression. The other part of me was blown off the map.

What about your family? What about your meaningful job? What about our dinner next week? *You will be better off without me.*

No, we will not. We will blame ourselves; we will wonder what we could have done to help you for the rest of our lives. We will miss you. We love you. *You do?* You have been a solid provider for your family, and you have done work that no one else could do. You are an integral part of a team. *I am?*

And just for the record, you have no idea how much love is blasting down upon you from the heavens. *Really?* Really.

No matter how dark it gets, remember that you are loved, that you are never alone and that life is a precious gift. You need help right now to see that all is not lost and that you are not alone. We are all broken and imperfect, but it's still possible to find meaning. And to love and be loved. Please stay.

In the World:

✳ If you or anyone you know is in a really dark space, tell someone. Don't wait; get help. You are unique and precious, and we need you here.

In the Heart:

✳ Even when I can't see my next steps, I know that I am worthy, valuable, courageous and infinitely loved exactly as I am.

※✝✦

Team Tranquility

I am constantly, relentlessly blessed.

With a precious day unfolding before us, there's a choice we can make that will send us down the path of divine flow, where we have support and guidance at every turn. All day, in every decision, we get to choose between going with the flow and holding on to control.

Choosing the path of least resistance does sound like the path to a calmer, happier day. But how do we do that? Wayne Dyer tells us, "By practicing thoughts of minimal resistance, you'll train yourself to make this your natural way of reacting, and eventually you'll become the tranquil person you desire to be."

Tranquil. We want that. Practicing minimal resistance leads us to a calmer place and the feeling of being in the flow of grace. It leads us to tranquility.

We always know in which camp we fall—flow or control—because the heart is like built-in radar for your soul. It tells us. When we feel peaceful, we are in the flow. When we are worried or trying too hard, we are resistant. Open to receive guidance from your heart. Then choose Team Tranquility.

In the World: Affirmations for Staying in the Flow

* Instead of resisting, I flow with the blessings and notice the gifts.

* Instead of controlling, I let go of what was never mine.

* Instead of being in charge, I surrender to divine wisdom.

* Instead of losing my balance, I maintain a calm center.

* Instead of being quick to anger, I am thoughtful and patient.

* Instead of holding on to darkness, I release it to make room for light.

* Instead of being rigid, I am flexible with my expectations.

* Instead of assuming the worst, I expect abundant blessings.

In the Heart:

* I believe in a world where I am constantly, relentlessly blessed. It is safe for me to let go of control and ask for guidance. I am listening.

~√~

Morning Momentum

May grace meet you where you are and take you where you want to go.

Our first thoughts and actions of the day are like the sunshine that warms the soil for the seeds. They set us up for what's to come. Anything we plant in that soil will have a head start, right?

I have found that starting off the day with a little morning momentum elevates everything that comes after it. There are two parts to this: how we feel and what we do.

The way we *feel* is what sends out the signal that draws abundance to us, so we want to feel good. We want to feel joy. We want to feel passionate and purposeful. We want to feel eager and enthusiastic. Think fist pump and a *woohoo!* That sounds like a lot to do before coffee, I know.

But it's not. The idea is to wake up feeling joyful and get one thing done quickly. We have already started the practice of waking up with gratitude and blessing the day. We can add to that practice by placing a positive affirmation on the nightstand where it can be seen first thing in the morning. It might simply say, "I've got this," or "This is an amazing morning." Then, before or after our morning spiritual practice, we do one thing. It can be a small thing, but we accomplish something on today's list in a joyful way.

Try this for a week to get in the spiritual habit of morning momentum. You will notice that the loving universe conspires to bring back to us even more of the energy we give forth. Prepare for an amazing day.

In the World:

∗ Wake with gratitude, bless the day and choose a short positive affirmation that will get you off to a beautiful start.

∗ Organize your spiritual practice and your schedule to accommodate five or ten minutes to accomplish a task first thing in the morning with joy.

∗ Give it a seven-day test run, and see how the morning momentum is working for you. Use a page in your journal to record your results.

In the Heart:

∗ I believe in a loving universe that flows toward joy and abundance. Today will be an amazing day.

~\/~

Bless My Soul

Bless my eyes to see goodness. Bless my words to speak kindness.
Bless my heart to feel compassion. Bless my soul to radiate love.

Today we revisit a sweet soul blessing that reminds us to turn our gaze ever so gently in the direction of our highest wisdom.

Bless my eyes to see what is good, loving and kind. Bless them to see what is whole, light and calm. Bless them to see the humble, the quiet and the small. Bless them to see the beauty in nature and in all living things. Catch my gaze when my eyes wander only to that which needs mending. Guard my vision when it strays to that which is dark and discouraging. Restore clear sight when they gravitate to violence. Bless my eyes.

Bless my words to speak only kindness and impart only love. Bless them to be used only to build up and create confidence. Bless them to put light into the world where there was darkness before. Hold my words when they might cause pain. Keep them within when they have the power to tear down and crush. May I never use them to harm. Bless my words.

Bless my heart to feel compassion for every being. Bless me to understand that the suffering of one of us is the suffering of all of us. Bless me to see a spark of divine light in every face. Bless me to see a piece of myself in all others. Keep my heart blind to the faults of others. May I resist a view of the world that creates separation and judgment. Lead me away from comparisons and jealousy for the experience of another. Bless my heart.

Bless my soul to shine love on all who cross my path today. Bless me to express gratitude for the small miracles of daily life. Bless me to joy and contentment for the gifts of this precious day. Gently remind me when I slip into lower vibrations of fear. Let me not linger long in the valley of self-pity. Nudge me out of needless worry. Bless my soul.

In the World:

✳ Use this blessing throughout the day as a loving mantra: *Bless my eyes to see goodness. Bless my words to speak kindness. Bless my heart to feel compassion. Bless my soul to radiate love.* Or write your own blessing to guide your way.

In the Heart:

✳ In thought, word and action, I am in perfect alignment with my highest and most compassionate wisdom.

꙳

Hava Nagila

There is only one today. Celebrate the small moments.

My brother Tommy calls Mom every Sunday afternoon without fail. They catch up on the family news, what his kids are up to, where his work has taken him that week. Until recently, their calls were a source of great joy.

Since he has been struggling with drinking again after almost sixteen sober years, it has been a turbulent sea of emotions for all of us. Mom and I compare notes after any contact with him, answering the timid question, "How did he sound?" We rejoice when he is clear. We are devastated when he is slow, slurred and confused. We ride the waves with him in an ocean of silent prayers.

Last Sunday he didn't call. Mom barely slept that night, imagining the worst. On Monday morning she called to warn me that something horrible must have happened. "Brace yourself."

Monday afternoon, Tommy called Mom, apologizing that he had missed his Sunday call. He was clear and playful. He and his wife had gone out to dinner on Sunday to celebrate their anniversary. They had a wonderful time and even saw a beautiful rainbow as they left the restaurant. Another rainbow!

After hanging up with him, Mom was so elated that she jumped up and began thanking the angels. Breaking out into a spontaneous dance, she started singing "Hava Nagila" at the top of her lungs, prancing around the living room. After many enthusiastic choruses, she stopped suddenly and thought, *What the heck am I singing? I have no idea what this even means!* So the Catholic Buddha turned to Google for a lovely surprise.

Let us rejoice, let us rejoice, let us rejoice and be happy.
Let us sing, let us sing, let us sing and be happy.
Awake, awake, awake my brothers.
Awake, my brothers, awake, my brothers, with a happy heart.

In the World:

∗ As you ride the waves of joy and challenge today, know that the angels are with you, lifting, supporting and encouraging you. And maybe even singing with you.

In the Heart:

∗ When I rejoice, the angels rejoice with me.

Hiding in Plain Sight

*The sunrise is my prayer; the horses are my prayer;
the rain in the field is my prayer for God is in all.*

If you are running short on time, don't worry about doing any spiritual excavation today. Fear not if your sneakers have hit the ground running. Don't be anxious if the day dawned with yet another emergency. The searching, the running and the attending are all in the field of God's love; and every step is the prayer, the yoga, the practice and the offering.

There's nowhere else to look when everything we need is planted within.

Our spiritual practices are important and irreplaceable. They quiet us to open the windows and doors of the soul. They calm our distracting fears and worries. They remind us of our magnificence and beauty. They build faith in the benevolence of a loving universe and an ever-present God. They help us remember the incredible growth and blessings that arise from challenges. They bring abundance and joy through gratitude. And best of all, they help us to remember all of this stuff all day long.

But should we forget, there is not an action in the day that is not of value, that is not precious and sacred. Even when our minds are not being mindful and our presence is not at all present, we are being held in the palm of the greatest love imaginable. At all times we are living out life as a shining ray of divine love, and we are surrounded by the God in all things. Spirit does not have to be persuaded to show up. She's already here.

Every thought and action are the prayer.

In the World:

✳ These words from Thomas Merton pried open my busy heart one day: "The sky is my prayer; the birds are my prayer; the wind in the trees is my prayer for God is in all." So I tried out my own version: "The sunrise is my prayer; the horses are my prayer; the rain in the field is my prayer for God is in all." What's yours?

In the Heart:

✳ In every step and every breath, I am incredible love in action. I am never alone and never outside the presence of God.

~✴~

More Room for Love

Forgive everyone.

Holding on to grudges, anger and resentment can take up a lot of valuable real estate in the heart. They swirl around in there, even when we are not paying attention to them, growing ever more complicated, painful and dark, blocking the free flow of our wisdom and love.

On the spiritual journey, we want to be as clear of energy blocks as possible, and for that, we need to consider enlisting the assistance of forgiveness. When we welcome it in, developing an ongoing friendship of sorts, we give the dark, heavy stuff permission to take a rest, and we make more room in the heart for love.

There are two parts to this:

Forgiving others: While the circumstances of our scars remain in our soul's history, it's possible to release the cloud of emotions surrounding them. It takes a lot of behind-the-scenes energy to hold anger toward a person or situation, distracting us from the present, and robbing us of our peace and health. When we forgive others, we choose to release our focus on the darkness. That's all. In the act of forgiveness, we make more room for love.

Forgiving yourself: We are expert critics of our own behavior, holding tightly to regrets for things done and not done, said and unsaid. We think that by punishing ourselves we might somehow right the wrong, but we only succeed in wounding ourselves. And that is not for the highest good of anyone. Forgive yourself and let it go. Make more room for love.

In the World:

✴ Forgiveness is an alternate way of looking at circumstances. It's a powerful choice, a chance, a blessing to your soul. You can approach it slowly, each day taking small steps in the process of releasing. Start by letting go of small transgressions, and move your way up to the more challenging ones.

In the Heart:

✴ I forgive myself and others with the assistance of divine grace, and open to the freedom of pure love flowing in and out of my heart.

~\/~

The Harvest of Kindness

Be kind to yourself. The seeds we plant within are the harvest we have to give.

In early spring during my walks around the sheep and llama field, I watched the farmer behind a local inn plant what became a flourishing organic garden. She tilled the soil and lovingly infused the Virginia clay with rich compost. She padded up the rows, planted precious seeds down the center, gave them a deep drink of well water and covered them with hay. One day when I arrived for a walk in the late afternoon, I saw her standing there, caked with dirt after a long day's work, just looking, smiling with arms crossed, admiring her co-creation with nature. *This. This is good. These beautiful, bountiful things.*

By midsummer, the garden was teeming with every imaginable vegetable. Flowers graced the entrance and cherry tomatoes climbed high on the border fences of the garden. Herbs lined the walkways and painted rock signs marked each row. The harvest was a mirror of the love with which the seeds were planted.

Like the farmer, we can think of every act of kindness toward ourselves as an investment in the harvest of kindness that we have to give to others. *Every act of kindness toward ourselves.* Like the process of preparing the soil, we can be loving to ourselves, even in moments of doubt or failure, when no tangible result of our effort is visible. Like the process of watering and nurturing, we can nurture our spirits when we thirst for encouragement, strength and grace.

Like a farmer at the end of a long day, we can stand back and gift ourselves with gentle kindness. We can admire the strength and courage it took to give what we had to give and love in the best way we knew how. We can forgive our missteps and notice the small victories. *This. This is good. These beautiful moments of today.* Plant seeds within with compassion and tenderness, and grow beautiful, bountiful things.

In the World:

* Be kind to yourself today, lifting, encouraging and loving yourself in thought, word and actions. You are a beautiful, precious spirit deserving of great love. Recognize your magnificence by planting kindness within, and you will have a bountiful harvest to give.

In the Heart:

* I nurture myself daily by being loving in my thoughts and actions.

❤

Unsubscribe

Thoughts are powerful. Think kind ones.

What we think we become. This is a wisdom quote often attributed to the Buddha. Today he might have added, *What we read or watch we become.* Everything that enters our consciousness changes our state of mind, and so, changes the world around us.

We have countless ways to stay informed. Our news sources have expanded exponentially, with articles and videos showing up in our news feeds, in the margins, popping up in little boxes with dire headlines. To receive essential free tips and tricks from the newest crop of experts, we surrender our email, and now our inboxes are exploding with mostly random and unnecessary tidbits and sales pitches. Thankfully, there's an easy fix.

Just because it's there doesn't mean it's worthy of your time or valuable enough to store in the files of your heart. You have the right to be discerning about what your interests are and what will feed your soul. In all things, be ruthless about deleting and avoiding *what you did not choose for yourself.*

Follow your intuition about what you really need to know. You will be kinder for it.

In the World:

✳ Delete impersonal emails with wild abandon. *Unsubscribe* is good too. Pass over posts if you don't recognize the origin. Honor your precious time.

✳ Don't feel the need to read or watch anything that shows up in your feeds. Read or watch what you choose from sources you know, and log in to yourself. Avoid negative, violent, divisive content even in the disguise of humor.

✳ Be mindful to fill your heart with images and stories that feed your soul, grow your life, inspire your path and resonate with your spirit.

In the Heart:

✳ I am the guardian of my time and energy, and I choose what enriches my mind, body and soul.

❧⚜❧

God Is in the Leaves

Find joy by walking in gratitude.

One of the most memorable moments of my life occurred when I was in fourth grade. Wearing my first pair of glasses, I was on the way home from the eye doctor in the passenger seat of my mom's Buick. My new eyes caught sight of the most amazing vision. Leaves. What used to be a pretty green backdrop to life was, in reality, millions of dancing, twirling, clapping *leaves*. We broke out in laughter at my incredible discovery.

We are accustomed to walking past the backdrop of life. We are preoccupied with life's drama while we stroll blindly past incredible beauty. It's easy to miss what is unclear. When we slow our step enough to really look, we find the secret at the heart of life: Everything is sacred.

Not in a formal kind of way but in a humble, amazed, everyday kind of way, when we allow ourselves to feel the magnitude of the gift of life.

When we really look, love and beauty become the new backdrop of life, impossible to pass by without notice. When we really look, gratitude rises as a way of being, a constant attitude of thanks for the endless blessings. Joy, then, is not found as much as uncovered. She is a by-product of our thanks. She was there all along. We find joy by walking in gratitude.

All of this can happen in the presence of any life circumstance. We make choices. When we are ready, we can put on our glasses and see things as they really are. Only then will we know that God is in the leaves.

In the World:

✳ Meet today with new eyes, opening wide to grace and beauty as the new backdrop of life.

✳ Be a witness to the sacred in small things.

✳ Be grateful for the gifts and allow joy to inhabit your heart and home.

In the Heart:

✳ I open my eyes and my heart to the sacred in all things.

ᕬᕗ

Grace Is the Wind

Even in the fog of challenges, there is a divine hand lifting us up.

I had some big middle-of-the-night worries last night. They swirled around me with thick, ominous energy, and it took me hours and countless prayers to relax enough to sleep again. I forgot that I wasn't in charge of everything. I forgot that I was not alone. I just forgot. Again.

Dawn broke into day with a breathtaking orange sunrise. The plants and trees were glittering proof of morning light; the bees and fireflies were happily working at their flower desks; the frogs took up their posts at their rock stations. Birds chatted good morning, and in a rush of joyous energy—I remembered.

Grace. *Right. Everything is in divine order.*

It was as if the dawn had raised the sails and the breeze was perfect. I had the momentum of divine support at my back, and all that had concerned me felt manageable. I was not in this alone. Grace would carry me through. The sails are the soul. Grace is the wind.

Grace is the gift of comfort and support when we feel immobilized by life's demands.

Grace is the dawn after the dark night of the soul.

Grace is the sun illuminating our every lesson and decision.

Grace is the light shining in the dark that guides our way back to the path.

Grace is the reminder that even in the fog of challenges, there is a divine hand lifting us up and lighting our way.

In the World:

✳ Right now, in this very moment, you have available to you all the grace you will ever need. You just have to do a few small things: Hand over the burden. Surrender the worries. Release the night and let the light in. Open your soul to grace.

In the Heart:

✳ The ever-present gift of grace strengthens my heart and lights my way today. There is nothing I cannot do. I allow grace to settle into the bones of stillness, acceptance and surrender.

Presuppose a Spark

*Treat others as if they already are the shining light
they are capable of becoming.*

Every day we are growing, changing, transforming, becoming. Each of us was born with a spark, a potential that we discover by following our passion and using our talents. Some of us nail it early on, and some of us search for a lifetime, looking for clues to the meaning of life, matches at the ready. Some of us have given up on feeling the fire.

Then something shifts because someone truly *sees* us.

Sometimes we can see the potential in others before they can see it in themselves. We see their goodness, their talents, their possibilities, even when they are blind to them. We encourage our friends by pointing out their strengths when they need them most. We teach our children by gently steering them toward what brings them joy.

Viktor Frankl, psychiatrist, Holocaust survivor and author of the groundbreaking *Man's Search for Meaning*, says that if we "presuppose a spark," we will contribute to the fulfillment of that spark. In other words, if we assume the best in people, they will rise to the assumption and become their best selves.

What a beautiful kindness we offer to others when we see, before they see, the potential of who they might become. What a wonderful world it would be if we looked only for the possibilities in everyone.

In the World:

* Today, with honor and respect for all beings, assume the best in everyone, treating them as the person they are capable of becoming (even when they don't act like it yet).

* If you are struggling with a particularly challenging person in your life, hold for them a vision of their highest, best self.

In the Heart:

* Today I see the potential goodness in all who cross my path. I assume the best of their intentions. I understand that they are doing the best they can do in this moment.

~◡~

Birthday Meditation Celebration

Every act of love, no matter how small, lives on forever.

Our birthday is not only a celebration of age but a sacred remembrance of our arrival on earth. On this day we honor our entry into humanity, where we experience the embodiment of divine love. From year to year, our birthday is a milestone that marks love given and received, and lessons learned on the path.

It is also a day when our energy is uniquely powerful.

Today is my birthday and also the anniversary of my father's death. Every year, I start the day with a meditation that my friend Maria taught me decades ago. Feel free to take it and make it your own as I have done. If today is not your birthday, you can still give it a whirl and surprise yourself with all the love you have shared this year. It all mattered. Every single act of love.

In the World:

✳ Take a comfortable seat as you would for meditation: spine straight, cross-legged or feet flat on the floor, palms up or down on your thighs. Take a few deep breaths with longer exhales to relax and become present.

✳ Begin by clearly seeing your birthday (or this day) last year. Then, slowly take a trip around the sun, month by month, reviewing major events and their impact on your life. Take each month slowly and separately, *In July I...,* allowing yourself to see and feel the experiences. Then move around the sun to August, etc.

✳ When you arrive again at today, step back and see your year as a circle around the sun. Then give thanks for each and every experience, all of the joy and pain, all of the beauty and challenge, all of the love given and received. Wrap it up in white light, and allow it to float up and away.

✳ Turn to the beautiful space before you, and open to receiving new lessons in love this year. Give thanks for the amazing blessings that are on their way.

In the Heart:

✳ I am a ray of divine love on earth. I open my heart to all of the good that is unfolding for me now.

Sacred Eyes

*May I see this day through sacred eyes, shape this day with helpful hands,
end this day with a grateful heart.*

There is another level of consciousness going on simultaneously to the material one that we see with our earthly eyes. Under the surface, on a soul level, we *feel* and *know* things—and access our divine connection—in ways that can be of great service to our material lives. Like the phrase, "I want to be *in* the world, but not *of* it," we want to be in the world but with consciousness of our spiritual wisdom.

When we see this day with sacred eyes, we are looking through the lens of our higher self. We recognize the precious nature of the day. We value the holy in the small. We reorganize our priorities to let love take the lead. We ask for guidance, faith and wisdom to get us through. We look for joy, flow and grace to lift us up. We release resistance and fear. We become lighter and clearer.

When we shape this day with helpful hands, we direct the focus of our day from ourselves to others. Energy flowing outward with loving-kindness opens a huge space within for blessings to flow toward us. Small acts of kindness perpetuate the cycle of giving and receiving.

When we end this day with a grateful heart, we see clearly from the overview of our highest self how many incredible gifts we have been given. We assume that challenges have purpose and meaning. We accept that what is undone will be accomplished in its perfect time. We lay our plans in the arms of the divine and know that all is well and we are loved. The day is done and we rest with a heart full of gratitude.

In the World:

* Endeavor to live the prayer below in the small moments of today. See goodness and beauty, allow love to flow from your heart and give thanks in all things.

In the Heart:

* May I see this day through sacred eyes, shape this day with helpful hands and end this day with a grateful heart.

~\/~

Chakra Love - Part 1

The energy of my spirit is radiant, powerful and connected with all things.

There is an elegant, powerful dance of light going on in our bodies at this very moment. Seven major energy centers—stacked, spinning wheels of spiritual power called *chakras*—are receiving, transforming and reflecting our unique imprint of embodied spirit. This ancient knowledge is derived from Eastern traditions and is used in wellness and healing practices like yoga, hands-on healing and Ayurveda.

Although we often refer to seven chakras, there are considered to be many other, smaller energy centers in and around the body.

The seven major chakras are lined up from the base of the spine to the top of the head in rainbow colors of progressively lighter energy, forming a bridge between earth and heaven. The root chakra grounds us to the earth and to our ancestors, and highlights our sense of belonging. Then the chakras proceed upward through higher and lighter vibrations to the crown chakra, which connects our energy with all beings and opens a window to divine love.

Each chakra is associated with a color, a developmental stage of life, emotions, gemstones, a body system and particular organs. Disease and imbalances can be related to a blockage in a particular chakra or chakras.

The ideal is to keep our energy centers as clear as possible for optimal health and healing. Working with an experienced energy healer can help us to accomplish this, and it can have enormous impact on our health and well-being. Looking holistically at mind, body and soul, we can expand into the miracle and power of our unique energy. More about the chakras coming tomorrow.

In the World:

∗ If the concept of chakra energy resonates with you, seek out the wealth of valuable wisdom about working with the chakras in areas of health, healing and spiritual transcendence.

∗ During meditation, sit with a straight spine so your energy centers are lined up for maximum energy, clarity and connection.

In the Heart:

∗ My mind, body and soul are in perfect harmony. The energy of my spirit is radiant, powerful and connected with all things.

~ \/ ~

Chakra Love - Part 2

We are balanced, miraculous creations of love.

Today we take a journey up the spine in this very simple introduction to the major chakras. Each is connected to the physical, mental and emotional bodies. Although the lower chakras have denser, more earthly energy, and the higher chakras have lighter, more spiritual energy, each one is essential for health and wellness. What miraculous creations we are!

In the World:

* The first, or root chakra, is centered around family, ancestors, grounding, foundation, belonging, survival, balance, trust, health and stability. It is located at the base of the spine and is physically connected to the bones, lower extremities and the immune system.

* The second, or sacral chakra, coincides with our relationship to others, abundance, pleasure, creativity, desires, nurturing ourselves and others. It is located at the level of the lower abdomen and relates physically to the reproductive organs and the lower back.

* The third, or solar plexus chakra, is about personality, ego, self-esteem, confidence, playfulness and humor, responsibility, control and spontaneity. It is located at the level of the upper abdomen and relates physically to the internal organs, abdomen and midspine.

* The fourth, or heart chakra, is related to love of self and others, forgiveness, empathy, compassion, giving and receiving. It is located in the area of the heart and physically relates to heart and lung health.

* The fifth, or throat chakra, is about communication, truth, speech, will, expression and decision-making. It is located at the throat level and is physically connected to the mouth, throat and neck vertebra.

* The sixth, or third eye chakra, coincides with intuition, imagination and emotional intelligence. It is located at the level of the eyebrows and is physically associated with the nervous system and the senses.

* The seventh, or crown chakra, relates to our connection with all beings, our divinity, spirituality and transcendence. It is located at the top of the head and is physically related to the brain.

In the Heart:

* I am a balanced and miraculous creation of light and love.

~\ /~

The Kindness Project

Think kind thoughts. Speak kind words. Seek kind friends.
Imagine a kind world.

Kindness has the power to change things. Even to transform something unimaginably tragic into something meaningful. Today is International Kindness Project Day, and Dr. Joanne Cacciatore shows us that we all have the chance to make a difference in the world in honor of our loved ones who have gone before us.

The saddest day of her life was July 27, 1994, when her baby girl Cheyenne was stillborn. The following December, in the midst of powerful grief, Dr. Jo anonymously purchased toys for disadvantaged children at a day care center in honor of Cheyenne. It changed her life. She felt as if she had shared her daughter with others and that Cheyenne's love was living on in the world through this act of kindness. She also felt a newfound sense of compassion within.

In 1996, Dr. Jo started the Kindness Project so others who had experienced losses could participate. They offered printable "kindness cards" and asked family and friends to mark the day with an act of kindness. It could be anything—buying coffee for coworkers, bringing toiletries to a homeless shelter, leaving a gift card under a stranger's windshield wiper. Since then, over two million kindness cards have found their way from bereaved hearts to strangers, as people from all over the world share their loved ones—and their kindness—with others.

In Dr. Jo's words, "No act is too small. Fierce compassion is a powerful force, one that is much needed and one that those who have known this kind of boundless grief can really channel into the world."

In the World:

* Mark this day with a random act of kindness in honor of one of your beloveds who has left the earth. You can print free "kindness cards" from the MISS Foundation Kindness Project website.

* Consider offering an act of kindness on the saddest day of your life. Even if you are the only one who knows, reclaim your day with something special that fills your heart and lights your path forward.

In the Heart:

* I contribute to the kindness of the world by reaching out with small acts of kindness from where I am today.

~∨~

Many Angels to You

You don't have to carry your backpack of life's heavy things alone.
Angels have wings.

We can use all the help we can get, and angels are ever-present messengers from God who assist us in any and every way. They are helpful in the smallest decisions and the most complicated matters of daily life. The angelic realm will not intervene unless asked, but once a request is made, help is on the way.

We can also ask angels to help our friends. Many years ago, after my mother had suffered several fractures, her friend Peg wrapped up a phone conversation with, "Many angels to you." Mom, who is intimately connected to her angels, felt an immediate rush of love and support.

We've been calling all angels with this phrase ever since. And you can too. *Thanks, Peg.* Wishing many angels to someone is to send them the most beautiful assistance.

Another way angels can assist us is with our relationships. We can ask them to work on a challenge from higher realms. I have seen misunderstandings and family fallouts melt away after diligent requests for angelic intercession. In situations when it feels like all is lost, there's always hope because angels are near.

Angels are present right now, awaiting your request. Share the assistance with family and friends.

In the World:

✳ For help with your most challenging task today, ask the angels.

✳ For relationships that need mending, ask the angels.

✳ For someone who needs extra assistance today, ask the angels.

✳ For help with a seemingly hopeless situation, ask the angels.

✳ For those who are sick and their families, ask the angels.

✳ For the disenfranchised of our world, ask the angels.

In the Heart:

✳ Angels assist me today in all of my challenges. I ask clearly for what I need and open myself fully to all forms of answers and resolutions.

Mind, Body and Soul

My mind is calm. My body is healthy. My soul is joyful.

We offer affirmations today for the unity of all parts of our being—that we may integrate our mind, body and soul into seamless, radiant beauty.

Take a deep inhalation, and on the exhale, say within, *My mind is calm.* Another deep inhalation, and on the exhale, *My body is healthy.* One more deep inhalation, and on the exhale, *My soul is joyful.* Repeat these three breaths and imagine mind, body and soul working together today as an integrated and powerful team, held safe in love by divine spirit.

May the light shine upon you
to illuminate your way.
May you stand on a mountaintop
and see a brighter day.
May all the separate pieces
of your world become one whole.
May spirit hold you safe in love
mind, body and soul.

May you flow like the river
as we kneel upon your shore.
May you bend like the tallest tree
in the winter storm.
May you fly on wings of freedom
in peace forevermore.
May spirit hold you safe in love
mind, body and soul.

May you always love with everything
and know everything is love.
May you never cry for what can't be
in your hand is just enough.
May you shine the light that shines on you
and teach us what you know.
May spirit hold you safe in love
mind, body and soul.

In the World:

✳ Return to your three breaths at any time during this beautiful day when in need of energy, spiritual connection and a little more love.

In the Heart:

✳ Today I am held safe in the arms of unconditional love and treasured as a precious and whole being—mind, body and soul.

~✦~

Sacredness in Tears

Tears are the legacy of our love and loss.

Though I am a relentless optimist, I've finally learned a big truth: Happiness is not meant to be a full-time job. We are born with intense feelings, and it's essential to allow all of our emotions to be seen, heard and welcomed for as long as we are feeling them.

Emotions are not a personality trait; they are transient visitors, like clouds in the sky. We don't freak out on cloudy days—we know the weather will change, and we accept that. We don't judge clouds as good or bad, and we know the sky will remain when the clouds have moved on.

Yet still, tears seem to unglue us and our loved ones. We are encouraged to stop crying and dry our eyes. We are told, "It's not so bad," offered a tissue and a distraction. There's little tolerance in most of our hearts for sitting with sorrow.

Tears are a sign of the courage it takes to dive deep with an emotion and stay present with it. They are the legacy of our love and loss. They are what burns us clean. They are a miraculous, natural release that opens our hearts to healing grace. They are a necessity of transformation.

Instead of resisting the vulnerability of crying, perhaps we can be still with it for a moment. Perhaps we can simply allow what is. Flow with the intensity of the feeling. Listen to it. Give it love. Be broken open by it. Be cleansed by it, and breathe in deeply its sacredness.

In Henry Ward Beecher's words, "Tears are the telescope through which we see far into heaven." May tears bless us with clearer vision, a deeper well of compassion and a glimpse of heaven.

In the World:

✳ Travel through this day with compassion for yourself and all beings, staying with emotions as they demand your attention. A multitude of feelings can coexist within us on any given day.

In the Heart:

✳ I give myself permission to feel all the feelings of my life. When I allow myself to be present with my pain, I am in the presence of healing grace. I feel deeply because I love deeply.

ꯙ

An Eye for Beauty

Search for something beautiful in every day.

Early this morning I opened the back door to look around. I noticed the tree limb that was broken by the bird feeder. Under the overgrown hydrangea, I spied red ants taking up shop in the jade plant. Algae needed to be scooped from the pond's surface. The table begged for washing.

Wandering in, I checked to see that my scheduled 7:00 a.m. post made it to my social media pages. It said, "Search for something beautiful in every day." In the comments section, this message awaited me:

"It is my daily mission. I live to find beauty and to try to make my surroundings beautiful. It keeps my mind beautiful!"

Tea in hand, I went back outside in search of beauty. A different world awaited me. The shiny, sturdy jade leaves were drinking up the morning sun. Pretty, fuzzy bees were visiting the lavender. There were at least fifty shades of green, and the sky was a deep, gorgeous purple-blue. The clucking rooster made me laugh. The smell of sage and thyme were intoxicating.

It made me think of a friend who visited Calcutta and said that so many children asked her for money that her heart closed and she ceased to feel compassion. The sheer enormity of need shut down her ability to hear the cry of poverty. Perhaps it is similar with beauty. We see so much of it that we have stopped letting it into our hearts.

Some circumstances require us to look a little harder than others. Beautiful things are often clothed as the small everyday moments. But if we search for beauty in today, we will surely find it. And it will keep our minds beautiful.

In the World:

✳ Walk in the world today with a keen eye for beauty. Notice with all of your senses. Breathe it in. Bask in the beauty that surrounds you.

In the Heart:

✳ With mindful awareness, I notice beauty in and around me. I allow beautiful things to make me more beautiful.

August Blessings

Stop now and rest your bones. Set the endless worries down.
Surrender what you can't control. Grace is here, you're not alone.

August wears a lot of hats. She starts out slowly in the heat of summer, then transitions into new school years and the first inklings of fall. So let's ease into the month with small steps. In spirituality, a little goes a long way. We don't have to have all the answers. We don't have to feel positive all the time. We don't have to save the world today. (Such good news.) We don't have to know the way forward in uncertainty.

Easy does it. Small steps, added up, make for big progress in our spiritual growth. This can look like reading something inspirational by the pool. Or writing down three gratitudes before bed each night. It can be offering a small kindness or a prayer for someone in need. Spiritual growth is the melding of simple steps that lead to the inner peace we long for. One step at a time, let's open to the blessings of August.

Be present.

Let the day flow with grace.

Expect joy. Be positive.

Serve with compassion.

Speak only kindness.

Impart only love.

Never forget you're not alone.

Give thanks for everything.

See goodness in others.

In the World:

✳ Invite these blessings into your heart as you begin a new day.

✳ Choose a word that will guide your month with ease and grace.

✳ Write some intentions for the month of August.

In the Heart:

✳ I relax into the arms of spirit and I am at peace in this moment.

The Gift of Stressful Thoughts

Phone down. Cup of tea. Say a prayer. Just breathe. Have faith.
Bless the day. Ask for grace. I'll be okay.

Sometimes there are not enough hours in the day to wrestle our work to the ground. Or so it seems from here. Our minds are dancing with stressful thoughts, and we're more than a little overwhelmed. When you notice this dissonant symphony descending on your brain, stop and do the most logical next thing. Make a cup of tea and sit. Herein lies the gift.

On the sixth day, God did *not* create stress. We did. In our minds. It's not even a real thing. It's our perception of some made-up future doom. It's the perception of lack, of fear and of mistrust. And we know better. We know that ours is an abundant universe with infinite support waiting to swing into action. We know the perfect outcome for all of our desires is already manifesting if we can just stop resisting and get out of the way of grace. We also know that peace and contentment are within reach.

But sometimes it takes those tea leaves to explain it to us. In a moment of silence, we might remember how infinitely loved we are and how the world will go on spinning just fine if we duck out for a moment. We might be reminded how when we reboot the attitude and plug into spirit, our highest energy flows.

It's the difference between climbing a mountain with a heavy backpack and floating down the river in an inner tube with a piña colada in hand. Where would you rather be?

In the World:

∗ Stressful thoughts are resistant thoughts. Notice when they infiltrate your mind today. And stop. Change gears. Pour a cup of tea and invite your highest wisdom into the situation. Say a prayer and just breathe for a moment. Have faith and bless the day. Ask for grace, then get back in the game with an army of angels by your side. Float. Flow. Know that all is well.

In the Heart:

∗ I live in an abundant universe, flowing with ease and grace through this day. I set stressful thoughts aside and find joy in each moment.

AUGUST 3

✦

Working in Angel Time

I have all the time I need for all I need to do.

In our quest to flow through today with ease and grace, we might have to get a little flexible with our usually rigid concept of time. Ever since my friend Lyndy told me about Angel Time, time has become more fluid and more, well, cooperative.

If I were discussing with Lyndy a certain looming deadline or upcoming trip, she would say, "Remember, Mare, ask to go through the day in Angel Time!" When we ask for Angel Time, somehow, activities we think will take longer steal only a fraction of the time allotted them. Other items seem to magically drop off the list. And then there is my favorite feature of all: You do what you are sure is an hour's work, and only thirty minutes have gone by. Oh how I love that.

Lyndy also shared the simple phrase she uses for her request, which often produces miraculous results: *May time expand to meet my needs.*

In the philosophical concept of time called eternalism, all moments, past, present and future, exist simultaneously. In my own philosophical concept, if the amazing dimension of eternalism is possible, then I can manage to organize my powers to wiggle out a few extra hours in this one day, right?

Spend a little precious time this morning on the most important thing you can do to give yourself some extra time today—connect with your spiritual support team. It's the best investment you will make in having the most productive and joyful day possible.

In the World:

✳ Center yourself by meditating for at least five minutes. Yes, you can find five minutes. Imagine your radiant heart beaming with light, then see your connection with divine light in your mind's eye.

✳ Now ask for the angels to shift time today to allow you all the time you need for all you need to do. *May time expand to meet my needs.* Give thanks in advance that this is so, and smile because you are going to have a really efficient day.

In the Heart:

✳ I'm thankful that I have all the time I need for all I need to do.

$\smallsmile\!\!\smile\!\!\smallfrown$

Little Breath, Big Changes

The light of our love can change the world.

Powerful joy can come in humble packages—like today's meditation using the breath as a guide. Ready? Here we go. As you read, sit comfortably and extend upwards from your seat, lengthening and straightening your spine, setting your shoulders slightly back to open the heart. Inhale deeply through your nose, and take a long exhale. Once again, inhale deeply and take a long exhale.

Now imagine your heart center glowing with radiant light and connected to an unending stream of grace that pours in through the top of your head.

- Inhale love and see it filling your heart.

- Exhale love and see it flowing around your loved ones and the earth.

- Inhale joy and smile as it enters your heart.

- Exhale joy and watch it envelop your loved ones and all beings.

- Inhale peace and allow it to fill your heart to overflowing.

- Exhale peace and see it wrap around the planet.

- Go back to the first step, and repeat with dedicated, blissful focus.

Isn't it amazing that something as small as a breath can make big changes in our mind, body and soul? Using the power of visualization, we can become a frequency of light that lifts the vibration of everything in its path. The light of our love not only changes us on a cellular level, but changes the world as well.

In the World:

✳ Take 5–10 minutes this morning or evening to practice today's meditation with focus and dedication. It is a gift to yourself and to each and every one of us.

In the Heart:

✳ I use the energy of my light and love to spread love, joy and peace to all beings.

✦

We Need You

You are a blessing to the world.

Your unique beauty, love and talent are gifts that no other being can offer. No one can replace you. No one radiates love with the same energy that you do. No one is an expression of God in the way you are. You are a magnificent, glorious, good, beautiful, whole reflection of divine love. And we, the people on the planet, need your light today.

This light in you is your essence. It is born and it blooms from within. It is your birthright. Nothing in the external world can ever change this.

You are not alone if you have trouble truly believing this. But the only way you can share the depth of your love and be the blessing you are meant to be is to recognize this truth. You must own the story of your power and grace in order to bless us confidently with the gifts that only you can give.

Release whatever might be holding you back from expressing yourself fully. Know that the only voice that can lead you is the voice of the heart, and it will never lead you astray.

Thank you for the way you bless all of us—by being you.

In the World:

✶ Give yourself permission to be less than perfect. Your precious and messy enough-ness is what makes you uniquely you.

✶ Remember that there's no competition ever. You are the only one with your gifts.

✶ Practice self-compassion as much as you practice compassion for others.

✶ Know you are a sacred being, here with the rest of us to share your love. You honor all other beings by becoming fully yourself.

In the Heart:

✶ I love and honor myself and all other beings, and courageously interact with the world as I offer the blessing of my gifts today.

~\|/~

Rooted in Gratitude

Keep your soul rooted in gratitude and your branches open to blessings.

In the early 1960s, three young spiritual seekers planted a garden out of necessity on the windy shores of north Scotland in barren, sandy soil. Having lost their employment, Peter and Eileen Caddy, with their three young sons and friend Dorothy Maclean found they had the assistance of nature spirits—angels who guided them in the cultivation of the garden. Through their loving care, the plants grew to enormous size, large flowers bloomed in radiant colors, and people traveled long distances to see their famous forty-pound cabbages.

The gardens of Findhorn are still in bloom today with the help of the nature spirits and the practice of gratitude. Maclean explains in her memoir, *To Hear the Angels Sing*, "Human affirmative thought protects and feeds plants, as it does all of life. Our thanks and appreciation unite us with the life of whatever we are thankful for and appreciative of, making a compatible blend of forces to help development on various levels, including the physical." Gratitude makes everything grow.

We know how gratitude helps us to see the abundance in our lives instead of the lack. But do we understand that our gratitude can physically change things? Maclean goes on to say that one of the angels taught her to view even sickly plants as healthy and robust by thinking of them in terms of light. "According to the *devas* (angels), gratitude and appreciation have enormous effects, making great swelling movements which complete the circle of life."

When we give thanks, we enhance the light around the object of our thanks. When we appreciate something, we change the very energy surrounding it. Now that is a beautiful thing.

In the World:

* Take along with you today an awareness of the power of your appreciation for all living things. Know that you are a being of light, and when you admire any living creation, you feed it with healing energy and change it from within.

In the Heart:

* Every day, I co-create my world by showing heartfelt gratitude and appreciation for all life and nature that surrounds me.

❤️

Lessons from a Brown Hawk

Listen quietly in the field of your heart.

The beautiful brown hawk sits tall and silent on the split-rail fence at the near side of the horse field. Only his head turns ever so slightly, taking in every movement in the trees and the grass. He alights and circles the cabin, soaring high above to get a wider view before coming in for a landing on a hay bale in the field's center. Vigilant, he watches, listens, trusts and waits with patience.

Mr. Hawk, I want more of your silence. I can only know what God would have me do if I listen quietly in the field of my heart. If only I can hold my noisy needs and wants at bay, muzzle them at the sidelines of my humanity, so my spirit can be directed by divine will. My will too, really. I don't want to fly alone. I want to absorb the wisdom that directs my every action.

Mr. Hawk, I can learn from your patience. You wait to make your move, unlike me, in constant motion, searching for direction, one challenge at a time. If only I can hold my waterfall of thoughts back and be more faithful in the waiting, knowing that the perfect plan will unfold for me if I allow it. I want to slow down in my incessant doing in favor of being the loving spirit that I am.

Mr. Hawk, I can learn from your sight. I want to turn my head ever so slightly, taking in each small moment of grace and sacred small happening. I dream of lifting up above the earth and gaining perspective, a holy vision of what really matters in my life today. I want to go forth with the sacred all-seeing eyes of guidance and love. Then I will come in for a landing on the seat of my soul, a high place from which I can see where to go, what to do, how to become an instrument of peace.

In the World:

✴ Mindfully take in the blessings of today with renewed and sacred sight. Use the tools of silence, patience and perspective to see the beauty in small things and to listen within for divine direction.

In the Heart:

✴ Today I slow down my thoughts and actions, allowing the day to unfold, one gentle moment at a time, through the soft focus of grace. I enjoy the blessings of resting, being and allowing.

~✧~

Faith and the Comet

Grant me strength when I feel small. Grant me faith when I lose sight.
Grant me hope when all seems lost. Grant me grace in morning's light.

Tiny pieces of the tail of a comet grazed my house last night. Yours too. They may as well have landed on the roof. Fiery wish-worthy shooting stars danced in every corner of the sky, lighting up the night and our dreams with ancient stardust. The Perseid meteor shower travels trillions of miles to put on a spectacular annual fireworks show—and to shake us out of our earthly coma. When we stare at the sky, we can't help but ask the big questions. After "How could forever be *that far?*" comes the inevitable "How can I be *this small?*" What kind of powerful God could have concocted this universe? Perseid gives us a pajama-clad chance to see how small we are and how great the universe is.

We are all part of this star stuff, this oneness. We are a tapestry woven from the same elements, made from an omnipotent force of love that envelops every being and entity as far as the eye can see and forever again farther. That's pretty comforting really, when we are brave enough to keep asking for assistance and small enough to lean in silently to receive the answers.

In the words of my daughter, "Sometimes it's good to feel small." *Yes, Maya, it is.* Because when we pray this prayer, *"Grant me strength when I feel small. Grant me faith when I lose sight. Grant me hope when all seems lost. Grant me grace in morning's light,"* we should have no doubt that the God of all things, the God of solar systems and stars, of comets and planets, of oceans and mountains, of you and me, will have no problem being the God of our pain and loss, of our strength and faith, of our fear and doubt, of our hope and grace, of our morning light. No problem at all. So I keep asking for assistance and leaning in silently for the help that always comes. Thank you, God, for tending to the stardust—and me.

In the World:

✳ The annual Perseid meteor shower is coming soon. Search the best viewing day and make plans. Sit outside where you can see the sky. You can even sit in the dark by a window. Forfeit sleep to open your mind to the vastness of the universe as you watch her show of beauty.

In the Heart:

✳ In my time of greatest need, I have perfect faith that when I ask with a humble heart, I will receive everything I need from the hand of God.

~∨~

I Accept

I focus on the blessings, and more blessings are on the way.

In order to open our hearts to the abundance of the universe, it's helpful to take a moment to look at what's holding us back. Why do we get stuck in habits and patterns that prevent us from moving toward the joyful life we want to be living? It might be a good time to revisit the concept of resistance.

Resistance comes in many guises, the most common symptoms being worry, fear, and the need to maintain control. This mindset keeps us spinning at a low vibration and draws low vibrational drama into our experience. On the other hand, acceptance of the experiences that come our way is reinforced by the practice of gratitude, faith and open-heartedness. When we surrender to what is, we are also sending out fireworks to the universe, eliciting assistance that is far greater than our ability to solve dilemmas or get through challenging times alone.

A few months ago, one of my dear friends was being haunted by an unending series of disasters. One night at dinner, I told her maybe she should just raise her arms, look up, and say, "I accept! No matter what you send me, I accept!" She was not amused. But soon after she performed this little ritual, on the verge of tears, she experienced a huge shift in her life. The resistance lifted, and the door of flow reopened.

What we focus on will be drawn to us by the feelings of love—or fear—that our attention creates. Our investment in tomorrow is to acknowledge the blessings of today and to trust that more blessings are on their way.

In the World:

∗ Today, keep your eyes on the blessings. Find them, great and small, everywhere you turn. You will be amazed by how they will multiply throughout the day.

∗ Release resistance by facing challenges with surrender, faith and good spirits. Activate spiritual alertness to notice when fear or the need to control slips in. Stop and wonder, *What is going right today?* With that one question, you will scatter new seeds of hope.

In the Heart:

∗ I accept what is. I focus on the blessings, and more blessings are on the way. I focus on the good, and more good is on the way.

✎

Today Is Not a Race

All else will fall into place when we slow down,
notice the gifts and give thanks.

One of my heroes in life, Maya Angelou, not only had a way with words, but a way with gratitude. "This is a wonderful day. I've never seen this one before," she noted. Her poetry, books and wide variety of other creative offerings drive at the truth with such force as to make us all wonder how we had missed so much depth in our own lives. The beauty of her inspired literature sweeps us away into her experience and lifts us with the hope of rising through our challenges too. No matter how dark things got, Maya found a precious ray of hope to celebrate. She reminded us, over and over again, that today is a gift.

Today is not a race; it is a gift. It is not to be rushed or hurried through, but to be savored and treasured.

Today is not a chore; it is a chance. It is not to be turned away at the door, but to be offered generous hospitality as an honored guest.

Today is not a duty; it is an honor. It is not an obligation that must be fulfilled, but an opportunity to rise into our highest selves.

Today is not a challenge; it is a choice. It is not to be wrestled to the ground and conquered, but loved and cherished and polished into beauty.

Today is not a cloud; it is a light. It is not to be traveled through blindly as a victim, but to be illuminated by the sun of our strength.

Today is not a solo; it is a chorus. It is not to be sung alone but to be orchestrated by a choir of angels and backed by a symphony of all those who love us.

Today is not a race. It is a gift.

In the World:

✳   Accept today as a gift, being mindful of the small miracles, and taking time to notice the beauty and the good, even in moments of challenge. All else will fall into place when we slow down, notice the gifts and give thanks.

In the Heart:

✳   There is no other day like today. I am thankful to be awake, to be alive, to be here. I walk through this day with a grateful heart.

~\⁄~

Lemonade and African Violets

You are never too young or too old to make a difference.
Dreams, at any age, can change the world.

I remember hearing a story of an eight-year-old boy who opened a lemonade stand and raised thousands to feed the homeless. When I searched it to check out the details, up popped seven other examples of kids who did the same thing, and that was just on the first page of the search. Way to go, kids! You are changing our world with love.

And way to go, parents. It takes our will and our example to open that window within a child's heart. It is said that kids are naturally compassionate, and I believe that to be true, but they learn quickly that their other choice is looking out for themselves only. When we encourage compassion at a young age and allow children to feel for themselves the beauty of unconditionally loving others, they will use that gift for the rest of their lives.

My psychiatrist brother, John, once told me of an older woman who suffered from severe depression. She lived alone and rarely left her house except to go to church. When asked what she did with her time, the only thing she mentioned was her love of propagating African violets. She had made many plants from one plant and loved her collection.

John encouraged her to share her plants with those in need. When someone from the church died or was sick, perhaps she could bring a plant to their family or to their room. She did just that, and within a few years, she became the African Violet Lady. She would quietly and lovingly bring beautiful plants and handwritten notes to the porch of those in her church community who were suffering. And she lifted many lives with her love.

In the World:

✳ It doesn't have to be a lemonade stand or an African violet. It can be a prayer or a prayer shawl or the results of your unique talents. You are never too young or too old to make a difference. Dreams, at any age, can change the world.

In the Heart:

✳ I am an ageless, timeless being of love. I share my gifts freely with those in need and change the world through acts of kindness.

꩜

Food for the Soul

If it doesn't feed your soul, have the strength to let it go.

In my twenties, I had a roommate with an aggressive form of cancer. His doctor, at a loss for treatment options, recommended a macrobiotic diet, which is based on whole grains, beans and vegetables. Wanting to help out, I picked up a few cookbooks and learned the basics. Within weeks, some unexpected changes began taking place. I had incredible energy and a sense of joyful lightness. I was sleeping better and dreaming beautiful colorful dreams. My intuition and higher wisdom became like a constant companion, complete with clairvoyance and clairaudience. Who knew that a diet could be so spiritual?

But alas, a diet only works when you stay with it. After a few years, I gradually added a greater variety of foods, and the mind-blowing benefits dimmed a bit. I have, however, always returned to this basic form of eating, more recently leaning toward a mostly plant-based diet, complete with morning green drinks.

My challenge is pausing to make healthy meals and snacks during the workday. Woman cannot live on tea and gluten-free ginger snaps alone. That will not feed the soul. So I take steps toward positive nutritional changes each day.

Our bodies are created to be calm, rested, energetic and clear enough to hear the voice of intuition. We are worthy of the finest treatment: healthy, vitamin-packed real food from Mother Nature. It not only heals the body and prevents disease, but it improves mind function and enables a clearer connection with spirit.

Now that's some food for the soul.

In the World:

* Identify some simple eating habits that are not serving your mind, body and soul. Choose to make one change today. You have the strength to do this!

* Do a little research to get inspiration about healthy eating. Find some new recipes you like, and introduce them one at a time.

In the Heart:

* I love and honor my beautiful body, and choose to nourish it with only the best and healthiest foods.

⌇

More Than Teaching Piano

With a loving thought or a silent blessing, you can share uplifting energy with someone who needs a little light today.

Between us, I never really was a great piano teacher for at least three reasons. 1. In my crazy love for the kids, I never got on their case for not practicing. I made the lessons fun no matter how unprepared they were. 2. If they wanted to learn the Star Wars theme by ear, I was happy to show them how, breaking the teacher code of keeping their eyes on the sheet music. As you can imagine, that's all they wanted to play from then on because their friends thought it was so cool. (Sorry, Beethoven.) 3. I'm not a great sight-reader, so the kids who *were* good readers surpassed me in about fourth grade.

But despite my shortcomings, most of them really loved coming for lessons. I always had a full schedule and a long waiting list, probably thanks to the kids who were playing the Star Wars theme and making their friends jealous. I knew that even if I wasn't teaching the next Yuja Wang, I was instilling a lifelong love of piano. These kids were never going to grumble about their parents making them take lessons. They would remember the fun they had at Miss Mary's house and what an awesome thing it is to make music.

They thought I was just teaching piano. But really, I knew that the most important thing I was doing was blessing them and their families. If somebody had a big test or audition, I would send up a prayer. If a family was splitting up, I'd shower them with blessings. If a kid was struggling at school or being bullied, I'd ask the angels to help. Everyone who came through my door got blessed, sent good energy and prayed for, and I like to believe it changed things for the better. And in the process, I know I was changed for good.

In the World:

✴ In any line of work, from carpenter to car salesman, from artist to CEO, we can hand out blessings generously and change the world with our love. Make blessing others part of your workday.

In the Heart:

✴ In all of my activities today, I look for chances to offer prayers and blessings where needed. I spread my light freely to all who cross my path.

꒦꒷꒦

Give of Yourself

Being yourself is more beautiful than anything else you could be.

In Anita Moorjani's book, *Dying to Be Me*, she tells the story of the terminal cancer that ravaged her body and the near-death experience that shed incredible light on her soul.

She shares this important wisdom: "When I'm *being* love, I don't get drained, and I don't need people to behave a certain way in order to feel cared for or to share my magnificence with them. They're automatically getting my love as a result of me being my true self. And when I am nonjudgmental of myself, I feel that way toward others."

Automatically getting my love. This. It happens as a by-product of loving ourselves. In order to give of ourselves, to another or to a greater purpose in our lives, we need to be completely ourselves. If we wish to share our unique gifts—our love, our talents, our precious time—then we must come to appreciate ourselves fully and nonjudgmentally. There's no way around it. We can't share something that we don't fully embody.

Moorjani goes on to say that it is not our purpose to inspire other people, but to learn what inspires us, then share that inspiration with others. Our joy becomes the gift, automatically. Because that's who we are. It's all love.

In the World:

✳ We have opportunities to give of ourselves daily by *being love* in each of our encounters. That means being true and nonjudgmental of ourselves so we can be less judgmental of others. We can then listen well, show compassion, give a compliment or share an insight without feeling drained. Instead of needing to change others, we are being lovingly present.

✳ We have opportunities to give of ourselves through service. Consider offering some time each month sharing your unique gifts with others through volunteering in your community.

In the Heart:

✳ I share the light and love of my spirit freely by honoring myself and by being completely present with others.

꒦ ꒷꒦

Are We Having Fun Yet?

Joy is a spiritual practice.

Someone asked me today what I do for fun. Uh-oh. *There's* a good question. Like a lot of you, I've been slogging through some pretty heavy stuff over here. I had forgotten about having fun! So this seemed like the perfect time to up my spiritual practice of joy.

I swung into action. I stopped at Peterson's for ice cream on the way home from the post office—before dinner. I took a left instead of a right and walked around the sheep and llama field before turning down Hunters Road. I went out back and talked to the plants. (Yes, my idea of fun.) I called a friend down the street and made plans for dinner next week. That's better.

Sometimes a few small things that we truly enjoy can lift our spirits and remind us that our soul selves—hidden under the weight of the world—*are* joyful. So today, stop and ask yourself, *What am I doing for fun?* And get to work. Make a plan. Joy is a spiritual practice.

In the World:

✳ Today, treat yourself to something that will lift your spirits. Small things go a long way if you haven't been having much fun lately. Go ahead. You deserve it.

✳ Experiment with using positive affirmations. Refer to your favorites in your journal. Allow negative thoughts and words to move naturally through you without taking up residence.

✳ Love yourself. Compliment yourself. Treasure yourself. Forgive yourself.

✳ Eat nutritious foods. Get plenty of sleep. Move your body.

✳ Read uplifting books. Listen to joyful music. Choose inspiring articles, podcasts and movies. Keep company with joyful people.

In the Heart:

✳ I open my heart to the possibility of joy. I am grateful for the gifts of today. I trust that the world is a benevolent place that flows toward my highest good. I deserve joy in my life.

~\/~

Always Becoming

We can't do anything about yesterday or tomorrow,
but we can pour love into today.

There have been many days this summer when I have been called out of my cabin on Hunters Road to another arena of life. There was the relocation of boxes and books as Maya moved out of one apartment and into another; there were ten divinely dazed days in Florida helping Mom edit and publish her book; there was the hospice patient on the precipice of life for weeks.

After each outing, I would wonder where my groove had gone, only to discover at this late date that I never really had a groove. Oh drat. As much as we try, life often refuses to assemble our days in any linear fashion. So what's the constant? We need some illusion of normalcy down here. Anyone?

Despite our best intentions, spirit doesn't seem to want to approach the co-creation of this day with an agenda or a list. There are only moments in which we are called to be present. Light bulb! The constant is *becoming*.

Each experience has the potential to grow us spiritually. Every daydream and adventure, every call for assistance, every interruption and distraction, gives us an opportunity to bring love to the current moment. Even waiting in line can be a precious chance to share joy, compassion and kindness.

It's not all about evolution and accomplishment. It's about being present and being ourselves for the unexpected awakenings that surprise us in an unscheduled moment. No time is wasted. No action is unimportant. We walk together on the road of perpetual becoming. So let's flow with it. Let's be in the moment, whatever it brings—and pour love into today.

In the World:

∗ As the day unfolds, be flexible and present, knowing that all experiences, even the unexpected, are precious opportunities to share joy, love and kindness.

In the Heart:

∗ I approach the mystery of this day with a lightness of being, knowing that all I need to do is be present and be myself.

⤚⥜⤙

When All Seems Lost

*We lift this day with a thought of love, an act of kindness
and a heart of hope.*

Tommy is drinking again. After all those sober years, he's sliding
backwards down the slope and out of reach. With each passing day, he's
disappearing into a shell of the man I used to know and the brother I
used to play with. He's almost out of sight.

After denying the truth along with him for so many months, I called him
yesterday and told him I loved him, no matter what. I told him I knew he
wouldn't stop drinking for me if he couldn't stop for his awesome kids
and beautiful wife. But there was one thing, I said, only one thing I
wanted. For us to be honest. As messy and messed up as this is, let's just
drag it out into the middle of the rug and let it live in the room. "I totally
agree," he slurred.

I hung up and hung my head in despair. I can't change this, or fix it, or
will it away with all my determined power. No, there is no power here.
He's powerless over his drinking, and I am certainly powerless over him.
Nothing can be done. I am utterly and completely helpless to assist.

Except...what if I just hold a space...where he's healthy and happy and
healed? What if I arrange my thoughts to think only brilliant ones of him,
where I envision his highest self, his already perfect soul, his humor and
light and radiance? What if I see him only as God sees him? What if I let
that be my prayer and my plan?

My Spiritual A-Team, God and I, we're going to hold my brother up to
the light knowing that on some level, he is already there.

In the World:

✳ When all seems lost, know that the best and most beautiful version
of the person or situation can always be found right here and now.
Enlist your Spiritual A-Team in holding your vision up to the light,
relentlessly full of hope.

✳ Revisit ways to connect with the assistance of your Spiritual A-Team
in the reading on May 5.

In the Heart:

✳ I lift this day, with hope in my heart, to my highest imagining. I
believe that all things are possible.

My Day Is Yours

*Bless me to be the hands of your work, the steps of your path
and the rays of your sun.*

Bless me to be the hands of your work. In the small moments of today, help me to put my highest self into every task. Remind me that I don't work alone, but for you and with you. My hands are yours.

Bless me to see with the sight of your eyes. In the small moments of today, help me to see you in the pile of notes that ask something of me. Let them be done with you in the fabric of each action and transaction. My work is yours.

Bless me to be the steps of your path. In the small moments of today, help me to know what should be done next and next, and how to stay in the flow of grace. Show me where to go, where you would have me be. My steps are yours.

Bless me to be the song of your voice. In the small moments of today, help me to remember that it is you who speaks through me, your kindness that flows from me, your encouragement that lifts others through me. My voice is yours.

Bless me to be the rays of your sun. In the small moments of today, shine your divine energy through me, so I may raise the vibration of everyone who crosses my path with the light of your radiant love. My love is yours.

Bless me to be an instrument of your peace. In the small moments of today, help me to be serene and to share this sense of calm with others. May I be peaceful in my thoughts of others and imagine a world of peace. My peace is yours.

In the World:

* Contribute to peace in the world by asking to be a worthy custodian of your spiritual gifts. In the small moments of today, be grateful for the gift of life. Turn your head to notice the sacred in the small and the holy in simple things. Be joyful and useful. Love your neighbor. Be compassionate. Bring kindness and peace to the part of the world that is within your reach. Offer up your day to be used for love.

In the Heart:

* Today, in each step and with every breath, I am an instrument of peace, acting as the hands and feet of the divine.

≁⥽⥺

Opening Doors

Every line on your face is a thousand sunrises to light my way.

My neighbor Gene was laid to rest today. I had never been to a military funeral at Arlington National Cemetery before. It was an honorable tribute to a man who came from little means and rose to became a well-respected, successful restaurateur. Not an easy path. Gene started his career as one of an early generation of Black owner-operators of multiple McDonald's franchises, at one time running the extremely busy stores at both DC airports, in addition to five other locations. Gene was also a master gardener, and passersby would slow their cars to marvel at the magnificent gardens he personally nurtured outside his beautiful home.

Gene was a door opener. It is said that we all get to where we are going on the backs of those who came before us. Those who broke down barriers before him opened doors for Gene, and he spent a lifetime opening doors for others.

My parents, both from humble backgrounds, made their way virtually on their own, to educate themselves and put four kids through college. They instilled in us the foundation of integrity, a strong work ethic, an attitude of gratitude and the belief that there was nothing we could not be. I took this rather literally, following my dreams through nursing school and on to careers as a singer/songwriter, a piano teacher, a yoga instructor, a graphic artist, an app developer and author. I did none of this alone. Courageous immigrants and braver women paved my way.

We owe a debt of gratitude to the Genes and the ancestors, the parents, the women, the leaders, the activists, and teachers who came before us and opened the doors or broke them down, then hoisted us up onto their backs and brought us across the threshold.

Now it's our turn to be the opener of doors.

In the World:

✳ Write, say or think a note of thanks to someone who paved the way for you. Even if only a few words, even if only in your mind, your gratitude will bless the sender and the receiver.

In the Heart:

✳ I am thankful for all those who came before me who have inspired me, led by example and brought me here to this place in my life.

—⁂—

The Wild, Wild West

Follow your own star.

The other morning as I was peacefully writing, four horses stampeded down the hill from the farm next door, just a few yards from the window, trampling the brush and racing into the clearing. One minute I was in a quiet Zen-like om-worthy cabin. The next I was in the wild, wild West.

They were totally psyched to be free, pirouetting on their hind legs and then taking off toward Hunters Road. Uh-oh—that can't be good. I ran to call Lorraine, the neighborhood horse whisperer. She had been my first call when Shadow pulled his escape trick into that same clearing a few months back. I'm sure she wondered what kind of horse vortex I have going on over here.

She told me to drive down to the street and block the horses from going up the road. Sure enough, they were in the middle of Hunters Road, acting wild. When they saw me, they charged off toward yet another farm. I hopped in Lorraine's car, and we chased them down to a barn where they had stopped to rest.

"How," I asked Lorraine, "will we get all these crazy guys back home?" It turns out, you only have to rein in the leader, and the rest will follow. She was able to halter the rabble-rouser, and sure enough, the others fell in step and walked peacefully, willingly home. *Impressive, Lorraine.*

It was a powerful image, watching the horses fall in. We, too, tend to follow the lead of those who seem to have more power than we do. But we have choices; we don't have to follow someone into the street.

Listen to your inner voice. March to your own symphony. Forge your own path. Shine your own light. Follow your own star. The world is in need of your unique ray of love today. Shine brightly.

In the World:

✳ Powerful messages from outside sources come at us from all sides. Today, turn down the radio, TV, videos, images and people who don't resonate with your highest good and align with your inner voice. Be bravely yourself.

In the Heart:

✳ I am the only one who can direct my path. I have a mind of my own and follow the lead of my highest self.

꜀ᐯ꜀

A Higher Perspective

The soul of you is always, always beautiful.

If you woke up today feeling less than beautiful, remember that, no matter what is going on with you, the soul is always beautiful and radiant beyond imagination. And not only that, it is capable of rising above any challenge you may face today to gain a higher perspective. Like being on an airplane high up over the clouds, the humans on the ground only see a rainy day, while the real you is getting all of the sunshine.

The soul is the immortal essence of your consciousness, which is one with all things, but most awesomely, with divine love. That's an enormous thing to grasp if it's still morning. You might want to grab some coffee.

The best part is, love is at the center of our soul, so it is also at the center of everyone else's soul, and at the center of all these circumstances and challenges that we pray for. Yes, everything is God, and everything is love, and everything can be viewed and solved from the higher perspective of the soul.

The soul can rise above fear and doubt; it can rise above pain and suffering; it can rise above confusion and uncertainty.

There is no judgment or regret. There is no competition or jealousy. Just a really accurate, ethereal GPS system to guide us to experiences that allow us to live deeply, to love ourselves and others unconditionally, and to constantly create with the tools of love and joy.

When it's dark below the clouds, rise to a higher perspective. The soul of you is always, always more beautiful than you could ever imagine.

In the World:

✳ You can handle whatever today gives you. If it feels like too much, rise above it, ask for assistance, listen for signs, and you will know what to do. Exercise your right to view today from above the clouds.

In the Heart:

✳ I am an infinite being of love, connected to all other infinite beings of love. Nothing can change the beauty of my soul.

~V~

I Have a House by the Sea

What we dwell on, we create. What we think, we become.
What we ponder, we empower.

I bought a house last week, and I wasn't even looking. It happened so speedily and seamlessly that I hardly feel like it happened at all. Olga calls it the power of manifestation. Lyndy calls it a slice of heaven. I call it crazy. The universe swooped in and organized the action, leaving me on the sidelines, an excited spectator in the game of awe.

Since leaving the house of my marriage, I knew I would one day land in Florida in closer proximity to my mom in her later years. My parents had lived across the street from the ocean in a sweet villa, and for over twenty years, I had been visiting this spot twice a year, falling in love with the mighty ocean, sunsets over the river, the big birds and the live oaks. In my Gratitude in Advance journal, I wrote the line, "I have a house by the sea," every day for six years.

In July, during my annual birthday pilgrimage to Florida, Mom and I were visiting some dear friends in the old neighborhood. I told them that next summer, I planned to move to Florida. "Well you should look at the place right down the street," Dolores said. "It even looks like you!" The next morning, hours before flying home, I did just that. It was perfect.

Upon arriving home, I lost my mind and my faith for a minute. This was *not* my idea of good timing. It was a year too soon, it was priced out of my league and I had the cabin lease to consider. How could this possibly be right for me? Then I quickly righted my ship and remembered that *I* was not in charge. I put the real estate postcard of the villa under a statue of Mother Mary with a candle and a note. "God, this is your house. If you want me to live there, allow it to happen with ease and grace." And I let go of all worry. Then, with love and respect, I put in a bid below the asking price, but what I could honestly afford. I wrote in my journal today, with tears of gratitude, "I have a house by the sea."

In the World:

✳ Revisit your Gratitude in Advance practice. Update it if necessary or begin one if you haven't already. The practice is described on May 14.

In the Heart:

✳ I believe in the power of my focused thoughts. I release control and leave room for the divine to work her perfect plan.

A Cup of Beauty

Music is the prayer the heart sings.

The language of music has shared chemistry with the language of spirit. Both are like the air in the room—behind, between, within and around everything. Music speaks to us in the beautiful trifecta of words, harmony and feelings, getting to the soul of the unexplainable and the heart of the ineffable. It manages to be both our love story and our suffering, sometimes in one song.

How does it do that? Perhaps music is the cleaner for the window through which we filter our world. When we allow it to do some soulful housekeeping, wiping away the grime and the streaks of the day, maybe we feel a beauty and understanding that was there all along, revealed by this clear, harmonic perspective. "Music washes away from the soul the dust of everyday life," explains Bertholt Auerbach.

Or it could be that music is an offering of sorts, as Saint Augustine so sweetly put it: "When we sing, we pray twice." Assuming he was talking about sacred music, we have the words of faith or devotion, with their prayerful value doubling when set to music. We can almost see the prayers lifting off the earth and wrapping around their heavenly audience.

My favorite attempt at defining music's magic comes from poet Frederico Garcia Lorca. He believes that the arts are created from the story of humanity, then offered back to the people in a "cup of beauty." When we drink of this cup (hear the song, see the art), we understand ourselves. And thirst for the beauty.

"The poem, the song, the picture, is only water drawn from the well of the people. And it should be given back to them in a cup of beauty so that they may drink—and in drinking, understand themselves."

In the World:

*   As you listen to your favorite music today, let your heart be touched by the language of music and spirit.

In the Heart:

*   I am in perfect harmony with the creative beauty of life. I allow the creative arts to expand me, to teach me and to bring out soul secrets from within.

Stand By Love

We can't heal the world today, but we can begin with a voice of compassion, a heart of love, an act of kindness.

Yesterday, while in the checkout line of the grocery store, I noticed that the man in the next aisle was very angry. He began to raise his voice at his partner. My first thought was, *What if he has a gun?*

I was upset by that thought and the ones that followed. *Where would I hide? Would I run or stay and try to help others?* I decided I would stay and help. Crazy line of thinking, right? And I only listen to the news once a week.

Last night, I confessed to my college-aged daughter what had happened. As if it were a fact of life, she said, "Oh, I think that all the time. Especially at school."

This mentality of fear is only as powerful as we allow it to be. Love is the most powerful force in our world, and we know that. Even if it is not what we *hear* about the most, we must consciously make it what we *feel* the most.

As my friend Gussie so eloquently put it in a post responding to gun violence, "We as a species need to reboot and find a way to embrace and respect our differences, discover that violence is never the answer, and learn to respond to the crisis state of our universe with love and compassion."

Love and compassion. Exactly, Gussie. The healing begins today with our voice of compassion, our heart of love, our actions of peace. We know how to do that. Stand by love.

In the World:

✳ Today, be an instrument of peace. Sow seeds of compassion for all mankind. Share the highest vibrations of love.

✳ Resist using divisive language online and in person. Build a more loving world through your thoughts, words and actions.

In the Heart:

✳ I take off the blinders of fear, and I see the world through the eyes of love. I am a powerful agent of peace in all I do today.

~✓~

The Gift of Listening

May I give the gift of talking less and listening more.

Each of us possesses the power to lift up others in such simple ways: a compliment, a thoughtful question, an email of love, a hug. An often forgotten way to show kindness to another is by practicing the art of listening. To be present to someone with interest and compassion is a rare kindness, and a healing and transformative blessing.

In conversation, our thoughts often wander off to how we might respond or to another topic completely. We talk over others before they have finished speaking, implying that what we have to say is more important than what they are saying. All of our stories are competing to be heard.

Think about it. We really awaken when someone listens to us. To speak our truth and be truly heard brings confidence, joy, connection and healing. We come alive when someone validates what we are feeling.

We can be that to someone. Dr. Joanne Cacciatore, an expert in compassionate bereavement and patient listening, tells us, "Compassion can be a practice. Holding 'space' for another who is hurting is a wisdom of the heart that we can hone."

With a little mindfulness in conversation, listening well becomes a simple practice of patience and compassion—a wisdom of the heart that we can hone.

In the World:

✳ When talking with someone today, make eye contact and give them your full attention. Actively listen by showing understanding and compassion. Resist the urge to interrupt with your own story.

✳ No matter how many notifications come in during a conversation, show respect and avoid looking at your phone while talking with someone. Wait until the conversation is over. Attention to people who are present carries more weight than attention to the screen.

✳ For important conversations, practice running your thoughts through the ancient wisdom of the Four Gates of Speech: *Is it true? Is it kind? Is it necessary? Is this the right time to say it?*

In the Heart:

✳ I give the gift of my full presence in conversation and listen to others with compassion, interest and understanding.

~∨~

Born to Fly

Friends lift us up on wings of love when we forget we were born to fly.

When we fly, we exercise our inborn strength to move forward in our lives with resilience, over and over again. When we fly, we allow what we love to instinctually carry us toward our purpose. When we fly, we have confidence in our ideas, our self-image, our hopes and dreams. When we fly, we are fully ourselves, divine reflections in the flow of grace.

And wow, is it easy to forget we were born to do these things. In the dark night of the soul, it's hard to be sure of anything. The drama of life can be a heavy mist, socking in our spirits and hiding the sky from our eyes. So that's why God gave us friends. Because friends can see us as we ourselves cannot.

After many years in the process of separating from my long-term marriage and finally moving into this cabin at the mountain's edge, I told my friend Liz that I had really lost my confidence. I told her that I wished I was that fearless musician she met all those years ago, who never second-guessed herself. I felt vulnerable and lost, nothing like the woman I used to be.

After a moment of silence, she quietly said, "But you *are* that. You have never *not* been that. The same fearlessness I knew in her, I see in you now. You just can't see it yet." *Wings of love, Liz, wings of love.*

I wish for you a friend who reminds you of the truth: that you are still you. You are precious, unique, irreplaceable and born to fly. It's time to lift off and soar.

In the World:

✳ If you have such a friend, let them know how much they mean to you. Open your heart to opportunities to be that friend to others.

✳ If you don't have such a friend, be that friend to yourself. Remind yourself of the truth of who you are, as many times as it takes to strengthen your precious budding wings.

In the Heart:

✳ When I lose my way, I call on my friends for perspective. I am honest in sharing my truth. When I have a friend in need, I remind them of their strength and beauty.

AUGUST 27

⋍⋎⋌

Synchronicity - Part 1

There is infinite wisdom in the silence of the heart.

A few years back, on a beautiful late afternoon in Acadia National Park in Maine, my husband, daughter and I were driving around the one-way perimeter loop of the park on our way to the exit. We looked forward to returning to our vacation cabin in Booth Bay Harbor after a long day of strenuous hiking. I was at the wheel when suddenly, as if the van had a mind of its own, we pulled over to the curb at an overlook. Ignoring the groan of complaint, and not really understanding it myself, I offered, "I'm just going to take a look. You guys can stay in the car."

The area was quiet except for one family just a few yards in front of me. The father was taking a picture of his wife and two children as they stood at the far side of the path with the valley and beautiful vista behind them. As I watched them, waiting for him to take the picture before I continued past them, the mother took a step...and fell backwards off the cliff.

I ran to the edge with them to see her crumpled body, quiet and bleeding, about thirty feet down on a rock ledge. The children were screaming; the father was holding his head in shock. I raced to the car, grabbed my hiking boots, and told my husband and daughter to come quickly. Maya sat with the children, the father paced frantically, paralyzed with fear, my husband stayed on the phone with 911, guiding them to our remote location, and I, without thinking, scrambled and slid down the dirt and rock wall to where the woman lay.

Clearly, spirit organized our vacation and trip out of the park so we would be here, in this very place, for just this moment. (Continued tomorrow.)

In the World:

✳ There are no mistakes. Synchronicity and coincidence are acts of spirit at work in our lives. Listen for their silent call, and follow your inner wisdom.

In the Heart:

✳ I am called to the people and circumstances where I can be of help. I listen each day to the wisdom of my inner voice in all things.

~y~

Synchronicity - Part 2

Listen to the gentle guidance of spirit.

Nothing in my nursing training prepared me for what I saw. She picked up her head and blood poured out as if from a pitcher. My thought: *No one can lose this much blood and live.* The men threw down their t-shirts, and I made pads, holding them gently to her matted broken skull. Her only words: "I think I am paralyzed." "No," I said firmly. "You will be well. Breathe. Don't move. Help is coming. The children are fine. Your legs will be perfect." I whispered slow, soft, dreamlike comfort until the EMTs finally found us an eternal twenty minutes later.

In the weeks that followed, I prayed for her constantly, all day and all night, blessing her hundreds of times an hour. I had the feeling of being within her body, knitting her spine to perfection, activating new healthy cells from within. I visualized her glowing and happy, walking with ease.

One morning about three weeks later, while I was doing yoga, I felt an urgent pull to call her right then. From news reports, I knew she had been airlifted to a large hospital in Boston, and within moments, she answered the phone in her room. She remembered nothing of that day, but she shared the most beautiful news of all: After three surgeries to repair her skull and broken spine, and an initial poor prognosis for walking again, the doctors thought she was making miraculous progress. They expected that in time, she would walk and make a full recovery.

In one step, everything can change. We never know what the next hour will hold. But to be sure, the divine will let us know where we are meant to be.

In the World:

∗ Every time we send positive light to someone through prayer, visualization or a loving thought, we co-create with the divine. Today, change the world with the power of your positive thoughts.

∗ Listen to your inner voice. Follow an urge, a prompt, a pull. Look closely at what attracts your attention. Notice signs and symbols. Keep an open heart for the guidance of spirit.

In the Heart:

∗ Today I listen for the voice of spirit in my life. I use the power of love to send light where needed.

Things We Are Made Of

I am one with all creation.

Delight. Happiness. Shining. Rays.
Compassion. Wisdom. Radiance. Grace.
Joy. Hope. Kindness. Love.
These are the things we are made of.

Songs. Harmony. Peace. One.
Silence. Power. Will. Sun.
Joy. Hope. Strength. Love.
These are the things we are made of.

Eagle wings. Angel flight.
Soaring. Dancing. Dark. Light.
Joy. Hope. God. Love.
These are the things we are made of.

Light. Stars. Skies. Moons.
Galaxies. Planets. Earth. Ruins.
Joy. Hope. Infinite love.
These are the things we are made of.

Water. Dust. Fire. Flame.
Wind. Rock. Clouds. Rain.
Joy. Hope. Faith. Love.
These are the things we are made of.

Roots. Branches. Blooms. Blades.
Mountains. Rivers. Forests. Lakes.
Joy. Hope. Divine love.
These are the things we are made of.

In the World:

✳ Approach the day from the highest perspective, as one with all creation. No one will know except you that you are seeing the world through sacred eyes. Enjoy the lens of magnificence and unity.

In the Heart:

✳ I am a radiant expression of earth and sky, God and love. I expand the loving energy of my heart to encompass all beings.

❧⟐☙

An Imperfect World

Forgive daily.

As much as we would like to live mistake-free lives, most of us are a mess of imperfection. We cut people off in traffic. We say hurtful things. We say them at the wrong time. We make choices we regret. We have accidents. We are clumsy. We break things.

What if our peeps held all of our transgressions against us?

We count on forgiveness. Daily. Hourly sometimes. We need to be surrounded by people who don't take our imperfections too seriously and see the goodness of our intentions. What a wonderful world it would be if we all held up a universal heart of forgiveness for our imperfect state of affairs.

Not quite there yet, I know. But as in all things spiritual, we attempt to do the most loving thing going forward—for ourselves and for others. We can't make others forgive us, but we can clear the air around us by forgiving them, as often and as much as we possibly can.

Our feelings are meant to be temporary visitors, all just passing through, travelers on a journey, each with something to teach us. We don't let them inhabit our personal space. We don't invite them to take up residence in our house. We honor them by allowing them to be felt and heard; then we release them without drama, without grasping.

Only then are we really free to be a most loving person in our imperfect world.

Forgive daily.

In the World:

✳ Start with the small stuff. Notice little grudges held against those who are close to you. Sit with it for a bit with a heart of love. Listen for a lesson. And then give it permission to leave.

In the Heart:

✳ I freely release all negative feelings arising from the behavior of others and perceived shortcomings in myself. I forgive easily, peacefully and often.

Meditation Extras

In the silence of my heart, I am one with love.
In the stillness of my soul, I am one with God.

If you have been meditating daily, your practice is getting stronger. It may become a calming oasis that enhances all aspects of your life. As you progress, there are some sweet additions you can make to your existing practice that will magnify your energy, focus and connection with the divine. The benefits can be truly exhilarating. Add what resonates within.

In the World:

* *Meditate for longer.* Think about increasing your time, adding five minutes to your usual morning and evening time, and experimenting with even longer times on the weekends. How does twenty minutes feel? Or thirty? What if there was no timer?

* *Add a mantra.* A mantra is a short sacred, soothing phrase that we float on top of the breath. Pick one that attracts you. My favorites are *I Am* and *Hong Sau* (pronounced "hong saw"). Both refer to being one with spirit. *I* or *Hong* is mentally said on the inhale, and *Am* or *Sau* is mentally said on the exhale. Your focus remains gently on the breath while also gently on the mantra.

* *Eyes gaze upward.* With eyes closed, draw the eyes upwards as if they are looking out between the eyebrows. In time your eye muscles will get used to this and it will accelerate your access to spiritual wisdom.

* *Shop around.* Enjoy exploring the world of meditation with some of the many reputable experienced teachers online. It might take a few methods until you find what's right for you. You will know.

* *Set up a meditation space.* Arrange a space that is reserved for meditation. It can be a cushion in a corner with a small shelf to hold a candle and some meaningful symbols of your practice, or a chair near a dresser with some special altar items on top.

* *Be devoted and dedicated.* Start and end your meditation with an intention to be in the presence of the divine and to make an offering of your practice. Make meditation a nonnegotiable part of your day.

In the Heart:

* In the silence of my heart, I am one with love. In the stillness of my soul, I am one with God.

September Blessings

May this day arrive in your heart with a beam of hope and a ray of light.

Today we find ourselves on the threshold of a new month that includes the autumn equinox. As we approach the change of seasons, when the hours of daylight equal the hours of darkness, it's a beautiful time to reflect on the pilgrimage of our daily spiritual path, and to rejoice in the harvest of the seeds we have planted with our monthly intentions.

We welcome September with a blessing to honor this new month and new season of the soul:

May this day arrive in our hearts with a well of peace and a field of patience. May this day arrive in our hearts with a helping of self-compassion and a serving of faith. May this day arrive in our hearts with a dance of joy and a song of kindness. May this day arrive in our hearts with a waterfall of love and a river of grace. May this day arrive in our hearts with a beam of hope, a ray of light and a whisper of gratitude.

Be present.

Let the day flow with grace.

Expect joy. Be positive.

Serve with compassion.

Speak only kindness.

Impart only love.

Never forget you're not alone.

Give thanks for everything.

See goodness in others.

In the World:

✳ Invite these blessings into your heart as you begin a new chapter.

✳ Choose a word that will serve as an inspiration for your month.

✳ Write your intentions for the month of September.

In the Heart:

✳ I welcome this new month and new season with an open heart.

~\ |~

Delight Is Gratitude

The more grateful I am, the more beauty I see.

This morning I took my tea out the back door as usual. I wasn't thinking about anything. I wasn't praying. My only agenda was delight.

The sun was just waking up behind the trees in muted rays that gently released the dark. The evergreens donned an ocean blue in the distance, and just above their tops lay a sliver of moon lounging on her back.

Inserting themselves into the dawning sky was a skein of geese surely flying south, silent with the effort of transition. A frog sat upright in the crevice of a rock, comical with only his big grin showing. From flower to flower, a tiny hummingbird flitted around, spreading her graces with effortless speed.

The rooster's insistent crow for day woke up my hearing with a laugh, and I tuned into a surround-sound chorus of birds singing of morning to each other. My arms felt the cool breeze of early fall as if she could blow from my memory the steamy mornings of late August.

Nature's work of art flashed by in mere moments as I witnessed her gifts, teacup in hand, heart in awe. There was nothing missing. Nothing wanting. No formal gratitude required.

God feels it when we notice beauty. Joy rises up at the sight of the rays and the blue, the geese and the moon, the frog and the hummingbird, the rocks and the evergreen. Joy rises up in the songs of the birds and the voice of the wind. When we notice beauty, we *are* grateful.

Delight is gratitude with a smile on her face.

In the World:

✳ Steal an unscheduled minute to go outside or sit by a window, and simply notice the beauty of creation in a spirit of joy. Allow yourself to be delighted, which is the prayer of gratitude that brings only more joy.

In the Heart:

✳ My heart is full of gratitude and delight as I stand in awe of the beauty that surrounds me now.

Silence

Still your thoughts and find the frequency of peace.

Spiritual messages can penetrate our awareness in a variety of ways, with the divine as the signal source and our hearts as receiver and interpreter of the messages. Tuning into the source, like searching for a radio station frequency, requires finding a place where the signal comes in clearly.

Our practice of meditation and contemplative exercises provides just this kind of clear signal. As we tune in each morning and each evening, we keep our line open for constant wisdom, guidance, support and unconditional love.

Be still and know that all wisdom lies within.

Be still and be vigilant for the promptings of the soul.

Be still and remember your magnificence.

Be still and trust in the presence of infinite support.

Be still and see the dawn of a new idea.

Be still and sense the next step to take.

Be still and feel the growing courage to follow your dreams.

Be still and believe the perfect plan is unfolding for you.

Be still and ask clearly for your heart's desire.

Be still and make space for the soft voice of the heart to answer.

Be still and offer your services to divine will.

Be still and feel oneness with all creation.

In the World:

✳ At least several times today, move away from the static and into a place of pure signal. Patiently still your thoughts and make way for amazingly clear wisdom and guidance. Find the frequency of peace.

In the Heart:

✳ I am an infinite being, connected with the source of all wisdom in the silence of my heart. I listen and receive.

Start in the Middle

Kindness begins at home with yourself.

Whenever my brothers and I got caught in a proverbial tug-of-war over a particular toy or game, my father would pull out one of his favorite mantras, "Charity begins at home." He would explain that if we could not be kind to each other and learn to share at home, we would not be able to be charitable people out in the world. I didn't really understand what being charitable meant back then, but I'm starting to get a bigger picture of his message now: Start in the middle and work your way out.

I'm seeing that how we treat ourselves when there is no one looking, be it over the weekend or in our minds, is very telling about how we are able to share our love in the world. If we can't love and honor ourselves, respect our limits, and most of all be kind to ourselves in thoughts and actions, we are limited in the ways we can love, honor, respect and offer kindness to others.

We are all in need of love and encouragement. It's up to us to begin the process of filling this need in the home of our own hearts. Even when we feel broken or inadequate, within us is a radiant being worthy of our gentle kindness.

When we love ourselves unconditionally, we are able to pour forth our love without holding back. We can be charitable without feeling like we're losing anything.

It's a circle. We fill our hearts so we may empty them through gifts of love for all beings, making room to fill them up again and to give once more. Kindness begins in the middle. At home. With yourself.

In the World:

* This morning I sat staring at a blank page for an hour. Not a single word was typed, not a lone idea sprouted forth. I wrapped up with, "Good job, Mary. You showed up for work today. Way to go." That little spark of kindness encouraged me enough to sit back down later in the day and investigate with words what it means to be kind to myself.

* Be kind to yourself today in small ways so your unique gifts might be recharged by tenderness.

In the Heart:

* I am a beautiful soul deserving and worthy of my kindness.

The Extraordinary Switch

Where our focus goes, our energy flows.

Is it possible that we can wake up overwhelmed and out of sorts, and transform the day into one of the best ever? How do we transition from cranky to joyful? Where is the Extraordinary Switch in an otherwise ordinary day?

If today is a day where you need to "call in sad" and snuggle down with a good movie, there's not a single thing wrong with that. What we need to remember is that there is always a choice. An alternate thought path can lead to a completely different day because the transition, the transformation and the switch—are in you.

As my mother would say, this change of attitude comes from looking at the world through "sacred eyes." It is a simple, powerful process that changes our reality in an instant. You will be immediately rewarded by the shift, and like any practice, it gets better with time.

We create more of what we believe is possible. We see beauty when we anticipate that it is there. We have an extraordinary day when we expect that it is so. Where our focus goes, our energy flows.

In the World:

✳ Breathe in deeply and exhale the thoughts that are not serving you. Breathe in light. Breathe out darkness. And again.

✳ Remind yourself: *I am an incredibly powerful spirit, and nothing is impossible. This day is a magnificent gift.*

✳ See this moment through the lens of gratitude instead of lack. Look for the gifts. Notice even one thing that is going right.

✳ Ask for assistance with a prayer like: *Thank you for making beautiful my path today. I offer it to you, believing that there is a perfect plan that conspires to serve the highest good of all. Support me in each moment as my day unfolds with joy, delight and surprise. I am listening.*

In the Heart:

✳ I believe that everything is possible today. I believe in miracles and expect to be surprised by joy.

Honor the Growth

Love is a balance of holding on and letting go.

As we journey through life, our growth process is not a linear one. There are periods of time when all is well and we feel satisfied with our lives. Then there are times when everything shifts: we experience losses, a change of job or location, or the need for a new sense of purpose. During these times of flux, we grow rapidly, transforming our lives and raising our spirits to a higher understanding. We have seasons of growth within us that must be honored.

Our relationships, much like the seasons, also have a rhythmic nature. We see this in the growth and development of children. There are times when the rhythm of parent and child is status quo, then periods when the child grows rapidly and becomes more independent. This calls for a redefining of roles out of respect for the person they are becoming.

With our partners and friends, we don't often think about this cycle of growth. We want the relationship to remain the same—in the easy way it was when we first met. But most people will go through dramatic transformation in a lifetime, and the greatest gift we can give them is to honor the ways they have changed and who they have become.

When we hold on to a former version of one we love, we are always disappointed. When we open our hand and let go of resistance, love flows with flexibility and grace, making space for the blessings of the next season of growth.

In the World:

✳ Think about where in the cycle you are now. Are you holding steady or beginning a season of transformation? Are you in full-blown transition? Set the intention to allow love and acceptance to flow with the changes in yourself, your children, your parents or your partner.

✳ Be genuinely interested in your loved ones, asking questions and learning about them as they change and grow, not assuming to know all of their secrets. Let go a little and allow the relationship to breathe new life.

In the Heart:

✳ I release my resistance to change and give the gift of unconditional love through life's transitions and transformations.

~⤳⤝~

The Art of the Pause

May peace be your companion and love be your guide.

Have you ever met someone who pauses after they hear something, taking an extra moment before responding? I love that. It reminds me of another kind of pause—one we witness thousands of times a day.

There's a little space, like a sixteenth note rest in music, after we inhale, appearing again after we exhale. Of the four parts of the breath cycle, we have two that provide silence amidst the activity of breathing life into our bodies: inhale, pause, exhale, pause. The calm is built right in.

In yogic breathing practice, or *pranayama,* this rest, called *kumbhaka,* is the point of perfect stillness. Yoga masters explain that during this pause, speech, hearing and perception are suspended, leaving tiny pools of pure peace to punctuate our hours. Ancient yogic texts tell us that the pause after the inhale is where God is united with the individual soul, and the pause after the exhale is when we surrender ourselves totally to God.

Just as there is an art to the practice of *kumbhaka,* there is an art to the practice of calm. It is the art of the pause. There is always a small window of choice between receiving information and responding to it. In this moment, we can slow down, take a breath and create space to reply mindfully.

By extending this pause, we give the heart and mind more time to avoid a *reaction* and to instead organize a useful *response,* keeping us in alignment with the source of all peace. If you're not there yet, no worries. Peace and calm don't just happen. We practice them. And when we do, we become more peaceful and calm. That's some mighty good medicine for all of us right now. Peace is in the pause.

In the World:

✳ Be mindful today of the moment between receiving information and responding to it. Practice responding with thoughtfulness and compassion rather than with a habitual reaction.

In the Heart:

✳ My soul is calm and undisturbed, serene and peaceful. I practice serenity in my heart, in my home and in the world today.

~ ⅄ ⁓

Thirteen Words

You are here for a reason. Your words matter.
Your thoughts matter. Your love matters. Your life matters.

My brother told me that the hardest thing he did today was stand up at an AA meeting and say, "Hi, my name is Tom, and I'm an alcoholic. I have five days."

Thirteen words.

He cried. He cried for the fifteen years and seven months that he was sober. He cried for the days when he was the leader of the meetings, hanging out at the coffee machine and taking out the trash so he was available for the newcomers. He cried for the days when he was his better self. He cried for the shame he felt saying those thirteen words.

He told me he is nobody now. Today he attended two meetings where he didn't know people and they didn't know him. There were more recovering drug addicts than recovering alcoholics. He doesn't want to tell anyone he blew fifteen years. He only says his thirteen words.

I cry with him. I tell him he's still in there. I tell him he's still that guy. What I'm tasting are the tears. What I'm seeing is his beautiful, magnificent soul. What I'm hearing is the most courageous story I have ever heard. What I'm feeling is proud to be in his life and of his thirteen words.

What I'm touching on but don't know how to say is that God doesn't mind about the fifteen years. There is no failure here. The only thing that matters is love. And being bravely true to who you are in this moment. What I say is, "You are loved beyond your wildest imagination no matter what."

What I meant was, *Today, you said thirteen words. And God felt love.*

In the World:

✳ Remember this: You are worthy no matter what. You are a beautiful child of God, and no one and nothing can change that. Walk with your head held high, and allow this day to flow forth from the love that you are.

In the Heart:

✳ I awaken to my worthiness, my beauty and my eternal soul of love.

SEPTEMBER 9

❧

Harmony: A Meditation

Today I choose calm over chaos, serenity over stress,
peace over perfection, grace over grit, faith over fear.

With a deep breath in, I welcome this precious day, and gratitude floods my heart with calming joy. With an exhale I allow all that is not for my highest good to leave me. I smile inside and out as I relax and release any overwhelming expectations for the day.

Today I choose calm over chaos. In all work, at home or in the office, my highest wisdom flows through my calm mind and heart. I am present in each moment, and I move from one task to another with easy transitions.

Today I choose serenity over stress. With clarity of mind, I accomplish all that needs to be accomplished with ease. I do one thing at a time with love, and I ask for the assistance I need from others and from my divine support team.

Today I choose peace over perfection. I do my best to use the gifts I have been given, and my best is enough. My priorities are to share love, to act out of kindness, and to allow myself to feel joy. All else will get done in its time. I am at peace.

Today I choose grace over grit. In the flow of divine grace, I am relaxed and supported in all I do. I listen for signs, knowing all that is meant for today will happen with little resistance.

Today I choose faith over fear. I trust that even in challenges, I am right where I need to be. I am present with my pain and aware of my blessings. I know that I am being supported and guided in every step.

With a deep breath, I bless this day and begin with calm, serenity, peace, grace and faith. Harmony surrounds me. All is well.

In the World:

✳ Spend a few minutes several times today with your favorite parts of this meditation. Slow yourself down with the help of some deep breaths, and be mindful of where your automatic thoughts are taking you. Our serenity runs as deep as our choices. Choose serenity and harmony over and over again.

In the Heart:

✳ In all that today brings, I am grounded in the center of deep peace.

~⅄~

Kindness and the Skunk

*Be the kindness that reminds someone
that the world is a compassionate place.*

A few days ago, a rustling caught my eye from the writing window. Heading straight for me was a large limping skunk with a very puffy tuft of white hair covering her back like a lovely fur coat. As she approached, it occurred to me that no one really prays for skunks, except maybe to think while driving, *Please God, don't let me hit this thing.* No, skunks, like stink bugs, have a bad rap, with very few people finding the good in them. And this girl had two soul-expanding features: she was a skunk, *and* she had a disability. A big spirit indeed.

Being nocturnal, or technically crepuscular (they come out at dusk and dawn), we don't see skunks around much. It was special that she came right to the window and looked directly up at me with her nearsighted eyes. Then my new buddy Samantha crossed the frog pond bridge and made her way, limping off to visit the horses. I prayed for her front paw.

Yesterday at dawn, she took the same path to the windows, but this time taking one labored step at a time, clearly on her last legs. Oh Samantha! She made it to the back patio, then fell in a heap on a soft pile of leaves in the flower bed. And lay there for hours. I went out, and she lifted her head toward me and put it back down.

I told her it was okay to die now and that all sorts of skunk angels were going to help her cross over. I was doing my "death doula thing" as Olga would say. Hours later I found her. She had moved herself to the compost area away from the house to die. What a thoughtful girl.

As you may have guessed, this morning featured a one-minute skunk memorial. It was a quiet, come-as-you-are affair. In attendance were two doves, four cardinals, a chickadee and a hawk. The horses watched from the field. A rooster crowed along with my hummed verse of "Amazing Grace." And Sam went off to new fields in style.

In the World:

✳   We never know. What we perceive as the least among us might just be the greatest. Powerful beings come clothed in humble circumstances. Be kind.

In the Heart:

✳   Today I reserve my judgment and give freely of my kindness.

One with Everything

Every prayer for peace and every act of peace
showers rays of peace upon the earth.

Today, the United States honors the victims and responders of September 11, 2001, with a National Day of Service and Remembrance. On this day, we are asked to unite in offering a charitable act of service, coming together in the spirit of love and peace.

We are, after all, one family. We are intimately connected as threads of a universal tapestry. Emanating from the same perfect source—God, love, universal mind—we all share the energy of this force. Today, each action we take and each thought we think will affect the whole. When we serve one of us, we serve all of us.

The major religions, sages, saints, mystics and scientists as well, agree on our interconnection. In her fascinating book on universal laws, *The Whole Elephant Revealed*, Marja de Vries explains: "The essence of all authentic religions, spiritual movements and mystic teachings can be traced back to similar mystical, direct experiences of Becoming-One-with-Everything." At our very essence, we are one. On the anniversary of the events that intended to divide our world, our service becomes a beacon of our shared spirit.

Our small acts of peace can begin healing the fabric of our world by overcoming fear with love, anger with kindness, separation with compassion, judgment with acceptance. Our tapestry can be mended, and we are all weavers working together hand-to-hand, heart-to-heart, using a common thread.

May our service today unite us in the spirit of peace.

In the World:

* Consider how you will join the force of charitable service at home, in your neighborhood or in your community today.

* You can check online to find local community organizations with volunteer opportunities near you.

In the Heart:

* I radiate the peace and love I feel within to all of humanity.

The Beautiful Gift of Today

Believe. Cherish. Enjoy.

No matter what you've done or left undone, no matter who you've hurt or who hurt you, no matter how it might seem to be an exercise in pride and hubris—relentlessly love yourself. No excuses, no caveats, just love yourself the way that you are so loved by the divine in this very moment.

And then present yourself with a few gifts:

BELIEVE in yourself. Believe that you have everything you will ever need to live a peaceful and joyful life. Believe in your goodness and unlimited potential. Believe in your capacity to love and be loved. Believe in the compassionate care of an all-loving divine source. Believe in a benevolent universe and the guardians that are sent to assist you. Believe in your strength, flexibility, and will to rise up under any circumstances.

Believe in the beautiful gift of today.

CHERISH yourself. Your tender self. Yes, you. Cherish your family and friends, your colleagues and clients. Cherish the birds and trees and animals and sky and the incredible beauty of nature. Cherish the chance to live out this day with choices and chances.

Cherish the beautiful gift of today.

ENJOY yourself. Enjoy the feeling of being an embodied, thinking, breathing human on the planet. Enjoy the smiles and laughter that reflect delight and awe. Enjoy the music and rhythm, the paint and the pencils, the creative expression of life. Enjoy the food and the drink, the love and the warmth, the peace and the kindness.

Enjoy the beautiful gift of today.

In the World:

* You deserve to be covered in a soft blanket of loving-kindness. Pay yourself a few compliments. Do something special for yourself today. Remind yourself that you are believed in, you are cherished and you are worthy of joy.

In the Heart:

* I believe in myself, in my goodness and in my light. I show myself how much I love myself, my life and the gift of today.

Simplicity

Simplicity is good for the soul.

Less can be so much more. Less stress, more peace. Less screens, more interaction. Less noise, more nature. Less worry, more joy. Less complaint, more gratitude. Less stuff, more space—in heart and home.

Simplifying our surroundings can bring a feeling of brightness and openness to not only the house but also to the soul. Our spaces reflect our state of being, and when we set them up to be clear, clean, bright, open, meaningful and loving, we naturally align with a higher vibration. And vice versa. The more clarity we gain through meditation and prayer, the more drawn we are to have our homes reflect the beauty of our expanding souls.

Donating to community organizations that serve those in need is a thoughtful way to simplify while sharing our abundance with others. A little research will save their volunteers time and energy, and get your reusables quickly and efficiently into the right hands.

Start today with one drawer, closet, tabletop or corner. Not only will you make space for more peace, but another soul will treasure your treasures.

In the World:

* Donate locally. Research the list of needs from each organization online, and separate your donations according to what they accept.

* Keep a bag for donations in an out-of-the-way place, and add to it regularly. When it's full, wash and fold the clothes, stack them in a paper shopping bag, and mark it "washed." Bring men's suits and outerwear on hangers. Avoid throwing unfolded clothes in leaf bags. These are gifts for souls.

* Most libraries accept used books of all kinds. Some police and fire stations take stuffed animals. Many counties collect used electronics once a month.

In the Heart:

* I take steps toward a simpler way of life. I divest easily of the possessions I don't need or use, taking great joy in sharing my abundance with others.

The Wisdom of Nature

A walk in nature walks the soul back home.

It was not the smoothest of mornings. Friends were sick and needed help. The inbox was overflowing. A brother needed to talk. Posts begged to be made. Writing beckoned. My desk was covered over in notes. What did I do? I walked out the front door with a smile of relief.

There's sage advice that says the busier we are, the longer we need to meditate. I agree, and would add to that a nice, relaxing midday walk. The more we decide to do, the more conscious we need to be—about being.

Our highest wisdom comes when we open the floodgates of our inner voice. The art of allowing this opening doesn't happen in a flurry of activity, but in the oasis of calm and beauty. So when we want to do our best, most creative work or our most insightful, patient parenting or caretaking, it's essential to take regular pauses to check in with divine wisdom and make space for answers that provide exactly what we need at just the right time.

Nature sits in wait outside our door, ready to share her gifts of spiritual expansion. Even a short walk with a keen eye for beauty and an open heart for joy can refresh our outlook and connect us with our soul's grace. If walking is not possible, we can think outside the box. I know a caretaker for a hospice patient who watches beautiful nature videos on YouTube when he feels stuck in his routine. My little mama, who can't always access the outdoors, watches birds in the oak trees from her chair.

Make time to experience nature's healing power—and walk the soul back home.

In the World:

✳ Open to the beauty of the natural world today. Enjoy, appreciate, and be in awe of the sights and sounds of nature. She is designed to plug us into our connection with all things and with the universal wisdom of the soul.

In the Heart:

✳ In gratitude, I appreciate the glory of nature. I allow the miracles of her calm beauty to bring me into balance and open my heart to my highest wisdom.

Grace Is Here

Grace is the gift of abundant blessings freely given.

Grace is here today. She's overflowing. Not only for the deserving, the perfect and the organized. But also for the humble, the weak and the messy. She brings abundant blessings. Grace is here today.

Grace is here today. There is nothing to fear. She will take the lead in uncertainty. She will rally strength in weary bones. She will raise you up on strong, soft wings when there is little hope. Grace is here today.

Grace is here today. Breathing the wind of guidance into your sails and bringing free fuel for your spirit. She is in your prayer of gratitude and your song of joy. She is in your cry of frustration and your tears of suffering. She is picking you up and laying you down. Grace is here today.

Grace is here today. All is well. She will quietly remind you of your worth. She will provide opportunities for your unique gifts to shine forth. She will quell shame and protect a vulnerable heart. She will remind you to love yourself fully, completely and always. Grace is here today.

Grace is here today. She is in your hands as you nurture. She is in your heart as you love. She is propelling you forward as you travel your path. She is in your mind planting seeds of divine wisdom.

Grace is here today.

And tomorrow, she will be again.

In the World:

✳ Grace is a gift from God, freely given. There is an endless supply flowing right where you are. Just turn your eyes slightly in her direction and you will feel her flow. Step into her. Ask for her. Use her many blessings.

In the Heart:

✳ I stand with an open heart, ready to receive Grace as she walks with me through every moment of this day.

SEPTEMBER 16

Small Things with Great Love

Our love inspires others to be loving. Our joy inspires others to be joyful. Our kindness inspires others to be kind.

We have power. Not the kind of power that needs victory over an enemy but the kind of power that rises up in us every day as we go about our work with love. It's everyday power. It never leaves and it never wanes. We always have it and can always use it.

The most effective power is not loud and aggressive. Power can be quiet and humble, especially when wielding the practices of compassion and kindness. The standard definition of *power* is "the capacity or ability to direct or influence the behavior of others or the course of events." That's just what we will do.

Today when we shower everyone who comes into our orb with love, we will change the vibration of everything around us. A loving gesture for your partner, a hug for a child or a compliment for a coworker will actually change the wavelength of the energy in the room. And the best part is that they will rise to your level of loving vibration. That is changing the world.

You don't have to believe me. Scientists are now concurring with what saints and mystics have known all along. That the more loving we are, the more love we foster in our energy field. The kinder we are, the kinder other people will tend to be. When we lift up someone, we not only lift ourselves, as George Washington Carver so beautifully said, but we lift everyone else up too.

We have that power in the small things we do today. Let's use it well.

In the World:

* Be mindful to distribute as much loving-kindness in your world today as possible. Monitor your thoughts as well; they are just as powerful as your words and actions. And remember, this is not homework. It's spirit work that will bring countless blessings to you and to all beings.

In the Heart:

* I am a walking, talking beam of endless light and love. I shine radiant energy on everyone I see and think of today.

Relentless Optimism

Oh happy day.

At a recent wedding reception, the father of the bride stood with a great grin, raised his glass to his daughter and new son-in-law, and said, "I hope you come to realize, as your mother and I did, that life is fun!"

Fun? Wow. This is surprisingly great advice.

What if we lived in a world of relentless optimism? What if, for an entire day, we thought positive thoughts, holding in our hands a glass half-full? What if we had an eye for beauty and delight and looked on the tasks at hand with purpose and a sense of creativity and joy?

I do believe that the father of the bride had it right. Life is not only supposed to bring us lessons through pain but also lessons through fun. The kind of fun that comes from allowing joy to hold a prominent daily presence.

Our joy is waiting to be set free from the suit and tie of seriousness and to burst out in awe of the miraculous world we live in. She's playful and she's ready to dance.

There is nothing stopping us but us. Yes, we have worries and problems and grief. But we also have joy and love and awe—demanding equal time.

In the World:

* Decide to make today a day of relentless optimism. Start by planting a joyful intention for the day. In thoughts, words and actions, phrase everything in the positive. Find the light in all situations. Do small things that bring you joy.

* Allow your soul smile to become your outward smile. Smile often.

* Then let that joy seep into the way you interact with others. Let your joy translate into lightness, loving-kindness and play.

In the Heart:

* I follow a path of joy, seeking out experiences that bring me happiness. I allow my beautiful light to shine joyfully on everything around me.

The Inner Oasis

The more we practice, the more natural it becomes
to see the world through sacred eyes.

Presence is bringing full awareness to the moment we are in, filtering out distractions and bringing our attention to the task at hand. The combined stresses of life fade into the background as we focus on being right here, doing whatever it is we are doing right now.

As we know, one way to improve our ability to come into the present moment is to calm the mind in meditation. Meditating has now become a morning and evening fact of life and the rewards are filtering into all aspects of life. Right? No worries. Any time is the perfect time to refresh or renew the practice.

Between our regular meditations, when we are "in the world," we can use short meditations—for even one or two minutes—that are refreshing, calming, centering and good for our health and clarity. They open the window of communication to our higher wisdom, returning us to our spiritual perspective.

We want to bring ourselves to this calming connection as many times a day as possible. The more we practice, the more natural it becomes to see the world through sacred eyes.

The following STOP method is adapted from a lecture by Deepak Chopra on mindfulness. It reminds us that we can always use the breath to calm the body and mind—and enter the inner oasis of the soul.

In the World:

STOP method for when you want to return to your spiritual center:

* Stop what you're doing.

* Take three deep breaths, and smile everywhere in your body.

* Observe what is happening in your body and mind.

* Proceed with loving-kindness, joy, compassion and love.

In the Heart:

* At any time of day, I can use my breath to calm my body and mind, and enter the inner oasis of the soul.

꒷

The Light Enters You

Be the love that reminds someone that we belong to each other.

Yesterday, as I unloaded my items on the belt at the grocery store, I noticed the cashier adjusting her headscarf over fuzzy wisps of hair. I don't know much about chemo hair, but instead of ignoring what I had seen, I softly said, "Growing back?" She said, "Yes, finally. But I don't have eyebrows or lashes yet." It opened the door to a conversation that lasted the duration of my checkout, during which I was honored to hear about her courageous journey through cancer. In that small exchange I could feel that something meaningful had happened for both of us.

My post office is a small place where people talk about their lives as they buy stamps and mail packages. From my regular Etsy mailings, I learned that Tina's beloved friend was suffering from a serious illness. After the grocery run, I stopped by the post office to mail my usual packages, and asked Tina about her friend. She reached a hand over the counter and told me things were not so good. We held hands, and I told her I would be praying for them both.

Moments of grace spontaneously erupt; waterfalls pour into a split second. One minute we are in the safe zone of greetings and weather, and the next, a window opens to something deeper, giving us the chance to connect on another level.

Perhaps our common experience of pain cracks our outer shells, and we recognize each other on the inside. "The wound is the place where the light enters you," Rumi reminds us. A crack in the armor gives us an opening to be the love that reminds someone that they are not alone.

In the World:

✳ Be awake as you interface with the world today. Notice, listen, look outside yourself. Be a force of love in gentle ways. Sometimes even a smile can turn around a dark day in someone's heart.

In the Heart:

✳ Today I am an instrument of love, connected to all beings. I am awake to my heart of compassion. I am the love that reminds someone that we belong to each other.

﹀ㇽ

Absence as Presence

Hear the angels sing.

When I was a teenager, my mother gave me a book that would change my life: Raymond Moody's *Life After Life*. Dr. Moody was a pioneer in the study of near-death experiences (NDEs), and his personal interviews with people who had clinically died, spent time in the afterlife, then were revived, were groundbreaking. Today there are many books detailing personal experiences of life after death and several websites of doctors who are currently studying them, where we can read countless stories of NDEs from all over the world.

The hallmarks of almost every story bring comfort to the bereaved and peace to anyone who fears the moment of death. This is real—and really beautiful.

Having the context of a beautiful afterlife didn't take away the pain of the loss of my daughter, but it laid the foundation of a deeper peace. I celebrate her presence daily, knowing that beyond her physical absence she is here, she supports my life, she loves me beyond words and I will see her again.

The main concepts from Dr. Moody's book are the same ones that are told over and over again in the NDEs of people of all races and religions. I list below those that have meant the most to me over the years.

As we go out into the world with our joy and our pain, may we be a little more at peace, lifted by the knowing that we never lose our beloveds and that our love is without end. Listen—and hear the angels sing.

In the World: Inspiration from near-death experiences:

∗ After death there is a light of unconditional love (God) that is so bright, so pervasive, so beautiful that we want to stay forever. We have no pain and no sadness. We feel a oneness with all things.

∗ Our consciousness remains intact and we have an almost immediate understanding of the events in our lives and their impact on others.

∗ We are not alone. We are greeted by loved ones who have gone before us and angels or guides who assist us in the transition.

In the Heart:

∗ I am an eternal being living in the light of unconditional love.

Building a Prayer

Be wise. Be strong. Be kind. Be you.

Decades ago, a prayer that would organically enter my heart every day was very simple: *May I be wiser and kinder.* That mantra was useful to me in the small moments of my busy life, encouraging the growth of wisdom and compassion.

Years later, the prayer would grow along with the understanding that in order to practice wisdom and kindness, I needed a lot of strength and courage. The growth of spiritual knowledge, although the most natural thing for the soul, doesn't come so naturally amidst the noise of the world. Like any other educational process, it requires devotion, dedication, persistence, focus, strength, tenacity and *tapas* (burning desire) to stay the course.

And the prayer became: *May I be wiser and kinder and stronger.* I chanted this within for years while swimming, walking or running.

They say that all roads lead home, and this is surely true of spiritual paths. Everything we learn is processed through our hearts, so how we think of ourselves becomes vitally important. Being honest about who we are, authentic about how we express ourselves, and sure about how completely loved we are by the divine become the most important building blocks of all. Self-compassion and self-realization are the foundation upon which we transform.

So in all things we must be ourselves. There is no wrong way when it is the authentic way. If we find joy in it, if we find love in it, if we believe in it, if we are passionate about it—we have found our road sign. We cannot take a wrong turn using the GPS of the heart. So the prayer became:

Be wise. Be strong. Be kind. Be you.

In the World:

❋ You can reinforce your lessons by coming up with short prayers to steer your learning. Yours might include: *Be open. Be grateful. Be joyful. Be calm.* Come up with your personal version for today's path. Record it in your spiritual journal, and use it as a daily mantra.

In the Heart:

❋ I am a unique and beautiful soul embarking on the journey of today with authenticity, joy and divine guidance.

SEPTEMBER 22

In Perfect Time

*May we have patience for all the things that have not bloomed yet
and gratitude for all the things that have.*

The gentle onset of a new season can bring about a welcome change.
When we open our hearts and surrender to transformation, we flow
through the seasons of life with grace.

The change of seasons in nature offers the chance to reflect on the
change of seasons within us. May we open to new experiences that will
bring inner growth as we release what is no longer serving our spiritual
journey. We are always becoming new. Have faith that everything
happens in its perfect time.

There is a time for everything,
and a season for every activity under the heavens:
a time to be born and a time to die,
a time to plant and a time to uproot,
a time to kill and a time to heal,
a time to tear down and a time to build,
a time to weep and a time to laugh,
a time to mourn and a time to dance,
a time to scatter stones and a time to gather them,
a time to embrace and a time to refrain from embracing,
a time to search and a time to give up,
a time to keep and a time to throw away,
a time to tear and a time to mend,
a time to be silent and a time to speak.
Ecclesiastes 3:1–7

In the World: An Equinox Blessing

✳ *May the outgoing season be covered in blessings and released with love.
May the harvest of previous intentions bring abundance in your heart
and in the world. May the balance of darkness and light bring greater
balance into your home and life. May this new season of gratitude and
letting go gift your heart with open space for miracles to grow.*

In the Heart:

✳ I release the past season of my life and open my heart to new
beginnings. I have faith that everything happens in perfect time.

The Joy of Milkweed

There is nothing too small for gratitude.

My friends Paul and Cheryl teach songwriting to elementary school children. This year, their organization, Kid Pan Alley, got a grant to partner up with the National Park Service. This is how it works: A class takes a field trip to the park and with the guidance of a park ranger, they wander through fields and along rustic paths looking for native plants and creatures. Then they use their common experience as a muse for writing a song together under Paul and Cheryl's musical direction. Creativity at its finest.

Yesterday the bus went up the mountain in the early morning in time to catch the dew on the morning grass. The children were given their instructions to look closely, to walk slowly, to feel with all their senses. Someone spotted a milkweed and was fascinated by its seed pod. Others gathered around in excited interest, noticing its pattern, colors and strength. Some sat down in the tall grass to study the miracle of caterpillars, butterflies and goldenrod.

This is soul food for a kid who has no grass in the yard, an amazing expedition even for a kid who is a master at video games, a spirit of wonder for a kid who was never encouraged to look at nature this closely. Cheryl summed it up beautifully when she wrote, "Life will gift you with wonderful experiences when you are present to receive them." Oh, the joy of milkweed.

When we take a pause to really look at the beauty that surrounds us with a heart of wonder, gratitude rises in abundance for the humble, the simple and the small. When we live in awe of the unfathomable miracle of our lives, there is nothing too small for gratitude.

In the World:

* Walk through this day with a grateful heart, mindful of the small wonders.

* Voice a whisper of *thank you* from deep in your heart for even the little things that bring you joy.

In the Heart:

* My heart is open with awareness of all of the gifts that surround me now. There is nothing too small for gratitude.

Blue Love

*Each day, may we let the noise of the world drop away for long enough
to hear the voice of love, peace and compassion.*

When we close our eyes, each of us enters a personal oasis. With a few breaths to still our thoughts, we find that our oasis is calm, wise and serene, always at the ready to send out and receive an endless store of divine love.

Entering the calm of the soul, we know that although our experience is completely unique, it is connected to the soul of all beings that have ever existed or will ever exist. As part of our shared fabric, what we feel, what we imagine and what we create transforms everything around us.

One way to impact the energy within our homes, in our communities, and on our planet today is to send out a wave of love on the breath. Small meditations can make a big difference in our own mind, body and soul. And when we change ourselves, we change our world too.

Love is the greatest gift we can give.

In the World:

* Take a comfortable seat, feet on the floor or cross-legged, spine straight and face relaxed.

* On the inhale, imagine a wave of peaceful blue love pouring into your heart, filling the infinite space within and magnifying unconditional acceptance and love.

* On the exhale, see the wave of blue love moving from your heart and surrounding your home, your community and the earth with peace.

* Spend a few minutes inhaling and exhaling the wave of blue love, magnifying your beautiful energy and sending it to all beings and to the earth.

In the Heart:

* I am filled with an endless supply of love, and I freely share it with all beings.

Puppy Downshifting

Rest is not an option—it is a necessity.

My inner goddess is strongly relating to a passed-out puppy at the moment. She is worn out from the daily dance. Running around, retrieving things, sitting, staying and loving people can be exhausting. I hear my wise inner voice ordering me to rest. And what do I do? I keep on going so I can complete just one more thing. And then one more thing.

And what does a puppy do? She collapses into the soft shag rug for a deep rejuvenating nap.

You would think that after all the reading and writing I do about the essential value of self-care and the spiritual anchor of self-love that I would be a master at taking naps and resting when my eyes, wrists, body and soul are weary. No, my Off button seems to be busted, but I have promised myself to do better with this.

Rest is not a reward that comes at the end of a long day of doing small things with great love. Rest is not an added bonus, a cherry on top or something we do if we have time after everyone else is served and happy.

Rest is not an option—it is a necessity. When we release, relax and wind down, clarity and calm rise up. We cannot give from an empty well. When we are replenished and energized, all else flows with greater ease and grace.

Puppies rest without guilt, and so can we. I don't know about you, but this goddess is taking a nap today.

In the World:

∗ When your wise inner self sends the message that it's time to rest, stop and listen. Set a timer and close your eyes. Invite deep rejuvenation into every cell. See yourself surrounded by light and peace. Ask that you awaken refreshed, alert, calm and ready to focus.

In the Heart:

∗ I rest when I am tired, and feel deep peace surrounding me. My body fills with light and energy, and I rise refreshed, clear and calm.

SEPTEMBER 26

Grief 101: Comfort That Comforts

My love is with you.

During our lifetimes, most of us will have occasion to console someone who has suffered the loss of a child. And we want to do it in a way that is most compassionate. No one teaches us what to say, so we flounder in the uncomfortable void, and frequently, despite our best intentions, we utter phrases that end up being hurtful. The information here is usually confined to grief groups, but I knew you would want to know. Next time you have the opportunity to comfort someone, your love will be truly felt and heard.

In the World: These phrases can be unintentionally hurtful:

* *Things happen for a reason.* We don't know what that reason might be right now and in the moment, it's hard to fathom that unbearable suffering would be inflicted on anyone for any reason.

* *You are young. You can have more children.* But we don't know that. And even if I had a whole crop of live children, I would never have that one. Children are irreplaceable.

* *It's God's will.* This can feel like a harsh judgment being handed down to the bereaved parents. No matter how spiritual or religious the person is, it's best not to be in God's shoes right now.

* *I know how you feel—my grandmother just died.* The loss of a child is very different from other losses. Resist sharing your own story.

* *At least...* It's not a good time to remind the bereaved of a silver lining.

* *Call me if you need something.* Simply drop off a comforting gift.

These phrases might bring comfort:

* *I'm so sorry for your loss. My love is with you.*

* *I've been thinking about you and your family. I'm here for you.*

* *I will always remember your beautiful Simon.* (Use the child's name.)

* *You are in my heart, my thoughts and my prayers.*

In the Heart:

* I am open to learning how to be a more loving and compassionate person in the world.

~⌄~

Grief 201: What We Need to Know

I cannot lose you. You live in my heart.

I know you're tempted to skip this page, but hang in there if you can. Take a moment and clear your mind of death discomfort. Deep breath. This won't be painful, I promise.

So many of us slip through life avoiding conversations about death and grief like the plague. So why not stop, turn around and look her in the eye? Death will happen to us, but before that, it will happen all around us. People we love will die, and we might find ourselves completely unprepared to face grief. When you know a little about it ahead of time, you won't feel like you've completely lost your mind when it's your turn. It's just another sacred part of life.

In the World:

✳ Grief demands our attention. It is important work that requires soul space. Learn about it.

✳ There's no timetable. It's a personal journey, and you walk at your own pace. There are no wrong ways to grieve.

✳ Grief is not a linear process; it ebbs and flows, possibly for the rest of your life. Stay with the feelings as they arise. Let them flow through you without judgment.

✳ Tell your story to a compassionate listener. Connect with others who have had a similar loss. Speaking your truth puts your experience into words and weaves the loss into your life going forward.

✳ Accept the help of loving people who offer it. They want to do something for you, and you need the support. Ask for what you need.

✳ Working with your hands—knitting, gardening, coloring—can be soothing. Writing letters and journaling can be comforting. Exercise can be helpful. Extra sleep can be necessary.

✳ You are the guardian of your grief. Be incredibly kind to yourself. Set limits where you need them. Do only what you feel up to doing. Go back to work part-time to ease your way in.

In the Heart:

✳ I allow the feelings of every stage of my life to move through me with compassion and without judgment. I am at peace where I am today.

～✲～

Mending with Kindness

Kind words are a gift of healing. —*Tiny Guru*

When my mother spoke this phrase to me—*Kind words are a gift of healing*—I was moved by the idea that kind words were a gift *and* had the power to heal.

I could see the words surrounded in light and knitting together a hole in the heart where self-esteem should be. I could see the words becoming the salve that finally prompts the mending of a wound that would not heal.

Our words wield power, especially the beautiful, kind ones. We lose nothing by spreading them generously throughout our day, and as these loving beams of light come through us to others, we find ourselves in the path of that gift of healing too.

Look for the possibilities, the chances, the openings, the opportunities, the small words, the humble moments—to be kind. Make a habit of formulating words of kindness, and allow them to replace other thought habits.

Instead of negative words that might open wounds in ourselves and others, let's contribute to the healing of hearts and of our world.

We mend and we knit with one kind word at a time.

In the World:

＊ Ask: *How can I be kind today?* Imagine what kind words would lift your spirits and gift them to others. Keep it simple and real.

＊ If you know someone is in a challenging situation, offer words of encouragement.

＊ Consider volunteering for a group of people who are going through a life experience that you have been through. Kind words from someone who is farther along the road can be especially helpful and healing.

In the Heart:

＊ Kind words flow from me naturally to those who need them most.

⌣⅃⌣

Archangel Prayers

You don't have to do it all alone. Ask your angels.

Archangels are radiant healers and protectors in the higher realm of angels. They assist us in meeting the challenges of our lives and help us to deepen our spirituality, love, compassion and peace. There are many archangels, all messengers from God, who deliver important signs, guidance and the most tender loving care. The prayers below can support us in times of need. We are not praying *to* them as much as *through* them. Our relationship with the archangels opens us to their unconditional love and companionship in each moment of this day. They are here for us.

Dear Archangel Michael (Who Is As God): Please defend, protect and guide me as I face each decision of this day. Cleanse me of darkness and negativity, and keep me safe from harm. Lift the walls of doubt, fear and worries, filling me with strength, peace and divine wisdom. Remind me of my worthiness as a spiritual being and of my soul's constant connection with God.

Dear Archangel Gabriel (Strength of God): Please open my heart to messages of spiritual insight. Help me to clearly express my truth with kindness and love, and to creatively use this day in alignment with my divine purpose. Assist me in overcoming fear, and fill me with strength, love and grace. Guide me through changes in my life.

Dear Archangel Uriel (Fire of God): Please light the fires of illumination, and facilitate any necessary transformation and rebirth in me. Assist me in realizing my goals and aspirations, imparting ideas and insights that light my way. Guide me in unlimited possibilities, so I may be used by divine will for the highest good of all.

Dear Archangel Raphael (Healer of God): Please bring to me the divine light of complete healing—physically, mentally and emotionally—restoring me to my spiritual wholeness. Help me to activate my own healing and creative energies. Shine healing grace on all humans, plants and animals, and on our beautiful planet earth.

In the World:

* For the challenges that you now face, ask for guidance and assistance from the archangels. Invite them to keep company with you today.

In the Heart:

* Archangels are present with me, helping me to become my highest self and providing loving support in every decision of the day.

⌒ᐟ⌒

Inspiration from the Inspired

It is in doing what inspires you that you become an inspiration for others.

In 1873, American lawyer and Presbyterian church elder Horatio Spafford was detained from a family holiday in England. He sent his wife and daughters ahead, and the *Ville du Havre* was struck by another vessel and sank. Two hundred and twenty-six people, including his four daughters, died that day. Crossing the ocean alone to meet his wife, he wrote the beloved hymn of hope, "It Is Well with My Soul."

In 1905, Canadian-American writer Civilla Martin and her husband were visiting the Doolittles. Mrs. Doolittle had been bedridden for twenty years, and her husband had disabilities that confined him to a wheelchair. Yet, they brought inspiration to all who knew them. "What is your secret?" the Martins asked. Mrs. Doolittle replied, "His eye is on the sparrow, and I know He watches me." Her simple testament of faith inspired Ms. Martin to write the hymn, "His Eye Is on the Sparrow."

In 1994, during the Rwandan genocide, Immaculée Ilibagiza spent ninety-one days hiding silently with seven other women in a tiny bathroom in her pastor's house. She walked in a joyous student of 115 pounds and walked out at sixty-five pounds, alone, nearly all of her family murdered. During that time, she taught herself English with only a Bible and a dictionary, and prayed unceasingly. Once freed, she forgave those who killed her family and got a job at the United Nations, where she continues her work for peace, faith and forgiveness.

In 2012, at age twenty-four, Aimee Copeland was zip-lining when she fell into a river, gashing her leg. She contracted a rare form of flesh-eating bacteria that ultimately claimed both of her hands and feet. She says that her accident led her clearly to her purpose—inspiring others with severe disabilities. She shares her enthusiastic love of life, her powerful strength of spirit, and her faith in overcoming challenges through the Aimee Copeland Foundation and a constant stream of motivational speeches.

In the World:

✳ Today, we celebrate life. When we focus on what inspires us and share our enthusiasm for life, we are an inspiration to everyone around us.

In the Heart:

✳ With a heart of gratitude, I celebrate my life, despite my challenges.

October Blessings

Autumn leaves are reminding me to release and just let go,
to open space with ease and grace for miracles to grow.

Cycles in nature often reflect the wisdom of the soul. So on this first day of October, we turn to some important lessons from our friends the falling leaves. Just think about how they let go and float for awhile, how they release what is no longer needed, how they open up space for the next season, how they trust and let the divine take over. It might help us to aspire to be more like them—especially on busy days.

Inspired by the leaves, let's welcome October with a blessing that floats on the wind of this new month and new season of the soul:

May we trust that we can rest now to rejuvenate the soul. May we let go of what no longer serves us to make room for new growth. May we remember that there is spring and the light will come again. May we have the faith of nature, knowing that every ending is also a beginning.

Be present.

Let the day flow with grace.

Expect joy. Be positive.

Serve with compassion.

Speak only kindness.

Impart only love.

Never forget you're not alone.

Give thanks for everything.

See goodness in others.

In the World:

✳   Invite these thoughts into your heart as you begin this precious day.

✳   Choose a word for the month that inspires rejuvenation.

✳   Write some intentions for the month of October.

In the Heart:

✳   I release what no longer serves me, and I make room for new growth.

Love Is Who We Are

You are playing a sacred role that was created just for you.

I have long held on to the belief that we live in a benevolent universe where the power of good far outweighs the power of fear. In the relentlessly positive world that I envision, there is always an available beam of light shining out from the depths of even the weariest soul to illuminate the darkness. Mean-spiritedness withers in the face of kindness; hate and racism fold in the presence of love and truth. But the continuing affront to the heart by acts of terror on the innocent and undefended has even my beam flickering in the wind of change.

With each story of suffering around the world, we grieve for anguished families and friends, for shattered hearts, for communities. We carry deep sadness for the unimaginable tragedy endured by our fellow souls and their beloveds who live on. But a beacon of light calls us home.

Unspeakable acts of violence beg us to make decisions about what kind of energy we bring to the world. And ultimately, we have to choose where our focus continues to go. Do we make a conscious decision to bless the world and raise it up with our love, or do we feed the darkness with fear? If we choose love, our every thought, word and action will reflect our choice.

We begin the process of healing right where we are. We use our calm, our presence, our song, our joy and our most tender kindness to brighten dark corners. We use a voice of compassion, a heart of love, a prayer of faith and an act of benevolence to lift the vibration. We take daily actions toward building a more compassionate world.

Love, peace and prayer are not the stuff of spiritual lightweights but the greatest, most powerful forces in the universe. Our united message of love can become a massive beacon of divine light. We are together now for just this reason. Let's light the way, shoulder to shoulder, heart to heart, lantern to lantern. We can rise to this. Love is who we are.

In the World:

* Today, be the embodiment of love in thoughts, words and actions. Create a better world—right where you are.

In the Heart:

* I am an instrument of peace and share the highest vibration of love.

~v~

Gifts from the Garden

Friends are flowers in the garden of the heart.

Like a perennial garden, our old friends follow us through the seasons of our lives. They know our secrets, they know our families, they know our stories. They easily bridge the time and miles, supporting us during transitions and losses, diagnoses and dilemmas. These friends ground our lives with perspective; they see the whole picture through the lens of unconditional love.

Like annual blooms, our new friends beam into our lives as blessings, providing daily comfort and joy. These friends walk us through moves, marriage and divorce; they companion us through grad school or when we go back to school; they are the like minds from yoga, work, the neighborhood, church or volunteering. These friends bless our lives for a season and lift us up by sharing our day-by-day burdens and celebrations with understanding and grace.

Each friend is a flower in the garden of the heart, making our hearts home to exquisite beauty. Each flower is unique and irreplaceable. Each season is unlike any other, enduring time, bridging miles, rejoicing in common experience. Each friend is a treasure, entering our lives at the perfect time and place.

Thank you, dear ones, for making life infinitely more colorful and beautiful.

In the World:

* If you are feeling alone or in need of counsel today, call on a friend. They will be honored to hear from you.

* If you regret the lapse of a friendship, it's never too late to reach out. If it doesn't rekindle, know that some of the most beautiful flowers are annuals. Perhaps they have already graced your life in the way they were meant to.

* If you haven't found your people yet, they are out there. Open your heart to planting the seeds of new friendships. They will grow.

In the Heart:

* I am eternally grateful for the soul companionship of my friends. I bless them, old and new, for the infinite beauty they bring to my life.

Surprise and Color

Be in the moment and notice what is.

I just sat down to write and the shy paint horse Little Joe came right up to the fence, his white and brown patches brightly beaming in the pouring rain. My favorite cardinal flew in front of the window and sits on the eave of the cabin, tail fluttering right over my head. They are messing with my plan to extoll the virtues of an ordinary rainy day, throwing in a splash of surprise and color.

Now a blue jay has arrived and is perched on a high branch for perspective, while a tiny yellow guy is leaping and flipping from branch to branch, a goldfinch version of breakdancing. I'm laughing and wondering if it's a cosmic joke or just nature's way of reminding me that a lot happens when I really look.

But that's all we need to do, right? Just be in the moment and notice what is. When we don't project our mood onto this brand-new, shining day, we are open to surprises and delights. We respond as we are led to, listening with an open heart, loving all the way. We will know what to do moment by moment.

The only difference between an amazing day, an average day and a disastrous day is the way we think of it right here in this moment. And clearly, we can't assume what we might find in this moment, or the next, or the next. We arrive with an open mind and accept what is with gratitude. And usually, it's pretty amazing.

In the World:

∗ Wipe the slate clean. Assume only that this day will be a work of art and will unfold exactly as it is meant to.

∗ Offer up a note of gratitude for whatever perfection is about to transpire.

∗ Ask for guidance to keep you in the moment, to keep your heart light, to keep you blessed, safe and open.

In the Heart:

∗ Thank you for this most amazing day. I am blessed with whatever unfolds in my life today and accept it with an open heart.

The Highest Goal

Life is fragile. There is nothing more precious than love.

One of my hospice patients has lost almost everything. When she first received the devastating diagnosis of a rare degenerative disease, Claire was retired and living a joyful life in Florida, where she tended a garden of orchids and sat by the ocean with her feet in the sand, reading for hours daily. She treated herself to a set and style once a week, along with a mani and pedi. She had a radiant smile and an infectious laugh, and beneath that, she was strong-willed, brutally honest and fiercely independent.

First she lost motor control in her right foot and gave up driving. So went the salon, shopping and reading at the beach. Her son moved her up north to assisted living so he could see her daily and supervise her care. In that move, she lost her home, her dear friends and her independence.

When I met her, she was in a wheelchair, unable to walk for any distance. I watched as week after week she endured new losses. Her left arm, then her right, thus her ability to talk on her phone, change the TV channel, feed herself. A few months ago, she stopped speaking. I know. It's a lot to fathom.

And still, Claire's room is alive. Caregivers spend their breaks watching TV with her, painting her nails, doing her hair, doling out sips of water and bits of chocolate. They call her Mama Claire. On the outside, it seems as if Mama Claire has lost everything, but she has not lost her ability to love and be loved.

Psychiatrist Viktor Frankl, in riveting reflections on his experience in a Nazi concentration camp concludes, "Love is the ultimate and the highest goal to which Man can aspire." He goes on to say that when our only achievement is in enduring our suffering honorably, we can still find fulfillment through love. When all else is lost, love remains. We always have the power of love.

In the World:

∗ Imagine being Claire and how the power of love would manifest in your life. Know that if you were faced with an unthinkable challenge, you would rise to it with a strength you never knew you had.

In the Heart:

∗ I believe in the enduring and transformative power of my love.

Love at Work

May I approach all work in the spirit of joy and creativity.

Sometimes our work life gets the smallest portion of ourselves. Not in the amount of time we spend there, but in the amount of love and energy we bring to it. It's not that we intend to withhold our greatness at work, but we tend to look upon it as separate. There's work life and there's home life. There's the me that goes to work and the me at home.

When we lift up to a higher perspective, our work and our personal lives are one and the same. It can help to think of work as a chance to make an offering of our talents to serve a greater purpose; to arrive as our best selves, powered by unlimited stores of love, putting joy and creativity into every task. Tension and resistance dissolve as we relax into the flow of creation and the energy of accomplishment. *Use me,* might be the prayer.

Beloved Indian guru Paramahansa Yogananda speaks to the integration of our personal, spiritual and professional lives in his book *Metaphysical Meditations*: "I will do everything with deep attention: my work at home, in the office, in the world—all duties great and small will be performed well. On the throne of silent thoughts, the God of peace is directing my actions today."

When we bring to work the awareness of our connection with infinite guidance, nothing is too challenging. When we make a special offering of our work, nothing is ever boring.

When we work for a higher purpose, our work life and our home life unite as a ministry, anchored in love.

In the World:

∗ Treat your work today as an important ministry. Bring special attention to each conversation and to every task. Spread positivity, peace and joy as you go.

In the Heart:

∗ I approach all work with a sense of purpose and in the spirit of joy and creativity. I make an offering of the results of my work to something greater than myself.

~⤙⤗~

Meditation for Calm

I am filled with serenity and calm in mind, body and soul.

Most of us feel the effects of stress, sometimes first thing in the morning. So before we go any further, let's get off to a beautiful start by practicing this calming meditation with exhales longer than the inhales. Breathe as you read:

Inhale peace. Exhale stress, 2, 3. Inhale calm. Exhale worry, 2, 3.

Bring your attention to the breath. We can use it to calm the nerves, focus the mind and center the soul. Let's do this again:

Inhale peace. Exhale stress, 2, 3. Inhale calm. Exhale worry, 2, 3.

Great. Next we will reel in our thoughts. This gets a little tricky because they have a life of their own. So you have to hijack your thoughts from your mind and give them a new assignment. All they have to do is think these phrases on the breath for a moment. Thanks, Mind. Breathe as you read:

Inhale peace. Exhale stress, 2, 3. Inhale calm. Exhale worry, 2, 3.

That's better. Back to borrowing your thoughts from your mind—you can do this anytime but your thoughts are not going to stop playing around on their own. You have to give the orders and tell them it is time for a rest. Write yourself a note, set your phone alarm or do it on your lunch break. When the time comes:

Inhale peace. Exhale stress, 2, 3. Inhale calm. Exhale worry, 2, 3.

Now sit for just a moment with eyes closed and a quiet heart.

In the World:

＊ The big happy benefit here is that when you calm down, you connect more with the real you. When you're not in a spin, you are more authentic, you can feel your intuition, you can shoot off a focused prayer, you can look outside yourself and be present to the blessings. It's a humble practice with lofty goals.

In the Heart:

＊ Today, I am filled with serenity and calm in mind, body and soul. I use my breath to remain relaxed, healthy, focused and connected to spirit.

OCTOBER 8

This Glorious Day

Write through me this unwritten chapter of my life.

The special prayer *This Glorious Day* was penned during one of the most difficult times in my life, and I have said it every morning since. You can freely substitute the name of the higher power that you are comfortable with. May every aspect of this day be covered with the most tender and unconditional love, and guided by the gentle wisdom of spirit.

Divine love, come into my heart
and create with me this glorious day.
Walk through me
so I know where to go.
Speak through me
so my words may be of kindness and peace.
Pray through me
so I know how to assist.
Praise God through me
so I know how to serve.
Think through me
so my ideas lead me
to what you would have me do.
Be joyous through me
as I celebrate the beauty of all creation.
Parent through me
so I may be respectful and helpful.
Be a friend through me
so I may love and be loved in return.
Work through me
so I do my work in the consciousness of God.
Write through me
this unwritten chapter of my life.
Divine love, come into my heart
and create with me this glorious day. Amen

In the World:

✳ Say the prayer slowly, imagining each scene as it plays out. Write it in your journal or create your own prayer to add to your practice.

In the Heart:

✳ I invite divine love to act through me to create this glorious day.

~~✧~~

In the Arms of Angels

You can never go wrong with purple.

Aunt Sissy grew wings today. She took on a lightness that she never knew in her earthly life, nor, I expect, ever thought she'd know. Sissy didn't expect anything for herself. She was taught from a young age that she would not amount to much, and mostly she believed that.

But not when it came to her painting. During her best years, she painted with wild abandon, decorating furniture, walls, ceilings and canvases with a whimsical fairyland of flowers, trees, streams and wings. One weekend, she came to the house and painted vines interlaced around a gallery of family photos on the hall wall. Another weekend she painted flowers on Maya's dressers. She adorned shelves with angels and trees, and trays with fields and fences. She was generous, free and joyful with her paints.

She taught every child and grandchild that came to her tiny house to paint too. She let them make messes and was the first to laugh at accidents and spills. They could use any colors they wanted, and she would always advise, finger toward the heavens, "You can never go wrong with purple!" She told them that everything they painted was a masterpiece and that they were important and, oh, so loved.

You'd never know that Sissy suffered from severe depression most of her life. You'd never know that when the paintbrush was not in her hand, she was in bed watching movies through the dark sleepless nights. She lived the very difficult existence of not recognizing her irreplaceable beauty, light and power.

All that changed today. She grew wings just like the ones she painted countless times, and she's lighter than air now. All the dark has lifted, and she rests in the light of unconditional love. She understands what she came here for, and her radiant, magnificent spirit is in the arms of angels.

In the World:

∗   Remember today that there is no scale on the planet grand enough to measure the importance of your life in the world. Celebrate your magnificence.

In the Heart:

∗   There is only one love like mine. My talents are unique and valuable. My life is an irreplaceable gift to the world.

~\|/~

Love over Fear

I choose faith over anxiety, hope over worry, love over fear.

These simple words can serve us in two ways: as an affirmation and as a practice. When fears arise, affirmations can move us gently toward the light, even as we face the darkness. They make us mindful of our thoughts and of our choice to direct them with faith and hope. Choosing to do this, over and over again, is the practice. When worries settle in, we always have the choice to look at them through the eyes of love.

When we make an offering of our challenges with a brave, patient and open heart, we surrender to the highest possible outcome. With affirmations and the practice of faith, hope and love, we can turn this day into something beautiful.

Today I choose faith, and when I do, my anxiety dissolves and my focus becomes the right outcome for the highest good of all. I believe that all things are possible, and I trust that incredible blessings walk the path right beside impossible pain. I know that I will live through this, thrive through this, become new through this. Today I choose faith.

Today I choose hope, and when I do, my worries retreat and my focus becomes a better outcome, one beyond my ability to see. I imagine a future where my concerns are solved with the ever-present support of spirit. I surrender my need to control, and I offer my problems, great and small, to divine guidance, knowing I am heard. Today I choose hope.

Today I choose love, and when I do, my fears fade and my focus becomes seeing all things through the eyes of love. Every decision I make today comes from a heart of love. Every thought I think today is sent out on the wings of love. I have nothing to fear. I am an eternal being, and by the power of love, all things can be solved. Today I choose love.

In the World:

✳ When you recognize signs of doubt and fear, stop and recite this calming prayer from Julian of Norwich: *All shall be well, and all shall be well, and all manner of thing shall be well.*

✳ Send light and imagine the highest outcome for all concerned. Then let it go and open your heart to the possibility of perfect solutions.

In the Heart:

✳ I choose faith over anxiety, hope over worry and love over fear.

Give Kindness Wings

We never know where our kindness might go.

The small everyday act of kindness that you shared didn't end with the act itself. It went right into the grocery store and on to the cashier. From the cashier it spread to every one of her customers for the remainder of her shift.

It went into homes and traveled via conversations in kitchens and in texts through phones. It traveled by car and train, by bus and plane, where it flew over mountains and crossed over state lines.

From there it rained into lakes and rivers, where it flowed around turns and trees until it reached an ocean of souls.

Your kindness was heard by welcoming ears, felt by weary hands, tasted by hungry souls and it warmed needing hearts. From the hearts and souls, it went on infinitely like seeds of love on wings of flight.

It all got started when you carried the bag for the elderly man or held the door for the mother with the double stroller. It was all set in motion when you complimented a stranger or wrote a thoughtful note to someone in their season of grief.

It never stopped. You sowed the seeds of love, and they took off on wings of flight.

You gave kindness wings.

In the World:

＊ We will never know how our simple acts of kindness have been paid forward from heart to heart. Be generous with compliments, smiles and encouragement.

＊ Be on the lookout for opportunities to be helpful, expecting nothing in return.

＊ Be kind in your thoughts about yourself and all other beings.

In the Heart:

＊ Genuine kindness flows with ease from my heart to all who cross my path today.

⤳⥿⤳

View from a Boat

Beneath my thoughts, I am a crystal clear reflection of divine love.

In the land of dirt roads and one-lane bridges, my kayak and I got lost this morning finding a new lake, but the end result was stunning. Nestled between mountains was the stillest body of water I had ever been on. It was so clear that you could see all the way to the bottom from the middle of the lake. The surface was a perfectly smooth mirror, capturing the exact reflection of the fall trees that were towering red and gold above it.

This beautiful image of a still lake can be used to illustrate the mind in meditation with the image of the colorful trees as divine love. When our thoughts are active, there are ripples on the surface of the lake of our mind. It remains deep and it has the potential to reflect the trees clearly, but as long as the ripples are on the surface, the reflection is out of focus. Divine love is always present, but we don't provide a crystal clear reflection of it like the mountain lake I was on today.

When we calm our thoughts in meditation, the surface of our lake becomes clearer. With practice, we become more tranquil until we are an exact replica of the divine love that surrounds us. It's an amazing process and one that we can all experience.

In his journal from Walden Pond in the 1840s, Henry David Thoreau echoes the same excitement about meditation, how "we become like a still lake of purest crystal, and without an effort our depths are revealed to ourselves. Such clarity!" Yes, such clarity. And such peace and love. "To be calm, to be serene! There is the calmness of the lake when there is not a breath of wind... So it is with us." So it is with us. *We are that.*

In the World:

✳ With newfound enthusiasm, recommit to your meditation practice for at least five or ten minutes twice a day. Move up to fifteen minutes if you feel ready or add longer sessions on the weekends.

✳ In addition to countless spiritual benefits, you will experience decreased anxiety and negative emotions as well as increased memory and joy. You will be more focused, healthier, calmer and more joyful.

In the Heart:

✳ Beneath my thoughts, I am a crystal clear reflection of divine love.

Center of Gravity

I call upon divine guidance to show me how to take action without forcing, to work without pushing and to love without depleting myself. —Maya Davis

It's easy to get thrown off-kilter and lose our center of gravity when we have too much work and too little play, too much stress and too little calm, too many screens and too little nature, too much world and too little silence. If this sounds familiar, consider taking a seriously lighthearted look at balance.

I am not the poster child for this topic. Ahem. I'm the queen of overworking, blowing past lunchtime, scratching out mile-long to-do lists that no human could ever accomplish. For the sake of a little illustration here, that is *not* balance. However, I do recognize the perils of my overenthusiasm, and when I notice I've lost my center of gravity by working too many straight hours, I implement practices that distribute my time more evenly. One small step at a time toward equilibrium. And it works no matter how far afield I've strayed.

It only takes a mindful moment to remember to eat (good idea!), to take a deep breath, to connect with spirit, to ask for assistance from our guides or to walk outside. We can say *thank you;* we can talk to our angels; we can organize a bit of time to feed the soul; we can set phone reminders.

And we can do it all in the spirit of fun and enjoy the process of reeling in our adventurous minds and schedules before we flame out. No self-blame. It's all in a day's work.

Balance is defined as "the stability produced by an even distribution of weight." No problem. We know when we are tipping to one side. And we know how to come home to the powerful, magnificent center of ourselves again and again.

In the World:

✳ Be aware of areas of your life that are out of balance. Show self-compassion when considering how to cut back. Revive spiritual practices that are grounding for you: walking in nature, meditation, gratitude practice. You will know exactly what you need.

In the Heart:

✳ I am centered, balanced, joyful and calm. I take steps to restore equilibrium to my life.

~\⁄~

Peaceful, Joyful, Thankful

Believe in yourself and in the power of your dreams.

I'm going to get through this. No matter what today holds, I'm ready. I am peaceful. I am joyful. I am thankful.

I've got three positive thoughts to get the day going on a high note. That's all I need. I am peaceful. I am joyful. I am thankful.

No opinion of me matters except my own. I love myself unconditionally. I am peaceful. I am joyful. I am thankful.

I have dreams. I have goals. I'm not giving up on them and will hold them in my heart until they come true. I am peaceful. I am joyful. I am thankful.

I am lighthearted. I love my life, and I use each day as an opportunity to make the world a better place. I am peaceful. I am joyful. I am thankful.

I am strong, courageous and steady. I am confident in my abilities, and the right plans unfold for me with ease and grace. I am peaceful. I am joyful. I am thankful.

I matter. What I do today matters. I'm an integral part of the workings of the world. My energy is needed. I am peaceful. I am joyful. I am thankful.

I am guided by spirit. I am never alone. Unlimited support is available to me in every decision of this day. I will ask for assistance. I am peaceful. I am joyful. I am thankful.

In the World:

*   Any positive affirmations you choose for today will steer you in the direction of a better outcome—even if you're not quite there yet. Believing in yourself and in the power of your dreams is the first step.

*   Add some new affirmations to your spiritual journal to use on days when your energy needs a boost.

In the Heart:

*   I have complete faith in myself and in the benevolence of the universe. I open my heart today to all the blessings that will come my way.

Faith and the Fawn

In all things the spirit remains calm, steady, wise, strong and whole.

The squirrels are collecting and burying nuts; the horses are circling the field in the rain. The leaves are beginning the long slow process of changing hue; the wind is gently sweeping away the ones that have volunteered to fly first. All is well out my window on this fall afternoon, as if nature was born of faith.

And all is well with the spirit too. Even in dramatic changes and challenges, the spirit remains calm and steady. Even in confusion and indecision, the spirit remains strong and sure. Even in depression and defeat, the spirit remains wise and well. Even in our most profound brokenness and exhaustion, the spirit remains whole.

The other day as I stood on the split-rail fence visiting the horses, I saw two tiny fawns grazing on the other side of the field, sharing the space with their muscular friends, looking up at me with happy curiosity. Every few minutes they would jump straight up, bump sides in a midair high five, then frolic a bit and go back to grazing. The joyful little guys bravely migrated closer and closer to me, daring each other to go first.

I stepped quietly off the fence, offered them love, and started walking slowly back up to the cabin. When I got to the door, I turned to see them right behind me, with ears up, trusting, wondering, waiting. They were too young to be afraid.

They were born of faith, believing in a benevolent world.

And so can we be—open, patient, vulnerable—trusting that all is well with the soul. We have learned fear, but we were born of faith. And to faith we can return.

In the World:

✳ Remember today that the spirit is always complete and unbroken. Have faith that all is well and that this season of the heart is unfolding as it should.

In the Heart:

✳ I have nothing to fear because I am an eternal spirit, and through all experiences my essence remains calm, steady, wise, strong and whole.

~✓~

Namaste

The divine light within me honors the divine light within you.

Although I miss being in the community of a yoga class, in my soul my mat is right there in line with the group. Since being diagnosed with osteoporosis, I find it more comfortable to practice at home, where I can modify poses and tailor the practice to suit my needs. But wherever we practice from, we share moments of common expansion, creativity, compassion, grace, wisdom and joy. We are together in the yoga class of the heart.

I have discovered something in the last few years that has breathed a lot of life into my yoga practice. It gives me a great fullness, or *purna*, and contentment. It raises me up with a lightness of being. And it's perfectly simple.

I give it away.

Not every pose. Not every day. But when someone is on my mind, I offer them a breath. When a situation is troubling me, I offer it a pose. When the concerns of my heart or the needs of a friend join me on my mat, I surrender and bring them into the fold.

Yoga is the union of mind, body and soul. The word means *to join*, or *to unite*. The practice is one of movement on the breath. We bring all aspects of ourselves together in one moment using the breath as a tool of calm and focus.

What a beautiful opportunity to be in union with others also, directing some powerful love to where it most needs to go while easing the anxiety of what might be troubling us. Unity within ourselves. Unity outside ourselves.

More on this practice tomorrow.

In the World:

✳ Today, choose part of one activity to offer up to something or someone other than yourself. It could be your commute to work, folding laundry or your morning walk. *I offer this breath to...* Then send a few loving breaths to your intention.

In the Heart:

✳ *Namaste.* The divine light within me honors the divine light within you.

✦

The Sun Within

The whole universe is in my heart.

Before we begin any yoga practice, we take a moment to get centered and set an intention. I love this part. These precious moments set the tone for everything to come. First, let's get centered.

For me, once I'm seated on the mat, I imagine my heart as the center of my being. Right there in the middle of my chest, right here in the body of little me, is a spark of divinity. So instead of divinity being outside myself where we might converse during the day as friends, the whole universe is now in my heart. There is a brilliant golden light, pulsating with overflowing love and joy. I am the sun. No, *everything* is the sun. I sit and center until I feel this brilliant sun clearly.

We can close our eyes and give it a try right now.

Next, we set an intention for our practice. This is usually an internal vow to focus on a quality that we want to enhance in our lives. It can also be an offering—a gift to something other than ourselves. Our intention could be for a friend in need, for those who are suffering, for peace in our world. And with that, we empower the entire practice that follows.

As we talked about yesterday, we can offer our loving energy to a special intention with a single breath or pose, slowly, evenly, breathing into the light within and then out to the intention. Each breath is taken deliberately and with complete focus, as if honoring a precious guest. Compassion begins to draw us in, tie us to the breath, to all love, to service, to the joy of the unending circle of giving and receiving.

Sometimes I write down a list of names, but more often a name crosses my mind, and I flow with whatever images I have of those in need. On some days I offer one pose; on others it's a series of sun salutations. Sometimes a whole practice is for one person or situation, or for the world. It need not be planned. The right intention always arises and directs us to where it is most needed. More thoughts on yoga tomorrow.

In the World:

✳ Give the beautiful gift of your loving energy to yourself or someone else on your mat, in your exercise routine or during chores today.

In the Heart:

✳ I freely share my endless compassion and love with all other beings.

OCTOBER 18

Lift the Veil

We are one with all things.

On the surface it may seem that yoga is just a series of poses; however yoga postures *(asanas)* are just one of many branches of yoga leading toward enlightenment. Yoga is much deeper than the poses alone. It can be an opening to a world so vast that we might spend a lifetime exploring but one sandy beach of this mighty ocean. No matter how far we get in our journey toward enlightenment, the truth remains:

We are one with all things. We are one with the infinite. And it's all love.

It's easy to let that basic precept fade in a world that sweeps us ever more fiercely toward self-interest and self-defense. But every day we can choose to meditate on the infinite, to practice mindfulness, to approach stillness so that we might discover our true nature during this lifetime— that we are made of one divine love. And the source is infinite. The well will never run dry—there is always enough to share with those in need of love and healing.

Yoga on the mat can become yoga in the world.

All of the practices we use on our spiritual journey join to softly lift the veil that covers who we really are. When the curtain is moved aside, the beautiful light shining forth is your unique ray of divine sun. And that light is always at the ready to be shared with another precious being in the form of a loving thought. The well of compassion runs deep.

Share the love. Shine the light. And may we have the deepest compassion for each other as we walk this path together. Namaste and blessings.

In the World:

* You are a ray of divine love with the power to lift and to heal from afar. Practice using the breath to guide your soul's energy toward a specific intention. Begin in small ways with a few breaths. Expand the practice to other contemplative activities such as walking, praying, yoga or simply as a meditation.

In the Heart:

* I use the power of my love and light to share beautiful energy. In the process of sharing it, I recognize my oneness with all beings—great and small.

~ᵥ~

Gratitude in the Dumps

Fill the rooms in the house of your heart with gratitude.

Oh no. The dogwoods that were stripped bare by the hungry caterpillars think it's spring and are trying to grow new leaves. A black bear climbed the redbud tree to steal birdseed and broke the beautiful branch. Meanwhile, inside the house, Tommy called me, confused and slurring. The leaves, the branch and my heart are broken. And so opened the floodgates of brokenness.

Once there was momentum, all kinds of trouble ensued. I found myself suddenly in the company of tragedy and challenges, worst-case scenarios and fear. Which can be a healthy thing to do sometimes—to sit with the pain for so long that we are in it, one with it. It tells a story. It teaches and enlightens. It releases tears. It sets the compass to a new north.

Then there are times like this one when I really don't want to do all that. I choose to be done worrying for today. I've examined the pain, and I know it well. I've listened and learned and changed. I've offered my prayers, lit the candles, sent my light, taken the steps, imagined the best and have faith that spirit hears me. I want to feel better in this moment. *Now*, please.

And I find that gratitude is my way through. As I keep my eyes on the horses, the trees and the birds, I see beauty. As I keep my heart on abundance while cooking my meal, I feel blessed. As I focus on my work, I'm totally content. As I consider my health, my friends, my family, my music—I am grateful. So grateful.

And this gratitude does not depend on the leaves, the branch or my brother's health. It's something I make inside myself.

In the World:

✳ In the moments of today that beg for relief from troubles, turn your sights in the direction of beauty and abundance, reminders of the many gifts that render us infinitely blessed.

In the Heart:

✳ I look around me now and focus on the many ways that I am fortunate. I am blessed. I am content. I am grateful.

Forgiveness Manifesto

I release the past and let it flow out to the sea of my soul,
to blend with my waves and become part of my strength.

I want to be free and present in the only moment in which I can live my life: this one.

I resolve to stop reviewing past mistakes and missteps made by myself and others.

I decide to release the anger I hold that is directed at those who have hurt me.

I choose to trust in the goodness of the human heart while being aware of my vulnerabilities.

I believe that the universe is benevolent and conspires to assist me in the manifestation of my highest good.

I honor myself and know I am worthy of love and joy.

I unchain myself from thoughts that bind me to unwanted memories.

I open my heart to that which is loving and light, and leads me to the fulfillment of my purpose.

I declare that I forgive all past actions and request that any residual pain be reflected away from the light of my sun.

I release the past and let it flow out to the sea of my soul, to blend with my waves and become part of my strength.

I am whole. I am worthy.

I am light. I am free.

In the World:

✳ Forgiveness is freedom. Copy this out or write your own Forgiveness Manifesto in your journal in which you declare your intention to forgive yourself and others. The written word is a powerful mobilizer of our future goals and dreams. Be free.

In the Heart:

✳ I forgive all past actions and request that any residual pain be reflected away from the light of my sun.

~·\/~

A Worry Break

*May I let go of all I can't control and open my heart to receive
the blessings of this moment.*

We all know this—that we have the power to release what we can't control. But we can use a little reminding every now and then when we forget the beauty of our lives minus the weight of the world on our shoulders.

There is precious little that we have control over; most especially not the way other people act or what they believe to be true. We don't control the world or the actions of anyone in it, except for ourselves. Our work today is to be present, to create with love and joy, to take care of each other and to respond from a place of peace.

The habit of control gets sticky when we allow things that are outside our jurisdiction to take up residence in our minds for long periods of time. Our anxiety is often rooted in other people's lives and in decisions that they alone can make. We can't fix them. Meanwhile, our precious present moment is hijacked by worry, and the things we can't control end up controlling us. Not the outcome we are looking for.

Whenever we choose to, we can take a break from the negative cycle and release what we can't control. Simply set the burden down if a solution is not being crafted right now. If we are not actively solving it, we put it aside.

Then turn inward and notice that there is a new space in the heart. We breathe deeper. We become present to the moment we are in and notice that there is beauty right where we stand.

Within each of us is a well of peace that never leaves. When we open our hand and let go of the weight of the world, we open our heart to receive the blessings of this moment. And see that the peace we seek was right here all along.

In the World:

✳ Just for today, take a worry break. Practice allowing your anxiety or fear to take a reprieve, and focus your love on the activity of the present moment.

In the Heart:

✳ Today, may I let go of all I can't control and open my heart to receive the blessings of this moment.

A Higher Vibration

Surround yourself with those who reflect the beauty in you.

Ever wonder why some people feel great to be around and others, not so much? We all have an energy field that is in constant interaction with those around us, and their energy field is interacting with ours. The energy of those who are around us matters to the well-being of our spirit.

Whenever possible, be around honest people who encourage you, mirror your goodness and see the best in you. Your highest self shines through in the presence of people who reflect your best qualities and bring them out in you. These are souls who see your beauty even when you can't see it.

We don't always choose who we get to be around. Members of our own families or people we work with might not be so good at reflecting the beauty in us. With some conscious tools, we can make the most of our energy spent in the company of lower vibrations. It's good practice and gives us a chance to make a positive difference in our surroundings.

Always remember that the energy we project to people—and the energy they project to us—makes a difference. The strength of the vibrations we give and receive today can change our world.

In the World:

* When it's possible, surround yourself with those who reflect the beauty in you.

* Expect the best of people. For those who are close to you, imagine them as their best selves so they might rise to your expectations.

* Visualize yourself enveloped in white light and ask for protection when spending time with people whose energy feels low or dark.

* The law of vibration says that everything is made of energy, and energy always flows in the direction of the higher vibration. Keep vibrating high, and in turn, raise the vibration of those around you.

In the Heart:

* My highest and most beautiful energy is what I give to this day. I gravitate to people who bring out my best self.

Molding Love into Things for God

Use me today.
I am a willing instrument of love and peace.

Today we get to make something brand-new. It doesn't really matter what—we could make a birthday cake or make a deal or make someone smile with our kindness. Every single thing that we create today wasn't there before. Not the cake, not the deal, not the smile, not the energy we bring to this day. We are the creative tools of the divine, molding love into new things.

I often wonder if that might be what this whole experience on earth is for—molding love into things for God.

Brother Lawrence was a seventeenth-century Carmelite lay brother in Paris, known for the practice of finding God's presence in even the smallest task. He performed menial jobs in the monastery for decades, cooking and repairing sandals, keeping God in his thoughts at all times. For him, even the smallest action put him to use as a channel for God's love. When he was doing it for God, every lowly task he was given took on great value. People would seek out the wisdom of this humble brother because he exuded such an abiding peace.

If we were assigned a duty from someone we deeply respect, we would pay special attention to the smallest details, bringing excellence and our best selves to the task at hand. The work would be considered the highest honor.

Let's be used like that today. Let's be an implement, an instrument of incredible love. Let's be present and attentive as the hands of the divine, creating with tools of humility in the field of thanksgiving—molding love into things for God.

In the World:

* Consider being a present and attentive channel of divine love today. In every small thing you make, create something beautiful for God.

In the Heart:

* Use me today. I am a willing instrument of love and peace.

A Soft and Peaceful Blessing

Today may peace settle into your heart, may joy measure your success and may thanks rise with each step.

Today may peace settle into your heart.

May it soften the sharp edges of concern and loosen the tension around your seams. May this peace take up residence, quiet at first, hidden below the fray but faithfully there. Today you are aware of her presence. It releases your shoulders and lets your guard down. It tells you it's okay to relax—that it's safe here. *You can put your burden down*, it says. May peace settle into your heart.

Today may joy measure your success.

May it measure a small success, like enjoying a quiet moment for yourself, and a big success, like being kind to yourself in your thoughts for a whole day. May joy transform your experience, just for today, even in the face of small disasters, and allow you to laugh at the absurdity of life in those moments. May your happiness color this day with awe for the amazing beauty that surrounds you. May joy measure your success.

Today may thanks rise with each step.

Everywhere you look, may you see another blessing, with every footfall leading to another precious gift. May it bubble up and over the top—this feeling of being grateful for this and grateful for that. May it add up to a critical mass like a mountain of thanksgiving for the gift of your life. May thanks rise with each step.

In the World:

* Introduce a soft and peaceful blessing into your heart. No matter what the day brings, you will walk on the foundation of calm, joy and gratitude. Allow this special day to bless you back.

In the Heart:

* I walk through this day with peace in my heart, with joy as the measure of my accomplishments, and with gratitude rising with each step.

✦

Deer Independence

You have more strength than you know, more calm than you believe,
more power than you imagine, more courage than you dream.

A family of seven deer has been living in the woods nearby and visiting the field, grazing alongside the horses for a few weeks now. The stars of nature's show are the two spotted fawns, gleeful and adorable. Whenever I see them from my writing window, love leaps out of my heart and down the field.

Last week in the dark of night, I was awakened by a chilling, unfamiliar howl. It was joined by a chorus of what might be a pack of eastern coyotes—the coyote-wolf hybrid that have been seen around these farms. The next morning the deer were not in the field. For a full week, there was no sign of them.

Then one rainy morning, one of the babies walked slowly across the field alone. After grazing, he curled up, unprotected in the pouring rain and lay there for hours. I imagined the worst and wanted to save him.

Yesterday, *both* little deer, now losing their spots, wandered slowly past my writing window. Oh joy! The rest of the family joined them later after the young ones had exercised their independence. Like creatures great and small, they were learning the power of using their own instincts, strength and courage. The young deer on the field in the rain last week wasn't lost, only venturing out to discover the world on his own.

To grow spiritually is a little like leaving home. We treasure the field of spiritual wisdom that informs and inspires us daily, but we must also trust the wisdom of our own voice and venture out independently sometimes. We need to sit in a field of rain, open and alone, and let tears wash us clean. We need to face challenges and joys by listening to the voice within and having faith in that constant presence. We have all the power we need to find heaven on earth. And to find our way back home.

In the World:

✳ Just for today, put down the books and practices. Listen with focused attention to your inner wisdom. That *is* the practice. Have faith and follow your divine lead.

In the Heart:

✳ I have more light than I know, more guidance than I believe, more love than I imagine, more beauty than I dream.

~✔~

The Joy of Simple Things

May the joy of simple things color the canvas of your soul.

Sometimes joy shows up like the muted colors of dawn—soft, slow, gentle, serene. This is not the usual celebratory way we think of joy, but it's joy even so. This calm bliss can rise in us like the sun, awakening our souls to the awareness of our incredible good fortune.

We are alive.

An opening in the heart is all that is required. Even a crack, really, is enough. This awe can bubble up through this tiniest of openings at the sight of something beautiful like a sunset, a bird or a flower. It comes without asking; it comes without calling.

It's built in, this sense of appreciation for living. Like grace, we don't have to earn it, chase it down or be extra well-behaved. It creeps into our awareness and showers us with gentle joy unbidden.

Appreciation and joy are inseparable partners. If you have one, you have the other. Sources of joy, like sources of gratitude, are countless. Be present. Be open. Breathe it in deeply. Be in awe. Savor the moments.

These are your paintbrushes. Notice and honor the simple things, and you will have lifted the brush to the canvas and painted her with joy.

In the World:

* Take a look around, and bring to mind something that sparks joy. Count the simple and the small. Whisper a thank-you for the coffee, for the sunrise, for the birdsong.

* Bring this soft focus of joy with you on your daily round. Notice small blessings in new ways. Whisper thanks as you go.

* Notice how those around you become drawn to you and to your soul painting. Your joy is contagious.

In the Heart:

* I notice and appreciate the simple things and small moments that surround me each day and bring me joy.

~⟡~

Speak Love

Even in the silence of the heart, without a single word,
love can build a bridge.

A friend of mine who had been estranged from her sister and brother-in-law was nervous about attending a wedding where she would be seeing them for the first time in years. Hurtful things had been said, but the pain had mostly faded with time. She knew it was an opportunity to build a bridge.

Afterward she told me that although they seemed to have little in common with one another, she was overcome with love at the sight of them. She realized that she didn't have to talk about anything in particular, she only needed to speak in a loving way and that the *feeling of love* was silently spoken. They laughed, danced and built a bridge.

Last Friday after roller-coaster months of sobriety highs and drunken lows, Tommy called me, smashed. He was lighthearted, funny and child-like. I somehow had the grace to resist my urge to launch into a scolding lecture. Something told me to just be love. So I laughed with him, I let him tell some rambling stories, I encouraged him, and I'm sure he doesn't even remember making the call. But I know he received the *feeling of love* and that was all that needed to be silently spoken.

Love has many languages. They all hold the same power because love speaks volumes all by itself. When words seem inadequate, when you've done your best explaining and you're just not getting through, remember that love comes with a feeling that always heals, always empowers, always lifts, always endures. And can always build a bridge.

In the World:

✳   Sometimes people just need to be loved. Even when they have made mistakes. Even when they have been mean. Even when they get a tattoo that you don't love. Sometimes we just need to speak love.

In the Heart:

✳   Today I release my instinct to judge, and in its place, I offer a gift wrapped in the language of love.

~∨~

Awakening Together

We are one with the light of each other and one with the light of love.

When the earth turns away from the sun, we don't fear that the light has been extinguished. We know the sun is there; we just can't see it. In the same way, we can trust that the light of the soul cannot be extinguished. It's always there, always brilliant and always connected to the light of divine love and all other beings.

Together, we are travelers on the road to awakening. Every day, we discover ways of connecting with and giving rise to our eternal soul. As we progress, we begin to see that we are much bigger than we thought we were, recognizing our divinity as an integral part of our being.

This recognition of the soul self *is* the awakening. We see that we have the light of the divine within us. It's always there, even when our smaller selves are hard at work keeping the dark of night in place.

We are waking up to this knowledge together. We know that we are eternal beings in finite human form. We know that we are made of the light and that this light is a common aspect of all beings. We know we are one with the light of each other. We know we are one with the light of divine love.

Darkness is the absence of light, so the real work is to relentlessly shine the light of our love in all the dark places where it is needed. Eckhart Tolle says it this way: "You cannot fight against the ego and win, just as you cannot fight against darkness. The light of consciousness is all that is necessary. You are that light."

As we walk together in this global awakening, we will tip the scales toward a lasting good by the light of our spirits. We will stand strong in the light of love. We will shine on and shine brightly.

In the World:

✳ Recognize yourself as the beautiful light that you are. Use your presence, your joy, your calm, your peace and your love today to brighten dark corners.

In the Heart:

✳ I am a brilliant being of light. When I remember my eternal nature, I am able to bring light into the darkness.

The Path of Others

May I respect the path of others and refrain from thinking
that my way is the only right way.

Sometimes we feel really confident about the way we are living and the choices we are making in our lives. And with the very best of intentions, it seems like a good idea to weigh in on other people's lives on topics like diet, exercise, housekeeping, parenting, politics or religion. It seems like we know what's best for our family, friends and even strangers. We have great ideas of how we would propose to fix things if we were them.

And we try it out to find our efforts are met with anger or resistance, and it doesn't turn out the way we planned. Oops.

The only life we really get to make choices for is our own.

With regard to the choices of others, it helps to consider that maybe what we see as a misstep will be the gift of grace that propels them to their own right path. Maybe the challenge they face is necessary for their growth. Maybe they are just not ready or able to release the habit, anger, fear or grief just yet.

It doesn't mean we have to stay in the presence of dark angry energy, but we do need to respect the individual journey of all souls and refrain from judgment. We can trust that all is in divine order and remember that what everyone *does* need is support and encouragement, compassion and prayer, grace and a hot meal.

In the World:

∗ Always reserve the right to refrain from discussions on politics and religion with people you don't know well—and family for that matter.

∗ Offer support and be thoughtful about suggestions.

∗ Remember the power of prayer when it's hard to know how to assist.

In the Heart:

∗ I respect the path of others and refrain from thinking that my way is the only right way. I honor all beings and withhold my judgment.

~\/~

Step into the River

The river of amazing grace is always right here—
waiting for us to step in.

The river of grace is always right here beside us. Steady and strong, she is endlessly flowing, ready to offer her gifts anytime, anywhere. To allow her divine blessings to work through us, we need only to acknowledge her presence, open our arms and open our hearts. And we need to step in. Every request for grace is a baptism of sorts, a holy moment when we wash away our merely human skin and accept our need for a higher power.

After the *Speak Love* talk with my brother a few days ago, I was once again completely devastated and at a loss for how to help. I asked for the grace to lay it in God's hands. I wrote, "Thank you for bringing Tommy to complete health and healing," and I put it in the God Box. I prayed rosaries for him, imagining him only as his happy, healthy self, surrounded by white light. And I let it go.

Today my intuition nudged me to call him, and I knew immediately when he answered that he was sober. Without waiting for me to speak, he launched into an enthusiastic (from the Greek *en Theos:* in God) plan for his wellness. It was all the same stuff I had heard before. But this time *he was the one who asked for the grace.* He wanted to be in the river. This was his idea. He said it perfectly: "I realize that I can't do this without my higher power."

Grace. He asked for grace.

It seems counterintuitive, but it is in the moment of surrender that we are granted the power of spiritual assistance. We usually discover this when we are completely beaten down, desperate, knees on the cold hard tile. But it doesn't have to be this way. The river of grace is always right here—waiting for us to step in.

In the World:

✳ Set down your armor. Give up your will to do it alone. Let go of control. Accept the army of angels that is here for you. Step into the river of grace.

In the Heart:

✳ I open myself completely to receive the abundant gift of grace in every moment of this precious day.

~~◡~~

Liminal Time

May the heavenly power of spirit guide your every earthly step.

Many of the traditions we will take part in tonight were passed down to us from the Feast of Samhain, a Celtic New Year's festival that marked the end of the abundant harvest season and the beginning of the cold dark of winter. This very night was considered *liminal time*, when the veil between the earthly realms and spirit realms was very thin, allowing ghosts and fairies to roam freely. Food and drink were set out to appease the spirits—now represented by the treats handed out to small costumed sprites on Halloween night.

Liminal time, derived from the Latin word for *threshold,* is a time of transition, an in-between space where one thing has ended and another has not yet started. The dawn of the day is an example, when it is no longer night, but not fully daylight. It is a place that asks us to suspend doubt, having faith that the light is on the way.

The most exciting of all thresholds is the one between heaven and earth. It is the space we access every time we pray, every time we invite divine assistance into our day, every time we rejoice in the beauty of nature. It is the holy ground of sunrise and sunset, birth and death. It is in liminal time where great saints and sages, healers and mystics, Jesus and Buddha walked with one foot in the spiritual world and the other here on earth.

Even though we can't see it, the benevolent power of spirit is always present, always available, always assisting us from just beyond the veil. We can trust that the spirit of great love is roaming freely—on All Hallows' Eve and beyond.

In the World:

✳ After the candy is put away, the kids are in bed, the party is over and the screens are off, take a quiet breath to go within and use this night of liminal time to say hello to the divine ones who guide you. Ask all the hallowed ones for the power of spirit to guide your every earthly step, to untie your every knot of concern and to remind you of the radiant benevolence of that which you cannot see.

In the Heart:

✳ Powerful sources of good work through me from heavenly realms, assisting my journey on earth.

November Blessings

*May this new day go easy on your heart, be gentle on your soul,
comfort your worries and grow your hope.*

The days are growing shorter, inviting us to slow down and turn within in preparation for the holiday season. As our schedules become fuller, we can be mindful of keeping our balance. When thoughts of the future get worrisome, we can gently reel ourselves back to the present. When it all feels like too much, we can remember the divine always has our back. When we need help, we can send out an SOS in the shape of a prayer:

Help me to slow down and make space for uncertainty. Help me to trust in an outcome that I cannot see. Help me to lift my fears and point me toward a ray of hope. Help me to be grateful even in the unknowing.

As November sets sail, may we pace ourselves, ask for the help we need, hold on to hope and allow anxious thoughts to melt into a sea of faith.

Be present.

Let the day flow with grace.

Expect joy. Be positive.

Serve with compassion.

Speak only kindness.

Impart only love.

Never forget you're not alone.

Give thanks for everything.

See goodness in others.

In the World:

∗   Invite these blessings into your heart as you begin this new day.

∗   Choose a word that will serve as a lighthouse to guide your month.

∗   Write your intentions for the month of November.

In the Heart:

∗   I am calm. I am guided. I am blessed. I am creative. I am strong. I am resilient. I am joyful. I have all the help I need.

~~√~~

Your Life Has Changed Mine

You are always and forever in my heart.

The impact of a single life is immeasurable. No matter how short their time on earth, a soul is a soul, coming here for a reason with a mission and a purpose. Every person who has touched our lives and passed on before us changes us in countless ways. Their lives have been gifts to ours, and their essence lives on through our love.

The highest honor we can give someone is to recognize the importance of their time on earth and to offer gratitude for the indelible mark they made on our hearts. Ceremonies—even small informal ones—help us to connect with their memory after death. We can set aside time on their birthday or day of passing. We can visit a gravesite, prepare a special cake, light a candle, create a memory book, write a letter or simply take time to feel how we were touched and changed by their presence.

In the World: *Thank you for your life. You have changed me forever.*

∗ Thank you to our parents, who gave us life, who loved us the best they knew how and taught us the lessons we needed most.

∗ Thank you to our children, gone too soon, who broke our hearts by their absence, only to transform us into something new, richer and deeper for having shared the beauty of their love.

∗ Thank you to our spouses, the one who walked with us, the one who left first, the soulmates who live in our hearts.

∗ Thank you to our friends, who were companions on the road of life, who supported us through the joys and sorrows.

∗ Thank you to our ancestors, who braved the challenges of their lives so they might pass on a better way of life for us.

∗ Thank you to the brave men and women who gave their lives willingly in protection of our beliefs and freedoms.

∗ Thank you to our teachers, guides and mentors who expanded us and enlightened us with their wisdom.

In the Heart:

∗ Today I radiate blessings of thanksgiving to all the souls who have left this world before me. Thank you for changing me with your life.

~↴↥↲~

Drive-By Love

Lift up someone somewhere today.

I don't know many people in my little country town, but I know that Sharron is everyone's right-hand person. She cares for countless horses and maintains their stalls. She feeds dogs and cats when their owners are away. She takes care of the llamas and the sheep behind the inn. She takes care of her large family. And she takes care of me.

Yesterday, I set out on a walk at dusk, my tired, achy body and soul moving slowly under the weight of Sissy's memorial service over the weekend. Sharron's pickup truck slowed to a stop when she saw me, and I leaned in, relaxed by her easy presence. From under her baseball cap, her brown eyes inspected my face. There was no hiding.

"Just got back from my aunt's memorial service, Sharron. I'm spent." She reached out and held the hand that rested on her window. "I'm so sorry about your aunt," she said with such love that tears welled in my eyes. She told me about her friend Margaret's funeral last weekend, and how her kids spoke about their mother. She warned me to be careful walking; there were wolves spotted at the next farm. Rummaging around on the seat, she pulled out a whistle and tucked it into my palm. In five minutes, in the middle of the road, Sharron had taken care of my body and soul.

When I got back to my driveway, I stood still in the dark by the road and just listened. Under the half-moon, the birds sang their *good nights* from tree to tree, the horses quietly enjoyed a hay dinner, the frogs emerged around the pond, and I took my first deep breath in days. The world had righted itself. Love had cracked open my heart and diluted the dark with her light. In the presence of simple drive-by love, gravity released me into the welcoming arms of an unspoken, "I'm here with you in this moment."

This, I thought, *is the feeling of being lifted up by love.*

In the World:

* Today, in simple ways, be the love that lifts up someone else. Be lifted too, knowing that your love has changed another for the better.

In the Heart:

* From my deep well of love, I share freely with others, lifting them up through small acts of kindness and compassion.

Rebirth and Renewal

Speak to yourself as you would speak to your best friend.

I was once my own worst enemy, berating myself for things I'd done or left undone, said or left unsaid. Perfectionism run amok. I would hold on to my sadness and shame, as if they were life preservers in the ocean of mistakes. If you join me in being a harsh self-critic, or if you have made a life-altering mistake that is difficult to forgive yourself for, remember this:

Holding yourself hostage for actions of the past does not serve you. It won't right any wrongs, even any scores or facilitate any new growth. It dims the light of self-love, self-esteem and confidence. Negative self-talk is not humility, but a destructive force that hides the radiance of your organic beauty.

Self-forgiveness is merely an acceptance of our imperfection and an invitation to once again align with divine love. It's a process and a practice that brings rebirth, redirection and renewal. It's a chance to recognize our innate goodness and begin again. When we forgive ourselves and release regrets, we find the freedom to go forward and live the lessons we have learned, pursuing our passions with newfound wisdom and an open heart.

So practice a little love directed at you. We all make mistakes, and we are doing the best we can. Forgive yourself. Release it. Breathe deeply. Begin anew.

In the World:

* Be aware of negative self-talk. Notice the harmful dialogue and stop. Your heart is listening.

* Speak to yourself on a soul level. Use an affirmation or repeat the following: *I forgive myself, and I have learned from this. I have received the lessons. I release it now. I am a new person going forward.*

* Soul-to-soul forgiveness is helpful when there is another person involved who has died or is not present. Have the conversation with them anyway. Tell them what you are regretful about. Thank them for the lessons. Then release.

In the Heart:

* I release regrets and forgive myself for past mistakes. I honor lessons learned and the person I have become through my experiences.

~\/~

Ask Your Doctor If It's Right for You

Peace and love are the best medicine.

Oh what a beautiful day to share with each other a salve that immediately makes everything feel a little better. It's a prescription medicine that you can give under the radar, without anyone knowing, without appointments and medical insurance. It is a drug from the spirit for the spirit. Today we give out free Peace and Love to everyone who passes by the office of our heart.

In the World: Prescription Insert for Peace and Love

∗ Clinical Description: Peace and Love are organic compounds found in the spirit of every individual. In cases where a patient is worn down by the weight of the world, a few doses from a kind soul will wake up the latent Peace and Love within the spirit of the patient.

∗ Indications and Usage: This prescription is indicated at all times, especially on days of low vibration. It is particularly effective against negativity and hopelessness, complaint and feelings of lack. Administering Peace and Love in conjunction with one another compounds their effectiveness.

∗ Side Effects: Reactions may include but are not limited to: increase in gratitude, spontaneous singing, being kind to others for no apparent reason, joy as evidenced by smiling, laughing, dancing and a general amount of lightening up, as well as a notable increase in vibration. There are no contraindications.

∗ Dosage and Administration: The administering clinician first takes a few moments to acknowledge her own overflowing stores of Peace and Love. She imagines the remedy in her heart center, radiating out to a radius of about ten feet from the body. She can see the energy as blue, green or white, although pink and gold work nicely also. Administration is automatic; however simple thoughts like—*Peace to you, Claire* and *Love to you, Annie*—may increase strength and effectiveness. The patient will receive the perfect dose. Repeat as often as necessary.

∗ Ask your doctor if it's right for you.

In the Heart:

∗ I am one with divine love and have unlimited stores of light to share. I change the world today by sharing peace and love with everyone.

~ ⅃ ~

Book of Thanksgiving

I'm seeing the good and the gift of each breath.
All is well with my soul, feeling thankful and blessed.

When Maya was two, we started a Thanksgiving tradition. A few days prior to the holiday, we'd make a blank book from construction paper, a hole punch and some yarn. On the front it said, "I am thankful for..." and on the back we wrote the year. Then, surrounded by crayons, colored pencils or markers, depending on her age, she took her time over the following hours or days to write and illustrate one thing on each page.

The book was spontaneous, imperfect, messy and honest. Without prompting, the early books included God—drawn with white crayon in a tiny fist making a tight circle of light—Mom and Dad, milk, juice, her blanket, her favorite stuffed animal, the cat. As she grew, the books included friends, extended family, music, the moon, the sky. Simple things. Everyday things. The things that surrounded her all the time.

In the fall of each year, as we gather supplies for the current year's book, we lay out past books on the dining room table as a colorful and hilarious reminder of small special things—the gifts and blessings that graced each year. They are a treasure.

Thanksgiving is a day of gathering with loved ones, centered around a bountiful meal. It's also a chance to remember the sweet small things that bring meaning and joy to our lives every day of the year. Come home to your heart for the holiday, making an offering of your gratitude.

In the World:

∗ Make your own list in your journal or on the back cover of a recycled greeting card. Keep it going in the days leading up to Thanksgiving, adding to it along the way. Open to the idea that gratitude can extend to the intangibles of faith, hope, grace, love, compassion and peace.

∗ Help kids (yours, your nieces and nephews, kids at a shelter, kids down the street, your students) make a Thanksgiving book. Cut special paper in halves or quarters. Punch holes every inch at the top or along one side. Thread ribbon or yarn through the holes, adding beads or charms as you go. Get out your crayons and play.

In the Heart:

∗ I open my heart and offer gratitude for each small joy. All is well with my soul, feeling thankful and blessed.

✺

Waging Peace on Our Health

My mind is calm. My body is healthy. My spirit is joyful.

One afternoon, after a particularly stressful conversation on the phone, my mother had an outbreak of a strange illness. Her lips swelled painfully, her mouth became severely dry, eating caused a stinging sensation and swallowing was difficult. These symptoms came and went relentlessly for six months, during which time she lost weight and almost all interest in food.

She reluctantly saw five specialists, each doctor finding nothing and sending her on to the next. When she returned full circle to the first doctor, he shook his head and said he had no answers for her. "Well, that's okay," my mother replied. "I've decided I'm not going to have it anymore." Just like that. And the symptoms have been in remission for months.

What we believe about our health has a powerful effect on our immune system. If our approach to a diagnosis, a treatment plan or a diet is driven by fear, we miss out on the benefits of our loving inner wisdom. It's always a good time to make positive affirmations about our health. Make use of the toolbox within.

In the World:

✳ *My mind is calm.* Our bodies are constantly communicating with us. Take the time to be still and ask your body what you need to know. Ask what course of treatment is right for you. Ask what changes your illness or ailment is leading you toward. Listen. You will know what resonates with you.

✳ *My body is healthy.* We should spend at least as much time thinking of our bodies in perfect wellness as we do focusing on discomfort. Thank your body for its service, its health, its strength, its energy. The placebo effect works because what we believe to be true impacts our healing. Believe in your wellness.

✳ *My spirit is joyful.* Instead of waging war on illness, we can wage peace and treat ourselves with loving care. Do something that brings you joy every day. Laughter has been known to improve outcomes with no adverse side effects.

In the Heart:

✳ My mind is calm. My body is healthy. My spirit is joyful.

~~\/~~

Beacons That Light the Way

Blessings abound.

Beautiful gifts of insight come to us from those who walk the spiritual road before us—saints, gurus, prophets, sages, our spiritual heroes, mentors and teachers. Even a single thought or word from an enlightened master can spark an understanding within us, illuminating our path. There are men and women of all faiths who have spent their lives in pursuit of a personal experience of God, and their stories are like beacons that light the way for our own spiritual progress.

On the first of the month, Christians worldwide celebrated All Saints' Day, honoring the holy teachers who shared their journey to divine love. Saint Francis de Sales says that we can "unite our hearts to these celestial spirits and blessed souls" and learn from them like "the young nightingale learns to sing from the older ones."

May their simple and encouraging words remind us that not only saints and sages, but all of us, are on the spiritual adventure of finding the holy in the small and the sacred in the everyday. Small things. Great love.

Teach us to give and not count the cost. —Saint Ignatius of Loyola

Remember who you are and whose you are. —Sister Thea Bowman

Pray, hope and don't worry. —Saint Padre Pio

Be who you are and be that well. —Saint Francis de Sales

God lives also among the pots and pans. —Saint Teresa of Avila

For love is the beauty of the soul. —Saint Augustine of Hippo

All the darkness in the world cannot extinguish the light of a single candle.
—Saint Francis of Assisi

In the World:

* Consider reading some biographies of great teachers in your faith tradition. Incorporate into your heart the teachings that resonate with you and your personal journey.

In the Heart:

* I remember and honor the great teachers who came before me as beacons to light my way and deepen my understanding.

◝↓↲

The Value of Virtues

Find the frequency of peace.

I have no TV, radio or cell reception in the cabin, but the few hours a week I spend in the company of my car radio have me searching the stations for the frequency of peace. Political stress is all around us, and it feels more challenging every day to bridge the waters of the great divide.

Call it a new normal, but our souls know this is not *their* normal. In a famous poem, thirteenth century mystic Rumi writes, "Out beyond ideas of wrongdoing and rightdoing, there is a field. I'll meet you there." His poem goes on to remind us that the mere idea of division makes no sense to the soul. In spirit, there is no separation. So what's a *human* to do?

The coming holidays will bring us together with beloved family and friends with varying points of view in tow. Even differing philosophies and religions agree that good moral standards are inherent to the development of our common humanity. Here's a small recap of a few virtues that might come in handy when we are searching for Rumi's field.

In the World:

* *Courtesy:* being mindful of how we speak to people and giving them the feeling that they are valued and understood.

* *Honesty:* expressing our unique point of view truthfully and sincerely. Anger and cruelty don't usually help us express honesty.

* *Kindness:* showing that we care about the other person. It aims to assist and uplift, and to avoid hurting the other unnecessarily.

* *Tolerance:* accepting differences and understanding that our way is not the only right way. It is refraining from judging groups of people based on their appearance or beliefs.

* *Integrity:* having moral principles and a compass by which we steer our actions. It means if someone dehumanizes another in our presence or on our page, we speak up and explain the house rules.

* *Respect:* treating others with dignity and honor. When we respect others, they often rise and treat us in a dignified manner in return.

In the Heart:

* I treat people with respect, even those whose opinions differ from mine. I stand for my beliefs without harming others.

❧

Love Stayed Standing

Surrender what you can't fix. Offer up what you can't carry.
Have faith in what you can't see.

It's a most glorious day outside. A brilliant sky holds the warm fall sun, and a soft wind has the bright gold leaves dancing their way to the ground. The field takes on a radiant glow, and countless birds, large and small, drift by with no particular destination. It's pure peace outside my window. And pure torture in my heart.

Crashing again, this time harder and longer than ever, Tommy timed his drinking binge with a Sunday visit from three of his kids and their significant others. The resulting mess set off dominoes of pain, one by one knocking down the newly built and fragile blocks of hope, trust, forgiveness and faith.

I asked the questions within: *Are there times when grace is not enough? Are there problems that we cannot solve through prayer? What happens when we pray our hearts out, ask angels endlessly, implore the God of all things, imagine, lift, cajole, support—and the boulder insists on rolling back down the mountain?*

Olga assured me that all the prayers were heard, which raised me up to a new perspective. Perhaps the scenario could have been worse. And just maybe, his plight in this life is a gift for all those around him—an opportunity to practice compassion, to love beyond boundaries, to dig deeper into the understanding of unbearable pain, to respect the path of others, to surrender to that which we alone cannot fix.

Olga also suggested that I call him for the sole reason of telling him I love him. Which I just did. And in that small moment, our love radiated through the mountain, the boulder, the dominoes and us. Love stayed standing.

In the World:

✳ In impossible things, in unbearable pain, in unfixable situations, have faith, stay hopeful, and above all, show love.

In the Heart:

✳ My life intersects with all other lives so I might learn the lessons of unconditional love.

Trust in the Abyss

When you can't see the path, believe in the power of a single step.

Most of us don't like the feeling of not knowing where we are going. We like to have a plan that gets us to the goal by the quickest route. Living in the space between chapters of life is everyone's worst nightmare, prompting us to scramble out as soon as possible. It tests the limits of our faith and our ability to trust in providence.

When I was writing songs, I used to treasure being in the space I call *the abyss*. Being in the abyss means you have creative permission to *not* know where a song is going when you first start to write. It is trusting that if the first idea is allowed to come forth, the next, better idea, will present itself. If you judge too early, you miss the keeper line. Floating in the abyss sends out an invitation with no limits; whatever comes through you is equally welcomed and considered. Nothing is ruled out during this most valuable part of the creative process.

We all experience these times of in-between, where waiting for direction can be torture. Maybe we've outgrown our job, but a new possibility has not presented itself yet. We feel stuck in the abyss, not sure what will unfold for us next. We may be emerging from the end of a marriage, but new life has not yet begun. We feel unsure, every day in uncharted territory. Hey, wait! I know that story.

All of life is creation, and being in the abyss can be fertile ground. It is a time of listening and being open to every lead. It is a time of dreaming and giving yourself permission to welcome whatever flows through without judgment. It's a time to have faith that divine order lives even in the places where there seems to be no order at all.

It's a time of trusting that something beautiful is being created—even when we can't see it yet.

In the World:

✳ Send out an invitation to all of your guards and guides to light your path with clear direction and perfect timing. Listen. Relax. Have faith.

In the Heart:

✳ I give myself permission to trust what I cannot see.

~⁂~

Fearless and Filled With Love

I let my worries go so I can open to the good that surrounds me now.

The things we worry about are the things that we fear *might* happen. I'm not a big worrier, but for the sake of research, I took a scrap of paper just now and wrote down what I was worried about. I got eight things in about thirty seconds. So much for not being a worrier. Hmm. I don't want to admit to that. I don't want to live my life *afraid*.

I want to be fearless. I want to be courageous and unshakable. I want to face this day with the joy of believing in myself—having faith that with this brush of love, I will paint a most beautiful day. A masterpiece. Which is impossible to do if I'm afraid of all kinds of disastrous things happening.

I propose we transform our worries from a list of things we are afraid might happen to a list of things that we want to happen—changing worst-case scenarios into ideal end results.

So when the worries arise, instead of being swept away down the slippery slope of doom, we can think, *Our holiday travel will flow with ease and grace,* or *Send extra angels to Louis and Ryan.* When the familiar dark cloud settles in, we can say, *Bless me to finish this project on time,* or *Send healing light to Lu, Deb and Angelina.* If we apply this little rewriting tool to both thoughts and words, the worry list becomes obsolete.

We have talked a lot about choosing love over fear. Perhaps the best definition of *fearless* is to be filled with love. That's it. I don't want to live this day afraid.

I want to live this day fearless and filled with love.

In the World:

✳ Experiment today with transforming your worry list. Be mindful and diligent in converting what you are afraid will happen into what you want to happen. My one-woman research shows incredible results.

In the Heart:

✳ Today I transform my fears into ideal end results. I let my worries go so I can open my heart to the good that surrounds me now.

❧

It Is Good

Simply loving your life today is the most beautiful thing you can do.

Today we go easy; we start where we are. This day, as it is, is enough. *We are enough.* Today, we allow our possessions to be enough, our homes to be enough, our jobs to be enough, our families to be enough, our friends to be enough.

We embrace the beautiful gift of this moment in time.

And we simply love it. We love our lives, right where we are, right now. We become whole in our brokenness. We become whole in our gratitude. We become whole in our acceptance of what is.

Today is the unique place where our life journey has taken us. We breathe and give thanks for the breath of life. Look around and give thanks for every single blessing. The whole mess that love and loss has made.

Just love it completely.

Today, the most spiritual thing we can do is to love our lives fully. We find joy without asking for more. We give deep thanks with no qualifications. We open our hearts, raise up our hands, shake our heads and wonder how the heck we got so lucky.

We relax from striving and racing. We become whole in our smallness. We become whole in our pain. We become whole in our vastness. We become whole in our awe. We become whole with the Creator of all things.

Today, we step back and think, *Yes, it is good. This life of mine is so good.*

In the World:

✻ Just for today, rest in the acceptance of what is. Don't judge it or analyze it. Rest where you are in your heart. Allow gratitude to pour freely from your soul. Decide to love your life today. Just as it is. Especially as it is.

In the Heart:

✻ I focus on the incredible abundance and beauty that surrounds me now. Today I celebrate, with my divine ones, the gift of my life.

꠸

The Sparrow and the Envelope

Life is fragile. Love is eternal.

I witnessed a death this morning, and I am still shaken. Everything started out fine. As I sat at the window to write, a woodpecker flew straight to the roof over my head and peeked down to say hi to me. I laughed out loud. The Carolina wrens were being pretend roosters on the now bare redbud trees, singing for dawn. A ruby cardinal hopped down the path, and a flock of sparrows flew in to join the bird party.

It was during the sparrow commotion that I heard the sickening thud of my little friend flying into the window. I looked up in time to see where he landed, wings out and beautiful, in a thick pile of leaves. I waited for him to move. I prayed that he was not scared or in pain. I admired the miracle of his feathers and the enthusiastic wings that carried him on his flight home.

Oh life, how fragile we are. One minute we are playing with friends; the next, silent in a pile of leaves, soul in the next world. Which is why I am going to finish My Envelope today.

A few years back, I read an article about making end-of-life preparations that would ease the paperwork burden on loved ones. I downloaded a handy form, where I filled out information, noting where important documents could be found. I also downloaded a medical directive, which sits blank in My Envelope. I plan to include a few recordings from my songwriter days and a note for my daughter. Not a big time capsule, but a gift of making the paperwork of death a little lighter for those who are not enjoying the benefits of a stress-free afterlife.

Now, I'm off to a sparrow funeral. The program includes a few verses of "Amazing Grace" and a eulogy thanking this sweet bird for being an inspirational friend.

In the World:

✳ Consider starting Your Envelope or asking your loved ones to start theirs. I used a form called "Valuable Documents at Your Fingertips," and you can find a simple medical directive form for your state. Fill it all out, add something personal and fun for your loved ones, then tell someone where Your Envelope is.

In the Heart:

✳ I am brave, wise and compassionate in all ways.

Sparrow Turned Phoenix

Rise like the sun and give thanks for mornings,
miracles and second chances.

He rose from the dead! The little sparrow—he's alive! After writing the solemn piece honoring his airborne death, I dutifully donned my gardening gloves and rubber boots, and wrestled the shovel from the back of the porch closet. I rounded the corner just in time to see him hop out of his leafy tomb and compose himself on the walkway. He stretched out one wing, then the other. After a few hops, he flew to a low branch on the redbud tree, wondering where the bird party had gone.

No need for "Amazing Grace." He had plenty of that.

Not many of us will get to witness a resurrection, but most of us will find, over and over again, that our worst fears never materialize. Life has a beautiful way of continuing to give us mornings and second chances. Just when we think the story is over, we get surprise endings and miracles. There are all kinds of ways that we survive the dropping of the other shoe. Like the little sparrow, we dust ourselves off and carry on.

A variety of cultures look to the sparrow's larger mythological cousin for a hopeful symbol of new beginnings. The phoenix goes down in flames, only to rise from the ashes reborn, spreading giant wings of renewal and transformation. To the sparrow, that might be a dramatic analogy, but to us, it's yet another in a long line of comforting stories throughout the history of mankind that say we are not easily deterred. We have incredible stores of strength. We get back up.

As Maya Angelou wrote, "Still, like air, I rise."

In the World:

∗ When we don't know how the next chapter will end, we can look toward the clouds or we can look on the bright side. We can place our bets on the dead sparrow or keep an eye open for the risen one. We can be defeated or have inimitable faith and a happy knowing that today, anything is possible.

In the Heart:

∗ With a spirit of courage and strength, I have faith in the perpetual possibility of positive outcomes.

Tabula Rasa

May today be the dawn of a shining new beginning. I release the past and open to receive blessings beyond my wildest dreams.

Welcome to a new day, a clean slate, an open book. It features a sunrise that has never existed before, marking the dawn of a shining new beginning. Today is a *tabula rasa* made just for you. It is a pure gift.

Today is not merely a continuation of yesterday, but a chance to be just a little bit more: more patient, more compassionate, more joyful, more mindful, more forgiving. We can accomplish this incremental growth by taking a few moments each evening to give thanks, to review the day and to release regrets.

Saint Ignatius of Loyola, a sixteenth-century Spanish priest and founder of the Jesuit order, published a volume called *The Spiritual Exercises*, which holds one of his most beloved prayers—the Daily Examen. In this five-part prayer, we look over our day with an eye for its blessings and how they have changed us.

We can use the Daily Examen or our gratitude journal to end the day with a mindful offering of appreciation and a request for tomorrow's grace. This way we make each day a blank slate upon which to write our unique story in the best, most beautiful way. May your today be blessed.

In the World:

This version of the Daily Examen is inspired by Father James Martin and Anne Kernion:

* Presence: Allow yourself to be in the presence of God and ask for assistance with this prayer.

* Gratitude: Think of what in the day you are especially thankful for.

* Review: Review the day, being mindful of where you felt God's presence most. Recall feelings of loving and being loved.

* Regret: Notice what you regret and ask for forgiveness.

* Grace: Ask for a portion of grace for tomorrow.

In the Heart:

* May today be the dawn of a shining new beginning. I release the past and open to receive blessings beyond my wildest dreams.

◂〰▸

You Can't Take It with You

I live in the heart of all I have truly loved.

Soon after the sparrow died and rose from the dead, I got to work on my envelope. I updated the form, listing where important documents could be found, and dutifully filled in my medical directive. There were some squeamish moments in there—imagining my loved ones making decisions for me as I lie there surrounded by angels. Yikes. This is the ultimate reality check. But we forge on, spiritual warriors! We can get through this and it's a gift. Really it is.

After the forms were completed, I moved on to the fun part. I whittled my collection of recordings from my songwriter days down to just a few CDs and made some new covers for them. Into the envelope they went, followed by a little happy dance celebrating the completion of the packet.

Then a thought stopped me mid booty shake. Why would I wait until I'm gone from this earth to give Maya the songs from my career that I am most proud of? That seemed to be strange timing.

So I busted back into the envelope, took the CDs out, and sealed it back up. I wrapped them in tissue and gave them to Maya next time she came home from college. That felt better! A few days later, she called me to say she had been driving around with my CDs and really loved having them. She had questions about the songs and about that time in my life. By sharing a piece of what I loved, we opened up a new conversation between us. She's learning more about my heart and soul—*before* the angels come to escort me home.

In the World:

✳ Think about what you love that you might share with your beloveds while you are still here. It might be your favorite recipe, picture or gardening tip. Maybe a painting or favorite quote or prayer. Could be a pair of earrings, rosary beads, mala beads, your class ring. Half the fun is thinking about what you have loved that will live on. The other joy is sharing a piece of you.

In the Heart:

✳ I am an eternal being who lives on forever through the people and things I have loved in my life.

~⭒⭒⭒~

Autumn Horse Therapy

Every ending is also a new beginning.

I've been spinning since I got to Hunter's Road. Literally. Out on the horse field or down the middle of the street, I spin down the hill like a whirling dervish, arms out to the sides, laughing. Breathless and stumbling, I then raise my arms to the sky, welcoming guidance, delighted to be completely alone in nature, watching, listening, following her lead of growing and releasing.

Yesterday, after a spinning episode, Shadow and Brother Time were nearby grazing, and we struck up a conversation. We looked around and agreed that nature was putting on quite a show, with the whole field reflecting a brilliant glow of golden leaves. Spaced throughout were breathtaking splashes of neon orange and ruby red.

I mentioned to the horses that the trees were raining leaves that were spinning through the air. Sort of like me. With the slightest breeze, they would release what they had nurtured; faithfully filling the sky with floating investments in the future. Sort of like me.

"Hey, you guys," I said quietly to my friends. "Do you know that I'm releasing my old life? Leaf by leaf I'm letting go, making room for new growth." They nodded with understanding. Horses are the best therapists.

"Let's bless the leaves, then bless the space," I suggested. "We can bless the ending that will create the emptiness that holds the new adventure." *Good idea,* was their sweet, silent reply. Then Shadow, Time and I stood still in the golden world of constant motion, with blessings spinning and falling, trees swaying and releasing, encouraged by the wind to rain down leaves.

In the World:

✳ Think about what you might release to make room for new growth. Acknowledge your transition from one season of life to the next.

✳ Journal about what you are releasing and what you are inviting in. See if any of these items should to be added to your Gratitude in Advance practice from May 14.

In the Heart:

✳ I freely open and release all that is fulfilled and completed. I create an inviting space for future blessings.

The Eyes of Gratitude

The more thankful we are, the more blessings we see.

When in need of ways to lift the spirits, we need look no further than the practice of gratitude. Every time we whisper a prayer of thanks, we immediately transform the feeling of the moment from lack to abundance. The simple act of noticing the blessing shifts the energy from mundane to miraculous.

Waking up to another day of life is a magnificent gift. So we can start right there with a gentle and heartfelt, *Thank you for this day.*

Within this precious day will come countless opportunities for gratitude —small moments that might ordinarily fly by without much attention, small moments that offer choices and chances, small moments in which we can notice the blessings. *The sunset is beautiful today.* Simply notice. *I love the first sip of coffee in the morning.* Just take it in.

After we notice, we can acknowledge the gift by following up with a short offering of appreciation—*thank you*—and we begin to shift. This humble act of expressing gratitude opens our hearts to the abundance that lies within us and around us all the time. When we nurture this awareness, looking for beauty and miracles, we find beauty and miracles. The more we give thanks, the more blessings we see and the more abundance we feel.

Notice the gift and say *thanks* from right where you are, and watch how gratitude chases away the mindset of lack and makes sweet miracles of small moments. This vast perceptual change manifests through something as simple as seeing the world with a different set of eyes. The eyes of gratitude.

In the World:

✳ Use your journal to start or recharge your gratitude practice, writing three or more things you are grateful for every morning or evening.

✳ Use a kitchen counter note or calendar alerts to remind you to stop and be thankful for the gift of this moment.

In the Heart:

✳ Today I notice all of the small blessings that surround me. I am grateful for the countless gifts of beauty and love.

~✢~

A Little Soul Care

Take care of the soul that takes care of others.

Thanksgiving is just around the corner, and we're already as crispy as a deep-fried bird. This *can't* be good. The gratitude in the air can be sucked out of the room by lists that are worthy of a three-ring binder. Our morning practices are shortened in the time crunch, and our souls are in need of some serious tuning up. I think it's time for tea.

There will be no shortage of demands on our resources, so there's no time like the present to implement a little soul care to reconnect, tune in and calm down. This is when we ask for assistance in getting through the sticky note jungle of tasks. Yes, our soul care time is when we get the clarity and support to get through the day with joy, ease and grace. We should not have to function without our biggest source of support.

So when we get flustered and cranky, let's stop, drop and roll over to the nearest teapot. Let the world spin without us for a few moments. It's totally possible to get through incredibly busy, stressful days while feeling a center of calm balance. It is our natural state of grace. We can totally do this. We just need to put on our own oxygen mask first.

In the World:

* Whatever happens, don't skip your morning spiritual practice, which will start the day in the grounding presence of your divine support team and center you for all of your tasks going forward. During the day try implementing a few sweet treats for your soul.

* Take a tea break with some deep calming breaths as you retool your plan.

* Take a short stretch break on your yoga mat or a quick walk in nature.

* Use prayer, affirmations or a mantra as you work, cook, or walk.

* Play music that lifts your spirits.

In the Heart:

* I care for myself as well as I care for others. I treat myself with love, patience and respect, knowing that soul care is not selfish, but essential.

~\v/~

You Are Not Forgotten

For the grieving, a kind friend. For the discouraged, grace and ease.
For those in need, help and hope. For the troubled, a moment of peace.

Facing the holidays is especially hard for those who have less and the many who have suffered a loss or endured a tragedy. You are not forgotten and you are not alone.

If you are grieving, we acknowledge your loss and will remember your loved one in our hearts. We understand that a holiday table is an especially painful reminder of those who are missing. Make space for your feelings, allowing them to move through your open heart. Let your family and friends be of help.

If you are lonely, sad, sick, discouraged, in financial need or other trouble, we remember you today. May our prayers rise to meet you and lift you up to a moment of peace. May you continue to hope, in the face of all darkness, that the light will shine again.

We are here with you, in this moment, in spirit. We are all together at the table of our hearts.

In the World:

✳ Be gentle with yourself, and be the guardian of your time and your tenderness at the holidays. Do only what resonates with your heart.

✳ Don't keep things locked inside. Talk to a friend about your feelings.

✳ Find a way to honor your special circumstances this holiday season by lighting a candle, journaling, or sharing a story or picture online.

✳ Accept help from others—or be of help to others in need. There are countless ways to lift each other up at the holidays and beyond.

✳ If you have a friend in need, ask if they might want to join you for a holiday dinner. Consider a special way you can honor their story.

In the Heart:

✳ I honor my unique circumstances at the holidays, acknowledging my challenges in ways that make me feel most comfortable and comforted.

~⌣~

Gratitude Now

Being thankful isn't all about what's going right.
It's about finding a little light in this moment we're in.

During Thanksgiving week, we might gather around a table to share a meal with family and friends. But there's more. Whether we are alone or in a group, we also have a chance to give thanks for another year of living and loving. My wish for you is that you have so many things to be grateful for that you can't get your heart around it all. However, if this is not your finest hour, that's okay too. Being thankful isn't all about what's going right. It's about finding a little light in this moment we're in. The reverberation of gratitude expressed *now*, in spite of all we are feeling, is a gift for the future. Like an affirmation, it changes our trajectory and we find ourselves in a new story—one that transcends the darkness.

Gratitude now becomes a light, a beacon of hope. It shines into the darkness and illuminates the next step and the next. It brings the dawn to the dark night, takes some fear out of the fire. It's a lantern, a candle, a ray of sunshine that shows us the rewards of faith.

Gratitude now becomes a vehicle, our wind and our wings. It provides momentum when our lives have stalled. It lifts us up so we can catch the draft and sail effortlessly for a few miles. It's a jump start, an angel wing, a breath that gets us from here to there.

Gratitude now becomes an offering, our prayer and our song. It speaks of promise and sings notes that harmonize with our souls. It connects us to our highest selves and with the flow of grace. It's a familiar melody, a whisper, a prayer from the heart.

Gratitude now becomes food for our soul and connection with spirit. It feeds us with laughter and reminds us of our strength. It nourishes us when we are starving for good. It's sweet contentment, an inner smile and a reminder to give thanks for this moment we're in.

In the World:

 * Create a Thanksgiving that reflects your heart. You might open to new traditions, update the menu, simplify the table, light a candle for those you've lost, honor indigenous people. It's your day and your gratitude.

In the Heart:

 * Today I give thanks for my life, for the chance to love and for the wealth of gifts—all things great and small—that surround me now.

~᷍\/᷍

Lighting Up Black Friday

Be kind to anyone who crosses your path or crosses your mind today.

Dear Black Friday, are you really a thing? Do we have to lose half our clan to shopping on what could be a family-and-friends weekend? On the day after Thanksgiving, I want to stay in my sweats and glean wisdom from the matriarchs in the kitchen while heating up leftovers. I want to read a book and catch up with my journal under a cozy quilt. I want to play with the kids and take a long walk with the cousins. Oh, Black Friday, tell me it has all been a bad dream and that you will place the day after Thanksgiving back into the warm, welcoming arms of relaxation.

I know it's not going to happen. And who am I to judge the glory of Black Friday when I'm really not much of a shopper? For many, I'm sure there's a lot of fun and a nice dose of holiday spirit in the Black Friday shopping tradition. And offering a little extra kindness can make it even brighter.

If you find yourself out there among the other gold rushers in the name of incredible deals, you might take this golden opportunity to exercise some holiday cheer by way of kindness. As this is the official start of the holiday shopping season, it stands to reason that the spirit of the holidays should be present: kindness, love, compassion, generosity, joy, peace. These qualities are at the heart of this time of year, and they can bring big light into all your shopping adventures.

In the World:

* Consider ways to brighten your shopping experience with kindness. You can chat with others while waiting in line, share your unused coupons, offer a kind word to the mom with the crying baby, compliment what someone is wearing, let someone go ahead of you in a line, pay for the next person's coffee.

* In your mind, you can excuse the people who jostle you, refuse to let anyone else's behavior jar you from your calm kindness, bless people who seem to need blessing as they cross your path.

* For online and phone shopping, be patient, kind, and ask your spirit guides for help in making loving choices within your means.

In the Heart:

* I radiate kind, calm and compassionate energy, especially in times when those around me are anxious.

꒷꒦꒷

No One Shines Like You Do

*You hold within you all of the strength and grace you need
for all you were born to do.*

My niece Mary was a track star from a young age. She won countless long-distance titles and was being scouted by elite colleges as a sophomore in high school. But low bone mass led to a string of stress fractures, and eventually, on a sad spring day during her junior year, after yet another crushing MRI, she knew she had to take a break from running. Mary grieved as any of us would when we lose the very thing we are most passionate about.

Then one morning she woke with a thought: *Today is a special day. I will never have today again.* She didn't want to miss any more time being angry and disappointed. She was ready to face the day with a new kind of energy—one that focused on what she had instead of what she lost. Her circumstances did not change. She did.

We have within us the courage to face life's challenges. We have a choice about what kind of energy we carry with us. We can focus on love or focus on lack; we can embody a positive attitude or perpetuate a negative one; we can become a beacon of light or remain in the void. Sounds simplistic and it really is. We bring our energy with us wherever we go, and we decide what it's going to be.

If you are in fresh grief or a deeply challenging time of your life, you need to be with that. You will know when the time is right to take small steps toward trusting life. It doesn't have to be now.

When it is time to shine the light of your love, it will be an amazingly beautiful addition to the light of the world—and to your own life. We need you here, beaming beside us, raising vibrations. You might not be the old you, but there is a light within that only you can offer. No one shines like you do.

In the World:

✳ Be aware today of what kind of energy you are bringing with you. Make a conscious choice to be who you want to be going forward.

In the Heart:

✳ I cannot control the world, but I can choose my path forward. I choose love. I choose hope. I choose compassion. I choose gratitude. I choose peace.

꧁

Like a Who Down in Whoville

*May you be inspired by giving, changed by love, filled with peace
and touched by miracles.*

It was Thanksgiving, and I was in high school when my mother made a proposition to the family. Actually, it was more like a decree. She said that since two of my brothers were in college and the other two of us were in high school—and it was challenging to know what everyone wanted for Christmas—we were not going to give Christmas gifts within the family anymore. Instead, we would make a priority of spending time together at the holidays, and we would give special status to birthdays. It was a radical idea for the time, and in her gentle little speech, Tiny Guru stealthily stripped Christmas down to the bare wood of a manger.

I remember feeling like it was daring, trusting that Christmas would be wonderful even without gifts, sort of like a Who down in Whoville in *How the Grinch Stole Christmas*. I told a few friends, and they expressed their deepest sympathy, but secretly, my heart grew three sizes that year. "It came without ribbons. It came without tags. It came without packages, boxes or bags... What if Christmas, he thought, doesn't come from a store. What if Christmas, perhaps, means a little bit more." Dr. Seuss and Tiny Guru had us thinking.

We kept up our tradition, and even now I buy few gifts at Christmas, usually somewhat small and somehow meaningful. I like giving angels, ornaments and small framed prints of quotes that the recipient might like. I don't spend a lot of time or money. And if I'm not inspired or am feeling rushed, I make up for it later, and the right gift idea usually comes sweetly and easily.

A gift is only a symbol of love. It's a mirror of the light. It's a reflection of the brilliance. We are all just as whole and beautiful without them. So worry not about giving the perfect gift. That has already been given.

In the World:

✳ Don't sweat the gifts unnecessarily. Write a loving letter and wrap it up. Donate to a charity you know the person supports. Plan a lunch instead of a gift exchange. Each gift is only a placeholder for love.

In the Heart:

✳ I am inspired by giving, changed by love, filled with peace and touched by miracles.

I Am the Ocean

When we reach our limit, healing asks us for gentleness in loss,
patience with tears, kindness with the heart and hope for tomorrow.

Next week I will enjoy a sojourn in Florida and close on my house by the sea. In preparation, I traversed the long empty road to the house of my marriage with the goal of going over some finances and picking up a few pieces of furniture. Seemed simple enough.

We did well with our tender hour of untangling our lives, but when we finished our casual meeting, there was still an ocean of feelings left unsaid. The years we shared in that house floated in the air just above the kitchen table. They were in the counters, in the walls, in the pictures. *I need to let go again,* I thought. Our kindness to each other reminded me of our sweet and loving early years together. *I need to let go again.* Then came yet another unexpected wave of longing, yet another love letter of the soul to let go of. The beloved crazy cat.

Living with Ollie was like living with a beautiful wild tiger. He spent most of his life prowling outside, rarely sitting on a lap, and he had a very limited ability to accept love. But I learned how to love him mightily anyway, and he became my silent companion when I lived there alone. I am using past tense because he is dying. And seeing him for the last time undid me. It was too much to ask to let go of him too.

I thought I had handled the mountains of letting go, and still there is more. Maybe there will always be more. Maybe I am the ocean. I crash down in a broken wave on the shore of what was my life and wash away every footprint in my path. I am the ebb and flow of constant change. I am letting go, then I am receding back into wholeness. I am flowing forth with the moon of newness and rebirth, and I am ebbing into healing, quiet, relative stasis. I am erasing every footprint; I am creating new ones with each step.

In the World:

✳ The constant growing and releasing during big life changes can seem unending. Be patient with yourself in the ebb and flow of transition and transformation. Breathe deeply and feel it all without grasping.

In the Heart:

✳ I am strong and whole. Through the constant change in my life, everything I have loved still lives in my heart.

꿏

Your Old Self

I honor the sacred journey that has brought me to this day.

In the process of moving, sometimes we discover remnants of our old lives and pieces of our old selves that have been relegated to the past and all but forgotten. Just as we look upon our future selves with love, imagining that the best will unfold, we can look upon our past selves with love, not to dwell or lament, but to honor and offer gratitude.

When I went to the old house the other day, I carted out boxes of old tapes from my music career. There were lots of studio recordings, but also live tapes, which can be a tad scary to listen to. Feeling brave last night, I took out a random tape of myself and my dear friend and sax player Al Williams, performing at our decade-long house gig at a local restaurant. I braced myself for what might be disappointment. I was expecting "her," the old me, to be pretty rough, because I remember mostly her flaws.

But something very different happened. I listened with new ears. I wasn't critical or horrified. I marveled at our confidence and our unique sound. I could hear the hours of practice that went into the set and was amazed by the soul in some long-forgotten songs. We were having fun and playing our hearts out. I called Al, and we listened together through the phone, laughing about those times, those songs, about living the dream.

And I saw in that moment, that in order to love ourselves here and now, we have to love the person we once were, the person who learned the lessons, who was in the trenches, who made mistakes, who survived the pain to get to this point. We need to love her too.

In the World:

✳ Take a moment to thank the many versions of you that learned the lessons that brought you to this moment. Look upon her with compassion and unconditional love. Forgive her. Accept her. Invite her to be part of you. Honor her for paving the way to who you have become.

In the Heart:

✳ I am here in this moment because of every experience I have had along the way. I look with compassion on my journey from there to here.

All We Need Is Less

Simple joys can be our greatest earthly gift.

Sometimes all we need is less. Especially now. To be grateful for less.

If you're having a hard time remembering that this season of the year is filled with holidays that celebrate gratitude, light, love, rebirth, transformation, peace and joy, perhaps we can turn that around a bit, my friend.

We can reclaim this sacred time for ourselves and those we love by doing a little planning ahead of time. We can create some precious space for what feeds the soul and opens our hearts a little wider to the spirit of the holiday that we're celebrating. We can weed out what is depleting our time and energy, and make room for traditions that hold meaning, for practices that bring us peace, for friendships that give us joy, for divine connections that fill us with hope.

We can simplify and feel richer for it.

In the World:

Here are a few ways we might simplify the holidays and make more room for joy, downtime and togetherness:

* Refine the gift list, shopping and buying for fewer people.

* Connect with friends ahead of time and suggest not exchanging gifts. Plan an ornament exchange or a lunch instead.

* Aim to be finished shopping by mid-December with serenity intact.

* Bring out only the decorations that truly bring you joy.

* Think about the most meaningful way to send cards. Or not. Begin with enough time to send them, or hit send, with thoughts of love.

* Think about what nourishes your soul that you'd like a little more time for—music, reading, quiet contemplation, a special spiritual practice, time with family and friends, unscheduled downtime, traditional services, volunteering. Make time for the meaningful.

In the Heart:

* This year, I connect more deeply with the meaning of the holidays. I have time for what is joyful, loving, peaceful and light filled.

Advent Waits

Listening. Waiting. Patience. They are all acts of love.

It's quiet. The leaves have finished falling except a few that have held on the longest. I am in solidarity with them. I have waited a long time to move on with my life. In a few days, I close on my house. Then back to Hunters Road for a few more precious weeks of preparation before I make my move.

Often in life we find ourselves in wait, not there yet, but in a place of mystery, expectation and hope. It's not altogether comfortable to be in the space that precedes the main event. It requires patience while we watch and listen for signs. The fact is that most times when we are waiting, we are wishing the waiting was over and the next chapter would ensue already.

But waiting is not idle time or merely a void between meaningful places. Waiting has sacred purpose. Even our souls love preparation. The holy repose. The quiet that fills us and grows us, readying us for higher consciousness and deeper understanding.

When I was a child, we always had an Advent wreath in the house this time of year. Four Sundays before Christmas, the first candle was lit, carols sung, prayers whispered. The next Sunday, two. On the Sunday when all four candles were lit, Christmas was days away. It was an exciting natural calendar marking the patience before the celebration.

Our bodies and minds might be shopping, but our souls naturally want to wait. In this season of lights, we are preparing a place in our heart where rebirth takes place. Let's listen. And be patient. And wait. Let's open and receive, preparing the way—for new life.

In the World:

* Be still for a moment now. Allow yourself to thoughtfully examine what makes this time personal and special for you. You can enlist the help of a higher being to help you to find more depth in the holiday season. Make space to contemplate your sacred traditions. Your quiet time will add meaning to every gift, every party, every song.

In the Heart:

* I make space and prepare my heart for the brightest light.

~᷍◡᷍~

Rest, Dear One, Rest

To simply be is to do something very important.

When we step away at the height of busyness in a nonstop day, often we are gifted with the clarity, focus and flow to get back in the game and accomplish twice as much in half the time with more quality. In a society that values doing, it's good to remember that *to simply be* IS doing something. Something very important.

I know. It's a time of year when life just doesn't allow us to slow down much. A mere fifteen minutes with a cup of tea while the kids are coloring can shift things. A power nap can leave us refreshed and clear. Checking something off the list for today to make breathing room helps enormously. Taking a time-out to rest, however short, has benefits that will reverberate into the rest of the day.

My friend Jen is a nurse practitioner, mom of three and runs a popular inspirational page. She wrote today that she was shutting down the page for however long it took to "feed her soul." Maria, who teaches yoga non-stop and is the mom of hungry teenagers, always makes time in her busiest days for yoga nidra. When Lyndy burns out from her caretaker job, she takes a hot bath with an inspirational book. You can find Olga on a long walk in nature when she needs an oasis from her work as a teacher of yoga, meditation and Reiki. In the wise words of self-care leader Eleanor Brownn, "You can't serve from an empty vessel." Amen, my friend.

The actual *doing* that results from this kind of *being* comes in many forms. Below are just a few benefits to encourage you to move *being* up on your list today. It's not a luxury. It's a necessity. And maybe the most productive thing you can do today. Rest, dear one, rest.

In the World:

* During rest time, resistance falls away, so when we resume our tasks, our intuitive wisdom is readily available and solutions more visible. Rest serves our overall health, allowing our bodies to recover from stress. Downtime also brings renewed energy and vitality to mind, body and soul. Last but not least, a holy pause gives us the chance to ask our Spiritual A-Team for a little assistance.

In the Heart:

* I honor myself enough to slow down when my mind, body and soul need rest. I am precious and worthy of tender loving care.

December Blessings

In the middle of it all, wishing you a moment of harmony.

As we enter into the sacred stories and the winter solstice of December, let's continue the inner journey of grounding in soul care even when our days are full. The seeds of our love in the world are planted in self-compassion and self-love. May we create precious time for soul nourishment so we might shine like a candle in the darkness of someone's day. This is how all sacred stories begin. With love.

In the middle of it all, let's welcome a moment of harmony: the melding of separate parts into oneness. On busy days, when we feel scattered into many pieces, it's helpful to remember that in the precious present moment, we are always connected to the source of all wisdom and all love. *May we listen and allow guidance to lead us. May we trust and allow hope to comfort us. May we have faith and allow light to lift us. May we open and allow love to surround us.*

Be present.

Let the day flow with grace.

Expect joy. Be positive.

Serve with compassion.

Speak only kindness.

Impart only love.

Never forget you're not alone.

Give thanks for everything.

See goodness in others.

In the World:

✳ Invite these blessings into your heart as you begin a new chapter.

✳ Choose a word that will serve to light the way for your month.

✳ Write some intentions for the month of December.

In the Heart:

✳ In the middle of it all, I welcome into my soul a moment of harmony.

~v\~

Army of Angels - Part 1

Angels go where we go.

I finished packing the car in the predawn pouring rain, covering my computer and printer with towels and tucking them into the only available space in the car—behind the driver's seat. The back of my SUV was stuffed like a jigsaw puzzle, with bankers boxes topped off by my heavy and precious green kayak. I had only slivers of visibility out any given window, so my plan was to drive from Virginia to Florida in the right lane. Yes, things were a little iffy from the start.

Buoyed by the vision of closing on my new home, I was undaunted as I drove over the mountains in a blinding storm. I took my time, my tea was hot, and I enjoyed the relief of knowing that the hard work of this transition was behind me. That's when I hit a dense wall of fog. I couldn't see five feet in front of me for a long half hour in southern Virginia. Then there was the hour plus of stop-and-go traffic in North Carolina for some poor soul's vehicle fire.

As my enthusiasm was starting to wane, traffic began to move and the sun peeked out of some small spots of bright blue sky. *Woohoo! Smooth sailing ahead.* And just then, a car with two young girls pulled up next to me on the highway, pointing to the back of my car and mouthing the words, *Flat tire!*

Angels. I need angels, I thought. I remembered a beloved angel prayer: "Powerful angels are protecting you, your loved ones and our planet right this very minute. You are safe." I took a deep breath. An exit ramp appeared almost immediately, and I slowly made my way to the stop sign. There was nothing to the right. Nothing to the left. Scrubby wheat-colored bushes filled fields as far as I could see. I wasn't even sure what state I was in. I kept my mind silent and open to direction. And the answers came. (Stay tuned. To be continued tomorrow!)

In the World:

✳ In every decision we make today, let's consult with our inner voice—and our angels and our divine ones. We have access to all the guidance we need. Ask and remain open.

In the Heart:

✳ I embody more courage, more peace, more strength and more divine support than I will ever realize. I am growing into my spiritual energy.

꙰

Army of Angels - Part 2

I always know the way when I listen with a quiet and open heart.

I knew answers would be forthcoming, and I needed to be still. But I was painfully aware of my vulnerability. I resisted getting out of the car to look at the flat tire so as not to call attention to my aloneness—a small woman, traveling solo with a car packed to the gills, in the middle of nowhere—literally.

I started out slowly to the right and *immediately got the hit to make a U-turn.* It felt like a strong urge. Almost a voice but not quite. I listened and reversed course, rolling down the empty two-lane road until I spotted an old gas station sprouting up in the distance like a mirage. Pickup trucks dotted the dusty parking lot; men outside laughed and chatted. I pulled off the road on the far side of the station, wanting to stay under the radar until I knew what to do.

With an open mind, I turned over the options. I have roadside assistance, but the spare was buried under everything I owned plus a kayak, and the spare was not going to get me to Florida. Then *I got the strong feeling that my first step was to find out where on earth I was.* With a deep breath, I strode confidently into the old shop and asked the man behind the counter for the address. As he wrote, he looked up with kind eyes and said, "Are you all right?"

I replied steadily, "Do you have a mechanic here?" "No," he said, "but see that dirt road across the street? You'll find a mechanic down there." *It felt right.* I slowly bumped and prayed my way to the only building on that tiny road—the open bays of an auto repair shop. A cheerful mechanic wiped off his hands and took a look at my packed, limping car, shaking his head. "I'm so sorry. We don't do tires." But I *knew* there was a reason I was there. (Story ends tomorrow!)

In the World:

✻ Let's ask for guidance today and listen with an open mind for answers in the form of intuition, a kind stranger, a strong feeling, a song, a sign.

✻ If you get the *feeling* you should do something, follow your instincts.

In the Heart:

✻ I have access to universal wisdom through my intuition. I always know the way when I listen with a quiet and open heart.

~✦~

Army of Angels - Part 3

Angels guide me to perfect solutions with ease and grace.

The happy mechanic went on to advise me not to wait for roadside assistance as it was getting late in the day. "How about I put air in the tire and that will get you to the Goodyear place about two miles away?" His directions included turning left at Mary's Diner, which felt like a very good sign indeed.

A few minutes later, I turned into a tiny Goodyear shop at the edge of a small South Carolina town. A young man behind the counter looked up as I entered, and asked how I was. Like my other two angel messengers, he exuded compassion. It was just enough to melt my composure, and I dissolved into tears as I explained that I got a flat tire driving from Virginia to Florida. In my mind, I finished that sentence with *to start my life over after my marriage ended.* I was suddenly exhausted and could barely breathe.

"Give me your keys," he said. He started out the back door. "Don't you want me to tell you which car is mine?" I asked. "I'll find it," he said as the screen door slammed. Alone in the shop, I paced in circles as tears streamed down my face. These were more than flat-tire tears. These were years-of-tired tears.

About ten minutes passed when I had a stomach-churning realization. My car held everything of material value to me—all of my computers, my phone, my kayak—and I had just given my keys to a stranger. I ran out the front door to where I had left my car, and it was gone. I reentered the shop just as the young man was coming in the back door. He set my keys down on the counter and said, "You're all set. That will be twelve dollars."

I'm sure the people back at Mary's Diner heard me scream. The amazing army of angels had me back on the interstate in thirty minutes...flat.

In the World:

✳   When things go sideways today, suspend judgment and trust that an easy resolution is in sight. Believe it. Enlist the help of angels. Ask and listen. Receive and follow your intuition.

In the Heart:

✳   My angels lead me to perfect solutions with ease and grace.

~∨~

Choices at the Crossroads

I trust my inner voice.

By looking at the moments in the previous story where spirit interceded, we can see how it's possible to be transported from one helpful circumstance to the next when we ask for assistance and listen to our inner voice. The choices made at each crossroads can apply to almost any situation we might find ourselves in.

Listen to the call of spirit in your life to assist others. What if the young girls in the car on the interstate didn't tell me I had a flat? I hadn't heard the rumble yet. I may have passed the exit that held all of the solutions for me at that moment. Something compelled them to flag me down. Spirit works within us for the highest good of others too.

Trust and act on your instincts. They are always right. As I turned right at the bottom of the exit ramp, I had the feeling I was going in the wrong direction. I immediately turned around. If I had not, I would have missed all the angels who helped me. I may have missed the closing on my house. Rumi's wisdom reminds us, "There is a voice that doesn't use words. Listen."

Sometimes messages from spirit don't make perfect sense. Follow them anyway. As I sat outside the gas station deciding what to do, I could have checked Google Maps on my phone to see where I was. That never occurred to me. The clear message was *Go inside and ask where you are.* If I didn't go in, I would not have been led to the happy mechanic.

Trust your gut feelings. They, too, are signposts. I didn't have to trust the happy mechanic's plan. But as soon as he mentioned Mary's Diner in his directions, I got a zing and an overwhelming sense that all was well.

In the World:

* Today, in a moment of uncertainty, silently ask spirit to lead. The request can be directed to God, angels, spirit—whatever or whoever is your higher power. Then gently listen for direction. Let it be easy. Trust and act on it.

In the Heart:

* I thank my mind for its wonderful work, then ask it to take its marching orders from the inner voice of my soul.

Sanderling Gurus

Find the beauty in imperfect imbalance.

I am centered. I am balanced. I am calm. But it's the holidays, so no, not really. I have the nagging feeling that I should be these things at all times, which sort of adds to the imbalance. Maybe wanting to be centered all the time is not a realistic ideal. Do ya think? And perhaps imbalance has some perks.

I went to run things by my favorite little beach birds. Sanderlings are hilarious, bulbous little guys, teetering on stick legs upon which they sprint, leaning forward at lightning speed—like the Usain Bolt of the Sand Olympics. They have amazing instincts and timing, chasing the surf out as it ebbs, wildly poking around for a fresh meal, and racing back toward shore as the tide flows in, so as not to be washed out to sea. Down and back they run.

Then I saw that one of them had only one stick leg, hopping in rhythm alongside his friends. He was perfectly balanced, even when standing still—a little ball atop a stick, calm and steady. Oh no! There was *another* with only one leg! What happened here? Shark appetizers? A mysterious rash of Sanderling amputations? Then, a miracle. They untucked their other little legs!

I came to learn that, like other long-legged birds, they stand on one leg *on purpose* to save energy and retain heat. They get so comfortable on one leg that they don't bother to untuck the other one for a while. They practice balancing in challenging circumstances. What wise little Sanderling gurus.

So instead of wishing our imbalance away, maybe we need some time here on one leg, getting used to it. We can approach it as practice for retaining strength, facing challenges and increasing our joy in *all* circumstances. We can be open to surprises and soften a bit. Then when we put our other leg down and come back to full speed, we will know the depth of our soul's energy, and how truly blessed we were all along.

In the World:

✳ Be with your imperfect imbalance today. Find the beauty in it. Let the day flow with grace as it is, instead of as you wish it would be.

In the Heart:

✳ I am centered. I am balanced. I am calm. And if not, that's okay too.

~\⁄~

Saint Francis Returns

Love is the best gift of all.

Of all the kind souls on the planet, some are of the angelic, exceedingly thoughtful variety. They are those people who remember unique things about who we are and what we love. They are those souls who have a special knack for giving meaningful gifts that we treasure.

Dick and Helen are two such people. After years of spending their winters in Florida, they decided it was time to sell their second home and stay put in their native New Hampshire. I was the fortunate one who bought their home, just down the street from where my parents lived for decades. In fact, they knew each other back in the day, before Dad died and Mom moved inland to assisted living.

On the back patio of my parents' house lived a beautiful Saint Francis statue that was my nature-loving mother's pride and joy. He holds a cross and has a peaceful bird on his shoulder. Mom painted him a light chalk blue distressed with white, giving him a heavenly glow. She washed and blessed him often, and I'm sure he blessed her right back. When she moved, she gave the heavy, holy, cement mystic to her neighbor Ray as she no longer had a yard to admire him in.

Remembering this, the week before the closing on my house, Dick and Helen visited Ray, and they made a beautiful plan to relocate Saint Francis to what would be my new patio. When I arrived for the walk-through with my mother so she could visit with her old friends again, there was Francis, beaming his familiar love to us from the patio. Mom and I could barely breathe through our tears. Our hearts overflowed with gratitude and the honor of witnessing such thoughtfulness.

Love transforms little things into big things.

In the World:

* In this time of gift giving, we might consider what someone really values and finds meaningful: gifts of the heart, of the spirit, of love, of joy; gifts that reflect who we are and what we love. It may be something you already own.

In the Heart:

* Each day I become a kinder, more thoughtful, more mindful version of myself.

꙳

When Things Are Too Good

I am blessed. I am content. I am grateful.

I am a walking, breathing *thank you*. All of the small treasures of beauty and light that surround me elicit overflowing gratitude—every warm sunrise morning, each breath of salt air and glimpse of the ocean. Yet still, I am just a little "off." I'm not sure how to handle so much joy and alignment. Can things be *too* good? After years of struggle and challenge, alongside countless affirmations that all is well, I don't seem to know how to act when all is...actually well.

Maybe I need some joy therapy. Happiness practice. What is wrong with me that I can't feel the big dancing *Woohoo*!? I just bought the little house of my dreams, and it's about a hundred steps from the ocean. The previous owners left me countless beautiful things in a most thoughtful way. I have family close by, and it is the perfect place to begin my new life. Don't get me wrong—it's not that I'm not happy and exceedingly grateful. It's that I know there is another level of the *acceptance of abundance* that I have not allowed into my soul just yet.

Which got me thinking about something called *impostor syndrome*. That's when we question what we've earned and have difficulty believing we are worthy of our accomplishments. We tell ourselves that we are not deserving of what we have, and we resist owning our value, wisdom and worth. Perhaps that's it. Somewhere deep down, I feel unworthy. So I ask for the grace to offer deep gratitude while learning to accept abundance. I ask for the grace not only to believe in miracles, but also to receive them.

In the World:

* Ask for the grace to open and fully receive, believing that divine mind puts no limits on abundance. The limits are all in your mind. Release them.

* Ask for the grace to accept yourself, faults and all, as a person worthy of great joy, beauty, fulfillment—and dreams that come true.

In the Heart:

* Even when I am unable to reciprocate, I receive graciously. When a friend or God gives me a gift, I know my gratitude and joy are enough.

A New Standard

I make room for the joys of the spirit and the voice of my soul.

Most of us gain weight at the holidays because so much is on our shoulders. We are expected to be psychics as we shop online for the perfect gifts for our beloveds, sight unseen. We are expected to clean and decorate the house, host the family in addition to their pets, and cook for the troops while looking our brightest in an ugly sweater. We are expected to be the communications director, sifting through barrels of extra emails, texts and social media posts, wishing well to friends, extended family in other countries, and everyone we ever went to school with—in addition to keeping up with our real jobs.

Yes, despite our best poinsettia hair bands, we might be stretched a little thin.

So I suggest we revise our standards and allow the messages of the season—peace, love and joy—to serve as our guide. Similar to the Marie Kondo method, where an item is salvaged or pitched based on the joy it brings, let us consider each extra activity on our list and ask the question, "Can I do this while still retaining my peace (composure and calm), love (goodwill toward all people and pets), and joy (a good mood)?" If the answer is *no*, we have options. When we revise our standards, we actually lift our spirits.

In the World:

* Make shopping easy on yourself: an ornament, a gift card with a thoughtful note, something that you have or can make easily, a lunch in January, a donation, a loving letter, school supplies for a shelter. Start your list early next year, picking up meaningful small gifts along the way. Suggest ending or replacing the gift exchange.

* Remember you don't have to cook and bake *everything*. There are lots of premade options that will leave your peace, love and joy intact.

* Don't feel pressured to reply to every electronic card that comes in. Put them in a folder and read them at your leisure. They are a gift, not homework.

In the Heart:

* I respect myself enough to allow peace, love and joy to be the measure of my activities this week. I protect my right to make room for the joys of the spirit and the peace to hear the voice of my soul.

⌇⌇

Loving Messengers

Spirit speaks in ways that only the heart can hear.

I returned from my Florida adventure yesterday and took off for the post office this morning to pick up my mail. Deep in thought as I drove down Hunters Road on my way home, a brilliant red cardinal sailed across the street, nearly grazing my windshield. Oh joy! One small bird on one little road, and I knew that heaven and earth had merged for a moment. I laughed and sang out a hearty *"Thank you!"* knowing I was on the right track with what I was pondering at that moment. My cardinal always appears at the crossroads.

For many years, cardinal sightings have been spirit messengers for me. They have appeared as signs of hope, grace, faith, joy and confirmation of a particular direction or validation of a thought. Their unmistakable color and unique song catch our attention even in the most turbulent, distracted moments, and they bring us gifts of love from the spirit realm in all seasons.

The day my mom turned sixty, a cardinal visited her home and tapped on the window for the entire day. Since then, he has visited regularly at auspicious times and she sees her "angel bird" as a spiritual gift. A friend of mine had a cardinal turn up the evening her friend died, and she had the distinct feeling it was a sign from her friend that she was safe and sound on the other side.

There are countless stories of cardinals or butterflies showing up in prominent places soon after a death or when one is thinking of a loved one who has passed on. It's the feeling of *knowing* that makes these events especially significant, as the inner voice of intuition is our litmus test of truth. We know when something holds meaning.

Spirit speaks to us through an open heart, loud and clear, and sometimes in a beautiful shade of red.

In the World:

✳   Allow the comfort of spirit messengers into your soul. Nature, in communion with spirit, speaks in ways that only the heart can hear.

In the Heart:

✳   I am open to receive comfort and joy through the beauty of nature. What catches my eye may be a loving message for me.

꜀ᴠ꜀

A Gift from Spirit

Invite love to think through you today. Invite grace to act through you today.
Invite kindness to speak through you today.

Yes, spirit is always speaking to us with messages that guide our way. These messages arrive through "angel birds" and friends, through moments of silence and through our very thoughts. And *just* as I wrote these words, a cardinal flew into the tree closest to the window, singing an enthusiastic song of agreement!

In the days since Tommy's last drinking adventure, I have been considering a completely different tactic: to back off my phone calls nudging him toward meetings, sponsors and steps, and just offer loving-kindness and silent prayer. I have been torn, and it has been taking up space in my heart. I don't want to give up on him in any way, but I have the nagging feeling that my constant pressure is hurting his already open wounds.

This morning, as I sat at my writing desk distracted by deer, a frog chorus, a bigger-than-usual snake and some Carolina wrens and their mini-mes, I was clearly prompted by spirit to open a drawer in my desk that I hadn't cleaned out in years. My eyes went to a tiny gem, *The Pocket Pema Chödrön*, and I opened it randomly to a little story about one of her meditation students, Dan. He had been doing well with his drug and alcohol problem until a recent binge that had Chödrön quite upset. *Well isn't this a timely story*, I marveled.

"You should never have expectations for other people. Just be kind to them," her teacher Chögyam Trungpa told her. He said she should help Dan in small ways and bring happiness into his life by any means possible. He reminded her that setting goals for others is asking them to live up to our own ideals. Instead, we should just be kind.

That was *exactly* the spirit message I needed.

In the World:

✳ Pure unconditional love and kindness are always healing, always helpful, always welcomed. When in doubt, just be kind.

In the Heart:

✳ Today I notice when I am confusing my goals with the goals of others. I support my loved ones with kindness, right where they are.

꙳

The Soul Voice

We are one with all wisdom and love.

The flat-tire story is still in my heart, now more than a week later. It's a roadside example of what we all have access to—guidance from something greater than ourselves. *A Course in Miracles* puts it sweetly: "Let me remember I am one with God...for God is our Companion as we walk the world a little while." Or drive as the case may be.

We can actually live in this space of connection and clairvoyance. We are made for divine companionship. So let's take a closer look and reel in these lessons to serve as reminders when we next forget.

In the World:

✳ The soul voice that speaks through our intuition is available to all of us. We are each made of the same particles with a consciousness that can tune in to the frequency of universal wisdom and divine love.

✳ The clarity of this internal GPS is dependent on our ability to quiet the chatter of the mind. Once we turn down the static—and we *can*—positive messages for the highest good of all are more easily intuited.

✳ This connection with source is what we are always seeking: all love, all joy, all wisdom. Being one with God is not a grandiose idea or one reserved for the holiest of holy people. It's ours to experience now.

✳ We don't have to try hard to tune in; it's like an underground spring that bubbles up when we *let go* of the many details we feel compelled to hold on to and the countless things we want to control. It's like suspended animation, an exhale in which we trust the unknown and *allow* the guidance to come.

✳ In the space of listening, everything is holy. Our awareness is heightened, and every person, creature and thing plays a vital role. We see ordinary things in a new light. We stand taller, strengthened by newfound insight. Contentment settles in. We feel more generous. When the soul voice leads, an elegant harmony ensues.

In the Heart:

✳ I am always connected to the source of all wisdom and all love. I listen and allow guidance to lead me. My mind, body and soul are in harmony.

~\ /~

Mindfulness and the Send Button

Anger is multiplied in the presence of anger.
Anger is divided in the presence of love.

I almost hit Send last night on an angry letter, but in the nick of time, I was jolted out of my self-righteous coma. Thank you, angels.

A few times a day, I check my daily posts on four social media sites to see what's going on and answer comments. I'm sure you know that when a platform decides it's time for a change, things on your page can go sideways. Business pages have extra options that seem to change just when you've gotten yours the way you want it. On their behalf, I am grateful for the opportunity to connect with the precious community of souls that I love so deeply. But as a businessperson, it's uncomfortable when someone else changes what my community sees first.

Last night I opened one of my pages to find, front and center, images from over two years ago. I had ads running and wanted new visitors to my page to see current material. I tried to get rid of the dinosaur posts, but they wouldn't budge. So, I searched the problem, and there were pages of rages from businesses with the same issue. I read many of them, and it got me all stirred up. We talk here about kindness being contagious. Well, methinks anger is too.

Someone posted a direct link to give feedback on the matter, so I hammered out a scathing letter that started with, "Are you crazy? On what planet would a business want to be introduced with two-year-old photos?" As I read through it to edit my zingers, I thought, *What am I doing? There's a person who is going to read this. There's a soul on the other end who is going to get my blast of dark energy. Is this who I want to be?*

So, I added, "Dear beautiful friends: I really appreciate your hard work, but..." and that changed the whole tone. I signed off, "With love and light to you tonight." And no lie, ten minutes later, my page was fixed.

In the World:

* In all you write today, be aware of the way it might feel to be on the receiving end. Be peaceful. Especially in the line of customer service, be patient and compassionate to those who are trying to assist you.

In the Heart:

* I reflect peace and kindness in person and in the cyber universe.

~⥂~

The Playbook of Saint Nick

*May your holidays be filled with the spirit of joy, the wisdom of sight,
a heart of love and a soul of light.*

Saint Nick was a bit more fiery than jolly. Born in the year 270 to wealthy, devout parents who both died when Nicholas was young, he was raised by his uncle and became a monk, and later a beloved bishop in what is now Turkey.

It is said that from the time his parents died, he was devoted to giving away his wealth to the poor. There are stories of him as an anonymous benefactor, throwing bags of gold into windows under the cover of darkness. These bags sometimes landed in shoes and stockings left by the hearth to dry. He became associated with gift giving but was also known to assist sailors at sea, protect children who were in danger, and was a vocal defender of his faith, paying the price with long years of imprisonment. So many miracles are attributed to him that he was called, "Nicholas the Wonderworker." Saint Nick was love in action.

Bringing some wonder and miracles into our gift giving might be just what we need to fire up our holiday spirit. This fierce, compassionate, opinionated monk created his own playbook of living and giving. And this year, we can too.

In the World:

* We can fill the holidays with *the spirit of joy* by putting as much emphasis on enjoying our families and friends as we do on shopping.

* We can fill the holidays with *the wisdom of sight* by making space and time for personal contemplation of the meaning of the season in our hearts.

* We can fill the holidays with *a heart of love* by being miracle workers of thoughtfulness, giving within our means, and passing on by example some creative and loving alternatives to traditional gifts.

* We can fill the holidays with *a soul of light* by channeling Saint Nick through our generosity to those in need during the holidays.

In the Heart:

* I create space in my life for contemplation and define for myself what form of giving resonates with joy in my heart.

~\/~

Into the Hands of God

Be the strength, Lord, in my struggle. Be the dawn in my dark.
Be the calm in my chaos. Be the haven for my heart.

We need not carry our burdens alone for another day. Stop now and rest for a moment. Breathe deeply and exhale fully. Then put your pride aside, and surrender everything to your higher power. Surrender your mind, surrender your fears and surrender your darkness to the divine. Today is a new day, and you are not in it alone.

Surrender comes first. It is a humble act that brings us power far greater than our own. We step aside and let the divine take the lead, and on this alternate path, we become a channel through which unlimited clarity and wisdom can flow. We align with divine mind and become fertile ground for breakthroughs, miracles and infinite possibility.

We don't surrender once or twice, but over and over again. Any time we feel ourselves sinking under the weight of the world, we let go and let God. In every struggle, we ask for strength. In every dark night of the soul, we ask for the dawn. In every situation where chaos overwhelms the heart, we ask for calm. In every storm, we ask to be moored in a safe haven. It is through surrender that the comfort appears and the answers are made clear.

When we surrender our burdens into the hands of God, we are no longer alone, but lifted by a force of love far more powerful than our pain. We are always heard and always answered with grace.

In the World:

* Today, tear down the veil of separation and make an offering of your situation. Allow limited thinking to be replaced with calm, hope and light.

* Each time fear returns, surrender with a gentle prayer, having faith that a perfect plan is manifesting miracles for you in its perfect time. *Be the strength, Lord, in my struggle. Be the dawn in my dark. Be the calm in my chaos. Be the haven for my heart.*

In the Heart:

* I surrender my burdens into the hands of my higher power and make an offering of every part of my life.

❦

Be Amazed

Every moment is a sacred moment.

Every day we bear witness to the sacred as it spins by in the guise of a plain old everyday moment. It's in the sweet sunray that warms the skin. It's in the softly falling snow that blankets the earth in silence. It's in the full moon that shows her face at sunset as we carpool home. It's in the paint-chip colors of flowers and birds.

Maybe the sacred is a little harder to locate in overwhelming stacks of paperwork on the desk, in car repairs, in dental work. The sacred can be impossible to find in the pain of a child, the death of a spouse or a terminal diagnosis.

But there is love in the fabric of all things outside in the world and inside the universe of the heart. To locate the coordinates of divinity, the only tool we need is awareness. And maybe to gently remember that each moment bears the gift of life and the chance to love. This small moment, this precious day will not come again. We have never seen a day like this before.

If we turn our gaze ever so slightly and view our day as saturated in sacred sights and sounds, then this moment right here, right now, broken and messy, becomes a holy moment.

As Rabbi Abraham Heschel reminds us, "Our goal should be to live life in radical amazement, get up in the morning and look at the world in a way that takes nothing for granted. Everything is phenomenal; everything is incredible; never treat life casually. To be spiritual is to be amazed."

Maybe we could just listen and be held. Maybe we could stop and be present to what is right here, knowing that something greater is between the lines, beneath our wings, over our heads, at our backs. Right where we are on this hard, beautiful, amazing day, every moment is sacred.

In the World:

✳ Allow yourself to be amazed today. In the best and worst possible moments, be aware, be in awe, be grateful and be transformed.

In the Heart:

✳ I am thankful for this precious moment and for the chance to love. I look at the world in a way that takes nothing for granted.

Beautiful Small Things

Notice something beautiful. Appreciate the gift. Give thanks.

It's almost sunset, and I sit weary in pajama pants and my coziest sweatshirt at the little table outside. The sky is a dark ultramarine blue, and the sun has already caught the edges of the clouds, painting them orange and gold. The birds are starting their evening conversations—more relaxed, melodic versions of their morning songs. The tree frogs are revving up, and the pond frogs are croaking. A half-moon spies down on me from a perfect vantage point directly overhead.

The horses were on the field just moments ago, and I was excited for a visit to sort through the events of the day, but they have moved on. I need them now.

I circled this very table, round and round on the altar of this morning's sunrise, offering thanks. With my move coming soon, my gratitude for this place of sweet energy is overflowing. I drink in the sights and sounds with great love and thirst. I take pictures with my heart. I marvel at the gift. I am in awe of the inhabitants of this plot that I borrow.

But between sunrise and sunset swirled decades of memories as I made my last trip to the old house, carrying out, among the pictures and CDs, the box that holds my wedding dress and the container that once held Angela's ashes.

Now, as darkness descends on the field and on this day, as the nighttime creatures stir and their daytime friends rest, I stop and notice the beautiful small things. The beautiful small things that bring my heart home to this moment. The beautiful small things that resurrect my pain and lingering sadness. The beautiful small things that heal me, that bless me, that embrace me.

The beautiful small things that remind me of the gifts.

In the World:

 * When your energy is fragmented, noticing the sights and sounds of the small gifts of this moment can center your soul and bring you back to joy, peace and gratitude.

In the Heart:

 * I notice beauty. I appreciate the gift. I humbly give thanks.

Tangled Lights and All

Treasure the moments. Be present for the grace. Be awake for the joy.
Dwell in the peace.

My father was very nearsighted, so when he took off his glasses to don his yearly Santa suit, he couldn't see a thing. My mother, holding back laughter, would lead him from the laundry room, where the pillows were stuffed in and the white beard was attached, to the front door, where he would ring the bell like any polite visitor. Even though we had a fireplace in our California home, Santa always surprised us by appearing at the front door about an hour after my dad left for the hardware store. Sad how Dad always missed Santa.

After gently holding each of us on his giant knee and asking us if we had been good, he would give us our gifts. Santa then left out the front door with my mother stealthily guiding him to the homes of some lucky neighborhood kids. Flanders Road lore has it that one year, blind as he was, Santa waved and joyfully called out, "Ho, Ho, Ho and a Merry Christmas!" to a mailbox.

I asked Mom about this many years later, and she said they had so much fun doing that each year. We were four children spanning six years, so there was about a decade of Santa visits until the last no longer believed. Ten years of laughing their hearts out on Christmas Eve.

The holiday season is a chance to bring new magic to old traditions. Each time we sit to untangle the lights, unwrap the ornaments or decorate the mantle, may we be present to the traditions and memories we are making in our hearts now. Each time we hear the songs, bake the cookies and light the special candles, may we be surrounded by the love upon which the holiday was born. May we be awake to the joy that lives right where we are—tangled lights and all.

In the World:

✳ Slow down, even if the world is speeding up. Be present, even if the world is distracted. Let your heart be light. Treasure the moments. Be present for the grace. Be awake for the joy. Dwell in the peace.

In the Heart:

✳ I enjoy the precious moments of this season and celebrate love in all of the ways that it enters my life today.

Be Still and Know

Take a quiet moment, just for you, to breathe in the beauty, the radiance and the gifts of this precious day.

Let's take a deep breath and remember. Inhale. Exhale and soften. We are in the flow of grace, and all is well. We have access to all of the wisdom we will ever need, and this moment of stillness is a precious gift. It is our greatest investment in today.

Here are just a few of the reasons why we find peace in the pause:

It encourages a sense of calm and well-being.

It allows us to make more considered decisions.

It activates the soul's wisdom from which we are guided.

It reminds us of our expansive nature.

It calms the chatter of the mind.

It lowers our blood pressure.

It opens the heart to the inner voice.

It heightens our intuition and clairvoyance.

It allows us to release our worries and fears.

It reveals the beauty and serenity that reside within.

It provides clarity from which to imagine the highest possible outcomes.

It connects us with our divine source.

In the World:

✳ Your contemplative practice offers countless gifts any time of year. Meditation and prayer soothe the soul and transform you through daily practice. The rewards reach across all aspects of your being. Take a quiet moment today and remember. Allow stillness to enter your bones and unfurl your soul. Be still and know.

In the Heart:

✳ I have a calm center from which all wisdom arises. In the silence of my heart I breathe in the beauty of this precious day.

~\/~

Lessons Learned from Loss

You live in my heart. You walk on my road.
You breathe of my air. You dance in my soul.

Today is her birthday. My daughter Angela would be twenty years old. She was quietly stillborn except for the sound of Kathleen Battle's sacred collection *Grace*. I am sometimes asked by newly bereaved parents what the view is like from here and what follows are my ever-evolving lessons. Every walk with grief is unique. Take only what resonates in your heart.

In the World:

* *There was the me before loss and the me after loss.* Nothing from my previous life seemed remotely familiar in my new reality. I cracked into a million pieces and was completely disoriented. It was impossible to return to who I was. A new me was assembled.

* *I lost the illusion that I had any idea what my life would look like tomorrow, or next week, or next month.* When something happens so traumatically, so tragically, so suddenly, it blows away the false belief that we have control over anything in our lives. We don't. Those who know loss are in on this secret, and it makes us live more in the present. I still don't hang my hat on any future plans.

* *I am now intimately connected to everyone who has suffered any kind of loss.* The details vary but the bond remains. I know the crushing pain in the chest that makes it hard to breathe, the burn behind the eyes, the constant lump in the throat. When her heart stopped, I was an instant member of the club of compassion for all loss. I treasure the honor of being one with suffering.

* *My life is a deeper ocean.* Small inconveniences are inconsequential. I don't spend time on small worries or small talk. I have little patience for negativity and a greater appreciation of the precious nature of life.

* *As far down as I had slipped under the weight of pain, I can now tolerate more joy on the other end of the spectrum.* Pain is more painful, yet beauty is more beautiful, joy more joyful.

* *I love her as much as ever, and her memory is comforting.* She continues to change me. I look forward to her birthday as a sacred holiday. When I cry tears for her today, they are tears of indescribable beauty.

In the Heart:

* You are always and forever in my heart.

‍

Lightness of Being

Solstice Blessing: May the longest night of darkness bring rest and rebirth. May the growing sun of daylight bring hope and new beginnings.

Today in the Northern Hemisphere, we celebrate the winter solstice, which marks the onset of winter and the darkest day of the year. From this place of darkness, we hold on to hope in anticipation of the light and warmth to come. We face the possibilities of birth and rebirth, of blessings and miracles. We have faith that from this cold yet fertile ground will grow new life from seed to bloom.

The winter holidays of many faith traditions begin in the dark and use light as an important symbol of hope. Hanukkah is the eight-day Jewish Festival of Lights, celebrating the miracle of one day's sacred oil lighting a lamp for a full eight days. The miracle is symbolized by the nine candles of the menorah candelabra, which are lit on successive nights until all are aglow on the last evening. Christians celebrate the birth of Jesus in the forty-five-day season of Advent and Christmas with wreaths, trees and Nativity scenes illuminated by candles, lights and stars. A special candlelight service is held on Christmas Eve to welcome the "Light of the World." In the seven-day African American celebration of Kwanzaa, light is used to symbolize seven principles, with one candle illuminating one principle each night until all candles are lit.

These and other winter holidays fall at a time of relative darkness in the bleak midwinter. They begin in the dark and are illuminated one candle, one light and one star at a time. They symbolize a gradual awakening of hope, faith and possibilities.

The harsh brightness of the commercial holidays is, in many ways, the antithesis of these celebrations. This time of year is all about gentle faith in miracles. Stay with the light of your heart, and remember that now is the time to begin again in hope. Now is the time to begin again in peace. Now is the time to begin again in joy. Tomorrow, there will be more light. And the next day, more light. And grace pours in with the light.

In the World:

✳ Celebrate the return of light today by burning a candle to represent light in the darkness and the illumination of your awakening.

In the Heart:

✳ My heart sings in the darkness with hope for the new dawn.

❧

Saying Goodbye

It is written on my heart.

Leaving is hard. Endings are difficult. Moving is disorienting. Changes descend upon us—big changes in addition to the small ones that are pelting us all the time—sometimes catching us unawares. It is the nature of life.

Last night, I ran an errand in my tiny adopted town, the town that welcomed me when I finally made the break from my old life, the town of 185 isolated nature-loving souls at the foot of the mountains. Snow had just begun to fall on happy garland-covered street lamps, and the Christmas lights danced on familiar trees and historic buildings. The church bells rang as I stood still in the post office parking lot. I looked hard at the scene that I would not see many times again. I wrote it on my heart. *Stay within,* I whispered. *I don't want to lose you.*

I did the same thing when my daughter died. I took a picture in my mind, and I wrote it on my heart. I knew I could never forget those moments holding her because they were written within. Over the years, the ink dissolves a little and becomes part of our cells, our blood, our energy.

It doesn't go away. It becomes one with us.

We will all live through a series of leavings. Spirit takes us on a scavenger hunt toward our purpose, yet away from people, places and things that we love and that have altered us. Ultimately these people, places and things accompany us from their new outpost inside. Everywhere we've been, everyone we've loved—they are all still here, written on our hearts.

In the World:

✳ Remember today that you have lost nothing in all of the leavings of your life. You grow fuller and stronger because of where you have been and who you have loved. Your experiences and your beloveds will always live on in your heart.

In the Heart:

✳ I now honor the loving memories of those people and places that I have moved on from in my life. I bless them, I thank them and I carry them with me always.

꾸

The First Christmas

We have within us a North Star that always leads back to peace, love, joy and abundant blessings.

Once my family was invited to a nativity party hosted by some dear friends who have traveled the world collecting nativity scenes along the way. They had set them up on tables throughout the house, with tiny lights twinkling around them like stars. Some were bright and celebratory, some muted and gentle. They were crafted from a variety of materials from wood, to ceramic, to banana leaves. Some were huge, taking up most of a table, and some were tiny, with figures no more than an inch high. And they all had one thing in common.

They all expressed great abundance in the backdrop of lack. There was great joy, yet an absence of most of the things we associate with fun. There was radiant peace in the midst of what we usually think of as turmoil—exposure to the elements, no clean beds or running water. There was great love in the presence of displacement and division. Each nativity showed wealth in the setting of extreme poverty.

It's no wonder that we sometimes have trouble feeling the spirit of the season. The level of gratitude and humility in the first Christmas story is unimaginable. Today we expect, we demand, we desire, we climb, and when we fall short, we consider ourselves lacking. We are disconnected; our outward idea of abundance is not reflective of the riches within.

Having material abundance of any magnitude is not wrong. It is when we substitute it for inner peace that we feel empty. What we have is not *who we are*. We are unchangeable, a reflection of the divine child in the nativity scene. We are already rich. We have within us a North Star that always leads back to peace, love, joy and abundant blessings. When we lead from there, we *are* the spirit of the season.

In the World:

✳ Take a few moments to contemplate the simplicity of the original Christmas story and the seasonal stories of your faith tradition. Allow their power to connect you with how you want to receive the season of lights in your heart.

In the Heart:

✳ I am an unchangeable expression of divine love, rich with blessings, abundant with peace and filled with light.

~\⁣/~

Silent Night, Holy Night

All is calm. All is bright.

Christmas was fast approaching, and Father Joseph Mohr had a problem. As pastor of Saint Nicholas Church, he was responsible for presenting an inspirational program for his congregation at the Christmas Eve service. Music played an essential role in the Mass, and the organ at the church was broken and would not be fixed in time.

Father Mohr remembered he had written a poem several years earlier, about the night when the angels announced the birth of Christ. He took his poem to the local teacher and church organist Franz Gruber, and asked if he would write a melody on guitar that could be sung at the Christmas Eve service.

On December 24, 1818, in the tiny town of Oberndorf outside of Salzburg in what is now Austria, the new composition, "Silent Night," was sung for the very first time. The people of Oberndorf adored *"Stille Nacht, Heilige Nacht,"* and it spread to several other Alpine communities. It was soon adopted by two well-known musical families (think Von Trapp Family in *The Sound of Music*), and the song spread through all of Europe, where to this day it is often reserved for December 24 only, in a simple, candlelit moment at the end of the Christmas Eve service.

"Silent Night" has since been translated into hundreds of languages and dialects, and is one of our most beloved Christmas carols. Would this sweetly inspired song have come to light if the organ had not been broken? From what seemed like a problem, or at least a significant inconvenience for Father Mohr, rose a song of great beauty—and a Christmas gift to the world.

In the World:

* Today, may you be open to the unforeseen ways that the divine works through your life. May you approach your challenges as possibilities. May you see your problems as opportunities. May you be open to receiving answers in creative ways.

In the Heart:

* I open to the possibility that my problems are gifts to grow me into my potential and to add richness to my experience of life and love.

Comfort and Joy

Rejoice!

May today bring us simple things in simple packages. Easy-to-use things. Things we can tuck into our hearts that don't require instructions or batteries. Simple things like love and peace, comfort and joy.

It's a simple day really. One that is filled with innocence, humility and lack of pretense. "Isn't there anyone who knows what Christmas is all about?" wails Charlie Brown in my favorite holiday movie scene. "Sure, Charlie Brown, I can tell you what Christmas is all about," says Linus quietly and calmly. He's got this.

He drags his blanket to the stage and asks for light. (Which is a good idea for us today—asking for light.) Then with the lisp of a child and the simplicity of just another day hanging with his friends, he recites Luke:

"'And there were in the same country shepherds abiding in the field, keeping watch over their flock by night. And, lo, the angel of the Lord came upon them, and the glory of the Lord shone round about them: and they were sore afraid. And the angel said unto them, Fear not: for, behold, I bring you tidings of great joy, which shall be to all people. For unto you is born this day in the city of David a Savior, which is Christ the Lord. And this shall be a sign unto you; Ye shall find the babe wrapped in swaddling clothes, lying in a manger. And suddenly there was with the angel a multitude of the heavenly host praising God, and saying, Glory to God in the highest, and on earth peace, good will toward men.'

"That's what Christmas is all about, Charlie Brown."

May today bring us simple things in simple packages. May the holiday you celebrate bring meaning and peace within. May the love of the season expand in your heart today, tomorrow and each day of the year. May there be peace on earth, goodwill toward all.

In the World:

✴ Breathe in the love. Imagine arms wide, face toward the sky, feeling peace and gratitude. Relax your mind, bask in your spiritual practice and perhaps even listen for the angels. You have the greatest love—right here, right now. Allow it to enter your soul.

In the Heart:

✴ My heart is open to receive the simple yet radiant moments of Christmas.

Take a Moment

Inhale gratitude. Exhale love.

For the joy and tears, relief and exhaustion, laughter and overwhelm of the holidays: *inhale gratitude, exhale love.*

For gifts given and received, for the light in our hearts that they represent, for the joy they bring: *inhale gratitude, exhale love.*

For the baking and cleaning, for the songs and the smell of evergreen, for candles and cardinals: *inhale gratitude, exhale love.*

For meals celebrated, family and friends united, miles traveled, moments shared: *inhale gratitude, exhale love.*

For vacation days, a moment of silence, a change of scenery, an insight: *inhale gratitude, exhale love.*

For those gone before us, whose love is still present in the room and in our hearts: *inhale gratitude, exhale love.*

For sacred traditions and ceremonies that ground us to ourselves, our families, our community: *inhale gratitude, exhale love.*

For the expansion of our hearts into a higher and lighter consciousness of love: *inhale gratitude, exhale love.*

For faith and grace to magnify in our hearts and hold us in hope through the coming year: *inhale gratitude, exhale love.*

In the World:

* Take a moment for silence, soul care and the space to *just be* while integrating the gifts of the season.

* Spend a few minutes several times today to *inhale gratitude* and *exhale love.*

In the Heart:

* As I breathe in gratitude, I give thanks for the gifts and lessons of the season, seen and unseen. With each exhale, my love flows into the fabric of everything I do today and into the hearts of all beings.

Grocery Store Inspiration

Peace on earth, goodwill to all.

We know now that starting the day off on a high note provides momentum for the rest of the day. What if we did that on a larger scale, starting the year off on a high note, providing momentum for the year ahead?

In the checkout line at Trader Joe's yesterday, I asked my cashier how her holidays were. "I am *so* glad it's over!" she announced with a big smile. Her relief was palpable. Then she added something interesting. "What really saved Christmas for me was going to a midnight service on Christmas Eve. It was the only time I felt happy and peaceful. Just singing the carols with others, and the candles...nothing earthshaking really...but it was just what I needed."

A simple connection with spirit and with others, a quiet moment, candlelight, songs of love and peace—that's what rose to the top. It seems like these are things we'd want to keep with us after the holidays are over. So, I ventured a little further since I had a pretty full shopping cart.

"Maybe instead of those feelings being over after the holidays, we should skim off the parts we really like and use them to jump-start the New Year. This way we get to keep the extra dose of love and peace."

"I like that idea!" she said. "Me too," chimed in the woman behind me. We laughed, I took my receipt, and when I got out into the parking lot, I was sure I felt the extra love and peace of the holidays, now behind us, catapulting me into the New Year with joyous momentum on wings of grocery store inspiration.

In the World:

✳ Think about what part of your holiday season brought you a sense of authenticity, peace and joy. In busyness or in loneliness, through connections or through isolation, what made its way through to your soul? When did you feel most like *you*?

✳ Write yourself a short note listing these special moments from the last few weeks. Pack it with your holiday decorations, where you'll find it next year and be reminded of what nourished your soul.

In the Heart:

✳ Every time I feel peace, my peace is shared in the world.

꙳

A State of the Heart

May joy bless you. May hope inspire you. May love heal you.
May light guide you.

I wake at dawn, wrap myself in a blanket, and head out to soak in the last sights and sounds rising up from this sleepy, hallowed ground. Today is my last day on Hunters Road.

I nestle in at the little table, and everyone shows up for the going-away party. The woodpecker provides percussion while the breakdancing goldfinch flips around on the closest tree. Male and female cardinals dart by in flashes of crimson. Throaty croaks come from the pond as the rooster, who has it right this morning, acts as emcee, announcing the new precious day over and over again.

The tiniest hummingbird floats past and, after a few attempts, turns off her motor and sits still on a low branch. She reminds me of myself.

Chickadees, wrens, sparrows, crows, hawks—they all pass through with a wave. The horses walk single file up to the field to graze, my beloved Shadow leading the parade. I hear cows in a distant field and think of Abraham and my first months here. *Will I ever feel this way again?*

Come to think of it, I didn't feel this way when I got here. I was distracted by the endless decisions of moving away from my home and my marriage. But like the little hummingbird, after a few attempts I turned off my motor here on Hunters Road and I perched on a branch. I stayed still.

And then I started to see beauty everywhere in the tiniest of things, and a great love rose up. The more I loved, the more love flowed out of everything.

Maybe Hunters Road is not a place, but a state of the heart. Maybe Hunters Road is where gratitude heals things, where grace finds us and where hope rises like the sun.

In the World:

✳   For a moment, be still and take delight in the tiniest of things. Allow a great love to rise up and wordlessly expand in a heart of gratitude. Take a breath of new grace, new light.

In the Heart:

✳   Right here, right now, my healing and my hope begin.

~⥁~

Ceremonies

May your New Year be grounded in love and graced with blessings.

Acknowledging transitions with spiritual ceremonies can transform our very souls and magnify the powers of healing and gratitude. They mark the intersection of where we've been and where we are going, creating a clear sense of before and after. Ceremonies can highlight the blessings of lessons learned or mark a new beginning. New Year's Eve gives us a chance to do both.

A few years ago, when Maya and I were visiting family over New Year's Eve, we found ourselves in a hotel room after an early dinner with a few hours to go before we welcomed in the new year. We went out on the beach and gathered handfuls of shells. Then we made lists: On one side, we listed the events and feelings of the past year that we were ready to be free of, and on the other side, we listed the events and virtues we wished to call into our hearts for the year to come. With felt-tip markers, we tattooed each shell with something from our list, making piles of keepers and of those we were ready to release.

With pockets full of shells and stars as our witness, we carried out a little ceremony on the beach. One by one, we took each shell from the release pile, privately imagined what we wanted to release, thanked it for the lessons learned, blessed it and threw it into the surf. The freedom was exhilarating. We repeated the ceremony last year, and the shells lined up on my windowsill reflect my keeper visions back to me daily.

This year, my niece Hanna was visiting the mountain cabin, and we did a variation on the theme. We wrote our messages on smooth stones, hiked up a mountain, and threw them off. Sacred space was once again made for the blessing of new beginnings.

In the World:

∗   Create your own ceremony, and release the difficult blessings of the past year to create space for a joyful year of your highest dreams.

∗   Record a list of blessings to keep and release in your journal for contemplation next year as you create your lists anew.

In the Heart:

∗   I release the year that is now complete and open to the unlimited blessings of the year to come.

﹀ ⅃ ﹀

The Daily Masterpiece

Be honest. Be kind. Be brave. Believe.
Lead with your heart and follow your dreams.

On my last night on Hunters Road, I had a dream. It was a beautiful day, and I was driving up the winding mountain road that heads west. From a simultaneous aerial view, I could see the whole country, sea to shining sea, laid out on the other side of the mountain in her magnificent beauty. A masterpiece of infinite possibilities lay ahead.

I started driving as I always do—on switchbacks that snaked steeply through dense forest. Then I realized something new. *I could create the road as I went along.* With no warning, there would be a fork leading in another direction. A wordless conversation ensued. *Right or left? Turn or don't turn? Shall we make a brand-new road where there is not one?*

I was clairvoyantly discussing every decision with a powerful and compassionate force. We were painting the masterpiece together, and it was a work in progress. The whole scene seemed to be a tiny thumbnail of co-creation with the divine.

The most awesome thing of all was, there were no mistakes. There was no judgment and no stress. The entire journey up the mountain, with a palette of unlimited choices, was for the fun of it—and for the joy of painting with a master.

What if every day we are being given the chance to co-create a masterpiece with our God—a constant conversation, a give and take, a friendly companionship that lifts all limitations and raises us to a higher version of ourselves?

We choose. Remember, there are no mistakes here. But hey, it seems like a worthy experiment to see what works better for us—to create alone—or to enter the dream and paint with a master.

In the World:

✳ Make today an experiment with co-creation. Bring a divine loving force into every minute, every hour, every decision great and small.

In the Heart:

✳ I invite the infinite wisdom of divine love to create the masterpiece of this day with me. With every brushstroke, I paint with a master.

✢

We Fly

My bird, one day you'll fly from this place. I hope you'll take with you this song; I hope you'll sing it with your grace. Oh my blackbird, sing.
—Maya Davis

Here we are, sitting on the edge of the split-rail fence on Hunters Road, ready for flight. We are traveling light, empty of the weight of that which no longer serves our highest good. We look forward in faith, knowing that when we listen to the heart, we know exactly where to go. We have learned that everything we need for sacred travel, we have within.

We have all of the wisdom we need to navigate the journey.

We have all of the light necessary to illuminate our way.

We have cultivated stillness and assembled the tools of calm.

We have established a friendly relationship with God.

We welcome divine guidance into the small moments of each day.

We have patience to hold space for the darkness.

We have listened and learned from the songs of nature.

We have joy that gently rises from within.

We have gratitude that liberates limitless abundance.

We have the eyes to see beauty in small things.

We surrender to the flow of grace and to the power of love.

We have practiced making an offering of our day.

We look outside ourselves with kindness, love and compassion.

Yes, today we are ready for the beauty and the light. So with outstretched wings and eyes to the sky, we open to grace...and we fly.

In the World:

✶ Receive in your heart this blessing for the precious year before you.

In the Heart:

✶ Bless this year with love and light. Bless this year with faith and sight. Bless this year with grace and ease. Bless this year with joy and peace.

Mary Davis is a wisdom seeker, spiritual teacher, visionary, graphic artist and mystic entrepreneur. Her wallpaper app, Every Day Spirit Lock Screens, brings a little love, beauty and inspiration to phones around the world. Mary received her BSN from Georgetown University's School of Nursing, after which she spent many fun years as a musician, songwriter, producer, piano teacher and yoga instructor. She completed her Compassionate Bereavement Counseling certification in 2017 and works with parents who have lost children, and in hospice care. She has a house by the sea and lives a contemplative life in harmony with nature.

Every Day Spirit

EVERY DAY SPIRIT WEBSITE: Let's stay connected! The website has lots of tools for your spiritual journey and newsletter sign-up forms. Find everything here: www.everydayspirit.net

EVERY DAY SPIRIT LOCK SCREENS APP: A mobile app of inspirational wallpapers that was the first spark of fire for this book. The app now has 1,000 beautiful wallpapers to lift your spirits every time you open your phone or iPad. Available in the App Store and Google Play.

SOCIAL MEDIA: Sharable artwork with quotes from the book and special messages in the captions can be found on Instagram, Facebook and Pinterest. They work in tandem with the book and amplify the message of the day. I look forward to seeing you there!

www.instagram.com/everydayspirit1

www.facebook.com/everydayspirit1

www.pinterest.com/everydayspirit1

REVIEWS: If you enjoy the book and the app, and have a moment to write a positive review, it would be so appreciated. Reviews are the single most powerful way to reach others and share the love. Thank you from the heart!

Prayers and Blessings

Divine grace, I step into your flow
and know that I will receive the perfect guidance.
Thank you for assisting me in each decision of this day.

Angels, be with me. Watch over me and guard my every step.
Guide me through the endless details of this day.
Let's walk together.

Bless me with a calm center in the storms of my life.

Archangel Michael, defend me, protect me and guide me.
Fill me with strength, peace and wisdom.

Archangel Raphael, heal me in mind, body and soul.
Fill me with clarity, creativity and health.

Archangel Uriel, light the fires of illumination.
Fill me with the energy of transformation and rebirth.

Archangel Gabriel, help me to overcome fear.
Communicate messages of clear guidance.
Fill me with strength of spirit, love and grace.

Archangel Metatron, shine your light, dazzling like the sun,
in my darkest corners.
Fill me with a clear connection with the divine.

I know there is a beautiful plan for today
and that you will help it unfold with ease and grace.
Thank you for showing me the way.

Bless my mind with calm and sight. Bless my heart with love and light.
Bless my day with grace and ease. Bless my world with hope and peace.

I am thankful for the divine plan that is in place for ___.
Perfect solutions are now manifesting with ease and grace.

Thank you for putting a perfect plan in motion
to relax my mind, body and soul.
Assist me in using my inner tools to find deep peace.
I trust that a beautiful plan is unfolding in my life today,
and that I have nothing to fear.
Thank you for helping me return to my natural state of calm.

May I be blessed with wisdom, patience and strength, and with all the
gifts I need to flow through this amazing day with ease and grace.

Thank you for pointing me to the best ways to use my energy now.
Show me what to do next, and help me to accomplish everything
with ease and grace in its perfect time.

Bless me to be the hands of your work,
the steps of your path
and the rays of your sun.

Dear Guardian Angel, Help me to honor my limits and listen for signs
of burnout. Help me to slow down before I wear thin. Remind me to
enjoy relaxation. Help me to trust that if I can't get through my list
today, you will help me accomplish things easily and in their perfect
time. Help me to know that this journey is meant to be fun and that
joy is a spiritual practice. Remind me to take myself lightly. Help me
to always lead from spirit, nourishing my soul so I may be able to
share with others from a place of abundance. Help me to wake up
every morning knowing that I am supported and guided,
and that when I listen, I will always know the way.

Be the strength, Lord, in my struggle. Be the dawn in my dark.
Be the calm in my chaos. Be the haven for my heart.

Help me to slow down and make space for uncertainty. Help me to trust in an outcome that I cannot see. Help me to lift my fears, and point me toward a ray of hope. Help me to be grateful even in the unknowing.

~\\ ⁄~

Thank you for this precious day. May I use it well. May I have a keen eye for joy, beauty and the delights of small things. May I spread love and kindness generously, laugh easily, and feel the ever-present peace of your light with every breath and with every step. Amen

~\\ ⁄~

Divine love, come into my heart
and create with me this glorious day.
Walk through me so I know where to go.
Speak through me so my words may be of kindness and peace.
Pray through me so I know how to assist.
Praise God through me so I know how to serve.
Think through me so my ideas lead me to what you would have me do.
Be joyous through me as I celebrate the beauty of all creation.
Parent through me so I may be respectful and helpful.
Be a friend through me so I may love and be loved in return.
Work through me so I do my work in the consciousness of God.
Write through me this unwritten chapter of my life.
Divine love, come into my heart
and create with me this glorious day. Amen

~\\ ⁄~

Mary, Queen of Angels, send an army of your angels to those in need today. Big and small, please send them for the highest good of all.

~\\ ⁄~

Thank you for making beautiful my path today. I offer it to you, believing that there is a perfect plan that conspires to serve the highest good of all.
Support me in each moment as my day unfolds
with joy, delight and surprise. I am listening.

~\\ ⁄~

Bless this day with love and light. Bless this day with faith and sight.
Bless this day with grace and ease. Bless this day with joy and peace.

Please cover me and this situation in grace. Shine a light on what I need to know today. Provide me with clarity and divine solutions in all things.

May the voice of our highest wisdom rise up from the winter stillness and offer comfort on our journey to loving ourselves within so we might be instruments of love in the world.

I know you are assisting me in all my work and bringing light through my hands, my eyes and my thoughts. With your help, everything happens with ease and grace. Please send extra angels for ___. Thank you.

May we invite love to think through us today. May we invite nature to be joyful through us today. May we invite faith to walk with us today. May we invite grace to act through us today. May we invite kindness to speak through us today. May we invite new blooms to grow through us today. May we invite our highest wisdom to work through us today.

May the warm sun rise in our souls and illuminate the precious nature of life. May the gentle winds of change blow through our uncertainty and remind us that we are beings of infinite possibility.
May the newness of spring awaken our hearts
with love, peace and the hope of new beginnings.

Solstice Blessing:
May the longest day of sunlight fill you with rays of hope.
May the growing nights of moonlight bring rest upon your soul.

Solstice Blessing:
May the longest night of darkness bring rest and rebirth.
May the growing sun of daylight bring hope and new beginnings.

Bless my eyes to see goodness. Bless my words to speak kindness.
Bless my heart to feel compassion. Bless my soul to radiate love.

May simple acts of kindness and unconditional love light our way today.
May remembering our magnificence
quiet the inner voice of judgment today.
May small acts of self-care and self-love nourish our souls today.
May amazing grace lift our spirits and bring us a ray of hope today.

May this day arrive in our hearts with a well of peace and a field of
patience. May this day arrive in our hearts with a helping of self-
compassion and a serving of faith. May this day arrive in our hearts with
a dance of joy and a song of kindness. May this day arrive in our hearts
with a waterfall of love and a river of grace.
May this day arrive in our hearts
with a beam of hope, a ray of light and a whisper of gratitude.

Equinox Blessing:
May the outgoing season be covered in blessings.
May the harvest of your previous intentions
bring you abundance on earth and in spirit.
May the balance of darkness and light
bring greater balance into your home and your life.
May this new season of gratitude and letting go
gift your heart with open space for miracles to grow.

May we trust that we can rest now to rejuvenate the soul.
May we let go of what no longer serves us to make room for new growth.
May we remember that there is spring and the light will come again.
May we have the faith of nature,
knowing that every ending is also a beginning.

May you be open to the unforeseen ways
that the divine works through your life.
May you approach your challenges as possibilities.
May you see your problems as opportunities.
May you be open to receiving answers in creative ways.

May joy bless you. May hope inspire you.
May love heal you. May light guide you.

Spiritual Practices

Self-Care - April 18 and June 10

Blessing Others - April 28 and June 5

Spiritual A-Team - May 5

Gratitude in Advance Practice - May 14

Calling Your Power Back - May 20

Loving-Kindness Meditation - June 7–9

Morning Momentum - July 13

Birthday Meditation - July 23

The Kindness Project - July 27

Angel Time Prayer - Aug 3

Love Joy Peace Meditation - August 4

Meditation Extras - August 31

Harmony: A Meditation - September 9

STOP Method for Mindfulness - September 18

Peace on Earth Meditation - September 24

Grief Tools - September 26–27

Archangel Prayers - September 29

Meditation for Calm - October 7

Yoga Offering - October 16–18

Forgiveness Manifesto - October 20

Forgive Yourself - November 4

The Daily Examen - November 16

Ceremonies - December 29

Journal Prompts

(With love from Mary and Maya Davis)

Welcome to a journey of discovery, spiritual awakening and healing. As you record the sacred threads of your soul story, create a safe space of honesty and curiosity. May the questions be a catalyst for what is stirring in your heart, and may you uncover the beauty of all you are and all you are becoming. May grace be your companion and love be your guide.

January

January 1: What word will be your theme for the month of January and for the new year? Write some intentions for the month and year ahead.

January 2: Make a list of some small gifts of beauty and simple moments of delight that lift your spirits.

January 3: What can you release from your heart or home that is not serving you now? What feels out of alignment with your spirit?

January 4: What can you invite into your life to feed your mind, body and soul? What can you look at with new eyes of appreciation?

January 5: What lessons can you take away from recent challenges? Who would you like to become this year as a result of these lessons?

January 6: What thanks would you like to offer up today? What fills your heart with gratitude in this moment?

January 7: Each of us is fulfilling a sacred role that only we can fill. What unique qualities and talents do you love most about yourself?

January 8: What small acts of kindness lift your spirits and spark joy when you offer them? In what ways can you model kindness to others?

January 9: Write about how your perfect day would unfold. Imagine that everything is possible. What would a day of miracles look like to you?

January 10: What simple delights can you treat yourself to today? What brings out the joyful, playful child in you? Start a joy list.

January 11: Is there a difficult truth in your life that you hold inside? How does it feel to know you have a support team always guiding you?

January 12: List three ways you can make today a co-creation with the divine. Consider asking for guidance, being mindful or giving thanks.

January 13: What lines in today's blessing can you use to turn toward the light today? How can you plant seeds of positivity in the world?

January 14: What qualities make you beautiful on the inside? If you were to radiate your inner beauty to someone, what would they see and feel?

January 15: Today's quote is a prayer for assistance. Copy it and add your own lines, or create a personal angel prayer.

January 16: What would it look like for you to surrender in the midst of a dilemma? How can you ask for and receive guidance in new ways?

January 17: After your meditation practice, write about the experience. What emotions or distractions came up? Simply freewrite, no judgment.

January 18: Write an intention for your daily meditation practice. How many minutes a day and for how many days will you meditate?

January 19: Begin a master list of all the spiritual practices that resonate with you. Update it as the year goes on.

January 20: Create your own daily spiritual practice. It can include prayer, meditation, sacred reading, walking, journaling, gratitude, etc.

January 21: Think back on a past act of kindness, and write out the details. How does it feel to know you may have changed a life?

January 22: What habitual thoughts of the past or future can you replace with more hopeful thoughts? What beauty can you find in this moment?

January 23: What practices would help you to slow down and rest more in the winter? A cozy blanket? A hot beverage? Fewer commitments?

January 24: When do you find yourself judging others? Challenge yourself to have a judgment-free day, and journal the results.

January 25: In what ways can you send love to those in the midst of tragedy? Reflect on some inner actions, such as prayer or blessings, and outer actions, such as a donation or volunteer work.

January 26: Thinking of the characteristics that make you unique and authentic, create three kind compliments directed toward yourself.

January 27: Imagine it is your last day on earth. What needs to be said? What situation resolved? What joy experienced?

January 28: Write down the three grace notes. Call on grace in your own words, opening to receive clarity, support and divine solutions.

January 29: How do you connect with the soft voice of your soul's wisdom? Meditation? Journaling? Ask for guidance. Record your results.

January 30: Write some empowering affirmations or borrow some from today's page. Every **In the Heart** section of the book is an affirmation.

January 31: Write out some of your own flight preparations. What would make you feel prepared, confident and ready to take one step over the side and soar into the next version of you?

February

February 1: What word will you choose for February to illuminate your way? Write some intentions for the month ahead.

February 2: Miracle preparation: Write three positive thoughts about your day, three kind thoughts about yourself and three gratitudes.

February 3: Make a list of things in your life that don't need fixing. What is going right in your heart, home and work life today?

February 4: Plan time to nurture your soul away from screens. Give it a name. (Mine is Spirit Sunday.) How will you use your precious time?

February 5: What dark parts of your life or your past need a little light today? What can you gently accept, learn from and release?

February 6: Gratitude Awareness practice: Write down twenty things you are grateful for each day for three days.

February 7: What desires can you surrender today, trusting in a greater plan? When has a disappointment later revealed itself as a blessing?

February 8: Where would you like to start simplifying? A desk drawer? A closet? What possessions can you release, opening space for growth?

February 9: Using the **In the World** list or your own, write a scenario where your patience is tested. What helps you pause before responding?

February 10: Write your own angel invitation as a list or letter, asking for assistance with whatever trials or challenges you need help with today.

February 11: In what ways do you put undue pressure on yourself? What can you release that has been taking you away from enjoying life fully?

February 12: Is there something especially loving you can do to nourish your soul on Valentine's Day? Lavish love on your beautiful self.

February 13: Write three loving thoughts for yourself and for our world. Write three things you can refrain from if you've gone adrift.

February 14: Write a love letter to Love. What do you want her to know? What would you like to thank her for? What does love mean to you?

February 15: Imagine yourself as a being that radiates unconditional love. Describe what you see through the eyes of love, light and oneness.

February 16: Write yourself a note, higher self to earth self, addressing yourself as a kind friend. What do you most need to hear?

February 17: Is there someone or something you need to forgive and release? Write it out, then make it an offering.

February 18: How can you move through the world today practicing ahimsa? Consider people, plants, animals and the earth.

February 19: Make a list of the benefits of going within and connecting with your inner peace using today's page or your own thoughts.

February 20: Write a declaration of commitment to your daily meditation practice. How can you enhance your practice?

February 21: What are your greatest fears and challenges? What can be surrendered in faith to the divine? What keeps you in the present?

February 22: What acts of kindness would you like to offer in the world today? What acts of kindness can you offer to yourself?

February 23: How can you assist and support the beautiful animals of our world? Write a note of awe and wonder for your favorite creatures.

February 24: What are your favorite bridge lines to introduce an apology? Reflect on any missteps that you'd like to apologize for.

February 25: If you are grieving, reflect on how you feel. There is no right or wrong, only what is true for you. If you are not actively grieving, reflect on any stars that brightened your darkest nights.

February 26: Write out a few affirmations that strengthen your faith, and a short prayer for your faith to outshine your fear.

February 27: What's your version of Monopoly? What activities or small moments spark joy, but don't often make it onto your priority list?

February 28: Create your own version of the hourly micro-break practice from today's page with a deep breath, a prayer and an affirmation.

February 29: What would you like to pour into this precious Leap Day? Your uniqueness? Your love? Your gratitude? Your joy?

March

March 1: What word will you choose for March to be your guiding light? Write some intentions for the month ahead.

March 2: What regrets of the past or worries of the future would you like to release? During what activities can you practice being fully present?

March 3: Start a list of small acts of kindness from the **In the World** section. In what other ways can you share loving-kindness today?

March 4: How can you open space for more wonder and awe today? Think about the things you can invite through your senses.

March 5: Are you feeling stuck or impatient about growth in a certain area of your life? What might the unknowing be teaching you?

March 6: Write a prayer for your intentions today. What support do you need? Who in your life or in the world needs blessings?

March 7: Write out some "I" statements for bringing peace into your relationships. How can you express your truth in the most peaceful way?

March 8: What phrase can you say first thing each morning in gratitude? What can you be appreciative of that you often take for granted?

March 9: Are there regrets that you would like to release? Is there one step you can take toward becoming a higher version of yourself?

March 10: What tasks and activities of today could be lifted by the intention of your love? Make a plan to center yourself, open your heart and ask for guidance as you transition from one activity to the next.

March 11: What can you do today to make your work more joyful? Ideas: mindfulness, gratitude, creativity, lightness of being, dance breaks.

March 12: What is the greatest challenge you now face? Would sharing your story with a friend, a counselor or in a group setting be helpful?

March 13: Create your lists: your tasks for today on the left, everything else on the right. Offer up the right side's tasks for divine assistance.

March 14: Sit tall and lengthen your spine. Take a deep breath. What shifts in your energy do you feel? When can you practice good posture?

March 15: Do you need to speak up for yourself about something? What truth of your soul is longing to be voiced through you?

March 16: What are your current favorite affirmations? Revisit your journal, today's page or any **In the Heart** section for ideas.

March 17: Which lines from today's Irish blessings resonate most deeply in your heart?

March 18: What are your three most important goals for today? Write a short note or prayer to ask for divine assistance in meeting them.

March 19: Using the template of today's blessing, what blessings would you like to ask for? Clarity of mind? Health? Patience? Inner peace?

March 20: What elements of nature bring you the greatest peace, joy and respite? How can you incorporate more of nature's peace into each day?

March 21: Enlist support to help with your worries using an affirmative prayer. *I am thankful for the divine plan that is in place for...*

March 22: Using ideas from the many examples on today's page, make your own list of where the divine is surrounding and supporting you.

March 23: What thoughts, words or actions can you commit to today that will contribute to peace and healing in yourself and in our world?

March 24: What worries will you place in your God Box? Write them out, add them to the box and affirm that a divine plan is in progress.

March 25–27: Build your own calming practice from the tools in the pages for "Fourteen Steps to Calm" and begin to implement your plan.

March 28: When have you experienced the vastness of the universe and yourself as a divine spark within it? How can you describe that feeling?

March 29: Create your own morning prayer or copy your favorite lines from today's page to transport you into the flow of grace.

March 30: What virtues would you like to nurture in the garden of your spirit? What seeds of love might this precious day plant in your soul?

March 31: Who are your dearest soul friends? Who are you most honest with? How could you tell them how much you treasure them in your life?

April

April 1: What word will you pick for April that will awaken your heart in new ways? Write some intentions for the month ahead.

April 2: What do you need special help with today? Write a note to your guardian angel asking for assistance or copy a few lines from the book.

April 3: Write a personal prayer that will help keep you in the flow of ease, grace and intuition through all the transitions of this day.

April 4: What is being sent through your joy channel today? What small things spark joy and celebration within you?

April 5: What kind words, encouraging actions or loving energy can you offer to gently invite someone to rise to their highest expression?

April 6: Write three of your own affirmations about choosing faith, hope and love, using the verses on today's page as a guide.

April 7: In what ways can you show patience and compassion to those close to you who are not yet on a spiritual path?

April 8: Take a few minutes to sit in the silence of your heart. How do a few beats of silence change your perspective on the day?

April 9: What gifts or talents do you possess that you could share through volunteering? Who might benefit from what you have to offer?

April 10: What element of grace do you want to rain down on you today? Compose your own request asking for just what you need.

April 11: Think of a situation that is weighing on your heart that you can't fix. Release it freely onto the page, then write a note of surrender.

April 12: What would you like to notice more of, and therefore *create* more of, in your daily life? Consider joy, beauty, peace, nature and love.

April 13: Write some positive affirmations to balance out the challenges you are facing with reminders of divine assistance and inner strength.

April 14: Is your body communicating a lack of alignment? Tune in to yourself and ask, *What are you bringing to my attention?*

April 15: Using *please* and *thank you*, write out your own conversation with God or your higher power. Share what's in your heart.

April 16: From right where you sit, what do you see, hear, taste or feel that brings you joy? What joyful experience could you plan for today?

April 17: What feels most natural: prayer as a conversation, prayers from your faith tradition or inspirational reading? Write out your favorites.

April 18: List the ways you can be kind to your beautiful self in mind, body and spirit. How can you prioritize self-care today?

April 19: What repetitive prayer or phrase would help banish middle-of-the-night worries? What peaceful thoughts could you plant before sleep?

April 20: Who can you share your deepest truths with? Consider your journal a compassionate companion. What is needing to be shared?

April 21: What is taking up space in your mind that you could set aside in favor of returning to the present moment? What gratitudes can you find right now for things that are going well?

April 22: What actions could you take to help heal our earth? How could you participate in protecting the environment?

April 23: In what areas of life can you practice releasing effort and perfectionism, and soften into surrender and possibility? Are there situations where you can let go of the need to control the outcome?

April 24: What special attributes and unique talents do you have that make you shine from within? Write yourself some loving compliments.

April 25: What helps you to relax and feel comfortable? What small joys bring you deep feelings of contentment, coziness and calm?

April 26: Who in your life could use a few kind and encouraging words today? How can you pass them on? How does it feel to share kindness?

April 27: Write a note of thanksgiving to the divine for the beautiful small gifts of abundance that are right here in the room.

April 28: Make a list of blessings for each person and world event that comes to your mind. When could you silently bless people today?

April 29: What can you say no to that will simplify your life and make space for what inspires you?

April 30: What prayer or affirmation could you use to make today's spiritual practice and the activities of your day into an offering?

May

May 1: What word will you choose for May to encourage your inner growth? Write some intentions for the month ahead.

May 2: What unhelpful thoughts of lack or discontent are on repeat in your mind? Recast them as: *I am grateful that I do have* ___.

May 3: Does listening well to others come easily to you, or does it feel challenging? What are some ways to deepen your active listening skills?

May 4: Who are your closest friends? If you were in a really challenging time, who would you choose as your support team?

May 5: Who are the deities and guides that assist you? If your soul was a small business, who would be your CEO? Your board members?

May 6: Ask a question or request guidance, trusting that the answer will come. When you feel an intuitive response or sign, record it here.

May 7: What aggravations can you reframe with a light heart today? What fresh spin can you put on the things that are out of your control?

May 8: Using the four guideposts from today's **In the World** section, describe how each applies to your future self and your future dreams.

May 9: When you shed the idea that your degree or field of work defines you, what yearnings of your heart come to mind?

May 10: Is there something you would like to try for the first time? If you could reinvent yourself, who would you become?

May 11: What kind of energy do you choose to bring to this day? What are some of your favorite ways to radiate love in the world?

May 12: Considering the fragile and precious nature of life, how would you like to live out this day? Would you include more joy, wonder, love?

May 13: If a parent, grandparent or child has left the earth, write them a letter for Mother's or Father's Day expressing what is in your heart.

May 14: Begin your Gratitude in Advance practice. Starting with, *Thank you for the blessings of this day*, make a list of future blessings in present tense, as if they have already come to pass. Read or write out daily.

May 15: Describe a magnificent sunrise, happening outside or in your mind. Write about the hope and possibility of a dawning day.

May 16: List some ways you can look outside yourself and serve freely and joyfully today. How would you like to offer the currency of love?

May 17: Think about someone who has made a positive impact on you. Write a short note of appreciation and share it with them.

May 18: If you could send light to any less fortunate people in our world, who would they be? Write a prayer to lift their lives and bless them.

May 19: When are your favorite times to disconnect from technology? Make a plan for short breaks today and longer breaks when you are able.

May 20: What situations are you ready to call your power back from? Create a ritual of your choosing to invite your radiant power back home.

May 21: We co-create this day with our thoughts and words. Write a positive prediction for today, painting a detailed picture with words.

May 22: How can you use your words for peace online or in your daily activities? What practices help you respond instead of react?

May 23: Are there people or situations that activate judgment within you? How do you envision the shared humanity behind our differences?

May 24: When people enter your orb with negative energy, how can you use thoughts, words, energy or actions to lift them up with light?

May 25: What calming activity could you turn to on your darkest days? What soothes your soul? Gardening? Cooking? Coloring? Walking?

May 26: Are there any past mistakes or missteps you need to forgive yourself for? Would you like to make amends for anything?

May 27: What are some simple ways you can practice kindness during your day? Write out a few affirmations reinforcing kindness.

May 28: What tools or practices help ground you in the present moment? Reflect on what self-care you are in need of today.

May 29: Who or what can you offer a prayer to today? Write your prayer and then send it off silently or aloud. How does that feel?

May 30: Define your ideal relationship–the one you believe you are worthy of. Can you improve your current relationship if you are in one?

May 31: Write a request for a bountiful portion of grace for all you need help with today, including your biggest emotions and internal challenges.

June

June 1: What word will you choose for June to light your way forward? Write some intentions for the month ahead.

June 2: What would you like your subconscious to work on while you sleep? Write some positive messages to plant within as your body rests.

June 3: What bodies of water do you have access to? List how you might connect with water, at home and in the world, for some soul care time.

June 4: Make your own vacation packing list for your next trip. What can you bring along or leave at home to allow for more rejuvenation?

June 5: Make a list of people, places and world events that could be lifted by your blessings. Add blessing others to your spiritual practice.

June 6: Around what situations do you carry self-doubt? Write yourself a few lines of support for courage on the journey.

June 7: Write out the phrases for first part of the loving-kindness meditation and add some of your own affirmations using, *May I be ...*

June 8: Who would you like to send blessings to in Part 2 of your loving-kindness meditation? Include those who are harder to love.

June 9: What does it look and feel like when you send compassion and love to all beings and all of nature in loving-kindness meditation Part 3?

June 10: When can you schedule in some holy downtime? What might delight your soul during this time? Meditation? A cup of tea? Cozy pj's?

June 11: What could you let go of to simplify your life? How can you shift your focus to make room for more love and spiritual growth?

June 12: What would lift your spirits and soothe your soul? Consider treats like flowers, a walk in nature, a new activity, a hopeful thought.

June 13: What practices can help you foster more inner peace? How can you best bring the power of your love to the world?

June 14: Write your own special prayer giving thanks for the gift of this precious day, or copy the Gift of Time prayer from today's book page.

June 15: What can you do today to make others feel safe, welcome and loved in your presence? How does that feel inside?

June 16: What concerns do you need help with from your divine ones? Write a letter asking for everything you need. Help is on the way.

June 17: Describe yourself as a beautiful being of divine love. Include details about the color and brightness of your light, the magnificence of your soul and your spark of divinity.

June 18: Name three things that are interfering with your inner peace. How can you release them to unveil the calm and love within?

June 19: If you carried on a constant conversation with the divine and had faith that you were always heard, how would it change your life?

June 20: When have you endured the feeling of failure or heartbreak? In hindsight, did this lead you to a more authentic path?

June 21: What spiritual practices could you add or release? Are you spending time with uplifting people? Are you nourishing your soul?

June 22: What would your inner dialogue be if you took a few minutes in the morning to greet the day in gratitude before other thoughts entered?

June 23: What complaints do you catch yourself giving energy to? How can you reframe them in the positive? Make today a complaint-free day.

June 24: Adding to your waking-with-gratitude practice from June 22, write a short morning blessing asking for anything you might need to feel uplifted and peaceful throughout the day.

June 25: What big changes are you navigating? Imagine your future life and write down what your new authentic self might look and feel like.

June 26: Write a thank-you note to your body for all it does for you each day. In what ways can you show your body extra loving-kindness today?

June 27: How can you become even more present today and make the day a moving prayer? What practices remind you to come back to the present moment with a light heart?

June 28: What current challenges can you begin to approach with faith rather than resistance? What past challenges have brought you closer to love and authenticity? In what way?

June 29: What is your soul here for? What are the qualities of your highest self? Write down some phrases that align with your visions.

June 30: Describe what unconditional love feels like to you. What emotions arise when you imagine being unconditionally loved?

July

July 1: What word will you choose for July to keep in your soul backpack? Write some intentions for the month ahead.

July 2: Write your own spiritual priority list. Under each element, describe some simple ways you can practice it today.

July 3: What do you need a little divine help with? Finish this sentence with your list for today: *May I be blessed with...*

July 4: How can you care for yourself through the biggest challenge in your life right now? Write down some activities that fill your cup.

July 5: How can you reframe your busyness as abundance today? What activities, lessons and connections can be seen as gifts?

July 6: Who are your spirit friends? If you are on a solitary journey, can you be that friend to yourself?

July 7: Our challenges come into perspective when we consider the suffering of others. Who comes to mind? Write them a blessing.

July 8: What activities can you bring more presence to with the practice of mindfulness? Listening to friends? A work project? Noticing nature?

July 9: Do you have a negative reaction to certain creatures like Jessie? What could you do differently to honor their little 'great' spirits?

July 10: Take a few slow, deep breaths. Close your eyes and say within: *I'm listening. What do I need to know right now?* Record your intuition.

July 11: Write a few lines of gratitude for the precious gift of life and the irreplaceable love you bring to the world. Use the phrase: *My life matters.*

July 12: Write a few of your own tranquility affirmations to take with you using the **In the World** section from today's page as inspiration.

July 13: Add a positive affirmation to your June 22-24 routine so you will wake with gratitude, bless the day and say an affirmation. Then complete a brief early-morning task with joy. Record your progress for the week.

July 14: Create your own prayer asking for assistance in turning toward your highest, most loving wisdom in the challenges and joys of this day.

July 15: Imagine your spirit guides celebrating you on your journey. What small wins are you and your soul team rejoicing over today?

July 16: Try out your own version of the prayer poem on today's page. What represents your world, reminding you that God is in all?

July 17: Is there something you need to forgive yourself for? Is there a resentment toward a person or situation that you can begin to release?

July 18: List some ways that you can cover yourself in kindness today through tender thoughts, encouraging words and nurturing actions.

July 19: What are you ready to let go of that is not enriching you? What content, news, emails or platforms are not serving your highest good?

July 20: What sacredness can you see in the small things around you? What seemingly mundane things can you give radical thanks for?

July 21: You are on a walk with Grace. She asks, "What can I do to help you? Where in your life do you need more ease?" Answer from the heart.

July 22: Think of a loved one who is not their best self right now. Describe what you wish for them instead. See them as their highest self.

July 23: In your last trip around the sun, what joys and pain have you experienced and what love have you given and received?

July 24: How might you move through this day *in the world but not of it?* What can you do to actively seek joy, generosity and gratitude?

July 25: Do you feel that your spiritual energy is clear, a little dull and foggy, or somewhere in between? Where do you feel light or heavy?

July 26: Which of the seven major chakras resonates most with you? Which of your chakras do you think might need some loving attention?

July 27: Choose a special day or use today to honor someone with the Kindness Project. What could you offer?

July 28: As if you are talking to a friend, write to your angels or spirit guides about your day. What could you use help with?

July 29: Name one way to relax your thoughts, one way to contribute to your physical health, and one way to feed your spirit today.

July 30: Think of what you would tell your best friend if they were going through a really hard time, and write it in your journal to yourself.

July 31: What everyday miracles surround you now? Keep looking until your senses awaken to the holy in the small. Make your precious list.

August

August 1: What word will you choose for August to guide you with ease and grace? Write some intentions for the month ahead.

August 2: Journal any stressful thoughts that are weighing on you. Then, bless and release them, and return to the flow of grace.

August 3: Begin by writing, *May time expand to meet my needs.* Follow with some affirmations validating a relaxed pace for today's to-do list.

August 4: Practice today's meditation and reflect on what came up. Is there anything else you'd like to offer to yourself and the world today?

August 5: Write a note telling yourself that you honor your unique gifts. Then write down five compassionate *I am...* statements.

August 6: What living things can you admire and infuse with gratitude? Your plants? Pets? Loved ones? How can you share this powerful energy?

August 7: In what ways can today hold more *being* and less *doing?* How can you bring sacred sight and a higher perspective into the day?

August 8: How does your perspective shift when you look at the stars, a mountain or the ocean, and remember your sacred place in the universe?

August 9: List the challenges you are facing with a blank line under each to write the words *I accept.* Then reflect on what is going right today.

August 10: What makes today a gift for you? What opportunities does it offer? What do you *get to do* today? What can you give thanks for?

August 11: Do you have a talent you could share to lift someone's spirits? What could you offer that would bring someone joy?

August 12: What are some eating habits that are not serving your mind, body and soul? What one small change can you make today?

August 13: What activities during your workday give you the opportunity to bless others? In meetings? During repetitive tasks?

August 14: *Being love* is being completely and fully yourself. Describe your beautiful, authentic self in the most loving, compassionate way.

August 15: What is your idea of joy? Start a list of things you can do to treat yourself and lift your spirits. What can you do for fun today?

August 16: What unexpected situations have you experienced in the past week? How can surprises become chances to share joy and kindness?

August 17: Who in your life could use today's practice of being seen as their highest self? Think of them from the perspective of divine love.

August 18: Imagine that all you do is in service to the divine. List some ways you can make an offering of your unique gifts today.

August 19: Write a note of thanks to a person or a group of people who have paved the way for your life to unfold with greater ease.

August 20: Where are you following others instead of following your heart? What outer noise can you turn down to hear your inner wisdom?

August 21: What events in your life can you see from a higher perspective today? How can you reframe the worries, fears or obstacles?

August 22: Take a moment to revisit and revise your Gratitude in Advance practice from May 14. What dreams or desires could you add?

August 23: What music feeds your soul and touches your heart? How is your memory stirred? How are your senses awakened?

August 24: What are some of the fearful thoughts that creep into your mind? Write some lines to affirm peace and compassion in the world.

August 25: How does it make you feel when someone mindfully listens to you? In what small ways can you listen to others with more presence?

August 26: Do you have a friend who reminds you of your authentic self in times of uncertainty? How would they describe you?

August 27: Have you experienced a pull to go somewhere or contact someone? Note any signs that might be calling for your attention.

August 28: Harness the power of your positive energy today by writing a prayer for someone's highest health, healing and perfect wellness.

August 29: Add your own verse to "Things We Are Made Of." What makes up your radiant, divine self?

August 30: What grudges toward yourself or those close to you can you sit with and then release? Process the emotions and let them go in peace.

August 31: List what you are doing daily for your spiritual practice. How is your meditation practice going? What could you do to recharge it?

September

September 1: What word do you choose as a beacon for September? Write some intentions for the month ahead.

September 2: What delights you? What elements of nature bring you joy? How can you invite more of those moments into your life?

September 3: What practices create the clearest signal to the divine for you? How are you best able to tune in to the whispers of your heart?

September 4: Kindness begins within. What encouraging words can you offer to yourself today? Write a note cheering yourself on.

September 5: What will you focus on to see the day through "sacred eyes"? Write an affirmation and short prayer to create the best day ever.

September 6: Relationships grow and evolve. Are you in transition? Find words for your growth pattern with your partner or loved ones.

September 7: What practices can you use to create more peace within and in the way you respond to others?

September 8: Do you have feelings of unworthiness? Write yourself a tender loving letter affirming that on a soul level, all is forgiven.

September 9: Write your own verse for today's prayer, or copy one from the page. Add in any affirmations that speak to what you need today.

September 10: Considering the natural world around you, what creatures do you feel close to and which do you feel disconnected from?

September 11: What can you do in service of love and peace at home, in your community or in your heart to honor this day of remembrance?

September 12: Following the topics on today's page, describe how you will believe in, cherish and enjoy the beautiful gift of today.

September 13: What items are you ready to release to make room for more simplicity? Where in your home can you begin?

September 14: How can you open to your highest wisdom by soaking in the beauty of the natural world today?

September 15: In what ways do you feel grace at work in your life? Invite the presence of grace into any particular challenges or concerns you may have today.

September 16: Come up with a few ways you'd like to shine your loving-kindness on others today in thoughts, words and actions.

September 17: Today is a day of optimism. What joyful intention can you set? How can you bring joy, playfulness and delight to the day?

September 18: Copy the STOP method from today's page into your journal if it resonates with you. Practice it and reflect on how it feels.

September 19: Is there someone in your life who is fighting a tough battle? How can you remind them that you see them?

September 20: Are there any particular NDE stories that have moved you? What do you imagine the afterlife to be?

September 21: Be patient. Be joyful. Be calm. Be kind. What "be" phrases would make a sweet and encouraging mantra for you today?

September 22: Today marks the change of season. What season of the heart have you been in? What season are you beginning? Write a few lines to bless the old and welcome the new.

September 23: What are some tiny wonders of nature that bring you joy and give you a sense of awe? Make a list of gratitudes for small miracles.

September 24: Imagine and describe the ocean of love within you, which you can use as an offering to yourself and to the world.

September 25: What kind of rest and rejuvenation can you make time for today? A nap? A cup of tea? Write about rest as a spiritual practice.

September 26: If someone you know is grieving, in what ways can you offer them love and encouragement?

September 27: If you are grieving a loss, write about how you feel today. What spiritual practices or grief tools do you find comforting?

September 28: What kind words would comfort *you*? When during the day could you use these words as a gift of healing for others too?

September 29: Do you feel a special resonance with any of the archangels? If so, write your own prayer through that angel or copy your favorite archangel prayer lines from today's page.

September 30: What are your favorite stories of inspiration, resilience and hope? How can they serve as reminders to celebrate the gift of this precious day?

October

October 1: What word do you choose for October that inspires rejuvenation? Write some intentions for the month ahead.

October 2: What does it mean to you to choose love over fear? How can you be an instrument of peace in your heart, at home and in the world?

October 3: Who are your most steadfast friends? What new friends are in your garden? Is there a lapsed friendship you would like to rekindle?

October 4: Set an intention for an amazing day ahead. Write a prayer asking for help staying in the present with flexibility and a light heart.

October 5: If you were faced with an unfathomable challenge like Claire's, how would the power of love manifest in your life?

October 6: Name three ways you could bring more purpose, meaning, joy or creativity to your work life and to your time caring for your home.

October 7: How did the Meditation for Calm make you feel? What are your favorite calming spiritual practices for stressful moments?

October 8: Write your favorite lines or ideas from today's prayer to use in your morning practice. How will you co-create today with the divine?

October 9: You are an infinite, magnificent spirit. As seen through the eyes of unconditional love, how might you describe your beautiful soul?

October 10: Choose faith, hope and love today by writing a few lines describing the highest outcome for an issue that's heavy on your heart.

October 11: What simple acts of kindness can you include in your day for yourself and others? Where can you look for kindness opportunities?

October 12: Write your meditation goals for the week. How long would you like to meditate each day? How can you deepen your practice?

October 13: Are there areas of your life that are a little out of balance? What spiritual practices might be especially grounding for you now?

October 14: Affirmations hold power by aligning you with your spiritual strength. Write your favorites and pick a few to use today.

October 15: What fears have you learned in the world that are keeping you separate from the wholeness of your spirit and the joy of today?

October 16: Is there an activity that you can make an offering of today? Write it in advance. For example, *I offer my morning walk to...*

October 17: What is your daily movement practice of choice? What intentions for yourself or others could you invite into that practice?

October 18: Imagine that you are in space. Look down and describe our planet as if we loved one another and lived together in peace.

October 19: What gratitudes might reframe your thoughts of worst-case scenarios? Write three ways that you consider yourself to be fortunate.

October 20: Write your own Forgiveness Manifesto or copy your favorite lines from today's page. What does forgiveness mean to you?

October 21: Imagine you can box up and set down worries that you can't control or work on today. Make two lists: *I set down...* and *I invite in...*

October 22: Is there someone in your life whose energy brings you down? How can you shield yourself? What is the lesson here?

October 23: What work, tasks or duties would you like to make a devotion of? How can you infuse greater love and purpose into them?

October 24: Write your own blessing for the day or borrow some lines from today's reading. What will you invite into your heart?

October 25: Today's practice is all about listening within. Spend a few minutes in silence, and then write what your soul is whispering to you.

October 26: Scan the room and your heart for things that spark joy. Make notes here as you open to the simple and small joys of this moment.

October 27: Who or what in your life might especially benefit from the gift of your pure unconditional love?

October 28: How could you shine your love to lighten dark places? What would it look like to cover the earth and all beings with light?

October 29: Are there people around you whose life choices cause you to feel frustration? How can you minimize their negative effect in your life?

October 30: What challenges can you surrender, accepting the need for help? What can you lift off of your shoulders and release in faith?

October 31: What would you like to release that is not serving you? What abundant new energy are you making space for?

November

November 1: What word will serve as a lighthouse to guide your month? Write some intentions for November.

November 2: Who has passed before you and left an indelible mark on your heart? Write a note of thanks for the gifts of their life.

November 3: When were you last lifted up by love? How did it feel? In what simple way can you pay that feeling forward to someone else today?

November 4: Do you berate yourself with unkind words over current or past mistakes? Write a kind letter to your beautiful self on a soul level.

November 5: How will it look and feel to send some beams of peace and love out into the world today? Describe it in colorful detail.

November 6: Start a list of things you are grateful for from this past year and add to it all month.

November 7: Ask your body what you need to know. Is an illness teaching you something? What does perfect health look like to you?

November 8: What teachings from great masters of faith or spiritual traditions resonate with you deeply?

November 9: How will you exercise respect and honesty during hard conversations? Where are your boundaries? What are your house rules?

November 10: Who or what asks you to practice unconditional love? Even in challenges, can you find one small way to offer that love today?

November 11: Write an invitation to all of your spiritual guardians and guides asking them to light your path with clear direction.

November 12: List a few current worries. Now convert each one from what you are afraid will happen into what you want to happen.

November 13: Without judging or analyzing, summarize your life just as it is. Journal on accepting and loving your life right where you are today.

November 14: If you were to make a quick transition out of this world, what would you want your loved ones to know?

November 15: Write about what your greatest challenge or concern would look like if it had a surprise, miraculous happy ending.

November 16: Use the Daily Examen or a similar daily review, and write a sentence or two in reflection of each section.

November 17: What favorite mementos could you share with your loved ones? What have you treasured that you'd like to be remembered by?

November 18: Think about what you have grown away from or grown out of. Journal about who you were and who you are becoming. What are you releasing, and what are you inviting in?

November 19: Take a few moments to start or recharge your gratitude practice. Write at least three things you are grateful for today.

November 20: Make a plan for soul care today. What tools will you reach for to help maintain a little inner peace amidst the day's demands?

November 21: If the holidays are bringing up memories of sadness or loss, write about it. Consider the joys too. Hold it all with an open heart.

November 22: How can you create a Thanksgiving holiday that reflects your heart? How might you balance gratitude with all you are feeling?

November 23: Write down a few ways you'd like to bring kindness and calm into your shopping adventures this holiday season.

November 24: What energy would you like to invite into this day? Who will you choose to be? What will you focus your attention on?

November 25: How can you simplify gift giving to minimize stress? Can you replace a gift with time together, a donation or a heartfelt note?

November 26: During what transformational life experiences have you found yourself letting go of the past a little bit at a time? Is there another layer to bless and release?

November 27: Write a note to your younger self who learned lessons and paved the way to this moment. Thank them for bringing you here.

November 28: In what ways can you simplify the holidays? What soul care practices might invite more meaning and joy to the season?

November 29: How can you honor the soul's yearning for patience and pause? What sacred traditions make this season special for you?

November 30: How can you nurture yourself with tender loving care, plenty of rest and spiritual support in the midst of busy days?

December

December 1: What word do you choose for December to light your way? Write some intentions for the month ahead.

December 2: What decisions will you face today that could be enhanced by a consultation with your higher self, angels or spirit guides?

December 3: In what form do you get your intuitive direction? Is it through gut feelings, signs, dreams, songs or people?

December 4: If you were in an emergency situation, what practices could you implement to stay calm and connected to guidance?

December 5: Write a prayer asking for spirit to take the lead in times of uncertainty, and for you to be there when you are called on to assist.

December 6: How can you soften into imbalance? Write a short note-to-self declaring that you will release resistance and allow the day to flow.

December 7: Is there a special gift of love that you feel called to share with someone this holiday season?

December 8: Are you fully open to receiving abundance? Write a note asking for the grace to see yourself as worthy of receiving your desires.

December 9: What part of your holiday to-do list is not sparking joy? Replace those items with an alternate idea that brings peace and joy.

December 10: In what form do your spirit messengers from the natural world show up? What do they represent? What message do they bring?

December 11: What situation could you step back from, offering love, kindness and prayers instead of suggestions?

December 12: When do you feel most connected to the divine? How could you open to more spiritual companionship?

December 13: Write an affirmation or two to remind yourself in moments of anger to communicate with peace. Start with today's **In the Heart** affirmation if you need a little inspiration.

December 14: How could you bring new meaning into the holidays? Consider time with friends, a special spiritual practice or making gifts.

December 15: What would it feel like to make an offering of every part of your life into the hands of your higher power?

December 16: "To be spiritual is to be amazed." What does that phrase mean to you? What everyday moments can you find amazement in?

December 17: How can beautiful small things around you bring you back to the present? Have you felt that sacred place between beauty and pain?

December 18: What holiday traditions are precious to you? How can you be more present, awake and mindful in these special moments?

December 19: Of all the reasons for treasuring your contemplative practices listed on today's page, which ones resonate the most with you?

December 20: What are the most heartfelt lessons you have learned through loss?

December 21: The holidays and today's solstice signify the birth of new light and new hope. How does it feel? What is being illuminated in you?

December 22: What people, places and things that are no longer physically with you do you carry in your heart?

December 23: Contemplate some of the seasonal stories of your faith tradition. What parts of these stories speak to your heart now?

December 24: What challenges can you reframe as possibilities? What inconveniences might be a chance to rise to your higher self?

December 25: In the quiet of your spiritual practice, breathe in the simplicity of pure unconditional love. How does it feel in your heart?

December 26: What scenes from today's gratitude list resonate most with you? What would you add to the list that you are most grateful for?

December 27: Write a short note listing your favorite moments from the past few weeks to pack with your holiday decorations as a reminder for next year of what nourished your soul.

December 28: In the stillness of this moment, what gratitudes, delights, sparks of grace or flashes of hope make their way to your awareness?

December 29: Make two lists, one with the blessings and one with the challenges of this past year. Create a New Year's ceremony.

December 30: What does divine co-creation look like to you? In what ways can you invite divine companionship into your daily life?

December 31: What are the most profound lessons you have learned during the past year? In what ways have you changed spiritually?

Bibliography

Aimee Copeland Foundation. "Aimee Copeland Foundation, Empowering People of All Abilities to Lead Fulfilling and Joyful Lives," n.d. https://aimeecopelandfoundation.org/.

Angelou, Maya. *The Collected Autobiographies of Maya Angelou.* New York: Modern Library, 2004.

Angelou, Maya. *I Know Why the Caged Bird Sings.* New York: Random House, 2009.

Angelou, Maya. *Maya Angelou: Poems: Just Give Me a Cool Drink of Water 'fore I Diiie, Oh Pray My Wings Are Gonna Fit Me Well, And Still I Rise.* New York: Bantam Books, 1981.

Angelou, Maya. *Rainbow in the Cloud: The Wisdom and Spirit of Maya Angelou.* New York: Random House, 2014.

Ban Breathnach, Sarah. *Simple Abundance: A Daybook of Comfort and Joy.* New York: Warner Books, 1995.

Bowen, Connie. *I Believe in Me: A Book of Affirmations.* Unity Village, MO: Unity Books, 2005.

Brownn, Eleanor. *Mile 9.* New York: Bookmark Publications, 2009.

Borysenko, Joan. *Pocketful of Miracles: Prayers, Meditations, and Affirmations to Nurture Your Spirit Every Day of the Year.* New York: Warner Books, 1994.

Brach, Tara. *Trusting the Gold: Uncovering Your Natural Goodness.* Boulder, CO: Sounds True, 2021.

Brennon, Barbara A. *Hands of Light: A Guide to Healing Through the Human Energy Field.* New York: Bantam Books, 1987.

Bryant, Edwin F. *The Yoga-Sutras of Patanjali: A New Edition, Translation, and Commentary.* Berkeley: North Point Press, 2015.

Burnham, Sophy. *Angel Letters.* New York: Ballantine Books, 1991.

Burnham, Sophy. *A Book of Angels.* New York: Ballantine Books, 1990.

Byrne, Lorna. *Angels in My Hair: The True Story of a Modern-Day Irish Mystic.* New York: Three Rivers Press, 2011.

Byrne, Lorna. *Love From Heaven: Practicing Compassion for Yourself and Others.* New York: Atria, 2014.

Byrne, Lorna. *Stairways to Heaven*. London: Coronet, 2010.

Cacciatore, Joanne. *Bearing the Unbearable: Love, Loss, and the Heartbreaking Path of Grief*. Somerville, MA: Wisdom Publications, 2017.

Cacciatore, Joanne. "The Kindness Project." n.d. MISS Foundation. https://www.missfoundation.org/kindness-project/.

Campbell, Joseph. *The Power of Myth*. New York: Anchor Books, 1991.

Carl Jung: The Wisdom of the Dream. BBC Documentary, 1989.

Carr, Kris. *I'm Not a Mourning Person: Braving Loss, Grief, and the Big Messy Emotions That Happen When Life Falls Apart*. Carlsbad, CA: Hay House, 2023.

Chödrön, Pema. *Always Maintain a Joyful Mind: And Other Lojong Teachings on Awakening Compassion and Fearlessness*. Boston: Shambhala Publications, 2007.

Chödrön, Pema. *The Pocket Pema Chödrön*. Boston: Shambhala Publications, 2008.

Chödrön, Pema. *Start Where You Are: A Guide to Compassionate Living*. Boston: Shambhala Classics, 2001.

Clark, Glenn. *The Man Who Talks with the Flowers: The Intimate Life Story of Dr. George Washington Carver*. Redford, VA: Wilder Publishing, 2011.

Clarke, Malcolm, director. *The Lady in Number 6: Music Saved My Life*. Documentary. Netflix, 2013.

De Sales, Francis. *Introduction to the Devout Life*. New York: Cosimo Classics, 2010.

De Sales, Francis. *Set Your Heart Free*. Notre Dame, IN: Ave Maria Press, 2008.

DeVries, Marja. *The Whole Elephant Revealed: Insights into the Existence and Operation of Universal Laws and the Golden Ratio*. Winchester, UK: Axis Mundi Books, 2012.

Dillard, Annie. *Pilgrim at Tinker Creek*. New York: Harper & Row, 1974.

Doty, James R. *Into the Magic Shop: A Neurosurgeon's Quest to Discover the Mysteries of the Brain and the Secrets of the Heart*. New York: Avery Publishers, 2016.

Easwaran, Eknath. *Your Life Is Your Message: Finding Harmony with Yourself, Others & the Earth*. Tamales, CA: Nilgiri Press, 1992.

The Forever Wisdom of Dr. Wayne J. Dyer. Hay House, 2016.

Foundation for Inner Peace. *A Course in Miracles*. Tiburon, CA, 1975.

Frankl, Viktor E. *Man's Search for Meaning: An Introduction to Logotherapy*. New York: Simon and Schuster, 1959.

Gandhi, Mahatma. *Gandhi on Non-Violence: A Selection From the Writings of Mahatma Gandhi*. Edited by Thomas Merton. New York: New Directions Publishing, 1965.

Gawande, Atul. *Being Mortal: Medicine and What Matters in the End*. New York: Metropolitan Books, 2014.

Gibran, Kahlil. "On Friendship." In *The Prophet*. New York: Alfred A. Knopf Publisher, 1923.

Harper Nichols, Morgan. *Peace Is a Practice: An Invitation to Breathe Deep and Find a New Rhythm for Life*. Grand Rapids, MI: Zondervan, 2022.

Hicks, Esther and Jerry. "The Abraham-Hicks Placemat Process." *Ask and It Is Given*. Carlsbad, CA: Hay House, 2004.

Hoff, Benjamin. *The Tao of Pooh*. New York: Penguin Books, 1982.

The Holy Bible: New Revised Standard Version. New York: Oxford University Press, 2010.

Ilibagiza, Immaculée. *Left to Tell: Discovering God Amidst the Rwandan Holocaust*. Carlsbad, CA: Hay House, 2014.

Iyengar, B. K. S. *Light on Pranayama: The Yogic Art of Breathing*. New York: Crossroad Publishing Company, 1999.

Iyengar, B. K. S. *Light on Yoga*. New York: Schocken Books, 1966.

Jackson, Laura Lynne. *Signs: The Secret Language of the Universe*. New York: Penguin Random House, 2019.

Judith, Anodea. *Eastern Body Western Mind: Psychology and the Chakra System as a Path to the Self*. Berkeley: Celestial Arts Publishing, 1996.

Kabat-Zinn, Jon. *Wherever You Go, There You Are: Mindfulness Meditation In Everyday Life*. New York: Hyperion, 1994.

Kadagian, DJ, Pim van Lommel and Gregory Shushan. *Life After Death: 100 Exceptional Near Death Experiences*. Project Shift, 2022.

Kernion, Anne. "Cards by Anne." Cards by Anne, n.d. https://cardsbyanne.com.

King, Martin L. "The Drum Major Instinct." In *A Knock at Midnight: Inspiration from the Great Sermons of Reverend Martin Luther King, Jr. 1968*. Edited by Claiborne Carson and Peter Holloran. New York: Warner Books, 1998.

Kondo, Marie. *The Life-Changing Magic of Tidying Up: The Japanese Art of Decluttering and Organizing.* Emeryville: Ten Speed Press, 2014.

Lamott, Anne. *Bird by Bird: Some Instructions on Writing and Life.* New York: Pantheon Books, 1994.

Lawrence, Brother. *Practicing the Presence of God.* Wheaton, Illinois: Harold Shaw, 1991.

Lindbergh, Anne Morrow. *Gift from the Sea.* New York: Pantheon Books, 1955.

Maclean, Dorothy. *To Hear the Angels Sing: An Odyssey of Co-Creation with the Devic Kingdom.* New York: Lindisfarne Press, 1990.

Martin, James. *Jesus: A Pilgrimage.* New York: HarperCollins, 2014.

Martin, James and Anne Kernion. *Daily Examen Card*, Cards by Anne, n.d. https://cardsbyanne.com.

McNamara, Patrick. "You Really Need to Be Tracking Your Dreams." *Psychology Today*, August 1, 2017. https://www.psychologytoday.com/us/blog/dream-catcher/201708/you-really-need-be-tracking-your-dreams.

Meera, Mother. *Answers Part 1.* Germany: Meerama Publications, 2004.

Merton, Thomas. *Contemplative Prayer.* New York: Penguin Random House, 1971.

Merton, Thomas. *Thoughts in Solitude.* New York: Farrar, Straus and Giroux, 1999.

Moody, Raymond. *Life After Life.* New York: Bantam Books, 1975.

Moorjani, Anita. *Dying to Be Me: My Journey from Cancer, to Near Death, to True Healing.* Carlsbad, CA: Hay House, 2014.

Moorjani, Anita. *What if This Is Heaven? How Our Cultural Myths Prevent Us From Experiencing Heaven on Earth.* Carlsbad, CA: Hay House, 2016.

Myss, Caroline. *Anatomy of the Spirit: The Seven Stages of Power and Healing.* New York: Three Rivers Press, 1996.

Nhat Hanh, Thich. *Living Buddha, Living Christ.* New York: Riverhead Books, 1995.

Nhat Hanh, Thich. *Peace Is Every Step: The Path of Mindfulness in Everyday Life.* New York: Bantam Books, 1991.

Nhat Hanh, Thich. *The Miracle of Mindfulness: A Manual on Meditation.* Boston: Beacon Press, 1987.

Nichols, Wallace J. *Blue Mind*. New York: Little Brown and Company, 2014.

Norris, Gunilla. *Being Home: Discovering the Spiritual in the Everyday*. New York: Bell Tower, 1991.

Norris, Gunilla. *Inviting Silence: Universal Principles of Meditation*. New York: BlueBridge, 2004.

O'Donohue, John. *To Bless the Space Between Us: A Book of Blessings*. New York: Doubleday, 2008.

Oliver, Mary. "Storage." In *Felicity*. New York: Penguin Press, 2016.

Paintner, Christine Valters. *The Love of Thousands: How Angels, Saints, and Ancestors Walk With Us Toward Holiness*. Notre Dame, IN: Sorin Books, 2023.

Pradervand, Pierre. *365 Blessings to Heal Myself and the World*. Winchester, UK: O-Books, 2018.

Pradervand, Pierre. *The Gentle Art of Blessing: A Simple Practice That Will Transform You and Your World*. New York: Atria Paperback, 2009.

Rasmussen, Olga R. *Meditation Pure and Simple*. Washington, DC: Meditation Pure and Simple Publishing, 2014.

Rasmussen, Olga R. *Walking in Darkness and into Great Light: Meditations for Advent, Winter, and the Solstice*. Washington, DC: Meditation Pure and Simple Publishing, 2011.

Rilke, Rainer Maria. *Letters to a Young Poet*. Edited by Stephen Mitchell. New York: Random House, 1984.

Rinpoche, Sogyal. *The Tibetan Book of Living and Dying*. San Francisco: Harper San Francisco, 1992.

Rosenberg, Marshall B. *Nonviolent Communication: A Language of Life*. Encinitas, CA: PuddleDancer Press, 2015.

Rumi. *The Love Poems of Rumi*. Edited by Deepak Chopra. New York: Harmony Books, 2008.

Rumi. *A Year With Rumi: Daily Readings*. Edited by Coleman Barks. New York: HarperOne, 2006.

Schultz, Charles, writer. *A Charlie Brown Christmas*. Directed by Bill Melendez. CBS, 1965.

Seuss, Dr. *How the Grinch Stole Christmas*. New York: Random House, 1957.

Shapiro, Shauna L. *Good Morning, I Love You: Mindfulness and Self-Compassion Practices to Rewire Your Brain for Calm, Clarity and Joy.* Boulder, CO: Sounds True, 2020.

Silver, Tosha. *Outrageous Openness: Letting the Divine Take the Lead.* New York: Atria Books, 2014.

Starr, Mirabai. *Caravan of No Despair: A Memoir of Loss and Transformation.* Boulder, CO: Sounds True, 2015.

Starr, Mirabai and Caroline Myss. *Saint Teresa of Avila: Passionate Mystic.* Boulder, CO: Sounds True, 2013.

Taylor, Barbara Brown. *Learning to Walk in the Dark.* New York: HarperOne, 2014.

Taylor, Barbara Brown. *An Altar in the World.* New York: HarperOne, 2009.

Taylor, Terry Lynn. *Messengers of Light: The Angels' Guide to Spiritual Growth.* Tiburon, CA: H. J. Kramer Inc., 1990.

Thoreau, Henry D. *Henry David Thoreau: A Writer's Journal.* Edited by Carl Bode. New York: Dover Publications, 1960.

Thoreau, Henry D. *Walden.* Boston: Beacon Press, 2004.

Tolle, Eckhart. *The Power of Now: A Guide to Spiritual Enlightenment.* Novato, CA: New World Library, 1999.

Tolle, Eckhart. *Stillness Speaks.* Novato, CA: New World Library, 2003.

Ware, Bronnie. *The Top Five Regrets of the Dying: A Life Transformed by the Dearly Departing.* Carlsbad, CA: Hay House. 2019.

Washam, Spring. *A Fierce Heart: Finding Strength, Courage, and Wisdom in Any Moment.* Carlsbad, CA.: Hay House, 2019.

Weiss, Brian. *Messages from the Masters: Tapping into the Power of Love.* New York: Warner Books, 2000.

Yogananda, Paramahansa. *Metaphysical Meditations.* Los Angeles: Self-Realization Fellowship, 1946.

Yogananda, Paramahansa. *Spiritual Diary: An Inspirational Thought for Each Day of the Year.* Los Angeles: Self-Realization Fellowship, 1964.

Yogananda, Paramahansa. *Where There Is Light.* Los Angeles: Self-Realization Fellowship, 1964.

Young, Sarah. *Jesus Calling: Enjoying Peace in His Presence.* Nashville: Thomas Nelson, 2015.

Bless my eyes

to see goodness.

Bless my words

to speak kindness.

Bless my heart

to feel compassion.

Bless my soul

to radiate love.